Praise for
THE WAYMAKERS

"This is simply the best book on diversity and inclusion I have read. Drawing extensively from research and unerringly told personal experience, author Tara Jaye Frank indeed helps us find a way forward. Hers is a must-read book for anyone who wants to be part of the solution."

Amy C. Edmondson, professor, Harvard Business School; author of *The Fearless Organization: Creating Psychological Safety in the Workplace for Learning, Innovation, and Growth*

"Tara's candid and incisive wisdom offers a fresh perspective on the future of work, empowering us all to take action around creating a more inclusive, equitable workplace. *The Waymakers* can and should change the way you lead."

Tom Hayes, president and CEO, Ocean Spray Cranberries Inc.

"*The Waymakers* shares with clarity the essence of what truly unlocks the promise of an organization. Rejecting the notion that well-intentioned people are enough, Frank sheds light on how choices and a commitment to lead can help us leverage the full potential of *every* person. Any leader who questions how to maximize their business outcomes through people in an equitable way will find the answers in *The Waymakers*."

Mike Hyter, president and CEO, Executive Leadership Council

"Pointed, practical, and powerful, *The Waymakers* serves as a guide to achieving and sustaining workplace equity, while reminding us—unflinchingly—that equity is not niceness and that successful leaders learn the difference."

Latriece Watkins, executive vice president, Consumables, Walmart US

"*The Waymakers* moves the cerebral equity versus equality debate to a place that is centered around 'heart work.' This fantastic read offers more clarity and insight into inclusion issues than any book I've read since college."

Nzinga Shaw, president, TurnkeyZRG; global practice lead and chief inclusion and diversity officer, ZRG

"Frank deftly outlines the keys to achieving true equity and inclusion—a gift for leaders who are ready to go beyond just diversity."

Anré Williams, CEO, American Express National Bank, group president, Enterprise Services

"Tara Jaye Frank's *The Waymakers* cuts through the noise, maneuvers around the excuses, and reaches beyond our self-imposed limitations to remind us that we, the people, are who make our companies great—one equitable choice at a time."

Michele C. Meyer-Shipp, Esq., former chief people and culture officer, Major League Baseball

"Too often in the workplace people stop talking to each other because we're afraid. We don't know what to say, or don't want to make a mistake, or feel too exposed to admit our own learning curves. *The Waymakers* teaches us how to become curious and connect—to live in community. Tara Jaye Frank makes it feel urgently possible."

Beth Andrix Monaghan, founder and CEO of Inkhouse

"Tara Jaye Frank's *The Waymakers* is an exceptional guide to building and sustaining a thriving and equitable workplace. Every business leader who is serious about making lasting and substantive change should read this book."

Soraya Chemaly, award-winning author of *Rage Becomes Her*

"Tara Jaye Frank's thoughtful insights and techniques pierce the heart of the inequity problem, which simply can't be denied after reading this book. CEOs who are serious about diversity, equity, and inclusion need this resource in their hip pockets at all times."

Dantaya Williams, executive vice president and chief human resources officer, Raytheon Technologies

"Waymaking should be at the center of every leader's agenda. Tara Jaye Frank's new book, *The Waymakers,* will help leaders effectively become better sponsors."

Minda Harts, NYT best-selling author of *The Memo*

"Tara Jaye Frank's work has inspired me and our NEW community to lead with great conviction and impact on behalf of all women. Now *The Waymakers* provides that same inspiration with actionable solutions to every leader who strives to unlock true equity. This is the life-changing invitation you simply cannot ignore."

Sarah Alter, president and CEO, Network of Executive Women

"True leadership isn't having all the answers; it's asking the right questions. It's having the self-awareness and vulnerability to put the team above yourself . . . to dive into the deep end to listen and learn. When it comes to creating equitable workplaces, many of us have held back due to a lack of knowledge, experience, or comfort. Tara Jaye Frank's *The Waymakers* provides powerful examples, insights, and a clear path for impact—and makes it plain that change requires courage."

Wendy Davidson, president of Americas, Glanbia Performance Nutrition

"Getting to equity requires two things: truth and action. In this book, Tara Jaye Frank shows us the way."

James Rhee, impact investor/CEO and John H. Johnson Chair of Entrepreneurship, Howard University

"I've had a front-row seat to Tara's unique ability to convey truths about workplace equity that well-meaning executives need to know but sometimes find difficult to hear. *The Waymakers* further cements that Tara Jaye Frank is the much-needed mind and voice of our time."

D. Keith Pigues, founder, C-suite advisor, and board executive

"Winning in any business during times of intense change comes down to people and perspectives. *The Waymakers* charts a path to unleashing both in clear, compelling, and infinitely actionable terms."

Kevin Samuelson, CEO, Infor

"Actionable and inspiring, *The Waymakers* is rich with tools and possibilities. Keep this book within arm's reach. I know I will!"

Dolly Chugh, author, *The Person You Mean to Be*

"Tara Jaye Frank *is* a Waymaker. She shines light, gives voice, interrupts patterns, and shows us the path to leading with integrity, heart, and humanity. Filled with wisdom, insight, and practical steps, *The Waymakers* will guide you toward becoming a better leader and human being."

Shelly McNamara, author, *No Blanks, No Pauses: A Path to Loving Self and Others*; chief equality and inclusion officer, Procter & Gamble

amplify

www.amplifypublishing.com

The Waymakers: Clearing the Path to Workplace Equity
with Competence and Confidence

For more information, please contact:
Amplify Publishing, an imprint of Mascot Books
620 Herndon Parkway, Suite 320
Herndon, VA 20170
info@amplifypublishing.com

Library of Congress Control Number: 2021915944

CPSIA Code: PRBANG1121A

ISBN-13: 9781637551806

Printed in the United States

To my husband, John,
who made a way for me to pursue my purpose unencumbered.
And to my children and yours,
whose equal right to opportunity fuels my work.

The WAYMAKERS

CLEARING THE PATH TO

WORKPLACE EQUITY

WITH COMPETENCE

AND CONFIDENCE

TARA JAYE FRANK

Foreword by **STEVE PEMBERTON**

CHRO, Workhuman

amplify

CONTENTS

Foreword

Disclaimer

INTRODUCTION
The Waymaker Whys

Why Me?
Why Us?
Why This Book?

CHAPTER 1
Power and Privilege: Sources of Stagnancy

Deep Roots, Sweeping Branches
Minding Our Business
Being Too Patient
Power Plays

CHAPTER 2
Start Where You Are: The Climate Test

What We Do, Not What We Say
Testing the Waters
What Great Looks Like

CHAPTER 3
Making a Way: The Path to Change

Embrace Realism
Take Responsibility
Build Relationship

CHAPTER 4
Heart Work, Right Mind: The Waymaker Principles

    Empathy

    Fairness

    Courage

    Ownership

    Integrity

CHAPTER 5
The Mountains We Miss: Four Core Issues

    Lack of Psychological Safety

    Low Representation

    Limited Opportunity

    Burden of Proof

CHAPTER 6
What Your People Want: Four Talent Needs

    To Be Seen

    To Be Respected

    To Be Valued

    To Be Protected

CHAPTER 7
What Your Company Wants: Performance Drivers

    To Attract Talent, Increase Diversity

    To Improve Culture, Cultivate Belonging

    To Support Retention, Ensure Equity

    To Drive Innovation, Unleash Creativity by Creating Psychological Safety

CHAPTER 8
When Waymaking Matters Most: Defining Moments

Doing Something New
Chasing Dreams
High Risks and Short Fuses
During Transformation

CHAPTER 9
Be the Way: Model for Results

Be Clear
Be Intentional
Be Consistent
Be Bold
Be Accountable

CHAPTER 10
Bring People Along: Model for Momentum

Be Available
Be Transparent
Be Collaborative
Be the Change
Be Humble

CONCLUSION
A New Thing: The Waymaker Life

Heal the Body
No More Excuses
Now
The Workplace We Deserve

Acknowledgments

Endnotes

Foreword

MY FIRST JOB OUT OF college was as a counselor for a program designed to provide high school students equal access to higher education. It remains among my most rewarding professional experiences, in large part because of the extraordinary, talented young people I met. Tara Jaye Frank was one of those young people. I most remember her natural curiosity and gifted pen, combined with her intuitive understanding of the importance of fairness. These qualities still abide in her, perhaps in even greater abundance now that life experiences have only deepened her natural gifts.

Had you told either of us back then that one day we would both be authors and change agents–influencing people and ideas–we might have questioned your sanity. Those doubts would not have been reflections of our interests or capabilities. Instead, we would have wondered just how something like that could happen, considering our somewhat limited exposure. What we could not see then were those who would make a way for us, quietly and humbly, by speaking our names out loud, revealing what was possible, and clearing the path forward.

This is a wonderful segue to the journey Tara is going to take you on with *The Waymakers*–and it comes not a moment too soon. Today

1

grandchildren are fighting some of the same equity battles their grandparents once did, and strong voices seem bent on creating a sort of second-class citizenship, pointing their hypocritical spears at communities who will never accept such a lowered bar. Polarization now pervades nearly every aspect of our lives. We are wrestling with a society that has traded legal segregation for a voluntary form that conspires to hold us all hostage.

This harsh reality, understandingly lamentable and yet stunningly transparent, requires new strategies that can point us toward safer shores and more equitable outcomes. This is a time of reckoning—and reconciliation—for all of us as individuals and as organizations. But all is not lost. We are, in quiet conversations and reflective discussions, asking how we can do our part. *The Waymakers* answers that question. And for as long as any society asks questions, there is always hope.

At this book's conclusion, you will no longer need to wonder how to find your way to an equitable workplace. Rather, a different question will be asked of you: Will you choose to *make* a way? For all our sakes—mine, yours, and generations to come—let the answer be a resounding yes.

—Steve Pemberton,
chief human resources officer, Workhuman, and
author of *A Chance in the World* and *The Lighthouse Effect*

Disclaimer

THE WAYMAKERS IS A BOOK for leaders and aspiring leaders who want to create or support a more equitable workplace for those who have historically been denied insight, access, and opportunity. Equity, as we know, covers a lot of ground. This book is not a catchall—it does not address societal structures, like public policy or education. The examples and strategies in these pages are heavily focused on leadership choices and behaviors that shape corporate workplaces in America.

Throughout my writing, I use various words and phrases to describe historically excluded, or underrepresented, talent and those who exist on the margins of corporate America. I emphasize the experiences of Black and Brown talent in *The Waymakers* because a lot of my work is centered on those experiences, but the principles apply to most situations in which people do not reflect a majority culture. Ultimately, inequity is rooted in power dynamics, and power dynamics exist everywhere.

There continues to be much debate about how people prefer to be identified or referenced, and I have come to understand that the only "right" way to identify individuals is to ask their personal preference and respect it. Since there is no way for me to do this in a book in which concepts apply to groups, I want to clearly state that when I use terms like *Black* and *Brown, people of color, marginalized,* underrepresented, *disenfranchised,* or *those who exist on dimensions of difference,* I mean people who have been (or still are) on the outside looking in. In some organizations, this includes white women, members of the LGBTQ+ community, older workers in companies that do not value them, and people with disabilities—both visible and invisible. Sometimes the terms are interchangeable, and other times I am very explicit about who is being impacted by the challenges and opportunities I explore.

My hope is that you, the reader, can glean the many insights, principles, strategies, and tools associated with Waymaking without getting distracted by the terminology I use to describe those who need Waymakers most. Equity is not a perfect journey, and this is not a perfect book. It is, however, a *true* book. I hope it inspires you.

The Waymaker Whys

WHEN I REFLECT ON ONE of the last conversations I had with my former employer, I do so with a heavy heart. It was shortly before I resigned.

My Hallmark career began with a campus visit, turned into a successful internship, continued with a full-time offer upon graduation from Spelman College, and lasted for twenty-one years. I grew up there, literally and figuratively—through marriage, the births of three children, years of unforgettable collaborations (including a decade-long stint as Maya Angelou's editorial partner), a divorce, a mental health crisis few knew about, a remarriage, a blending of families (into a bona fide Brady Bunch), and a move to another state. In many ways, my destiny felt linked to theirs.

It's important to me that I make this clear: The president at the time, who was my boss, is a very kind man. In fact, the entire Hall family is known for their decency, humility, and generosity—in all the ways people can be generous. It makes sense. They own and operate one of the most timeless and beloved brands in the world—known for products born of the fundamentally human need to meaningfully connect with other people.

Leading up to this pivotal discussion, I'd enjoyed an admirable run with the card giant. From greeting card writer to editor to editorial director. From editorial director to creative director to vice president, writing and editorial, and on to vice president, business innovation. I then designed, stood up, and led a multicultural center of excellence (MCCOE) at the request of my direct manager at the time, who led the North American greetings business. The MCCOE was an embedment arm meant to help company leaders better understand America's evolving population, then translate that understanding into consumer solutions. Toward the end of this stint, I got remarried and moved to Texas.

The move changed everything for me professionally. Before I announced I would be leaving Kansas City, it was a near guarantee that I would become a corporate officer in the role of senior vice president, creative. In fact, the business innovation role I inhabited was merely a way to broaden my business acumen and strengthen relationships with business leaders. But here I was, faced with a difficult choice between two life goals: reestablishing a sense of family for my three children and my dream job. I chose the former.

When I first told my boss I was planning to move, I had no idea my dream job would become available only six months later. To miss out on the role I'd been working toward for years was hard, but even harder was the feeling of aimlessness that followed. A career ascension that once seemed inevitable had been completely disrupted. I never aspired to lead a multicultural center of excellence in perpetuity. But because I would no longer live in Kansas City, where the Hall family was based and community connections were deeply entrenched, my corporate officer dream came to a screeching halt.

My final role in the company–corporate culture adviser–was one I defined myself based on my unreadiness to leave Hallmark and the CEO's unreadiness to let me. After serving in this role remotely for a year, I made the emotional call to resign. Hallmark had been good to me. But I wasn't done growing, and while the CEO and his brother, the president to whom I reported, had a genuine desire to keep me "in the family," I felt placated. My career had always been about impact. I wasn't about to let that change now. Simply staying around would not be enough.

In those final weeks of my Hallmark adventure, having completed an enterprise diversity, equity, and inclusion strategy I'd developed in partnership with a human resources colleague, I sat across from the president feeling both resolve and undeniable sadness. I was proud of the work we'd done. The strategy was rooted in robust conversations with employees about their experiences—both good and bad—as well as a thorough look at the existing makeup of the organization. I believed we had a good handle on the few things the company could commit to that would unlock opportunity for underrepresented talent. We framed bold choices under three pillars and shared our perspectives on table stakes versus efforts leaders might commit to through a lens of sustainability. I was confident that buying into the approach would drive progress. I was not, however, confident about what would happen with the work after I left. As hard as this is to admit, I believed much of it would end with my tenure.

In that last conversation with the president, I warned that the company was at an inflection point in its relationship with Black and Brown talent and, less so, white women. I encouraged him to hold leaders accountable for making deliberate choices—by setting goals and monitoring them—if he wanted to achieve his diversity and inclusion vision. As many presidents and CEOs have since, he said he believed setting targets was unnecessary because the leaders at the company were "good people" and wanted to do the right thing. I responded, as respectfully as I knew how, that their good intentions were not enough. That real culture change is not about good people or bad people. It's about choices. Ownership. And discipline.

I walked away with a distinct feeling of foreboding, fully expecting the company to lose talent in potentially dramatic fashion, initiating an exodus of sorts. I knew how disenfranchised people felt on the inside because they told me so. Constantly.

They didn't set targets. I was not surprised. And not long after I left, Black and Brown people began planning their exit. Thankfully, in the years since, the company has made some impressive choices and investments that I hope will help bring the very best employee experience alive for everyone.

You are reading this book today because I have worked with hundreds of well-meaning executives all over the world who have equated niceness with fairness, being welcoming with being inclusive, and who see scant representation—even when concentrated in nonexempt jobs or entry levels—as diversity. While all these things are *good* things, they are not the *same* things.

To believe equity can be achieved by relying on leaders to be kind and to "do the right thing" suggests that inequity exists because some unkind people did some wrong things, which clearly oversimplifies a system designed and propagated to advantage some and disadvantage others. Equity—technically defined as fairness and impartiality—is an uncomplicated idea with a very complicated root. It acknowledges that there have been more barriers for some than for others, heavier burdens, higher standards, and increased risk.

The idea of Waymaking—the simple yet profound premise that those with power and position have the opportunity and responsibility to make a way for other people—goes beyond fairness. It is a state of heightened awareness, a shared belief, and a commitment to lead. Awareness of the depth and breadth of challenge sweeping over many people and of the many reasons why we have failed to create sustainable change. Belief that every human being has value and potential. And a commitment to be the kind of leader who helps others contribute their value and fulfill their potential.

Waymaking creates space for those leading and those being led to learn and succeed together by waking up to the fundamental call of leadership. It encourages us to better understand *why* we are *where* we are—after decades of equality initiatives—and *what* we can do to accelerate change toward truly equitable workplaces where every employee has an opportunity to achieve their highest aspirations.

In full transparency, I am a person of faith, and the idea of making a way is both practical and biblical. In Isaiah 43:2, we read, "When you pass through the rivers, they will not sweep over you. When you walk through the fire, you will not be burned; the flames will not set you ablaze."[1] This verse suggests a sort of protection—a shielding from harm and an elevation that allows us to rise above and move through challenges without being irreparably damaged by them. Countless professionals in workplaces all over the world need that kind of shielding. They need that kind of support.

This book is an invitation, more than anything, for you—from whichever seat you occupy—to make a way for someone else. In it, I share everything I've learned about why companies are struggling to achieve their equity goals, how those making progress define and measure success and build inclusion competence and confidence, and what you as an individual can do—practically speaking—to create and sustain an equitable workplace. My hope is that you use it to help unlock true equity in your company and then bask in it.

I've been asked why I wrote this book. I wrote it because there are so many reasons why we've not made more progress on equity, and we can't overcome the roadblocks we do see. I wrote it because I've had Waymakers, and I've needed them. I wrote it because beyond all the theories and strategies and operational elements involved in achieving equity, I know that you—the person holding this book or listening to it—are one of the most powerful drivers of progress. I wrote this book to show you not only *why* you should make a way but *how*. Whether you realize it or not, you are the most important difference maker.

Why Me?

"Sparks of brilliance, but no."

This was the comment a Hallmark writing manager scribbled on the internship portfolio I submitted in the spring of 1995, during my junior year at Spelman College. It's atypical to ever see your own portfolio evaluation, but ten years later, when I became vice president of writing and editorial, someone thought it a fun gift to give me.

Becoming vice president at thirty was uncommon then. As with most corporations in the first decade of the twenty-first century, paying your dues was a thing. My journey to executive leadership was swift and expansive—filled with unforgettable experiences and people. Over the course of my twenty-one years at Hallmark, I worked on product lines featuring Bishop T. D. Jakes, Iyanla Vanzant, Chris Rock, Jill Scott, and Dr. Maya Angelou, to name a few. While ambitious, I never would have been in a position to see that critical portfolio comment or to rise to higher heights in the years to come if not for a handful of people who took an interest in my career, removed obstacles from my path, and shared their power with me.

I was fortunate. Still, I fell short of my highest aspirations inside corporate walls. I am not alone, and this is not new. The road to equity has been long and encumbered—painful for those who seek it, perplexing for those who strive to facilitate it. Today many keepers of corporate culture who want to create equitable workplaces don't know exactly what to do or where to begin.

As a Black woman who has experienced success in corporate America and who has also coached others through the maze, I can say with certainty that it's hard to know the best way to meaningfully participate in a system not built with you in mind. The pursuit of equity can feel like a never-ending game of keep-away, except the other players are standing on platforms. You can reach farther, jump higher, swipe faster for the ball, but you still won't grasp it. The distance is too great. If it drops, however, you might be asked to pick it up and clean it off. If you do a good job, maybe you'll get rewarded. Maybe.

If we want to change workplace systems so that more people are valued and can succeed, where and when do we enter? Should we bother? Or do we just throw the whole thing away and start from scratch?

I frequently remind myself and others that existing workplace systems—left to their own devices—perpetuate themselves, meaning they operate the way they always have and advantage people they've always advantaged. It's a sort of a gravitational pull. But the systems are only part of the equation. Shared humanity—familiarity, mutual regard, common ground, a belief in something bigger than us—is powerful too.

"We, the people" have creative energy and free will. We can also harness gravity and momentum. Said more plainly, if enough of us push in the same direction at the same time, change is indeed possible. But only if we see ourselves as having an active role in the change.

Why Us?

Who are the "we" in this situation? To state the obvious, it's not just Black and Brown people. It's also white people. And it's not just women. "We" are *all* people who believe society and its institutions should work for *all* people. In our workplaces, we are those who want better representation across gender and race and ability and sexual orientation. We are the ones who desire to create psychologically safe spaces where people can be themselves, challenge assumptions, and bring innovative solutions to difficult problems. We are the ones who notice that some are standing on pedestals while others stand in holes. The ones who want to fill in all the holes and give everyone pedestals. We are the people who desire more equitable workplaces and who are coming to understand–through painful incidents and tough conversations and rude awakenings–that our organizational cultures are not what we want or need them to be. *We are the people* who must get off the fence and into the equity arena, armed with not only passion and compassion but also insight and tools that help us show up, day by day, as the leaders we aspire to be.

Our inability to realize true equity has been, in large part, due to a series of interdependent systems. Patriarchy, white supremacy, and capitalism have worked together for centuries to keep women and Black and Brown people "in their places" by protecting information, insulating networks, and concentrating money and power. It is naive to think we can achieve equity without addressing these systems. There is no sustainable change without it. But when I consider the many individuals who live and work together every day–with their unique beliefs and behaviors–I know that equity is *also* about you and me. It's about searching our hearts for hints of the leaders we hope to be and our minds for glimpses of a new reality, then declaring that we are both *ready and willing* to do the hard work it will take to realize our goals.

Black and Brown people at work, and others who exist on dimensions of difference, have been conditioned to move about quietly, to minimize disruption, and to endear ourselves to everyone if we want to succeed, often while subjugating our own well-being. Underrepresented employees are publicly encouraged to behave in ways that bring about private criticism: *Use your voice (but not too loudly). Be bold (but not too bold). Pursue excellence (but not beyond existing markers).*

Many white men have been conditioned to believe the world is theirs to conquer, assuming that opportunity–including jobs and promotions and pay–is not only well within their grasp but that it is also in fact theirs to lose. This perspective is evidenced by the dozens of times I've been asked by clients how to respond to their white male colleagues who fear they will lose opportunities because of diversity, equity, and inclusion initiatives. They fail to recognize the underlying assumption they are making, which is that said opportunity was theirs to begin with.

Opportunity is, or at least should be, available to all people equally. Without artificial barriers in the way. This is not the case today, and it will take all of us to redefine the rules.

One of the reasons we turn a blind eye to inequity at work and society, or look for every possible cause other than bias or discrimination, is that if we acknowledge something as wrong or unfair, our conscience will require we do something about it.

In early 2021, Oprah conducted an interview with Meghan Markle and Prince Harry in which they discussed several instances of overt racism and media bias in the United Kingdom. One very clear example was how tabloids skewered Meghan in print over the same actions for which they praised Kate Middleton. One issue of the *Daily Mail* with a photo of Kate holding her baby bump read, "Pregnant Kate tenderly cradles her baby bump while wrapping up her royal duties ahead of maternity leave—and William confirms she's due 'any minute now.'"[2] A similar photo with Meghan on the cover of another issue read, "Why can't Meghan Markle keep her hands off her bump? Experts tackle the question that has got the nation talking: Is it pride, vanity, acting—or a new age bonding technique?"[3]

Buried in this headline are so many insults it's hard to stomach them all. Some are subtle, like how Meghan's full name is used, versus "Kate," which is a sign of formality and therefore distance. Some are not so subtle. The publication batched the typical complaints about Meghan into one headline—pride and vanity, "acting" as a dig at her less-than-royal career history, and "new age," surely a slam at her identity as an American girl from California. This is only one of over a dozen examples of the differential treatment Meghan received in the British media. And yet people made excuses, denying that she was treated differently at all.

In the workplace, whether we're talking talent perception, growth opportunity, or evaluation—it doesn't seem to matter. When dealing with outsiders, skepticism is higher, judgment harsher, and trust minimal to nonexistent.

I have a mentee, a Black woman, who applied for a role at a public relations firm. When she first inquired about the job, the title was vice president, and the salary was $185,000. She went through the vetting process, felt she did extraordinarily well, and was offered the job—as a director with a $150,000 salary. When she questioned the hiring manager about the unexplained changes, she was told they had to align the role with other positions in the company. But wouldn't you have known that before you posted the job and interviewed for it? What's more, they shamed her for challenging their decision by reverting with, "Well, it seems that titles are important to you—what do you want your title to be? We'll call you whatever you want." She didn't last a full year in that firm.

These stories have a common root—they assume the worst of and withhold rewards from those perceived as "less than"—less qualified, less valuable, less desirable, less ready. Still, many will say race is not a factor. Committing to such dramatic degrees of oblivion is something I will never get my head around, but I assume some just don't want to believe racism exists. Others know it exists but want to believe it is rare. And still others are unwilling to really examine it at all for fear they will see it in themselves.

This is also why we resist holding ourselves and others accountable. If you admit a harmful practice is alive in your company, then it is your responsibility to eliminate it. If it is your responsibility, all eyes are on you to act. And when it comes to equity, they should be.

Once we wake up to the idea that driving diversity, equity, and inclusion is not the sole responsibility of the underrepresented, or of the three-person team representing the underrepresented, we have to "get out of bed," which is my way of saying we have to shift from being "woke" to walking out our leadership. We know we can't lie in bed forever, staring at the ceiling. Waking up always means getting up. And getting up means getting going. What's hard for many leaders is not knowing where to go or what they'll do once they get there. Leaders, though, do not have to know everything before they act.

They are curious about the many factors influencing their businesses. They care enough about the employee experience to want to know the reality of it. They identify what's blocking people from winning. And they leverage talent fully and fairly to unleash the potential of their workforce so they can unlock better performance.

Why This Book?

Your good intentions may not be enough to create and sustain a truly equitable workplace, but it's an important start. In this book, you will learn to look at the workplace with new eyes so you can *clearly see* the talent challenges unique to your organizational culture. You will be inspired to imagine an inclusive future that works for everyone. You will discover *where* to look for the hidden bias in the system, *when* in an employee's professional journey it is likely to have the greatest impact on outcomes, *what* you can do to root it out and keep it out, and *how* to determine which choices and investments might actually get you closer to your aspiration. Whether you are "the big boss" or one of many voices pushing for progress, this book will help you make a way for others.

The Waymakers is structured to help you grasp the art and science of Waymaking and to act upon what you learn by:

1. discovering where you are on your equity journey today,
2. embracing the steps required to achieve true equity,
3. understanding what your employees really want from you,
4. developing a lens for the big barriers and intervention opportunities,
5. connecting the dots between meeting talent needs and unlocking company value,
6. recognizing when Waymaking matters most, and
7. showing up–day to day–as a leader who makes a way.

Ultimately, you'll have a reference that makes a compelling case for change and teaches you *how* to facilitate that change. You'll also be very clear about *who* is in the driver's seat. (Hint: it's you.)

The equitable workplace is not an easy place to reach, or we would have arrived a long time ago. Inequity is a crisis with deep roots and sweeping branches. From capitalism to white supremacy to the preservation of power, its drivers and consequences are found in everything we do and how we do it. A book about equity cannot be honest without acknowledging the role of systems in perpetuating harm–inside and outside company walls. But I will keep coming back to this simple and profound truth: Inequity is partly a systemic problem and partly a human one. And human problems call for human solutions. In fact, this is where the real power lies.

We have to know people to care about them.

We have to care about people to invite them in.

We have to invite them in to share our world with them–a world that includes power, position, and possibilities.

We have to see beyond our own discomfort and limited experiences, understand the role we play in driving equity and in unconsciously blocking it, and make a way.

CHAPTER 1

Power and Privilege: Sources of Stagnancy

Progress lies not in enhancing what is,
but in advancing toward what will be.
—Khalil Gibran

Deep Roots, Sweeping Branches

WHEN GEORGE FLOYD WAS MURDERED in Minneapolis, Minnesota, on May 25, 2020, Black people across America found themselves in unfamiliar territory. Not because Floyd was a victim of police brutality—sadly, that was not at all unfamiliar. What *was* unfamiliar was white America's awakening to a clear and institutionalized disregard for Black life. This rising consciousness seemed to roll across segments of white America like a wave. Many watched with horror as Floyd begged the officer kneeling on his neck to get up, then as he called for his mother, and then as he took his last breath. I've been told by white friends and colleagues that the apathetic look on the officer's face while pressing into Floyd's neck with his knee was a wake-up call. Of course, Black America was confused and somewhat offended by the revelation. There had been countless Black men and women who had died in this way. How was this time different? To us, it was just as egregious.

From my conversations, the newfound awareness appeared to result from a combination of things: a pandemic that slowed us down enough to notice and the more than nine minutes it took for George Floyd to die—long enough for the officer to choose to choke the life out of another human being. The mix of greater mental space to see it and the amount of time to process it shook some well-intentioned white people out of their stupor. I experienced my own moments of frustration with the rolling revelations. The downside of noticing scores of people care about Black life all of a sudden is, true or not, it conveyed to Black America that they did not care before.

America as a "safe" place for Black people to live and work and play has long been debatable. Driving while Black, being victimized by "concerned" citizens calling the police for no legitimate reason, and police violence are all long-standing and continuously occurring examples of a nation with different strokes for different folks. This experience creates psychological trauma that many Black people in America have learned to live with. And if they have learned to live with it, they have learned to work with it too.

When I work with executive teams, I don't mince words about "the causes and consequences of enduring racial stratification," to borrow a phrase from political scientist Naomi Murakawa.[1] The causes are many and are as old as time: Power or the desire to control people and situations. Supremacy or the need to see oneself as better than others to affirm a sense of importance. Capitalism or good old-fashioned greed. Self-preservation or the fear of extinction or scarcity.

With the very founding of America, white people built an inequitable system with a desire to be first and best. That system has been cultivated by greed and maintained by a fear of losing stuff–from money and influence to access to the very idea of who they are and why they matter.

I often ask people, "Who would you be without your racial identity and everything that comes with it?" This is a hard question for many white Americans to answer, in part because they seldom contemplate their whiteness. There has been no reason to–it doesn't adversely impact their fundamental rights, access, safety, or well-being. It's also a difficult question to consider because whiteness carries a host of advantages many of today's leaders didn't necessarily ask for but from which they continue to benefit. Privilege is a really uncomfortable idea to sit with and is of real consequence for not only white people in America but also for many who are not white. In fact, everyone who inhabits a corporate role has some degree of privilege–with access to capability building and financial benefit that the majority of Americans simply do not enjoy. In America, if you are white, you have privilege. You also have privilege if you are male, heterosexual, cisgender, safe, wealthy (or just financially stable), educated, or a fair-skinned person of color. Privilege isn't exclusive to white people–it's just concentrated in white communities and compounded by the benefits that have been reserved for white men and their families since 1776 and before.

Interestingly, when I ask other Black people who they would be without their racial identity and what comes with it, I can almost see them sit up taller. While they don't want to lose the joy or pride associated with their Blackness, they visualize a burden being lifted. Racism is, indisputably, a burden–affecting the health, justice, safety, economic, and social realities of Black and Brown people in tangible and persistent ways.

When COVID-19 hit in early 2020, it didn't take long for experts to sound the alarm about the virus disproportionately impacting people of color, many of whom were frontline workers and didn't have the option to work from home. Many had comorbidities, created and exacerbated by historical inequalities–lack of access to healthy foods in certain neighborhoods, lack of public resources or sufficient advocacy. There is also a broad-based mistrust of doctors due to past indiscretions with testing and vaccinations. Once in the care of a facility, there were reports of subpar care for Black and Brown people. These problems are not new, but they were magnified by a pandemic that swept the nation without warning, preparation, or rapid response. And as is always the case, when toxicity exists within any given construct, the marginalized suffer the most.

The justice system has been in the spotlight for decades now, but inherent inequities continue to come into sharper relief. Safety issues also abound–like higher incidences of domestic violence, in part due to financial strain, or stress fueled by discriminatory treatment. This discriminatory treatment starts young. UCLA professor Phillip Atiba Goff and colleagues published a piece in the *Journal of Personality and Social Psychology* that found Black boys as young as ten years old were viewed as older than–and not as "innocent" as–white boys the same age. Other studies Goff cites show that Black boys are more likely than white boys to be disciplined and sent to remedial programs for the same acting-out behaviors.[2] This early discrimination has condemned many young Black boys to the "school-to-prison pipeline," where they move from one system to the next without escape–would-be family men caught in a cycle of injustice.

Another significant disparity revolves around financial wellness. The wealth gap between white Americans and other racial and ethnic groups, which we'll talk about much more in chapter 5, is staggering. A whopping factor of ten times, impacting other inequities, including educational attainment and mobility.[3]

Many executives grew up in the "racism is over" era and have fully bought into a meritocracy mindset that says you get what you deserve. While a nice thought, it's inaccurate and dangerously disabling.

In January 2021, the *Daily Beast* released an article about Donald McNeil, a former science and public health reporter for the *New York Times*, on his language and behavior during a *Times* student trip to Peru. According to multiple parents on the trip, he used racist slurs, made sexist comments, uttered disparaging remarks about Black teenagers, opined that white supremacy doesn't exist, stated that he doesn't believe in the concept of white privilege, and said that racism is over. In a follow-up four-part essay, he denied most allegations and attempted to provide context for others. He recounted, through emails and reflections, that he didn't apologize initially, because he had nothing to apologize for. In one part of his lengthy defense, he wrote:

> Some of today's woke youth eager to "correct" us greybeards have no idea how normal it once was in America to slip into racism. I went to an all-male and nearly all-white Jesuit high school. It was, and still is, a good school. But it was the kind of place where it was much safer, for example, to be known as a racist than as a homosexual.[4]

I found it interesting that in the same essay, McNeil denied having behaved in a racist manner, while acknowledging that he grew up in an environment where it was acceptable and even easy to be racist. From where I sit, it is not a stretch to assume that racist ideas and conditioning might find their way into his words and actions, but he was adamant. This instinct to preserve self-image at all costs has kept us stuck as a society. When we care more about defending our idea of who we are than we do about how we impact other human beings, we get entrenched in racist (and other damaging) ideology—which includes feeling right about our actions and wronged when others call us on it—rather than leaning into the opportunity to learn and become more conscious and compassionate people.

There's nothing as frustrating to Black and Brown people as the claim that racism is "old news"—that their pain is unfounded. For those who've had racist epithets spray-painted on their garage doors or have been spat upon while walking down the street or told to go back to "where they came from," it is not old news. For those with extraordinary debt due to a lack of generational wealth and predatory loan practices, it is not old news. For those who go to the doctor in agony and are disbelieved or otherwise maltreated, the pain is fresh and visceral. And for those who've been stuck in the same job for thirty years no matter how hard they worked, that "history" is now.

When I join executives for conversations about institutional racism and its lasting impact on Black people and, by extension, other marginalized groups at work, participants express shock and disappointment that, in some ways, we seem stuck in the civil rights era. After facilitating almost one hundred of these conversations since July 2020, I can confidently say this idea of America's race reality "not changing enough" is something many white executives hadn't thought much about. What's more, they had an entirely different narrative in their heads.

This epiphany is prompted by the homework I ask them to complete in advance of our conversations, which is to read Dr. Martin Luther King's "Letter from Birmingham Jail" in its entirety.

Dr. King penned the letter in April 1963 from his Birmingham, Alabama, jail cell in the margins of a newspaper. He was jailed for defying a state court's injunction when he led a march of Black protesters without a permit and urged an Easter boycott of white-owned stores. A statement published in the *Birmingham News*, written by eight moderate white clergymen, criticized the march and other demonstrations.[5]

This prompted King to write a robust response, which was smuggled out with the help of his lawyer. The nearly seven-thousand-word brilliantly constructed and masterfully expressed call to action against unjust laws, and for the presence of "positive tension," became a landmark document of the civil rights movement.

Minding Our Business

The "Letter from Birmingham Jail" touches on several concepts that remain relevant for both citizens and leaders today, but in my conversations with executives, a few of the ideas seem to resonate most, igniting a shift in posture that opens the door for more honest conversation about the insidiousness of racism and its lasting effects. One such idea is our tendency to "mind our own business."

In the first third of the work, Dr. King wrote:

> "Injustice anywhere is a threat to justice everywhere. We are caught in an inescapable network of mutuality, tied in a single garment of destiny. Whatever affects one directly, affects all indirectly."[6]

Let's be honest, Western society is relatively self-interested. Those who have enjoyed some degree of success surround themselves with people like them because they can. They focus on the immediate and long-term needs of their own families and friends, who often look like them, and when things go awry in other parts of the world—aside from an occasional donation—they are secretly relieved it's not happening in their own backyards. Unfortunately, though, history has taught us that pain—and the very human response associated with it—spills over. It spills over, as it did in 2021 and in years prior, into our shopping malls and schools and taverns. It spills over into our working relationships and our workplaces. It spills over every time it grows too deep and too broad to be suppressed any longer. For Black and Brown talent in corporate America and beyond, it is constantly spilling over. And we are constantly cleaning it up.

We are often willing to acknowledge that human beings are connected, but not in the real and present ways that make us look and lead beyond our noses. When those with whom I work refer to this passage as one that really stuck out, what they simultaneously acknowledge is their ignorance of other people's pain and the ways in which that pain changes them. Beyond a lack of awareness about the mechanics of interconnectedness, they also admit a fear of not knowing if, when, or how to enter the racism conversation, never mind what to do when the conversation is active. This idea of being inextricably linked is something we will come back to time and again. It is, as amorphous as it sounds, the great accelerator in equity work and a concept all Waymakers must embrace to bring about lasting change. Bottom line: we need each other.

Being Too Patient

Another powerful idea in the letter has to do with the lack of urgency around equal rights and opportunity. Dr King wrote:

> "For years now I have heard the word 'Wait!' It rings in the ear of every Negro with piercing familiarity. This 'Wait' has almost always meant 'Never.' We must come to see, with one of our distinguished jurists, that 'justice too long delayed is justice denied.'"[7]

This is the part people point to when they are compelled to admit they have been living squarely in the "be patient" camp. In the work-place, these are the leaders who ask marginalized talent to "wait their turn." To do things "the right way." To understand that advancement is about "timing and opportunity." Except, for many, neither time nor opportunity arrive. There is always another delay, additional barriers, new rationales as to why they're not yet ready.

Waymakers find both long- and short-term ways to change systems, processes, and norms to unlock opportunity faster. They attack the blocks in the system from bottom-up and top-down, from inside and outside, with today's tools and toward tomorrow's promise. All directions and all at once.

On a recent call with peer equity professionals, we discussed pipe-line building as an equity lever. Building a pipeline of diverse talent into leadership roles is one important strategy, but it takes time. Pipeline building doesn't get you to equal representation overnight. In fact, many of the levers we have relied on to drive diversity and equity take years to deliver results, and as we create strategic partnerships to bring in new talent and adjust our policies to enable them, that same talent falls through cracks created by leaders who are ill-equipped to cultivate truly inclusive workplaces and teams.

People who have been sidelined, devalued, and underappreciat-ed are officially impatient. They do not want to wait, and as more companies recognize how urgent the talent war truly is, the leaders who take their time instead of making a way will fall further behind.

Power Plays

Another reason we've not made more progress has to do with power—who has it and who has proximity to it. In most companies founded in America, the answer is white men. Imagine any entity or organization as having concentric circles with the people in power in the center.

Those people hold the insight, access, and opportunity. The insight is, for example, the unwritten rules–a deeper understanding of how the company and its leadership operate, apart from what you may learn in an onboarding class. Insight includes stakes in the ground, sacred cows, hot buttons, intelligence regarding those in charge versus those with influence, and all the other pieces of data you only know when you're in the circle of trust.

Access is the connection to important business information like priorities or performance, and, most important, to networks–the people who have keys to doors that open rooms where great things happen. Opportunity is exactly what it sounds like–placement on business-critical teams or roles, including by way of promotion.

The more different you are from those in the Power Core, the further removed you are from insight, access, and opportunity. Which is to say, white men are closest. Then white women. Then Black and Brown men. Then Black and Brown women. You don't have to take my word for it. McKinsey's Women in the Workplace team has published a chart for the last few years that shows the representation of each of these groups as they enter the workforce, as they move through the leadership pipeline, and at the top of the house. The only group that expands as leadership levels increase is white men. All other groups decrease as a percentage of the total and in proportions that align with the degrees of difference between them and white men. McKinsey's data shows that women of color are in fact the most underrepresented visible minority in the workplace.[8]

The most important thing to know about how the Power Core operates is that it is fueled by affinity bias, and affinity bias is like a bullet train–it moves quickly and predictably. Left to its own devices, it will stop at the same places at the same times, serving the same people. More on this later, but human beings are wired to trust and surround ourselves with people like us. When we have something of value, those around us are likely to benefit indirectly. Those we trust are likely to benefit directly. Said another way, power begets power. Not always because it is earned but because it is the natural, uninterrupted order of human behavior. It flows to whatever and whoever is there to catch it. Those on the outer rungs of the Power Core cannot buy, earn, or fight their way to power. Power must be shared by the people who have it.

Many companies have begun to establish leadership development programs for talent segments with the intent of accelerating advancement. There are opposing viewpoints on this strategy, and people often ask my opinion. On one hand, Black and Brown employees resist the idea of a "special" development program for them because it suggests they are somehow less capable of performing to expectations and need extra help. I understand this concern; however, I am actually a proponent of cohort experiences—but not for training or development in the way we traditionally think about it. When I design cohort experiences, they are specifically created to deliver insight and access and to open doors of opportunity. Because many times, it's not knowledge or skill people are missing—it's all the intangible things that being on the outside looking in deprives you of.

Looking back at a few of the reasons we find ourselves standing still when it comes to achieving equity in our workplaces helps us appreciate the problem we are trying to solve. *The Waymakers* isn't a history book. Nor is it about systems design. But both have led us here, and if we want to make a way toward the equitable workplaces we deserve, we need to understand not only what we might do but also what we might need to undo.

Where do you stand relative to these four sources of stagnancy? Here are a few reflection questions to ask yourself to assess whether you may have unwittingly contributed to why we remain stuck in place.

1. Have you questioned whether racism (or other isms) is real, privately wishing people would just work hard and focus on what they can control?
2. Have you "minded your business" when peers have made assumptions or assertions not grounded in facts, when those assumptions had a tangible impact on the careers of others?
3. Have you asked people to be patient on matters of equal opportunity or equal pay or fundamental safety concerns inside your workplace?
4. Do you consciously share unwritten rules with people who are not like you, or do you keep important insight to yourself?

Throughout this book, I will ask you to think about both your conscious and unconscious role in making a way for others. John Dewey, American philosopher, educator, and cofounder of the philosophical movement known as pragmatism, once said, "We do not learn from experiences, we learn from reflecting on experiences."[9]

Reflection is an important step
toward becoming a Waymaker.

CHAPTER *2*

Start Where You Are: The Climate Test

Your words will tell people what you think.
Your actions will tell them what you believe.
—T. D. Jakes

I'M GLAD LEADERS JUST LIKE YOU want to jump into action on diversity, equity, and inclusion. But if you want your efforts to be successful, it's crucial to understand your current state before you make any major decisions or investments. If you don't know where you are today, you may end up taking a more circuitous route trying to get to where you want to go.

When I first engage with clients, they immediately ask what other companies are doing. While it's a natural question, it's the wrong question. Every company is unique. You may be earlier in your journey than the next company, but you could also be further along. If you chart your course based on others' actions, you could waste valuable resources and even damage your credibility internally (with employees) and externally (with customers and prospects).

One of my clients was pleasantly surprised when we held a dozen listening sessions with various segments of their employee population and discovered their culture was healthier than they thought. They didn't need an overhaul; they needed fine-tuning. I recommended they pursue a very targeted approach instead of a large-scale initiative, which helped them move toward their destination faster and make an impact where it counted most. This looked like reflecting back to them precisely what their employees thought about specific aspects of their workplace culture and systems. For instance, their employees felt that company leaders were genuine and accessible. They trusted their leaders' intentions. They loved their colleague relationships and described them as fun, collaborative, and familial. They also really enjoyed the work, with many people I spoke to calling out how much they learn every day and how energizing it is to be trusted to do their jobs well without being micromanaged. The feedback was honestly pretty incredible—better than I'd heard in a long time.

Their greatest area of opportunity, though, was related to advancement—clarity on what it takes to get to the next level, feedback quality, differential treatment in the promotion process. And while it was most pronounced for their Black talent, there were white employees who complained about gaps in growth and development processes as well.

Whether you are starting fresh or are refreshing your diversity, equity, and inclusion strategy, the first step any organization should take is to assess its readiness by conducting a thorough culture assessment. This includes understanding how a culture is defined and by whom, as well as learning the best places to look for data and how to meaningfully interpret it. You need to know who you *really* are, then declare your aspiration before you can become the company you want to be.

What We Do, Not What We Say

Before you dive into a culture assessment, it's important to thoughtfully reflect on where you are today. Who do you *think* you are? If your organization were a person, how would you describe them? How would your employees describe them? Would they say they're inclusive? Equitable? Diverse? Creative and innovative? If yes, how do you know?

Our conversations about culture are sometimes ambiguous. As we all know, it's near impossible to affect something we cannot clearly define nor measure. Culture is so much more than our beliefs and values. In fact, cultures exist on three levels: the claim, the policy, and the norm. And in corporate environments, there is a gap between who we say we are (claims) and how employees experience us (norms). The same is true for societies, and it's important that leaders recognize the myriad ways this chasm between claims and norms manifests in the daily work and lives of their employees.

When I worked with Dr. Maya Angelou, she had an interesting way of thinking about words. She would say, "Words are things—they get into the fabric of your furniture and into your floors and on your walls. They are in the clothes you wear. They are in everything." That's how I feel about norms. They are everywhere and in everything, and they represent—day by day, conversation by conversation, decision by decision—who you really are. Not who you say you are and certainly not who you think you are.

For example, a company may claim it supports gender equality. Its policies may include work-life integration strategies or parental leave or pay reconciliation efforts. But if every time a woman comes up for promotion someone raises her family as a barrier or her opportunities become limited because she is of child-bearing age or people excuse pay inequity based on history, the norms do not support the claims. Period. When we choose or behave in exclusive and discriminatory ways, our culture is exclusive and discriminatory. No matter what we say about it on the internet or in our marketing materials.

There was a time when companies could tell consumers what to believe about their products and services, and if they had a good enough advertising campaign and the right celebrity endorsement, people believed them. Those days are long gone.

Today a company may claim to have the best product, but the people who buy and use that product are the real judge and jury. If they like what you're selling, they'll tell their friends, who will tell their friends. Someone may make a viral video enjoying your product. Others will feel like they're missing out and buy it to see what all the fuss is about. In rolls the revenue. The momentum builds on itself.

If they don't like it, however, they'll tell their friends that too. They'll leave a lackluster review on Google or Yelp or Amazon. When people search for your product type, they'll see yours, with three stars, right below someone else's with five stars. If it's the same price or in the ballpark, they won't take a chance. They may tweet about how underwhelming your product is, which could trigger an avalanche of cosigners.

What's more, back when television ads were king, your product was the only thing people cared about. Now they care about not only what you make but also how you make it. And who makes it. And what you're doing when you're not making it. All to say that we have gone from a world where a great "thing" was all you needed to build and maintain your reputation to one where people care about your values, your investments, how diverse your leadership and employee population are, how sustainable your processes are, who and what you donate to and why, and what you're doing to make the world a safer and more equitable place. Brands do not decide they are the best. Consumers do.

The same is true for company cultures. Leaders can no longer tell employees or prospective employees their company is great. Employees decide, and they decide not based on what you say about your company or even by the policies you put in place to reinforce those claims. They decide based on your norms. The choices you make every day. Your consistently demonstrated behaviors. The people you promote or don't. The leadership attributes you celebrate and those you tolerate. The individuals you bring into the room when important decisions are being made and those who always seem to be on the outside looking in. The causes you support. How you hold people accountable when they violate your beliefs and values. These are the signals you send when you're not finessing your communications strategy or fine-tuning your campaigns. It's who you are when you think people aren't paying attention. Except these days everyone is paying attention. To everything. All the time.

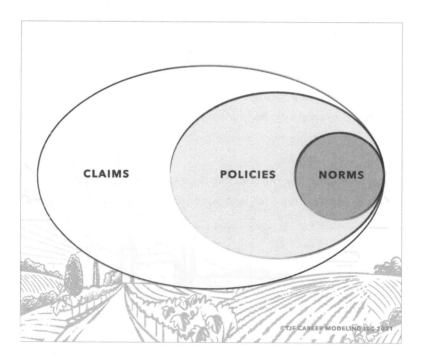

Testing the Waters

After you take time to reflect on where you are today, the best next step in conducting a thorough culture assessment is to gather new data and/or analyze existing data. It's not always clear to people what kind of data you should be gathering and analyzing. There are the usual suspects:

1. **Hiring:** Who you are hiring from which groups and into which positions over time;
2. **Representation:** Which groups are represented in which divisions and at various levels of leadership;
3. **Promotion:** Who gets promoted across groups and at what rates;
4. **Retention:** Tracking attrition, including involuntary and voluntary, with emphasis on regrettable losses;
5. **Exit:** The insight gleaned from exit conversations about leadership, culture, process, and experience;
6. **Engagement:** Any data from surveys conducted to measure leadership effectiveness, climate, and employee satisfaction; and
7. **Listening:** Conversations with groups of people that provide opportunities to dig deeper into both strengths and weaknesses.

In the next several paragraphs, I'll encourage you to look well beneath the surface and shed light on what each type of data can teach you about your company.

For every type of data explored below, collect and analyze *intersectional* data, if you can. Learn not only how many people of each gender, race, or ethnicity enter and leave your company but know also how many there are at the intersections of race/ethnicity, gender, levels, divisions, generations, sexual orientation (if you have access to this information), and tenure. More on this under *representation.* Let's start with hiring data.

Hiring

When looking at hiring data, pay attention to not only who you bring into the organization and at which levels but also what your candidate pools look like and the rate at which different groups of talent are selected versus others. Notice where you hire from—are you favoring certain talent sources over others based on historical success? Old habits can hamper your ability to bring diversity into your organization. In one company for which I conducted listening sessions, employees teased about their organization being a baby version of another company from which they repeatedly hired. It was a joke, but they clearly didn't find it funny. If you do what you've always done. . .you know the rest.

Representation

When it comes to representation, intersections become especially important. For instance, knowing how many Asian women are in your executive ranks and how long they stay, by division or operating group, will tell you much more than knowing how many Asians are in your company in total. You may find certain intersectional groups are concentrated in lower levels or in service teams, which will tell you where to dig deeper for both bright spots and problem areas.

A few years ago, I was working with a company on a culture assessment, starting with their existing representation data. The client shared how good they felt about their representation numbers, which reflected the general population. When we looked deeper, however, we discovered the vast majority of their Black employees were in building services, manufacturing, and in the call centers. There were literally two Black people in the product management division and a handful in the creative department. This was a huge deal for a consumer goods company whose talent must reflect the people they serve if they intend to stay ahead of marketplace needs. When a product organization doesn't have diverse representation in consumer-facing roles, they find themselves in a perpetual state of external discovery–always asking outsiders what works, what's relevant, what people need. Focus groups are great, but they should be a validation tool, not your sole source of insight.

Promotion

We need to look at promotion rates across intersections too, but promotions aren't the only thing to track. Movement–lateral moves included–is generally connected to advancement. Underrepresented talent not only suffer from slower promotion rates but when we look at job moves we find they stay in jobs longer, which deprives them of relevant experience, exposure, and skill-building opportunities. If you're able to uncover it, it's also interesting to triangulate aspiration with advancement. Meaning how much time has lapsed between an expressed desire to advance and actual advancement for certain groups versus others. This isn't a dimension many companies track today, but with human resources systems used in recent years, which ask employees to self-review and input their career goals, it's certainly possible. Do some people in your company wait longer for promotions than others? National representation data suggests they do.

Retention

Retention data is very insightful and generally easy to capture, but be sure to view it through multiple lenses. What you're basically looking for here is voluntary versus involuntary turnover, combined with tenure. *Who* are you losing that you don't want to lose, from *where/ which* levels, and *when* in their tenure with you? One of my clients found they were losing their Black talent in under three years, which suggests they were having some success with their recruiting strategy, but as talent experienced the true company culture and its leadership, perhaps learning more about growth opportunities or the lack thereof, they opted out. Data will not tell you everything you need to know, but when combined with other sources of insight and information, it can convey a pretty complex story about your (organizational) life.

Exit

Exit data is a hot button for me because people lie on their way out the door. I know that sounds harsh, but it's true. Black and Brown talent and women, to a lesser degree, are taught to not burn bridges. This means when they leave, they might say what they believe is tolerable for you to hear and what will allow for continued connection in case they need to revert in the future.

"I got an offer I couldn't refuse…"

"My partner's job moved to another state, so…"

"I love it here, but this new role will give me an opportunity to…"

Maybe. But the truth is often more complicated. There were likely several experiences that made the exiting employee feel less and less optimistic about their future with you. At a point of saturation, this feeling caused them to lift their heads and scan the employment landscape, at which time they saw something that piqued their interest, and the rest is quite literally history. To be frank, we need to learn to ask better questions of people when seeking to understand their true experiences at work. Which leads me to engagement data.

Engagement

Companies have been measuring employee engagement for decades. We know how this works. We administer a survey. The questions cover a range of topics–from best friends at work to tools necessary to do your job to manager effectiveness. Employees answer the questions, results are analyzed, and managers receive reports that tell them how engaged (or disengaged) their teams are, along with how effective their employees perceive them to be as leaders. Managers are supposed to gather their teams and create action plans to increase engagement. Sometimes they follow through; sometimes they don't. Gallup, the leading employee engagement company, reported that in the two decades since they began tracking engagement as a measure of employee satisfaction, engagement has risen ten points from 26 percent to 36 percent. In 2020 "not engaged" employees made up 56 percent of the total, and 14 percent of employees were actively disengaged.[1] If engagement were a valuable metric, and action plans based on engagement survey results were effective, why aren't we seeing more dramatic increases over twenty years of focused attention?

I have long held the opinion that engagement surveys are problematic. First, I'm not sure engagement as previously defined, along with its underlying assumptions, is as relevant as it used to be. As with everything else in the world, our expectations have changed dramatically. Beyond career satisfaction, people want to fulfill their potential. Beyond the tools to do their jobs, they want to learn new things and practice new skills. When it comes to diversity, equity, and inclusion, the surveys we administer are light on relevance and impact. Asking whether employees feel comfortable talking about diversity at work has no bearing on whether the company is diverse, equitable, or inclusive. Asking whether your company values diversity, equity, and inclusion is also not useful. I may answer yes because they *say* they do. That doesn't mean representation is increasing, equity is improving, or inclusion has been realized.

While most surveys can certainly provide insight at scale and suggest areas for improvement, which might facilitate more focused discovery, it's risky to rely too heavily on them. For one, our brains are conditioned to provide answers we think people want. When you consider that certain racial and ethnic groups tend toward optimism, it can be hard to trust the results at face value.

Another challenge is context and timing. My perception of my company may be strongly influenced by my last manager or former division, even though I've changed managers or roles. Or I may answer a question based on my unique situation, which likely differs from my colleagues. (Imagine a work-life balance question for a single mom with young children and an aging parent versus someone with older children in a two-parent household.) Surveys alone preclude us from clarifying the inputs that drive our responses. We don't have a safe way to go back and ask the most important question, which is "why?" Last, some broad-based surveys do not allow for data splicing combined with comparative analysis. Imagine a ten-person team with a 90 percent engagement score that has nine men and one woman, where all the men were engaged and the woman was not. Ordinarily, you would assume that team has above-average engagement based on the score. Imagine that same scenario played out across the organization, with all women reporting disengagement and the men reporting engagement. Without an ability to deconstruct this data and view it across multiple intersections, an employer would not know they have a major crisis on their hands. More companies are requiring their survey vendors to have data-splicing capabilities, or they're designing their own surveys that allow for a deeper and more textured view of the employee experience. This is a very good thing.

I created a survey for a program I designed to help remove barriers to advancement for multicultural women. The experience brings together a group of interdepartmental leaders across race and gender to build empathy and collaboratively problem solve and is being deployed across dozens of teams inside large organizations. The first time we used the survey, which all participants took prior to the live session, the leader was shocked by the results. The survey didn't ask whether the company valued diversity or if the participants felt confident in the company's mission. It was essentially a list of common work-related and societal microaggressions that many employees from marginalized groups have experienced. Each participant was asked to answer "yes" if they experienced the microaggression and "no" if they had not.

The team already had employee engagement data. That data suggested their operating unit was faring relatively well. While there was opportunity to improve in a couple of key areas, the results were promising overall. The microaggression survey uncovered nuances they were completely unconscious of, like how the majority of multicultural women on the team had no idea what leadership thought of their potential. Or how they've watched less experienced colleagues receive promotions that had been denied to them. Deeper than what the company claimed or the practices they put into place, these questions revealed what historically excluded colleagues were actually experiencing or had experienced. And in revealing these experiences, we were able to identify where bias might be hiding in their system. We used this survey not as a stand-alone data source but as fodder for the shared experience, which gave us an opportunity to learn more about the impact of those experiences through candid discussion fueled by both facts and story.

Listening

Data is critical. But there are some truths that can only be uncovered by listening to people share their truths in safe spaces where someone is really listening to understand, probing for context, and validating their story. I always recommend that leaders hire an objective party to facilitate listening sessions, by affinity group, to add dimension to your data. To dig deeper for accurate and complete understanding of the employee experience. I usually advise four areas of exploration, using a frame I learned during my innovation days at Hallmark that helps glean deeper consumer insight. The first is delights or what employees like about their experience, including culture, opportunity, and the work itself. The second is preferences or what employees wish were true about the culture, company, or work experience. (This is the "magic wand" question.) The third is frustrations, as in practices, norms, or realities of the work or work environment that drive them crazy and get under their skin. And the last is concerns, usually drawn out by questions like, "If your company changed nothing about its leadership or culture over the next five years, what might concern you about its long-term viability?" This question is about risk. Each of these lenses leads to a different dimension of understanding.

> *Delights drive satisfaction and can be amplified in real time.*

In our Waymakers research, a proprietary body of work we conducted in partnership with Brandtrust about key moments of connection and disconnection in the employee journey, one Latina shared a story about a time she felt really valued at work. She had been a recruiter with her employer for a couple of years. On a conference call with the larger team, her manager began to tell everyone how successfully she negotiated decision rights to make compensation decisions that would ensure alignment across teams. She didn't know her manager planned to recognize her publicly, but the recognition made her feel like a valuable business partner. She felt respected and validated. The delight here is public recognition. When you listen for what delights employees, you learn which practices you might implement more consistently or broadly.

Preferences are aspirational and can be implemented over time.

The preferences I hear employees express cover the gamut. From wishing they were assigned a mentor during the onboarding process to wanting more transparency on pay scales and advancement criteria to wanting to hear from leadership more often and in more casual forums. Preferences should be viewed as essentially free ideas that come directly from employee hopes and needs. There is no better source, and there is no clearer opportunity than a shared preference across employee groups that reveal patterns about how you manage talent.

Frustrations are here and now and chip away at our tolerance.

Some frustrations I hear are about small moments that seem fleeting but land heavily upon and stay with the perceiver. The actor often thinks nothing of it—not always understanding the baggage attached to the act. Frustrations and microaggressions usually travel together. Like being called articulate (as if it's surprising for people with education and years of work experience to speak clearly). Or someone sharing your idea in a meeting without mentioning where the idea came from—both an act of intellectual theft and a missed opportunity for the originator to be attached to great work. Or being confused with other people from your race or ethnicity, as if we all look the same, which conveys a basic lack of interest in others' individuality and a cultural laziness that casts a shadow on any existing or would-be relationship. If every person, at the very least, wants to be seen, then being mistaken for a different Asian person if you're Asian or a different Black person if you're Black deprives people of this fundamental desire. Other frustrations that arise are a lot more consequential. Like asking for feedback only to receive direction that is neither clear nor relevant, which pretty much guarantees the mark will never be met. Or a lack of transparency about what it takes to get to the next level, which sounds like, "When I ask about promotion, I'm told to keep up the good work. All I ever know is that I'm not there yet, but no one will tell me the way."

> *Concerns are long range and can have far-reaching consequences.*

When I ask people about their concerns, there is usually a personal lens, a company lens, and a competitive lens, and the answers are often similar across companies. The personal lens is pretty straightforward:

"I am concerned I won't reach my potential."

"I am concerned I will eventually have to leave if I can't reach my potential."

These concerns turn into concerns for the company:

"I'm concerned we won't be able to attract or retain talent."

"I'm concerned if we don't attract and retain talent, then we won't be relevant in the future."

The third lens, the competitive lens, stems from the realization that, increasingly, outside entities are choosing business partners based on their diversity, equity, and inclusion positions and outcomes. We are now in the era in which a retailer upon whose business you rely on may not carry your goods if you don't have a DEI (diversity, equity, and inclusion) strategy. Or a critical contract may be at risk. And we are squarely in the space where prospective employees are searching the web for your claims and comparing them to your executive leadership composition and your social justice stance, for example. And if your DEI portfolio is less appealing than that of another company, you will miss out. These concerns are legitimate, and they are becoming a reality for many American companies.

Listening is something we know is important but don't always do well, especially when we are nervous about what people might say. This is where objective parties help–they will keep asking "why" questions until they get to the root of concerns and frustrations and until they understand the drivers of delights and preferences. Often the truth is much more dimensional than we know or assume. And the truth is the only right place from which to begin culture work.

What Great Looks Like

No shortcut exists to creating a more diverse workforce, and even if there were, there certainly isn't a shortcut to retaining one. Leadership teams have to start at the beginning.

And the beginning is a simple question:

"When it comes to diversity, equity, and inclusion, what does great look like *for us*?"

I like to ask teams this question instead of "what is your vision?" because the point of this exercise is not to craft a perfectly articulated paragraph you can slap on a billboard or the company website. The point is to discuss what would be happening inside your company if you got it right. Here is, practically speaking, how I facilitate this conversation:

Imagine three years from now your teams are diverse, your pay and opportunity are equitable, and all employees feel included.

1. How is the business different?
2. What does it feel like in the office?
3. How are teams working together?
4. What do customers (partners and clients) think of you?
5. What do consumers (purchasers) think of you?
6. How have your products and services changed?
7. What's it like to work here?

This low-stress (dare I say fun?) way to imagine a preferred future is always effective. I ask these questions and simply write down everything everyone says on a flip chart or a virtual whiteboard as they call out words and phrases. The energy grows in the space as people think of descriptors for a company that is more inspiring, more productive, more successful, more respected, and more competitive. When we're done, I read every word on the page as though it were a perfectly crafted vision. And then ask them how they feel having heard it. They use words like *hopeful. Clear. Excited. Ready.* And *accountable.*

Aligning on what great looks like is an important step in this process because it inspires enthusiasm, builds optimism, and helps create alignment between team members. Collaboratively painting a picture of progress is a lot more energizing than only looking at and listening to all the ways you're failing to create a culture of belonging. Telling the truth about where you are is crucial. But allowing yourself to envision what great looks like is just as important.

As Erby Foster, a former corporate executive and equity expert with thirty years' experience, told us, "We must go from best practice to next practice to achieve true equity. There is no cut-and-paste approach. You must find out the ideal state for your company and work toward that. Look at your comparative set, yes. Define your playing field, yes. But chart your organization's unique path."

Questions to consider as you embark on your Waymaker journey:

1. Are you who you say you are? As a leader, a team, a company? How do you know?
2. What do others say about your leadership, team, or company?
3. How much do you really know about what's happening when you're not around?
4. How are others experiencing your company and leadership?
5. Have you defined what great looks like for you?

CHAPTER *3*

Making a Way:
The Path to Change

Behold the turtle.
He makes progress only when he sticks his neck out.
—James Bryant Conant

A COUPLE OF YEARS AGO, I facilitated a session about enabling Black executive talent with the CEO and executive team of a
multinational financial company. I planned to conduct the conversation as I typically do with high-level executives, by first asking what
they expect to get out of the time, making sure they have a firm grasp
on the problem or opportunity, discussing a preferred future, and
finally moving to strategic choices and what might get in the way.
It's not rocket science, but it's reliably effective.

Shortly after we began discussing what Black executives were experiencing inside the company, the CEO, who has a bias for action
(as most do), interjected with a plea to move toward solutions. I'm
always prepared for this reaction because successful CEOs who run

large, complex organizations are accustomed to flying at a relatively high altitude and doing what they do best–sensing problems, making decisions, removing barriers, and driving performance.

I knew that the people in the room, who were mostly white and male, couldn't possibly understand the problem well enough to make good decisions about what to do next. So I posed a simple question to the group: "How many of you can say you fully grasp what your Black executives are experiencing inside your company, along with how these experiences impact their careers?" There was only one person who raised his hand–the lone Black man at the table. The CEO sat back and asked me to continue.

As we've explored, the path to an equitable workplace starts with a good, long look in the mirror, but it doesn't end there. You can "see" a challenge, even know the facts behind it, and not fully understand it or how it impacts people's lives. When something is real, it takes up space and changes everything around it. Racism, sexism, xenophobia, homophobia, transphobia, ableism–these are real phenomena with severe consequences for both those on the receiving end of harmful actions and the actors themselves.

Making a way for others means facing hard truths, taking responsibility for your role in changing them, and building bridges between yourself and the people with whom–and for whom–you will forge the path to equity.

Embrace Realism

If we have any chance of creating the kinds of cultures we say we want tomorrow— diverse, equitable, and inclusive—we have to first be honest with ourselves and each other about who (and what) we are today.

In the summer of 2020, Arkansas representative Tom Cotton introduced legislation to prohibit public schools from using federal funds to teach the 1619 Project. The 1619 Project is a long-form journalism project developed by Nikole Hannah-Jones and writers from the *New York Times* and the *New York Times Magazine*. (Jones was granted tenure at the University of North Carolina at Chapel Hill as the Knight Chair in Race and Investigative Journalism after initially being denied, then rejected UNC's offer to teach at Howard University instead.) The work "aims to reframe the country's history by placing the consequences of slavery and the contributions of Black Americans at the center of America's national narrative." The project was first published in the *New York Times Magazine* in August 2019 for the four hundredth anniversary of the arrival of the first enslaved Africans in England's Virginia colony and later included a broadsheet article, live events, and a podcast.[1]

Cotton's legislation would also prohibit the allocation of federal professional development funds to schools that teach the project, effectively censoring educators by withholding needed resources.

His direct quote:

> "As the Founding Fathers said, it (slavery) was the necessary evil upon which the union was built, but the union was built in a way, as Lincoln said, to put slavery on the course to its ultimate extinction."[2]

There's so much to unpack here, but to shine a light on this idea of "necessary evil," I added this commentary to a LinkedIn post I published shortly after the story about Cotton's comment:

"Let's talk about how slavery as it existed in the 1800s might be over, but this mindset—which exists today—continues to fuel America's relentless injustice. Because murder, rape and all manners of abuse are acceptable as long as the outcome is good for those in power. People of color in society and in workplaces are often seen as a means to an end. Any suffering that transpires on the way to a goal is collateral damage. This is the sickness of racism. We must do better."[3]

I realized after reading a few comments on my post that what some Americans seem to have gleaned from Tom Cotton's statement and related position is a call to "focus on the positive"–an acknowledgment that slavery was bad but with the subtext that we should embrace America's good intent so we can move forward. It's a nice idea but deeply flawed, in my opinion.

To humanize the issue, I invite you to reflect on a time in your life when you expressed hurt over lasting harm, and someone in your circle asked you to "move on." No, really. Please take a moment to consider an actual example when you gave voice to residual pain or disappointment about an incident or circumstance, and a person who claimed to care about you suggested you move on. Maybe, as a proof point, they referenced good intentions or–at minimum–the absence of malice. How did you feel? Did you agree or disagree? Did the idea of moving on without addressing the source of your pain help lessen the pain? Did attaching yourself to the idea of a future without pain make the pain disappear? And if you did move on, how did you feel about that person afterward?

I ask because, when harm persists, moving on from pain without acknowledging how it has affected your life does little good in the long run. Even worse, it often irrevocably damages the relationship between you and the suggester. Instead of facilitating healing, it teaches victims to suppress their feelings, and it absolves the perpetrator (or purveyors of the harmful idea) of responsibility.

Sometimes, when we ask people to move on, it's a sign of our inability or unwillingness to join them on the path to healing. In the case of racial reconciliation, some simply do not want to participate.

Some do want to—they just don't know how.

When people say "let's move on" to someone who is hurting, I always try to understand what's behind it. Here are a few alternate meanings I've uncovered over the years:

1. This is too hard: "I can no longer sit in the discomfort of this (or my) transgression."
2. You're overreacting: "What happened (or what I did) really wasn't that bad."
3. It's over: "There's nothing we (or I) can do about it."
4. It's not my fault: "I am not responsible for your feelings or circumstances."
5. I meant well: "They (or I) didn't mean to hurt you, so you shouldn't feel hurt."

When you reflect upon your leadership posture in 2020 and 2021, when there was pain everywhere and no easy way to eliminate it, do any of these statements resonate? Have you, perhaps unconsciously, held one or more of these beliefs about how Black people in America should contend with the outcomes of slavery or how Asian Americans should feel about increased violence toward members of their community or even how women should process sexual harassment or assault that may be decades old? And if so, what does it mean to recognize yourself in these statements?

Talking about how racism, sexism, and institutionalized disenfranchisement continue to show up in many of our companies is hard. And I should know because between May 2020, when George Floyd was murdered by Officer Chauvin, and the writing of this book, I have facilitated these conversations for audiences totaling over fifteen thousand leaders.

So, hard yes. But we don't get anywhere if we let discomfort keep us from confronting hard truths. As difficult as it can be for people to talk about race or gender or sexual orientation or immigration or politics at work, so many of our deepest wounds are festering in exactly these corners. I've seen countless leaders find their courage over this last year or more—making statements about injustice and race-based violence, taking a position against rebellion in many forms, and simply standing in solidarity with people who are hurting and afraid. This is all good, but it isn't enough. Especially if the employees inside your companies aren't benefiting from that same empathy, that same declaration against harm, that same solidarity. Your values should shine from the inside—not the other way around. Being honest with ourselves and each other about what is broken in our systems and norms is the first step to recovery—to becoming the company you claim to be and nurturing the culture you say you want.

As discussed in chapter 2, there are many ways to get an accurate feel for where you are on the diversity, equity, and inclusion embedment journey. We've thoroughly explored the path to understanding. The path to change goes beyond gathering data and analyzing it. We have to internalize that data. Acknowledge it as real and problematic. Then own our role in doing something about it, which includes taking active responsibility for how we lead and not letting ourselves off the hook no matter what. And finally, we must commit to building bridges across difference and invest in relationships with people who are not like us so we can expand our circles of power and privilege to benefit more than the few.

Take Responsibility

Change requires not only awareness but also ownership—the knowing that we are indeed the change we seek and that without energy and accountability, all things remain stagnant.

In Malcom Gladwell's book *The Tipping Point*, he talks about how small actions at the right time, in the right place, and with the right people can create a "tipping point" for anything from a product to an idea to a trend. He also talks about the "Power of Context," which refers to the environment or historical moment in which the trend is introduced.[4]

Many called the civil unrest following George Floyd's murder a "tipping point." It woke people up to widespread racial injustice that had previously been ignored or minimized. Every Black person I know was being asked to share their "Black story" with their colleagues. My white executive friends were calling me, asking what they should do, how they should respond, and lamenting over how badly their first attempts were going. There is no manual for this.

In one of my "Race at Work: A Bridge to Progress" sessions—which are ninety-minute conversations about the current state of race in the workplace and our urgent leadership opportunity—someone asked if I had hope that company leaders would change. I think he was asking whether I believe the work I do makes a difference. I said yes because, well, I do. I believe there are many white male and female leaders who are listening in new ways. Who are recognizing their lack of engagement in racial equity as having had very real consequences. Who now see their past indecision as decision. Who have come to understand that silence does indeed "take a side." But, if I'm being real, I also said yes because hopelessness is not an option for me. I can't allow myself to consider a workplace—or a society—where progress is not possible.

Understandably, there are Black professionals who are not as hopeful. They have been up this hill dozens of times while carrying the weight of the world on their shoulders. Changing our workplaces and our communities will require a lot from us. It will take being honest about the bias inherent in our systems and acknowledging the ugly truth that some like it that way. It will take discovering where discriminatory practices hide and being bold and intentional about rooting them out. It will take courageous leadership—holding ourselves and others accountable to the values we espouse.

Going back to Dr. King's "Letter from Birmingham Jail," one part that struck my clients profoundly was the part about "white moderates" being more devoted to order than to justice.

> "First, I must confess that over the past few years I have been gravely disappointed with the white moderate. I have almost reached the regrettable conclusion that the Negro's great stumbling block in his stride toward freedom is not the White Citizen's Counciler or the Ku Klux Klanner, but the white moderate, who is more devoted to 'order' than to justice."[5]

This passage, by far, hits the executives in my sessions hardest. What they say, in so many words, is "The part about the white moderate was really difficult to read. This is me. I thought I was being a good person by not being racist. By being nice to everyone. I realize my inaction has been in fact actively harmful. And I need to rethink how to show up." I hear this weekly. Sometimes daily. Occasionally, multiple times in the same session. Too many of us have played the role of observer. We have to get off the fence.

In times of great change, there are usually three categories of people. There are those on the front end of the change—ready and willing, excited even, to push into new territory. I call this group the leading group. There is also a group on the other end, resisting the change. They like things the way they are. They want to preserve their norms and positions. I call this group the fixed group. But the largest group is always in the middle. Waiting and watching. Maybe feeling badly about what they see. Wishing it weren't happening. But simply observing—sometimes with apathy, sometimes with low-level anxiety, sometimes with cautious optimism. They are lagging.

This is known as the 20-60-20 Theory, which I adapted from Susan Lucia Annunzio for the purposes of this book, and takes a page from the Pareto principle, or the "80-20 Rule," which says that, in many situations, 80 percent of the effects come from 20 percent of the causes.[6] The 20-60-20 theorists suggest that 20 percent of people during culture change will actively lead and run with a new idea, 60 percent will sit on the fence, weighing the benefits and risks of moving forward, and 20 percent will actively resist the change, flipping only after critical mass has moved forward.[7] (Some will opt out if the new reality is untenable.)

When the leaders I work with say, in response to Dr. King's letter, that it could've been written yesterday, I nod my head. When they say they can't believe we are still having these conversations, I say, "I know." And when they ask earnestly why not much has changed, I tell them the truth. I say it's because of the fence-sitters. This is usually when they recognize themselves as the 60 percent. I also share that we don't have to remain stuck in time. And that if they begin to see themselves as conscious leaders in this paradigm shift, we can guarantee—together—that our children won't have this same conversation sixty-plus years from now. This is what I tell them. This is what I'm telling you.

It matters that we understand this harsh truth: We are not yet who we say we are. In many ways, we are standing today in the same place we were yesterday. Becoming a Waymaker means committing to a different future. One we imagine. One we own. One we make together.

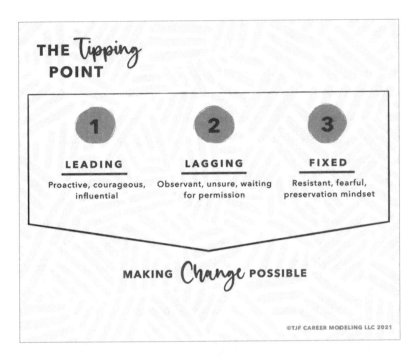

THE *Tipping* POINT

1	2	3
LEADING	**LAGGING**	**FIXED**
Proactive, courageous, influential	Observant, unsure, waiting for permission	Resistant, fearful, preservation mindset

MAKING *Change* POSSIBLE

©TJF CAREER MODELING LLC 2021

Build Relationship

Curiosity breeds familiarity. Familiarity makes way for trust. Trust builds relationship. Relationship opens doors of opportunity. The only way we achieve equity is together.

During one of my visits to Kansas City, I stopped by the home of a dear friend to see her and her husband, their curious (then) three-year-old daughter, and the brand-new baby girl they had recently welcomed into the world. Always enriched by the time we spend together, I made it a point to visit as often as I could.

My regular visits resembled those anyone might make to a good friend. The work heels were tossed aside in favor of a loaner pair of socks. My friend's husband (who became my friend too) would cook a healthy meal and pour me a less healthy but much-needed glass of wine. Sometimes I would read books to their vibrant toddler, who greeted me at the door with an enthusiastic hug and who had an acute fondness for Peppa Pig. My friend and I laughed. Told stories. Shared our exasperation over typical workplace dramas and expressed our gratitude for family, grace, good cheese, and each other. Once in a while, I would stay the night.

As friendships go, ours is right in line with the life-changing kind. This friend has been with me during my highest highs and through my lowest lows. Her rational mind has counterbalanced my ERS—emotional response system—more times than I can remember. She's brilliant, beautiful, funny, and loyal. And when I say loyal, I mean, "one-foot-in-the-ditch-with-you-for-leverage-so-I-can-drag-your-behind-out" loyal. At the darkest time in my adult life, she whipped out a flashlight, pointed toward the exit, then proverbially took my hand and led me into the light. I wouldn't have made it without her, at least not with my sanity intact.

By now you may be wondering why this is important. This friend is white. She has long blond hair and green eyes. Her extended family outings involve activities like hunting and skiing. I've never held a shotgun nor stepped on a slope. She grew up in Topeka, Kansas, and attended school in Iowa. I grew up on the East Coast and went to a historically Black college in Atlanta. We are seemingly opposite and yet so very intertwined. Our differences have broadened our respective views of the world, and our similarities have given us the most powerful baseline from which to appreciate difference. That baseline is familiarity.

Knowing and loving someone from another cultural background is one of the best enablers to truly valuing diversity. It's hard to generalize an entire group of people when your firsthand experience tells you the truth, which is that every group—no matter the attributes by which you define the group—encompasses both good and bad, right and wrong, beautiful and ugly. Systems are real. Cultural norms are real. And it is also true that human beings are unique individuals with the capacity to grow, learn, and change for the better.

Familiarity breeds trust. Trust opens the door to collaboration. Collaboration inspires creativity. And creativity solves business problems. This friend and I have achieved some pretty cool business results together over the years.

The combination of my educational, professional, and personal experiences cultivated in me a relationship agility that has helped me see, hear, understand, and bridge across difference. Bridging is a skill, and I believe anyone can learn it. I also believe that we *must* learn it if we want to be the leaders we aspire to be.

Many of the ideas I've implemented, the leaders I've influenced, the partnerships I've developed have been thanks to this bridging ability. In real time, it shows up as curiosity, reciprocity, vulnerability, concern for the person beyond the position, and—as a former leader of mine Teri Ann taught me—"holding my truths lightly" or a willingness to consider other points of view. Michelle P. Wimes, an attorney and chief diversity officer for a leading children's hospital in Kansas City, Missouri, says it best: "Relationships have the biggest impact on meaningful progress, and we build strong relationships one person at a time—balancing consistency with empathy, vulnerability with strength. We have to be available to people in order to build trust and credibility."[8]

Think about someone with whom you are now in a relationship. When you first met, you were curious about that person. You asked questions about where they grew up, where they live now, what they like to do. You asked about their family. You wanted to know what they thought about important issues. You sought to understand what they value and how they "do life." You learned what friendship looks like to them—in giving and receiving. In time, you came to understand more about what matters to them—what keeps them up at night and what their dreams are. You picked up on their gifts and were able to reflect their goodness back to them. They showed up for you when it mattered most, and you returned the favor. Your mutual trust built with each interaction. Now, you're there for them when the ish hits the fan and also during times of celebration.

What is a relationship if not a series of value-added interactions over time? People who are not like us are still people, and *just* like us, they have hopes and fears and needs and gifts. I don't think it's provocative to say that if we got to know and truly care about human beings who are different from us, we might be more willing to spend our capital (time, energy, advocacy, and resources) on their behalf. This sharing of capital is one way to clear the path to equity in our organizations and in our societies too.

Recently, while being interviewed for a leadership podcast, someone asked how we can build relationships with people across race and gender. I talk about the importance of this all the time because it's a crucial component of achieving more equitable outcomes, especially at work. Take the sponsorship factor. According to Coqual, formerly known as the Center for Talent Innovation, having a sponsor—someone who actively uses their capital on your behalf, who vouches for you "in the room where it happens"—enhances the perception of career progress by 23 percent.[9] But how do talented people find sponsors? And how do sponsors identify talented people they deem worthy of their most valuable asset—their credibility? Often they discover common ground early on. Over time they become more familiar with each other, build trust, and before you know it they have a relationship. When people ask how to build a relationship with someone across difference, my answer is deceptively simple: the same way you build any relationship.

The last few years have left us so divided. We are separating ourselves along countless lines of demarcation. We look for signs of dissent before we look for signs of agreement, and as human nature would have it, we usually find exactly what we're looking for. As citizens of the world, we are striving to preserve our value systems because they guide our lives, and we feel aimless without them. Preservation and progress, though, are sometimes at odds. But there is hope. Because while collectively we are closed to ideas that challenge our values, individually we are open to people who change our hearts. I am optimistic that we can meet each other here—in this vulnerable and unpredictable space.

Connectedness is one of the most powerful equity tools at our disposal. It inspires curiosity. Dispels stereotypes. Broadens perspectives. Creates value. And nurtures respect. But how do we use it? Not *instead* of systemic change but as a complement?

One thing I know for sure. We will not realize equity in the workplace without the active participation of the millions of people who sit between the poles of street-marching activism and power-centered preservation. This is the group who has, likely unconsciously, assumed the role of empathetic observer to discriminatory ideas and practices for years, not believing it was their place to intervene. I wish to appeal to all leaders who know equity is a worthwhile pursuit but who feel ill-equipped to actually achieve it.

Here are a few reflection questions as you contemplate your path to progress:

1. Are you being honest with yourself about where you are on your journey? Have you invited courageous conversations and opened the door to constructive criticism?
2. Are you taking responsibility for your role in shifting culture, or are you heavily relying on others to do the work while you simply "monitor"?

3. Have you made a concerted effort to build bridges across difference? Both at work and at home? When's the last time you had someone of another race at your house for dinner?
4. What can you do tomorrow to build a new relationship?

CHAPTER 4

Heart Work, Right Mind:
The Waymaker Principles

*A good head and a good heart
are a formidable combination.*
—Nelson Mandela

ANYONE CAN BE THE KIND of leader who makes a way for others, if they want to be. There is no profile, per se, and there are no experiential prerequisites. There are, however, principles that guide the kind of person who leads with intention and whose intentions include the betterment of other people, places, and things. This is all you really need if you want to be a Waymaker—an internal desire to use your power, position, and talent to leave the world and the people in it better than you found them. I realized, after talking with a friend who used to work for me, I have been a Waymaker all my adult life. My first leadership book was written out of necessity. Every time someone asked me to be their mentor, I'd say yes, until I literally ran out of time. I wrote *Say Yes: A Woman's Guide to Advancing*

Her Professional Purpose in 2015 as a proxy for myself and included everything I would normally share in a mentoring relationship.

Waymaking is a mindset, but it is also heart work. Waymakers see themselves as part of a larger community, where each individual brings all the gifts they have to bear. Together they determine what value they should exchange, and how, so the group might be whole. They know their success is tied to the success of others. They believe opening doors for people and holding them open is, at least in part, *why* they are here. But that's not all. Waymakers also see the act of bringing others along as a privilege—an opportunity to use the access they've been granted and the gifts they've been given to multiply good in the world. This is *how* they lead—from a place of curiosity and generosity and deliberateness. When we asked over thirty diversity and inclusion experts what constitutes a Waymaker, they used words and phrases like *strategic, confident, realistically hopeful, truth teller, learner, passionate believer, counselor, disruptor, growth mindset,* and *tired but not deterred.*

In the NIV Bible, Isaiah 42:16 reads, "I will lead the blind by ways they have not known, along unfamiliar paths I will guide them; I will turn the darkness into light before them and make the rough places smooth. These are the things I will do; I will not forsake them." *The Waymakers* is not a religious book. It is, though, a leadership book with a higher calling. And that calling is to lead *beyond*—beyond our objectives, beyond others' expectations, and beyond our own inner goals and desires toward a workplace where all employees can thrive.

As with any big, hairy, audacious goal, there are principles that help guide both the work and the person doing it, especially when there is no clear-cut success formula. In Waymaking, these are the principles:

1. **Empathy:** We care about and are sensitive to the lived experiences of others.
2. **Fairness:** We are free from prejudice in our choices and behaviors.
3. **Courage:** We do the right thing, even when it's hard or inconvenient.
4. **Ownership:** We own and carry out our leadership responsibility.
5. **Integrity:** We do what we say we will do so we can be who we say we are.

Empathy

I designed an immersive learning experience for the Network of Executive Women, a nonprofit dedicated to the advancement of all women based in Chicago, that brings together leaders across cultural and gender lines with the expressed purpose of creating opportunity for multicultural women at work. The "experience," which is what I call it as opposed to training, transpires over the course of two days, with day one focusing on insight and empathy and day two focusing on systems and collaborative solution development. We were deploying this session pre-COVID-19 and before the period of intense racial reconciliation. On the first day, we ask multicultural women to share three types of stories. The first being what it is like to be different in the world. The second—what it's like to be different in the workplace. And the third is about the talent journey, with emphasis on the interactions that enhanced their relationship with the company and those that created a disconnect of some kind. There are usually tears shed by the storyteller and sometimes by the listeners.

Inevitably, these stories—told by team members and direct reports and peers—touch a part of the observing leaders, whom we refer to as allies, that data cannot reach. They humanize and personalize the experience of "otherness," bringing painful accounts of being ignored, falsely accused of wrongdoing, sidelined, sabotaged, and even threatened to their doorsteps. The stories are told. The people in the room who have never been othered express dismay and compassion. People feel more connected in their humanity. And the cycle continues.

I always struggle, to be honest. Asking these multicultural women to lay themselves bare for the education of others can be dangerous. You're asking people to access their trauma so others can believe it's real. It's a dilemma. I don't like it on principle, but I have yet to see another tactic work as well. Showing videos of other people's stories is not as effective, because we are not connected to those people. There's something transformational about knowing that Sharon, who sits next to you every day or whom you see on Zoom multiple times a week, was asked to prove she worked in the building by a security guard once, even though she had a badge. Or that Sue's real name is Chunhua, but her white colleagues gave her a new one because they couldn't pronounce the name her parents gave her. These windows into other people's worlds have made the leaders who've not had these encounters more committed to making a way for their multicultural women colleagues. By the time we get to solution development, they are on fire—bold and intentional and appropriately impatient.

Empathy is foundational to leading inclusively. When we are unable to imagine another's experience, we struggle to meet them where they are. And if we can't meet them where they are, it's really hard to walk alongside them to new places where they might better thrive. The good news is, while there are multiple factors that influence empathy, such as genetics, neurodevelopment, and temperament, empathy can be developed.

In December 2020, PositivePsychology.com published several ways to build empathy, some of which I've listed below with a workplace twist on a few to help connect the dots to leadership.[1]

1. Cultivate curiosity

- Spend time with colleagues you know less well. Ask them about themselves, how they are, and what their life is like.
- Follow people from many different backgrounds—religious, ethnic, political—on social media and listen to what they have to say.
- Be present with people when you talk to them. Recognize the emotions associated with certain subjects.

2. Step out of your comfort zone

- Experience what it is like to be unable to do something or not know how to interact with where you are. (This is how many Black and Brown employees feel in corporate America, especially when they're new.)
- Reach out for support.
- Accept how helpless you may feel at times, and let it humble you.
- Use humility as a path to empathy.

3. Examine your biases

- Find opportunities to mix with people from other backgrounds.
- Talk to people about the important things in their lives.
- While recognizing the similarities we share, be interested, without judgment, in the differences.

4. Walk in the shoes of others

- Understand what it is like for people in other situations. How do they live, work, and share?
- Spend time with others and understand their worries. What gives them happiness? What are their dreams?
- Build relationships with people you see but don't usually connect with.

5. Have difficult, respectful conversations

- Listen and don't interrupt.
- Be open to new and different ideas.
- Apologize if you have hurt someone's feelings by what you have said.
- Research the issue. Understand where a point of view has come from and how it affects the people involved.

6. Work on something together

- Align on a business problem or project.
- Join others who have been through similar life experiences.
- Join a group of people from different backgrounds and help out at school, political, or church events.

Fairness

It's not fair. This is what one white male leader said to me during a session I facilitated about race at work. He found it unfair that we were spending focused energy talking about race and was concerned that conversations like this would lead to an unfair advantage for Black people in his company. Of course, the risk of disadvantaging white men in the corporate workplace is virtually nonexistent in our life-time. Systems, processes, values, linkages, and our human tendency to favor our own is built into the very fabric of our companies, and it will take a lot more than a conversation or several to counter the ecosystem of advantage from which they benefit.

I sometimes juxtapose the story of the man telling me "It's not fair" with one in which another white man said to me, "My colleagues don't want Black people in their building. What do you want me to do about that?" I was working with a passionate stakeholder who was desperately trying to educate a board of directors about diversity and inclusion. She worked for a prominent sports member organization with an exclusionary past. That day I learned their past was actually their present, and it was staring me in the face.

This concern people have about losing ground lies beneath all diversity, equity, and inclusion work—sometimes as a whisper, some-times a scream. We shouldn't pretend it isn't real, but we don't have to let it distract us from the important work of balancing the scales. The truth is, we are operating in a construct that has never been fair. Fairness is not a state we can return to; it is one we must create anew.

Waymakers realize that inequity is an intricate web, and the way we guide others through it—toward equal access—is with conscious leadership against the backdrop of systemic change, which should be addressed simultaneously. If we—those who hire and select and encourage and coach and reward and celebrate and promote—can learn to be more objective, more *fair* in how we lead by challenging our own assumptions and the assumptions of others, we will open doors of opportunity for people who have been shut out. Waymakers seek to be free from prejudice as they engage talent and collaborate with others. Easier said than done, of course, due to unconscious biases, which we'll talk more about in chapter 5. I will share growth strategies, with helpful questions to ask, in chapter 6, when we cover the four talent needs and how you can thoughtfully meet them.

Courage

*"Without courage, you cannot practice
any other virtue with consistency."*[2]

This is one of my favorite Dr. Maya Angelou quotes. I first read it in
my twenties while scanning her work for quotes to include in the
greeting cards we created for her product line at Hallmark. I didn't
fully appreciate the meaning until I got much older and had "lived a
little," as elders say.

Clearing a path to an equitable workplace takes courage in the way
that any worthwhile pursuit does. There is always a path of least resistance. In the case of equity and inclusion, many leaders try to make
everyone happy or at least not make anyone mad. A client once asked
how they can get everyone on board with their diversity and inclusion
strategy. They went on to explain how there were employees in parts
of the country who were calling them racist for talking about diversity
and sending letters to headquarters about reverse discrimination.
They wanted to get those employees to embrace the need to focus
on diversity because they knew the vast majority of their employees
wanted the company to be more diverse and inclusive, and the CEO
was committed to evolving. I asked two very pointed questions. First,
what percentage of your employee population do you think strongly
disapproves of your strategy? They didn't know but guessed about 1
percent. I then asked the more important question: "What will you do
if you can't get the 1 percent on board?" They were stumped.

Operating on the assumption that it is actually possible to get your
entire employee population aligned with an equity strategy is a recipe
for failure. It's not realistic. You will spend a disproportionate amount

of your energy playing an unwinnable game. You have to remember that some people do not want diversity or equity. They like being advantaged (who wouldn't?), and the very idea of disrupting a status quo that works for them is blasphemy.

I was driving in North Dallas recently behind a purple Jeep with a bumper sticker that read "F Diversity" and had two Confederate flags hanging inside the rear window, one on top of the other. No amount of encouragement is going to get that person, or people like that person, to embrace your strategy. Referring back to the Pareto principle, your focus should be on amplifying the 20 percent who are leading the way and encouraging the 60 percent who are sitting on the fence to get on the field. This is how you build toward critical mass and shift culture—you make a way and invite others to do the same. As time passes, it will become uncomfortable for those who don't agree with your values to stay with your company. And if you really are committed to equity and inclusion, you need to be at peace with at least some turnover.

Waymakers lead with courage, viewing people and process decisions through a lens of possibility instead of risk mitigation. There is not necessarily a "safe" way to drive culture change. You cannot be transformational and universally liked at the same time. True change always leaves something or someone behind. This is not to say that Waymakers ignore risk, but they recognize there will always be a reason to *not* change systems, especially when challenging power and position.

Waymakers decide how they want to lead and commit to a set of principles that consistently guide them.

How do we find the principles that are right for us? Through reflection, review, and revelation. Think back on times you showed up as the leader you aspire to be.

Reflection: What did you learn about yourself?

1. Which skills or talents did you use?
2. Were there clear patterns in your actions or arenas in which you operated?
3. What else or who else did you tap into to support your success?

Review: What did you learn about the work itself?

1. What was true about your mindset when you achieved your desired outcome? When you didn't, what was missing?
2. What did you notice about the process you used?
3. How did you adjust over time?

Revelation: What is your purpose or inspiration?

1. What did you believe about the work?
2. What is your personal "why"?
3. What are your leadership values?

This chapter is about the principles of a Waymaker, but you can and should consider what your personal leadership principles are as well. Waymakers are undeterred by opposition. When challenged, they stand on their principles and forge ahead. They accept the bitter with the sweet and stay the course—believing that what will be is greater than what has been and that, in this case, the benefits of an equitable workforce will make the momentary struggle worthwhile. There is also strength in numbers. Build yourself a coalition of the willing by connecting with other leaders who see the future as you do and who are willing to be courageous alongside you.

Ownership

Whose job is it to drive equity and cultivate belonging? Yours. It's your job.

A partner in a large nonprofit connected with me to ask if I could help them dig themselves out of a hole they created with a well-meaning (but misguided) attempt to create buy-in for their internal racial equity and inclusion efforts. Basically, they asked employees what they believed the company should focus on to help drive equity and inclusion. The employees came back with several areas of interest and aligned on the top four. Leaders then asked employees to choose which team they wanted to be on and whether anyone wanted to lead the team. One year later, only one team remains. That team has done some cool things in the community, but nothing has changed internally. In fact, according to the partner who called me, most of the executive leadership team doesn't really believe they need to change. And this, my friends, is how we get nowhere fast.

Cultures are defined and sustained by leaders. I will keep saying this, and it will keep being true. Asking employees to develop and own your DEI strategy is akin to my husband and I asking our children to organize and monitor their chores. They may start off strong, but if we don't actively engage, they'll fall off. Not because they're not smart and well intentioned, but because they do not lead the household–they don't make the decisions or investments, and they are not ultimately responsible for whether and how the household is successful.

You can't ask employees to do this work for you. You can't even ask your chief diversity officer, if you have one, to do it for you. Diversity teams are there to uncover opportunities to improve, help you frame strategic choices, and facilitate progress. But enhancing your culture, even at the team level, is work that only you can do. Your talent needs you to own it the way you own customer success or profitable revenue or quality–mindfully and mercilessly.

Integrity

Every time a company makes a claim about their diversity, equity, and inclusion efforts online, and I know differently, I cringe. I have over thirty-five thousand people in my LinkedIn network. Having nurtured this network for over ten years, I actually know a lot of my connections. Many are in human resources in large companies with offices all over the world. In the wake of George Floyd's murder, organizations were making statements and promises left and right. In cases in which I had insight, I quietly wished they had cleaned their own house before donating millions of dollars to external organizations. Generosity is great, but there is no integrity in saving other people while your own people suffocate.

Those who reached out to ask how they should proceed with messaging were met with my practical and measured advice, which was to say something but only say what is true and to speak for themselves instead of the organization. This looks like the CEO making "I" statements about how they feel, what they think, and what they intend to do differently. One person called to ask what they should say if they "want people to believe they care about what's happening in Black communities." I asked, "Do you actually care, or do you just want people to believe that you do?" I walked away from that company. (Not all money is good money.)

No one expected these companies who had been lax on DEI to magically become pillars of progress in a matter of days. We, those who were watching to see who would say what or not, recognized that many companies were newly committing or recommitting to change. We didn't want perfection; we wanted clarity—on their values, their stance on what was happening in society, and their intent to do better.

Integrity matters in this work. We should only promise what we are willing and able to deliver. When we do make promises, we must keep them. On the reward side, it expands our legacy when we commit to higher-order impact—when we determine that we will be better than we have been and do more than we have done. On the risk side, it compromises our credibility when we make commitments to employees and communities and do not honor them. We must do what we say we will do so we can be who we say we are.

I was inspired to add empathy, fairness, courage, ownership, and integrity as principles and not values after reading Ray Dalio's book *Principles*. I'm not sure they're fundamentally different to most people, but I'll admit that something about principles feels more active to me, which fits with my idea of Waymaking. I think of values as residing in our hearts, while principles are held in our hands—shaping, reshaping, drawing in, and pushing out. Values are connected to what we tolerate or do not tolerate, but principles guide what we do and how we do it. *Waymaking*, after all, is an action word. And a Waymaker acts by making a way every day.

Commit to holding these principles in mind on your own leadership journey. When faced with a tough talent decision or an opportunity to elevate talent, ask yourself whether you're being empathetic, fair, and courageous. Ensure you're owning your leadership responsibility and acting with integrity. I wrote my own work principles and posted them where I can see them every day. They keep me focused. They help me avoid making the same mistakes again and again. They remind me of what I've learned so far and encourage me to keep pushing toward the leader I want to be. I challenge you to make your principles a part of your every day. See it until you can be it.

CHAPTER 5

The Mountains We Miss: Four Core Issues

We wear the mask that grins and lies,
It hides our cheeks and shades our eyes.
—Paul Laurence Dunbar

I HAD NEVER HEARD THE TERM *"magical negro"* before Effie Brown, producer of the hit Netflix television series *Dear White People*, explained it during a talk at Hallmark Cards' Creative Symposium several years ago. In her explanation, she began naming all the "magical negroes" we know and love: Whoopi Goldberg in the movie *Ghost*. Laurence Fishburne in *The Matrix*. Samuel L. Jackson in *The Avengers*. Will Smith in *The Legend of Bagger Vance*. Michael Clarke Duncan in *The Green Mile*. Morgan Freeman in…well, everything.

In cinema, "magical negroes" are Black stock characters who come to the aid of the white protagonist. They are often people or beings with supernatural gifts. They talk to God or are godlike. They see things other people can't see and change lives with their abilities.

Inside the confines of a film, being magical is almost always a good thing. The character may experience hardship or even tragedy, but they are often untouchable in the long run or at least fully redeemed through their sacrifice. The deep or abiding conflict in the film is typically resolved in part because of the magical negro. All is well. The movie ends.

I remember half-listening to Effie's talk at one point because I couldn't stop thinking about all the magical negroes I'd seen beyond the film and television arenas and how being magical in other contexts can be a lot more complicated. "Magical negroes" in public life are often the first from their racial group to achieve superstar status in their area of expertise. Michael Jordan in the NBA. Tiger Woods in golf. Serena Williams in tennis. Bob Johnson in television and media. Oprah Winfrey in journalism. Ursula Burns as CEO—the first Black woman to hold the title in a Fortune 500 company. Barack Obama in the White House. We sometimes call them "unicorns" because they accomplish unbelievable things despite the obstacles in their way. As pioneers in their fields, they are celebrated but also held to unrealistic expectations. They must be beyond reproach, remain neutral on controversial issues, and never show emotion perceived as negative or weak, like anger or frustration or anxiety or sadness.

For Black and Brown people in America, the journey to the summit of any professional mountaintop is a treacherous climb. Not only because they often begin from a deficit (have you ever tried to climb out of a hole?) but also because the mountain seems to grow taller as they ascend. And when they do "make it," a minor breach of conduct can render prior accomplishments null and void, however spectacular they may have been.

To be magical and human at the same time requires a level of fortitude and emotional detachment that defies description. It means flying high while avoiding incoming debris. Highlighting what you have accomplished without seeming too proud of it. Moderating your superpowers so you can still fit in. While über-successful Black pioneers steel themselves for the down sides of success, and success is a gift for which no one should be pitied, it's still stressful living on such a tightrope. At that altitude, it takes a whole lot of energy just to stay put.

Before the creative symposium, I didn't have language for what it meant to be "the one" in a corporation—the one Black leader almost every white person feels comfortable around. The one they want to help and coach and create space for. The one who succeeds at an accelerated pace. I can tell you from experience that while it sounds sexy, being an "exceptional" Black person at work is a double-edged sword.

The seeming ease with which some leaders from any given racial minority rise in a white majority culture is often mischaracterized by observers and can be disorienting for subjects. To the majority population, it becomes proof of equity. The success of the few is weaponized against the many, as those who break through become evidence of why every other underrepresented employee can "do it too." This truth is at the heart of the "magical negro" figure as well as the "model minority" myth, which characterizes Asian Americans as a polite, law-abiding group who have achieved a higher level of success than the general population through inherently greater levels of intelligence and a willingness to work harder. While it may seem complimentary on its face, this myth erases individuals, their stories, and the struggles they face in favor of a romanticized tale.

When Barack Obama became the president, white people all over America said that racism was dead. *How could Barack Obama become the leader of the free world if racism still existed?* In life, there are always exceptions. That doesn't mean there aren't rules.

Many "unicorns" end up suffering from a sort of double-mindedness. A double-minded person is described as restless, confused in their thoughts, or in conflict with self. There was never complete and consistent joy for me when I was in this position. I'd feel pride in an accomplishment and immediately become aware of whom and what I was now responsible for–beyond my job requirements. Which reputations I needed to mend, which doors I had to open, which connections I had to make, which opportunities I had to create. (Being a Black executive in corporate America automatically promotes most to Waymaker status.)

Succeeding at that level in corporate America as a Black person requires extreme conformity and an extraordinarily high degree of emotional intelligence. You have to be nicer than other leaders to overcome a conditioned fear of you. A better listener because you're constantly monitoring both opportunities and threats. A better dresser because casual Friday looks different on you. You must learn to bring others along to places they may not intuitively want to go to. For white people, there is nothing instinctual about following Black people. Even when a title or leadership level suggests it is appropriate to do so.

The conflict comes from wanting to enjoy the wind at your back but feeling guilty because that same force keeps others like you stuck at the bottom. It's hard to fully embrace the pride of your accomplishments when your peers are stagnating en masse. No Black executive I know feels fully satisfied when they are the only one winning. If they are the first of their in-group to rise to their level of leadership, they are constantly trying to figure out how to not be the last.

To make matters worse, successful Black executives often have two jobs. In addition to their day jobs, they are–as I've described in other forums–the "Harriet Tubmans" of their organizations, running "underground railroads" of talent loss mitigation for the company. While most sizable businesses have long-standing mechanisms to monitor employee concerns, such as human resources and employee resources, a distrust of systems funnels underrepresented talent away from these paths toward the highest-ranking leader from their in-group. That leader coaches them, negotiates opportunities on their behalf, helps resolve interpersonal conflicts, and generally serves as a Waymaker, even as the interceding leader works feverishly to maintain their own standing. They know a good run is exactly that–a "run," not a permanent state. They are perpetually looking over their shoulder, not only for approaching danger but also to see who may have been left behind.

It took me longer than it should have to resign from corporate America. It had been evident for over a year that my trajectory, once a clear path to the C-suite, had shifted after I moved out of state. But I had to disentangle myself from the growing guilt of leaving people without a voice.

This inability to simply focus on doing your job well is just one pain point that many who exist on dimensions of difference experience at work. Each one acts as a silent killer of organizational culture–causing undue stress and compromising employee wellness, stifling innovation, adversely impacting results, and derailing careers. The four roadblocks that have the most profound effect on the underrepresented employee experience and, by extension, business outcomes, are:

1. the lack of psychological safety,
2. little to no representation,
3. limited opportunity, and
4. the burden of proof.

Each of these roadblocks is distinct, and yet they are connected by two interrelated concepts–power and otherness. Developing an inclusion consciousness is both a head and heart exercise. Here we become more knowledgeable about what is broken and how it harms the people in our charge.

Lack of Psychological Safety

The last few years have brought the issue of psychological safety to the forefront for a lot of Americans, not just Black people. When President Trump declared Mexico was not sending "their best people" to the United States and began touting his plan to build a wall, the Mexican children in our community school were taunted by some of their white classmates, who shouted "Build the wall!" at them in the hallways.[1] An increasing number of Spanish-speaking Americans were shamed on trains, in restaurants, on airplanes, and even on sidewalks for speaking Spanish. "Speak English! You're in America!" became a rallying cry for those who were encouraged to believe it was their job to preserve America's legacy. I spoke to members of the Latinx community who told me they would brace themselves when they left their homes, not knowing whether or when they might run into a person who would decide to take on the mantle of white supremacy at their expense.

Their fear was not unfounded. The FBI reported a 21 percent increase in anti-Latino hate crimes in 2018 over 2017—and hate crimes in general are increasingly targeting people instead of property.[2]

When COVID-19 began spreading in the United States, President Trump made a point to call it the "China Virus" and "Kung Flu," which placed a new group of people in the crosshairs of his followers' ire. East Asian people all over the country reported instances of harassment and assault. They were yelled at, spat upon, and told to "Go back to China." Never mind the fact that their families hailed from multiple countries of origin, not just China, and many of them were Americans. *This is their country too.*

In fact, it seems an American pastime to swap one derided group for another. People from Arab countries are no strangers to this kind of cruel and unwarranted treatment, as they were subjected to widespread threats and acts of violence in the aftermath of the 9/11 terrorist attacks. They reported being afraid to go outside, to speak out of turn—to inadvertently frighten anyone. According to the FBI, anti-Muslim hate crimes jumped in 2001 from 28 to 481, and while the number of attacks decreased in the years following, they never went back down to levels reported before 9/11.[3]

Why does all of this matter? It matters because employees are people first. They have families and hobbies and values and passions and health considerations and needs outside work. And as intentional as many are about compartmentalizing, when the climate is as stressful as it has been, it is impossible not to carry personal burdens into work. The societal view, however, is only part of the story. There's some pretty troubling stuff going on inside organizations too.

Enter the leadership connection to psychological safety. In a 2017 meta-analysis and literature review,[4] psychological safety was found to be significantly related to several domains: leadership—that is, inclusive leadership, transformational leadership, trust in leadership, and leader-member exchange; work design characteristics—that is, supportive work context, interdependence, and peer support; and employee performance—that is, employee engagement, satisfaction, commitment, and task performance.

Amy Edmondson, professor of leadership and management at Harvard Business School and the most prominent academic researcher in the field, defines psychological safety as "the shared belief among team members that the team is safe for interpersonal risk taking." She explains that "team psychological safety describes a team climate characterized by both interpersonal trust and mutual respect in which people are comfortable being themselves."[5]

Personally, I think of it as the freedom to show up as you are—with your gifts, your ideas, your personality, and your potential, without feeling the need to suppress or minimize your contribution for fear someone may not listen to it, understand it, like it, or value it (or you).

What does psychological safety feel like?

When team members feel psychologically safe, they don't fear threats to their personal, interpersonal, or professional identity or standing. In my mind, identity is our very essence—how we define ourselves, what we believe, and how we perceive our value as individuals and collaborative partners. Standing represents the perception of our leadership efficacy (how good we are at our jobs), our contribution impact (the distinct value we add to the work), and our relationship quality (the condition of our working relationships).

Team members who feel psychologically safe are able to freely contribute to the team, even when—especially when—they have dissenting opinions or unconventional ideas. They ask for help without fearing they will be perceived as inept and seek feedback more readily as a tool for growth rather than shying away from it as a weapon of criticism. People who feel psychologically safe not only bring their "authentic selves" to work, a phrase we've perhaps oversimplified in our conversations about inclusion, but they also bring unlimited creativity, business insights inspired by unique life experiences, and their counterviews, which can help organizations mitigate risk by pressure testing ideas and plans related to both people and performance.

There are far too many employees in organizations all over the world who lack basic psychological safety, and the implications are pretty far reaching. Perhaps most unnerving is the health impact. In a 2018 study on the emotional tax among women and men of color in the workplace, Catalyst found that a majority of men and women who identify with Black, Latinx, Asian, and multiracial backgrounds experience this "tax" to the detriment of their overall health, well-being, and ability to thrive. The study also notes that these employees are in a constant state of guardedness in response to being undervalued or discriminated against at work or in society. Fifty-four percent of those who felt different based on gender or ethnicity reported being on guard, compared to 34 percent of those who did not feel different. This feeling manifested in having to consciously prepare to deal with potential discrimination by bracing for insults, avoiding social situations and places, or fixating on their appearance as a way to avoid bias. What's more, when feeling on guard, women of color believe they have to outwork and outperform their colleagues. They also question the vitality of their careers, with 38 percent saying they are more likely to frequently consider leaving their jobs.[6]

Why should we care? There are very real business risks associated with the absence of psychological safety, not the least of which is a basic return on employee investment. Seventy-four percent of employees surveyed who did not feel different from the norm spoke up about important or difficult issues at work, compared to 56 percent of those who felt different based on either gender, race or ethnicity, or both.[7]

The challenge here is obvious. We have talented people on teams and in decision-making bodies who are overthinking whether and how to share their unique perspectives for fear of being ridiculed, even as we claim we need and value diverse perspectives to make our businesses more successful.

We may be hiring for diverse voices and insights, but in many cases, due to a lack of psychological safety, we are not benefiting from them.

Imagine purchasing a new computer that only worked 44 percent of the time. You would not feel good about your investment, and you wouldn't rest until you identified the root cause of the performance problem.

Like you, I've seen many advertising campaigns released by big brands that went awry in a racially and ethnically diverse consumer marketplace, only to wonder who was in the room when approval was given. From culturally insensitive to downright racist ads, the range of missteps has been broad and deep. I used to assume these decisions were made with no people of color in the room. My hypothesis now, however, is a little more nuanced. In some cases, they probably did have one or two in the room who could have spoken out against an idea or plan but didn't feel safe in doing so. Or maybe there was a dissenting voice that was ignored or overruled. It is unsettling being the only one in a room where your "diverse perspective" is supposed to matter but doesn't. Majority leaders still listen for threads they can relate to, and when they don't hear anything that connects to their lived experience or personal observations, they struggle to trust the insight.

Beyond the missed opportunities that come with sidelining unique perspectives, there is an innovation cost as well. According to Catalyst's emotional tax research, 75 percent of those who did not feel different reported being creative and innovative at work, compared to 61 percent of those who felt different based on race or gender.[8] A 2017 Boston Consulting Group Diversity and Innovation study revealed that companies with racial and gender diversity enjoy an average of 45 percent innovation revenue versus companies that are not racially and gender diverse, who report 26 percent of their revenue from innovation.[9] Some say this is because of the diversity itself. I actually believe diversity—which minimizes the outsider dynamic—enables psychological safety, and safety is what unlocks innovation.

It's not rocket science. If I'm worried about heightened scrutiny, I'm not likely to bring forward big ideas. Incremental ones, maybe, but nothing revolutionary. It takes a lot of courage to think outside the box when you fear you might not be allowed back in. It's no surprise then, that among those who *did not* feel psychologically safe, only 21 percent felt included, but among those who *did* feel psychologically safe, 86 percent felt included.[10] This research suggests you cannot have inclusion without psychological safety, making it perhaps the most important place to begin any journey toward culture change. Sometimes a lack of safety becomes evident in obvious acts of discrimination. Other times, the threat shows up more subtly.

My family and I live on a golf course in a mostly white suburb of North Dallas. We had been in our home for two days when an older white woman carrying a welcome basket full of flyers and coupons rang our doorbell. When I answered the door, she jumped back, whisked her hand to her chest, and gasped, "Oh, I'm sorry!" I remember a flush of heat running through my body as I realized she was shocked to see me, a Black woman, answer the door of *this* home in *this* neighborhood. Even though she rang *my* doorbell. I was not out of place. I was literally standing *in my place*—in my sanctuary—on the receiving end of her microaggression.

A few years later, my parents moved into a different subdivision within our community and a woman with a similar basket rang the doorbell. My mother, who could pass for white, answered and invited her in. The woman entered, welcomed my mother to the neighborhood, and struck up a conversation. My father, who is clearly Black, walked out from the back of the house to say hello, extending his hand. She refused to shake it. There was nothing "micro" about her aggression that day. Her refusal to touch my father while standing in his home conveyed a deep disregard for his humanness. It took my father—a man in his seventies who had been actively engaged in the civil rights movement—*weeks* to get over the insult. I'm convinced it was the same woman, since I later discovered there is no official "welcome wagon" in our community. Just a person who takes it upon herself to play the role. A welcome committee or a gatekeeper, depending on who's trying to get in.

According to psychologist Derald Wing Sue, microaggressions are "brief, everyday exchanges that send denigrating messages to certain individuals because of their group membership."[11] Others describe microaggressions as subtle verbal, behavioral, or environmental indignities that communicate hostile and derogatory messages to a certain group. Whether or not the offenses are intentional, they essentially convey to people in the group that they do not belong.

At work, those who do not fit a traditional leadership profile are microaggressed all the time. A high-ranking Latina at a local non-profit told me she was mistaken for the help at her office. In another instance, a Black woman took her team out to dinner, and when she asked for the check, the server brought it to one of her direct reports, a white male. A Chinese executive told me that she had to adopt an American name to make it easier for her American colleagues to communicate with her. A Black male executive vice president for a global tech company shared how he would spend weeks on the phone with a client, only to have the client ask, "Where's Phil?" when they first met in person. These slights are common occurrences in the lives of underrepresented talent, both inside and outside the workplace.

Black women and lesbian women experience microaggressions at a higher rate than women overall, at 69 percent and 71 percent, respectively. For members of the LGBTQ+ community, slights are waiting around every corner, from well-meaning questions about husbands or wives, to gendered stereotypes that rob people of their basic right to define themselves for themselves. Sixty-four percent of all women say they deal with microaggressions at work, with common examples cited as being talked over in meetings or labeled emotional when displaying even a modicum of passion.[12] Microaggressions are dangerous in that they are not only demeaning and contribute to burnout and turnover; they also emphasize racial stereotypes while diminishing an individual employee's unique characteristics, talents, and contributions.

Microaggressions can be rooted in any number of factors. Racism, sexism, xenophobia, homophobia–all fertile ground. But so are stereotype bias, fear, a good old-fashioned sense of entitlement, and just plain lack of exposure. Outright racist and discriminatory acts are less common than they used to be at work but still occur. (And, as previously noted, have been on the rise outside work.) Targets of microaggressions often drive themselves crazy wondering if group-based maltreatment is simply ignorance or something more insidious. It's important that we distinguish between the two whenever possible because the response strategies differ. Ignorance can be combated with intervention, education, and reconciliation. The only acceptable response to any "ism" is zero tolerance. We'll explore this idea more later.

Low Representation

Lack of representation in the workplace is a major barrier to equity and inclusion. I know—it is also an outcome, but this is a quintessential chicken or egg example. It's hard to pinpoint which comes first, and it almost doesn't matter.

When we talk about representation at work, we often focus on the numbers. "This percentage of this employee segment in this organization or role equals representation." But representation is so much more than data. It is, for many women and people of color in organizations, a sign of what's possible. If I join your organization as a Black woman and I look up, then to the left and right, and see no one who looks like me in positions of influence, I automatically question my ability to succeed. I figure if other Black women at your company, some of whom have likely been there for years, haven't broken through the barriers to advancement, what are my chances?

This skepticism regarding marginalized talent's likelihood to flourish at your company is a multifaceted problem for individuals and organizations alike. It adversely affects engagement, fulfillment, aspiration, trust, and internal and external credibility. It may even prevent talent from joining your company in the first place should they notice the homogenous leadership team on your website or the absence of diverse voices representing your company in the media.

In the five years since McKinsey has been tracking representation of women in the workplace, nothing much has changed regarding leadership, with women entering the workplace at 45 percent and representing only about 20 percent of top jobs. This top-line statistic is stark, but as is true with so much of the equity paradigm, it is incomplete. In 2020 white women accounted for 29 percent of those entering the workplace and 19 percent of top jobs. The big story here is the morbidly narrowing funnel for women of color, who entered the workplace at 18 percent in 2020 but only represented 3 percent of top jobs. Men of color are also underrepresented, entering the workplace at 18 percent and representing 12 percent of top jobs, but the double jeopardy Black, Latina, Asian, and Indigenous women experience on their journey to the top is undeniable. By contrast, white men, who enter the workplace at 35 percent and represent 66 percent of top jobs, are the only group whose opportunities expand as their careers progress.[13]

Why is this happening? Not because white men are inherently smarter or more "leader-like." We must examine mental models as institutional barriers to equity. One of these mental models is prototyping. We can't ignore the fact that, for generations, profiles of corporate leadership have been defined by and for white men, which means anyone who appears or operates noticeably different may be perceived as an anomaly–a person who does not "fit in." This can manifest as appearance-based qualities, like height or manner of dress. It can manifest in speech, like accents or word choice. It can also show up in ideas, like using sports or military analogies to make a point or get people on board. And it can certainly be perceived in behaviors, like how we use humor or how we celebrate success.

We are wired to lean into what has worked for us in the past, and this includes the kinds of leaders we value and promote. We'll explore in future chapters how avoiding the style trap when defining leadership profiles can make space for a broader range of leader types. Clearly, unconscious bias plays a significant role in perpetuating workplace inequity and preventing us from achieving equal representation. Confirmation and affinity biases are, in my informed opinion, the most harmful culprits. Left to their own devices, these two bias types can be blamed for much of why we continue to have the same conversation about diversity, equity, and inclusion year after year. Knowing how these and other mental models prevent us from recognizing the potential in others is just one of many blatant opportunities to reframe the way forward.

Underrepresentation also exacerbates the challenges that come with a lack of psychological safety. Forty-five percent of women of color and 37 percent of men of color are often the only, or one of the only, people of their race or ethnicity in the room, according to McKinsey and LeanIn.org's 2018 Women in the Workplace study.[14] In this scenario, they are more likely to feel excluded and scrutinized—and this is especially pronounced for women of color who are Onlys. In particular, Black women are significantly more likely than other Onlys to feel closely watched and to think that their actions reflect positively or negatively on other people like them.

There's evidence that carrying the emotional weight of representing your group is justified. If someone from a majority group makes a mistake, that mistake is usually individualized. That person is blamed for their error and judged accordingly. When someone from a minority group fails, however, their failure is often generalized—casting a shadow over other members of their group. I've been within earshot of leaders questioning whether it's a good idea to promote a woman into a big role "after what happened last time."

Can you imagine a scenario in which someone doubts whether a white man will be successful in a role because the last one wasn't?

Women and people of color understand all too well that while they may prefer their wins and losses belong to them alone, others are observing, seeking patterns, and drawing conclusions—often erroneously, always unfairly.

Part of why we draw false parallels is because we have no frame of reference for groups to whom we have little or no exposure. When our interactions with people across difference are limited, we are more likely to take the bit we discover and extrapolate. This is one of the lesser discussed risks of low representation—limited exposure means fewer data points. Fewer data points lead to generalization. Generalization prevents us from discovering the truth of others' identities and makes it easier to dismiss individuals and their ideas.

We should strive to have no more firsts. No more Onlys. No more unicorns. Just a diverse collection of talented individuals who are striving to meaningfully contribute—with space for everyone to bring their very best into every room.

Limited Opportunity

Conversations about inclusion are sometimes reduced to creating a sense of belonging. We think if we are kinder to underrepresented talent or more welcoming, they will feel like they belong and then feel included. I can't count the number of times I've spoken to CEOs about racism and institutional disenfranchisement, only to be met with a predictable "the people here are good people" retort.

This notion that nice people cultivate inclusive workplaces is faulty at best and dangerous at worst. If you believe it, you will not train leaders to lead across boundaries. You will not educate them about the blind spots inherent in their gut instincts. You will not ensure diverse decision-making bodies to mitigate bias. You will not set goals to increase diversity, which can enable equity, increase psychological safety, and foster inclusion. You will not hold leaders to certain standards of fairness, because you will assume that "good" people are fair people. I have said, verbatim, to CEOs I greatly respect: "Your good intentions are not enough." It may be hard for well-meaning leaders to hear, but let me say this again. Being nice and being equitable are not the same thing. This mindset is the equivalent of throwing water on a gas fire. While water is generally thought to extinguish fire, there are circumstances in which it would make harmful conditions worse. Similarly, trusting your and your leaders' good intentions to fix your equity problems will give you a false sense of security in your ability to fix what's broken.

To take it one step further, underrepresented employees do not go to work for kindness. Or for belonging, for that matter. Developing trusting relationships and even friendships at work is an important career enhancer, of course, but many employees from marginalized groups scratch that itch outside work. What they really need from their employer is what most people want in the workplace–to contribute, to grow, to be promoted, to earn the opportunity to impact the business, and yes, to make more money so they can care for their families.

We cannot oversimplify what it means to be included by talking about belonging as an emotional experience. It's nice when people are kind to you. It's even nicer when they respect and value your contributions in tangible ways. In fact, 75 percent of Black women and 65 percent of Latina women view themselves as very ambitious toward their careers, with 40 percent of Black women hoping to make it to a management position within the next five years, according to CNBC and SurveyMonkey's Women at Work survey released in early 2020. Despite this clear desire to advance, they face seemingly insurmountable odds. For every one hundred men promoted to manager, only sixty Black women and sixty-eight Latina women are promoted.[15] Achievement is a completely natural career driver and should be elevated above the idea of belonging if leaders want employees to give them credit for their equity initiatives.

Reflecting on my days as a corporate executive, I recall healthy debates about what was deemed acceptable motivation for wanting to be promoted. Achievement and higher income as end goals were frowned upon in the eyes of many leaders. Personally, the only motivation I was ever bothered by was the obvious power grab, but I understood the distaste some had for money as motivation. I now see how judging others' reasons for wanting to advance is privilege in action. It's easy to criticize from a position of power and prosperity.

I do believe that if more leaders better understood how wide and persistent the opportunity and wealth gaps are between white America and Black and Brown America, they would spend less time judging and more time doing what they can to help others succeed.

When I lived in Kansas City, I volunteered for an organization called Operation Breakthrough, which provides a safe, loving, and educational environment for children living in poverty and empowers their families through advocacy, emergency aid, and education. During orientation, we engaged in a financial empathy-building exercise reminiscent of the game Monopoly. At the beginning of the exercise, we were handed varying amounts of money (reflecting monthly incomes earned by the families we served) and a starter set of circumstances, which included household size, health conditions, employment status, and more. We journeyed between tables, each stop delivering some new life circumstance in the form of a playing card. As in real life, every circumstance carried financial implications. When the game started, I had a job and a car. Three minutes into the game, my car broke down. I didn't have enough money to fix it. I could have taken the bus to work, but it would have required me to leave the house earlier than my young children started school, and I couldn't afford childcare. Just that fast—one unpredictable hit to my limited resources—and I was having to choose between my job and the welfare of my children. I would say that I wondered how long it might take someone to face that choice in real life, but I know the answer. People all over the world are making these choices in the name of survival every day.

This may seem like a dramatic example to share in a book about equity in corporate America. But relative advantage and disadvantage exists everywhere. According to the Federal Reserve, in 2019, white median wealth in America was $188,200. Black median wealth was $24,100, and Hispanic median wealth was $36,100—a wealth gap of more than $150,000. Thanks to a legacy of discrimination, this chasm has existed for longer than any of us have been alive. The inconvenient truth is that white Americans benefit from an intergenerational transmission of wealth, either through inheritance or gifts. These methods account for more of the racial wealth gap than any other demographic or socioeconomic factor. Nearly 30 percent of white families report having received an inheritance or gift, compared to about 10 percent of Black families, 7 percent of Hispanic families, and 18 percent of other families. And of the families who receive an inheritance or gift, white families receive larger amounts.[16]

Families also make investments in their children that increase their ability to accumulate wealth, like paying for college or private schools or providing down payments on homes. Home ownership can be a reflection of the wealth a family already has or that their parents have and also serves as an investment vehicle. About 46 percent of young white families own their home, compared to just 17 percent of young Black families, who are far less likely than their white counterparts to receive down payment assistance from their parents. Last, we know that liquidity plays a significant role in overall financial health. Emergency savings dictates how well a family can weather a storm, like job loss, illness (self or family), or other unplanned expenses. The typical Black or Hispanic family has $2,000 or less in liquid savings, while the typical white family has more than four times that amount. Other families fall somewhere in the middle, with the typical family holding $5,000 in liquid savings.[17] The old adage "pull yourself up by your bootstraps" falls flat when some families are gifted boots with straps and others are not.

You may doubt the relevance of this data to the Black and Brown people with whom you work, since many may own their homes and make decent money. They likely have liquid savings, even if it is significantly less than their white counterparts. But you don't know how far they have traveled, what they've had to sacrifice to get where they are, and who is traveling along with them. In many cases, Black and Brown professionals who have "made it" are a source of financial assistance for their extended families and friends.

All this to say that employees have their reasons for wanting to advance and for members of marginalized communities, corporate jobs have historically been one of the more accessible paths to building generational wealth. Of course, the advent of social media and the rise of entrepreneurship is challenging that belief more each day. Corporate life remains riddled with obstacles for underrepresented talent—the valleys are deeper and there are many more mountains to cross. It would serve every leader to move beyond the idea of acceptable motivation for advancement, as it fails to consider the realities of systemic racism and other institutionalized barriers that have plagued marginalized communities for generations. The talent war is real, and—thanks to technology—the competition is increasingly fierce. It's time to open our minds so we can be employers of choice.

Where Bias Hides

Years ago I read an article suggesting that women of color (and Black women in particular) at work were perceived as either rock stars or underperformers. They didn't have the luxury of being "solid"–good, smart, reliable, well-performing talent who met their objectives. There seemed to be no box for people in the middle–only for unicorns or problem children. I know talented people who have been pursuing the same promotion for over a decade. Similarly, I've known talented people on "R1-2" (ready in 1-2 years) succession lists for just as long. In cases in which employees produce results but are denied the opportunity to advance time and again, what's happening? Why can't they get over the hump? While each case is unique, there are disturbing patterns of bias hiding in our systems and processes, and some of these hiding places hold significant roadblocks for under-represented talent. So where does bias hide? In the following pages, I'll cover five places bias can hide. In chapter 6, under the four talent needs, I'll share specific questions you can ask yourself and others to combat bias in real time.

Bias Hides in Our Beliefs

Inevitably, when I speak to executives about diversity and equity, someone will say that race, ethnicity, and gender don't matter to them when selecting and promoting talent. They just want "the best person for the job." On its face, this is not a controversial statement. Who wouldn't want the best person for the job? Every leader should, and every employee should want to be the best choice for an opportunity. The problem is this: The "best people for the job" are not born; they're made. And we are not making them equitably. Best people for the job are made on important projects. They are made with access to strategically important information. They are made with coaching and sponsorship and influential networks. They are made with tools and resources. They are made with encouragement and chances and faith in their ability to win. Opportunities are denied to underrepresented people every day because they are not perceived to be "the best person for the job." Sometimes they are exactly the right choice and we aren't conditioned to see value in them. Other times, they are not yet the best person for the job, and the reasons why have more to do with our norms than their potential.

More than fifteen years ago, when I was at Hallmark, a woman named Debora McDermed, who owned a company called The Vertical Dimension, came to speak to us about what we now call a growth mindset, researched and made popular by Carol Dweck.[18] Deborah shared the belief cycle, a tool I have used countless times since. The belief cycle is a universal concept that recognizes how any thought we have repeatedly becomes a belief, which creates emotion, which influences our behaviors, which impact our results. What we believe about other people changes how we feel about them, which changes how we treat them, which ultimately affects their opportunity to succeed.

Question your beliefs about people. Remember the cycle, and when you feel negative emotion toward a person or situation, ask yourself what you are believing about them or it. Then challenge that belief to make sure it is based on fact.

THE POWER OF Belief

BELIEF

FEELING

RESULTS

BEHAVIOR

THE VERTICAL DIMENSION

Bias Hides in Feedback

People of color are less likely to get timely, relevant, and specific feedback on their performance, which hinders their ability to make early adjustments for long-term success. I moderated a panel a couple of years ago with a diversity consulting leader who was a white woman. When I asked why she believed white women leaders, specifically, did not provide more timely and specific feedback to women of color, she said—without hesitation—that it was because they didn't want to be called racist. It took me a second to process her response, and every woman of color in the room was initially shell-shocked. The shock gave way to gratitude, however, when we realized the power of her willingness to give voice to what many of us intuitively knew. That some white women at work harbor a fear of

Black women in particular. And this fear prevents them from giving Black women and other women of color one of the most valuable gifts an employee can receive—timely, honest, and relevant feedback. This fear of sharing difficult news with people when they need it most is lengthening learning curves and depriving people of critical learning opportunities.

The lack of feedback is a huge problem, but so is discriminatory feedback. People who exist on dimensions of difference get negative feedback for doing the same things white employees do, but because of irrational fears (thanks to the media or other conditioning), the actions or words—even voices—of Black and Brown people are less tolerated.

We've all seen or heard about that one leader who is toxic. He may yell at his team or curse at people when he's upset. He "leaves bodies in his wake." People avoid triggering him, and his triggers are widely known. He drives results, however, so his toxicity is considered an acceptable risk. This leader is almost always a white male. I am not saying white men are inherently toxic. What I am saying is this: I have never known a woman or person of color who felt comfortable treating colleagues poorly in a work environment. Ever. Managing other people's fear and distrust is something Black men and women know a lot about. Thanks to decades of unchecked media portrayals, the stereotypes are deeply entrenched and easily brought to mind. Black men are aggressive; white men are assertive. Black women are angry; white men are passionate. For white women, the "emotional" trope gets thrown around like confetti (though we've seen how unfounded this stereotype is thanks to America's political landscape).

Stereotypes can end up being a default characterization of entire groups of people, and one negative comment about an employee that mirrors a stereotype often gets magnified because it reinforces a mental model that already exists. (Remember: too few data points.) Consider this: Julie says Kim is abrasive. Jen, Susan, Melissa, Eva, John, and Joe say Kim is fun and funny. But because Julie says she is abrasive, Kim needs to work on being less abrasive. This one negative comment about Kim from one person can be the solitary reason Kim's reputation is sullied, and it may very well prevent her from being promoted. I often tell leaders who call employees intimidating that there is a difference between someone being intimidating and you feeling intimidated. Your fear of me does not make me scary. If we can begin to understand that our negative reactions to people who are different are sometimes about us and not them, we can make space for the diversity we claim we want. We react emotionally to others based on any number of factors—and reality is but one.

Three simple ways you can interrupt bias in feedback:

1. Consider the source—is the source reliable? Is the feedback firsthand?

2. Determine if the feedback really matters relative to performance—is the behavior in question compromising the person's ability to do their job well, or is someone being sensitive?

3. Think about whether there is a solution that honors the person—be sure you're not asking someone to be perfect or clear more hurdles than others or neglect a part of themselves to satisfy your expectations.

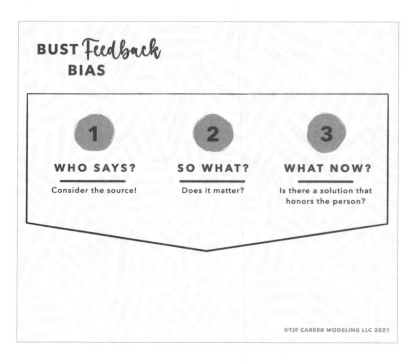

Bias Hides in Training and Development

Another reason underrepresented talent remains underrepresented is how we go about training and developing people. It's great that companies offer training and development, but three things often go wrong here. First, the "high potentials" we select for these experiences often resemble those making the selections. They remind us of our early career selves. We "get" them. They "speak our language." When we do not deliberately add a diversity lens on our selection processes, white employees disproportionately benefit. Second, we sometimes include one or two people in these programs who exist on dimensions of difference, but when they are the only or one of two people in the room who look like them, they feel less psychologically safe, which means they ask fewer questions, take fewer risks, and are likely to get less out of the experience than their white counterparts. Third, some training is formal, but a lot is informal. Without informal networks that include high-level leaders, many Black, Latinx, Asian, and multiracial professionals miss out on critical insight–like the sacred cows or unwritten rules referenced earlier–that could enhance their prospects for advancement. Without this insight, it's easy to miss moments to shine and, worse, to trip up. We must be more conscious about who we are teaching, training, developing, and informing and make it safer for all employees to take risks.

To make training more equitable:

- Check your high-potential lists for dimensions of diversity– both visible and invisible, and create learning cohorts if possible.
- Include diverse leaders as mentors or sponsors in training and development efforts to create safe spaces for all.
- Make the unwritten written and the unspoken spoken. This is part of the "training" that seldom makes it into manuals.

Bias Hides at Happy Hour

Okay, bias doesn't literally hide at happy hour. But bias hides in trusted circles and relationships, where the "in" crowd supports their own. If you're in the crew, your name will be on the list for that special project or new opportunity. You will be selected for a role before the job description posts. You will be ushered into high places by your people. You will benefit from secondary connections, too, because a friend of my friend is my friend.

The social distance concept holds true before people even get in the door. When comparing Black and white prospective job seekers, a 2019 study by Pedulla and Pager found that Black job seekers were less likely to know someone who worked as an employer and less likely to have someone from their own professional network who could reach out on their behalf. As a result, for every five white job applicants who receive a job offer, only one Black job applicant will receive an offer through job applications found on social network-based channels.[19]

When the system takes its natural course—when we neglect to consciously interrupt it—the train runs automatically, boarding some people and passing others by. What happens when you don't enjoy influential relationships? When you have to work harder to find common ground and no one is intentionally seeking you out to make a genuine connection with you? You stay outside. You miss the train. You get run over or you fall behind.

Make it a point to connect with people who are not like you. Don't plan informal gatherings at places that are inherently exclusive, appealing to some and unappealing to others, or where some might feel insecure about their knowledge or skill. Become familiar with new people so they can be included in your consideration set next time opportunities arise.

Bias Hides in Succession Planning

When I first became a corporate executive, we would spend a full day—sometimes two—discussing succession plans. Over the years, time grew short, demands grew long, and by the time I resigned from corporate America in 2017, what used to be a multiday event had been whittled down to a few hours. A few hours to discuss and debate the next generation of leaders and their readiness for the roles we inhabited. In years prior, we created space for the unusual suspects to emerge. For stories we didn't yet know. For challenging assumptions and each other. But like many business activities, this crucial exercise had been victimized by a shortage of time and attention. So much goes wrong when we compromise our people processes.

I will never forget my last succession-planning meeting. I was the only Black person in the room. Actually, I was the only person in the room who was not white. It was decided that we would only be discussing "top talent" due to time constraints. Before I walked in, I readied myself for the negotiation ahead because I knew that meant we would be discussing all white women and men unless I intervened. It was the same list we always talked about. Bright women and men, for sure. A couple had worked for me, and I had strongly advocated for them year over year. They deserved to be on that list. But they were not the only talented people in our organization; they were just the most visible and the ones in whom we had consistently invested. After we ran down the list, I started asking about a few other leaders who were not white. A colleague pointed out that they were not on the top-talent list. "I know," I said. "But we've not spoken about this person in a while, and if I remember correctly, she was once considered high potential. What happened?"

Her manager responded that she was "hit and miss." That she had "lost her spark." I asked what changed. He didn't know. I asked if he had spoken to her about it. He said no. I requested that he do so in the two weeks following and report back to us, and he agreed. He did not object to approaching her about her perceived inconsistency, but he hadn't thought to do so on his own. Why? Why do we naturally care to keep our fingers on the pulses on certain employees' careers and not others?

The truth is, if I had not been in the room, no one would have held space for her or others like her. No one would have asked why, then demanded we be more curious—that we stop making assumptions. In succession-planning conversations, this is our greatest error. We are too quick to "mind our own business," trusting that everyone else's talent thought process is thorough and fair. It isn't. We are all susceptible to bias, and unless we begin to challenge each other in the moment, we will remain stuck—doing the same thing on behalf of the same people and only those people—in perpetuity.

By the way, my colleague followed up with the employee, as did I. We both learned that she was ready for a new challenge. I ended up hiring her onto my team via promotion. Sometimes, the best and only thing I could do to bridge the opportunity gap was to take matters into my own hands. This is not an unusual move for executives from underrepresented groups.

There is no silver bullet to getting to equity, but if there were, it would be to diversify the very top level of leadership, so all employees benefit from affinity bias equally through a trickle-down effect. The most diverse divisions or business units in companies are usually led by people of color. This is because they have an intuitive diversity consciousness. When you are in the majority group, you have to cultivate that consciousness. Unless we slow down, ask new questions, and look at talent with fresh eyes, our biases will perpetuate the status quo. Inclusion is not natural for many of us—it requires deliberate interruption. Repeatedly. Until it becomes second nature to ask ourselves and each other "what else?" and "who else?"

To pursue progress is to take nothing for granted. Don't ever stop at your first decision when it comes to promoting and positioning talent. Know that you are unconsciously taking the easy route. But easy is not always best, and it is often not equitable either.

Burden of Proof

The last pocket of pain is what I call the "Hoop-Jumping Olympics," otherwise known as the burden of proof—a tremendous weight carried by countless employees who do not represent the norm, who have little in common with talent managers, and who find themselves in the unenviable position of proving their worth—over and over again.

Let's say I, a Black woman, have an important job to fill, and there are two candidates. One is a Black woman (like me) and the other is a white male. Now let's assume I have visibility to about 50 percent of what each of them brings to the table (from a results and experience perspective), but the other 50 percent is unknown to me. Thanks to affinity bias, which leads me to trust and associate with people who remind me of myself, I am likely to project what I know about me onto the Black female candidate. I will say things like, "She has potential," "I believe she will rise to the occasion," and "She has what it takes." Having nothing inherent to draw upon as a means to better understand the white male or his potential, I may suggest a stretch opportunity for him—a chance to demonstrate his ability to do the job. If he succeeds, my "gap" in knowledge has been reduced but not eliminated. I may continue to ask him to prove his ability until I am *sure* he will be successful. I ask him to go through this proving process not out of malice but because I am managing both his and my own reputational risk.

As leaders, we want to make the right people calls. And when we have no common ground from which to infer, we seek more information by (unconsciously) requiring more of the person to whom we can't easily relate. In time, the employee who endured rounds of proving becomes frustrated, and legitimately so. They recognize what you don't—some people are required to jump through multiple hoops in order to be considered for an opportunity, and some aren't. Now, they have a different problem. They appear negative or disengaged. It takes a lot of energy to keep running up a hill that never seems to peak. Especially when you notice that leaders expect you to fill every single gap while, for others, a hint of promise is enough. Since white men make the majority of hiring decisions at the highest levels, affinity bias advantages them most consistently.

This is not just a convenient story. According to LeanIn.org and McKinsey's 2019 Women in the Workplace study, 40 percent of Black women and 28 percent of white women say they have to provide additional evidence of their competence, compared to 14 percent of men. Forty-one percent of Black women say they are questioned about their judgment in their area of expertise, compared to 39 percent of white women and 29 percent of men. And 22 percent of Black women say their contributions are ignored compared to 16 percent of men and 16 percent of white women. For many Black women at work, the onslaught of disregard doesn't let up. Which is why it is no surprise that 49 percent of Black women feel their race or ethnicity will make it harder for them to get a raise, promotion, or chance to get ahead, compared to just 3 percent of white women and 11 percent of women overall.[20]

The burden of proof is real. We hire talented Black, Latinx, Asian, and Indigenous people into our companies, then we ask them to continually earn their right to succeed once they arrive. Sometimes we even let them flail in uncoordinated attempts to navigate our culture and its unwritten rules without guidance or support. Black women are often the most disenfranchised inside corporations, with four in ten never having interactions with senior leaders about their work. They are also far less likely to get help navigating organizational politics and balancing work and personal lives, and managers are less likely to promote their accomplishments. The same dynamic holds true for access to managers: Only about a third of Black women socialize with their manager outside work, compared to about half of white women.[21] Is it any wonder why employees from certain groups remain on the outside looking in?

Our tendency to more easily connect with and trust people who feel familiar to us has a direct impact on who ends up on the fast track and who stagnates. For some, potential is sufficient, and we come alive at the chance to develop that potential. But some must demonstrate their ability and agility until we feel comfortable.

How do we measure comfort—an ambiguous, unmeasurable feeling? It is a trap that leaders easily fall into, irrevocably harming talent that doesn't inspire them. Thanks to our lack of connectedness across differences and the dearth of diverse leaders making talent calls, this inequity persists. The burdens increase. And we can feel helpless to change it. Except we're not. In the following chapters, I'll make very clear what your talent wants from you and how you can give it to them, while setting both you and your business up for long-term success.

CHAPTER *6*

What Your People Want:
Four Talent Needs

I've learned that people will forget what you said,
people will forget what you did,
but people will never forget how you made them feel.
—Maya Angelou

I MOVED TO A SUBURB called Pine Hill Acres in the North
End of New Bedford, Massachusetts, when I was two years old with
my parents and my older brother. We were the only family on my
street of African origin (Cape Verdean, to be specific). In fact, I can
only remember one other Black family in the entire neighborhood,
which consisted of approximately four hundred single-family homes.

My most salient memory from those early days was meeting my
first friend at four years of age. I was sitting in the driveway playing
with dirt, and she walked over and began talking to me. I don't recall
what was said or what happened immediately after that. I simply
remember Keri's smile, which is still killer, her presence, and the fact

that this moment of openness led to a forever friendship filled with years of short-lived crushes, countless sleepovers, Halloween parties with spaghetti brains and peeled-grape eyeballs, breakfast for dinner, séances, and swim parties. As we grew into our teenage years, those swim parties turned into trips to Horseneck Beach and the crushes turned into boyfriends (still short lived).

This moment mattered because I was an extremely shy child. I now know there was anxiety at the core of my shyness, but as a girl it manifested in hiding my face in my mother's skirt. Turning away when adults spoke to me. And flat out refusing to engage whenever doing so felt overwhelming, which was most of the time. Even my family members—aunts and uncles—still joke about it. Some say I was skeptical. Others say, laughing as the words come out, that I was "mean." Keri was undeterred by the invisible shield I'd erected around myself. She saw the potential friend behind the brown skin and short, curly Afro, behind the head down and eyes focused on the dirt. She saw *me*.

During my freshman year in college, my mother called to tell me that Keri's mother—a woman who welcomed me into her heart and home almost every day for fourteen years—had passed away from a brain aneurysm. Mrs. Hebert was the first close adult figure in my life to die when I was old enough to feel the gravity of it. My heart broke for me, and it broke for Keri, who was undeniably changed by the loss.

In elementary school, I was one of three Black students in my entire school and the only Black girl. This was in the late seventies and early eighties, and while I remember most kids being nice to me, I also remember feeling on guard about my difference. I braced myself when I met my friends' grandparents. And when it was time to choose kickball teams during gym. And whenever spin the bottle was being played. I was in the crowd, but I was not a member of the "in" crowd, and the only time that feeling went away was when I was with my small, intimate crew. There were five of us. Four white girls with whom I laughed, cried, played, and learned to be okay with myself. Outside this safe space, I sometimes felt invisible and often anxious.

In middle and high school, there was more diversity but not necessarily more inclusion. I was different from the other girls—somewhat introverted, studious, and let's just say my awkward stage felt less like a stage and more like a lifetime. If not for my elder cousin Matt, whom I affectionately call "brousin" (*brother* plus *cousin*) inviting me into his friend circle, and my summers in Upward Bound—a college preparatory program for high school students from low-income families and families in which neither parent holds a four-year college degree, I doubt my circle would have expanded beyond what I came in with. My husband and I often joke about how differently we remember high school. He recalls being loved, respected, and centered in the middle of it all. I recall trying desperately to get out, driven by a deep need to reinvent myself from a reserved, nerdy "ugly duckling" to someone more connected and confident.

Enter Spelman College, a historically Black women's college in Atlanta, Georgia. My Spelman experience was a textbook example of belonging. I had never felt so seen, respected, valued, or protected by anyone other than my parents in my life. I saw versions of myself everywhere—in the dorms, in the classrooms, in the president's office, in the cafeteria, on the grounds. I saw myself in the lessons. The books I read. The stories told. The sheroes we celebrated. My classmates were much like me. They stood out in their high schools too—young women across the geographic and socioeconomic spectrum who wanted to define themselves for themselves apart from the complexities of race and gender. Inside Spelman's gates, our identities extended far beyond our Blackness and our womanhood. We knew each other by our quirks, our talents, our styles, our stories, our personalities, and our aspirations. There was Chae, my roommate, the comedic one, who would give anyone the shirt off her back. Toiya, the responsible one, whose laugh carried down the halls and into your soul. Jonica, the gregarious one, who never met a stranger and would also knock one out if necessary. Tracie, the sweet one, who was always about her business. Susan, the easygoing one, who was determined to grab life by the lapels (in my Maya Angelou voice). My sophomore and junior year, I lived with Tara–focused and fun loving and fearless.

It's probably hard to imagine what it feels like being surrounded by people who look and dream like you for the first time when this is your everyday reality. Feeling visible in this way normalizes who you are and what you stand for. When you succeed, you are not a successful Black woman–you are simply successful. Critical mass in any American environment allows people who are not white and male to be individualized–known and celebrated for who they are as people and not as members of a group. There is no substitute for the freedom that comes with being surrounded by people who also value what you value, and at Spelman, those values were scholarship, sisterhood, and service. In that place, I saw the best of myself in the eyes of my sisters. I learned to love myself because they loved me.

I felt respected at Spelman. My ideas and contributions were appreciated by my peers and professors. Not in relation to mainstream ideas but on their own merit–in a context that didn't compare or contrast my views with pundits or poets who didn't look like me (as though their lenses were the true lenses, and mine were being evaluated for accuracy).

I felt valued there. I earned decent grades, and I also earned opportunities to lead in ways that mattered to me. I was the college's poetry journal editor. I won the Spelman athletics logo design contest (a mark that still dons Spelman apparel today). I was chosen as the "guide" for Hallmark campus visitors–a coveted role I asked for and received, and that turned into a twenty-one-year career.

And perhaps most important, I felt protected at Spelman. For more than twenty-five years, my sisterhood has fortified me. Inside its embrace, I am safe to ask questions I don't know the answers to and to make human mistakes without reputational risk. I can be emotional when I am emotional and strong when I am strong. I can soar like an eagle or feel grounded as needed. The women with whom I came of age are still in my life—offering parenting advice, tips on aging well, and simply reminding me that I'm all the things I need to be, exactly as I am.

There is a limitlessness that comes with feeling seen, respected, valued, and protected. And there is also power in it. This human experience—truly being a part of something lasting with people who trust you and believe in your potential—unleashes children to conquer their fears, adults to bet on themselves, and yes, employees to contribute at a higher level than they thought possible.

In each of these scenarios, there are Waymakers. Parents who model for us. Loved ones who motivate us. And leaders who make a way.

These four needs—(1) to be seen, (2) to be respected, (3) to be valued, and (4) to be protected—are not exclusive to Black and Brown talent. But inside corporate America, they are met less frequently and to a lesser degree for those who are different from demographic and behavioral norms.

This chapter is filled with stories and findings from the Waymakers narrative inquiry study conducted in partnership with Brandtrust, a research firm that helps companies solve complex business challenges through applied social and behavioral science. We asked hundreds of underrepresented employees about moments in time that made them feel more or less attached to the organizations and people for whom they work. We then asked them to describe, in detail, the circumstances surrounding these moments: Where were you? Who else was there? What did they say or not say? How did you feel in this moment, and after? Was there any follow-up? How did this experience change your relationship with the company? Using their stories to elicit their most memorable experiences and the conditions surrounding them, we uncovered a rich landscape of intercession opportunities that clarify the role leaders can play in capitalizing on these moments for the good of the company and its employees. (And how they can avoid inadvertently sabotaging their efforts to create a more equitable and inclusive culture.)

The hundreds of employees across race, gender, and sexual orientation who told us their stories of feeling seen, respected, valued, and protected or feeling invisible, disrespected, underappreciated, and scrutinized are at the heart of this chapter. Their vulnerability has allowed us to show you—in the daily choices and behaviors I will continually emphasize—what it looks like to lead equitably and inclusively. I strongly believe that the more completely we understand what it means for underrepresented talent to experience these states of acceptance, along with how leaders have broken through perceived or invisible walls to facilitate them, the more confident we'll become in our own ability to do the same.

The choice to be a Waymaker can be made in a moment, but the ability to do it well takes skill and practice. In this chapter, I'll also share leadership skills and behaviors associated with delivering against each of the talent needs, along with specific ideas for how to cultivate your individual capacity to lead toward an equitable workplace. Depending on where you are on your Waymaker journey, you may benefit from some parts of this chapter more than others. I have chosen to be thorough and instructive because I know firsthand how elementary some people's knowledge of these issues happens to be. After more than a year of helping C-suite teams and their direct reports better grasp the cultural context in which we now work, I am now being asked, pointedly and with great anticipation, "but *how*?"

Leaders want to know how to talk about race and other sensitive issues. They want to know how to give difficult feedback across difference. They want to know how to interrupt bias on the spot. If you, too, have been wondering what to do and how to do it—as one person with the heart to make an impact and the determination to follow through—this chapter is for you. In chapter 7, I'll review systemic levers companies can pull, with tips that can be used to drive equity on a larger scale.

To Be Seen

Due to the nature of my work, I see a lot of tears, but I'm not often the one shedding them. That changed when an Indian woman in a large consumer goods company shared her talent journey with her peers—of all races and genders—in early 2021, during an experience designed to build empathy and understanding across difference. She called me the night before to ask how honest she should be. The very act of telling the truth in professional environments where Black and Brown people are accustomed to suffering indignities in silence is revolutionary, and she felt the burden of it—not knowing how her peers would react to her truth and being even more aware of how it might affect the other South Asian women in the room who looked up to her. I advised her to consider the importance of this moment— that she may never have a time carved out like this again to say what only she can say about her experience but that she should consult her inner wisdom in real time and only say what she felt safe to say.

Long after this experience, I am still marveling at her courage. She held nothing back. With tears, an unsteady voice, and occasional use of the "stop video" button, she painted a vibrant picture of a young woman's pursuit of excellence marked by racism, xenophobia (even though she was born in the United States), gender bias, and cultural expectations. I was transfixed, as was everyone else present. It was painful to hear and see her labor to get it all out, especially because she has been incredibly successful and has mastered the art of composure, as every Black and Brown woman executive must do.

Her story included all the usual suspects—from marginalizing comments about being a diversity hire to others taking credit for her work to having to intervene at various breaking points in the careers of other Indian women, effectively serving as a lone talent loss mitigator. As is true with all Black and Brown people at work, the barriers to potential she shared extended far beyond the workplace. They were also in her home, in her neighborhood, and in her memories. Everywhere she goes, racism and xenophobia go too.

Toward the end of her story, she made one statement I wrote down because it wounded me. She said, "Because I am different, I stick out in a crowd, but I feel invisible at the same time." This is the dilemma of underrepresentation. People notice you when you do something wrong or differently and ignore you when you do something right. It really does feel like a no-win situation at times.

There are many ways we can help people feel seen at work. When we have diverse representation at all levels of leadership, in meetings where decisions are made, on important projects, and in our product and marketing and communications, we are signaling to individuals and to the company that we see and value difference.

For years, we've heard people say, "I don't see color." Many white leaders who have uttered these words are caught off guard when met with poor reception. For Black and Brown people, it's simple: If you don't see color, you don't see me. You don't see the ways I am unique. You don't see how my experiences might add dimension to your efforts. And if you don't see me, you render me invisible. Seeing color isn't the problem. Anyone who has sight can and should see color. The problem arises when we attach negative beliefs to skin color and treat people unfairly as a result, which includes ignoring them and their contributions. An employee who exists on any dimension of difference can feel seen in two primary ways. And they are both important.

As discussed in chapter 6, the first way we feel seen is to see others who look like us in positions of power and as representatives of what we hold dear. When Barack Obama, a Black man, became the president, I felt seen. When Thasunda Duckett, a Black woman, was named CEO of TIAA, I felt very seen. When Rosalind Brewer, a Black woman and fellow Spelmanite, was named CEO of Walgreens Boots Alliance, I felt especially seen. When Stacey Abrams, who is a Black woman, a Spelmanite, and was in college with me, took the political world by storm, I felt extraordinarily seen. The more we have in common with people who are thriving in a given situation, the more "visible" we feel. You can think of it as being able to see yourself in a place as a result of someone like you being there.

According to our Waymakers study, the other way we feel seen hinges on the degree to which our work is noticed and appreciated by others at our company. These moments most often come from a superior validating our contribution publicly. Moments of visibility hold more weight for employees when they're surprised by the recognition because it shows that leaders are paying attention. Visibility plays a fundamental role in how we contextualize ourselves and our contributions. Do I fit in? If so, where and how? Feeling seen helps us find our place.

As you would expect, moments of visibility motivate us. Those we surveyed developed a newfound, or increased, sense of confidence in their work when they felt seen. In some instances, they were inspired to strive for even greater success in their roles. Feeling visible also makes us feel understood and cared for as a person, beyond output, which culminates in a sense of purpose and a belief that our work has meaning.

There were important insights across groups that might inform how we lead forward when attempting to make talent feel seen. For Black employees, visibility through public recognition is an uncommon experience. When initially singled out, respondents reported bracing for maltreatment, making it more difficult to process positive recognition in the moment. But once on the other side of the public recognition, these instances of visibility were recalled as watershed moments—even more surprising and especially memorable.

Indigenous talent shared stories of being recognized for their intelligence or contribution to higher-order thinking. East Asian respondents, similar to Black talent, were caught off guard by positive recognition, and some even expressed embarrassment for being singled out. They viewed hard work not as going above and beyond but as being adequate and articulated a degree of imposter syndrome in receiving recognition they perceived as undeserved. Interestingly, even with these mental models, they still interpreted visibility as lending credibility to their voices and perspectives.

We also asked people to share examples of when they felt invisible, as a way to better identify missteps leaders inadvertently make as they strive to create more equitable workplaces. These insights serve as warning signs for leaders who have a heart to make a way but are still figuring out the path by which to do so.

Generally speaking, moments of invisibility come from being disregarded or feeling isolated, as in iced out, cast aside, or marginalized. These moments show up as intentional acts of rejection, like being belittled, scapegoated, or targeted, as well as through passive forms of exclusion, like being ignored, not having their efforts noticed, or a lack of communication from colleagues.

One specific act that generates feelings of invisibility is when work is claimed by a peer or manager. Respondents told us they don't feel they have the support, credibility, or trust required to speak up against the bad actors. Some then placed blame on themselves, believing they didn't work hard enough or aren't good enough on their own merit, which caused self-doubt and disengagement from the work, the role, colleagues, and the company as a whole. As extreme as it may sound, people said moments of invisibility can lead to feeling dehumanized and rudderless.

Black employees characterized erasure as constant. Invisibility places responsibility on the marginalized for asserting their own value, yet Black employees feel compelled to perform in ways that are disarming to avoid potentially worse outcomes, like being painted as an aggressor. They reported feeling ignored, underrepresented, and discriminated against when passed over or paid less than those with equal or lesser qualifications. For Black women, the intersection of race and gender is keenly felt.

For Latinx employees, invisibility seems to exist on a spectrum. Like all groups, invisibility feels like being ignored, excluded, or isolated. But Latinx employees conveyed increased emotional intensity when misunderstood, such as when others considered them less intelligent or experienced than they are. In short, it felt worse to be misrepresented than to not be represented at all. These moments were often cited as the reason Latinx employees began their search for a better opportunity.

Stories shared by East Asian employees showed that invisibility can lead to a sort of learned detachment. Constantly being talked over and disregarded wears on them until they choose to no longer put in the effort to be included. It's important to note that being ignored at work isn't just about hurt feelings. It can also have an adverse impact on the work itself. One East Asian woman said her emails were often ignored, and she was continually being redirected for information. When she asked questions so she could do her job effectively, she received cursory answers that were either incomplete or inconclusive, which resulted in an ongoing search for input that took time and energy away from performing her duties.

How do we, as leaders, facilitate moments of visibility? What leadership skills might we tap into or further develop, and which new questions can we ask ourselves to be more effective liaisons between our talent and the moments of visibility that matter to them?

Three leadership skills that help people not only feel seen but *be* seen, resulting in greater diversity, are forethought, influence, and accountability.

On Forethought

A friend sent an email recently asking how I recommend she address a member organization she belonged to who was publicizing a panel on diversity. The speakers on the panel were two white men and one Asian woman. My friend reached out to the organization to express her disappointment that, with everything going on in the world between 2020 and 2021, they would host a panel about diversity with majority white male voices. I personally appreciate when white men engage in conversations about driving diversity, but a panel of three people with two white men in a year of racial reconciliation is bad optics and just poor planning, no matter the topic. It shocks me, honestly, that I still see majority or all-white conferences, panels, marketing campaigns, and so on. We are living and working during a time when the call to diversify is at fever pitch, and still many simply do not have a lens for it. And because they do not see opportunities to diversify faces, voices, and perspectives, Black and Brown people do not see themselves.

Because many leaders have not yet developed a diversity lens, changing this means you have to plan for diversity. It means being more proactive, thoughtful, and thorough in everything you do–in the big things like product development and talent planning and in the small things like responding to emails and meeting invitations.

On Influence

The second way to help people feel seen at work is to use your influence. While a simple concept, I can't emphasize enough how powerful it is. I've had literally dozens of mentees over the years receive visibility opportunities because a leader who trusted my judgment hired them or invited them to participate in an important body of work or made sure they were not left out of critical conversations. That's it. That's the reason. In some cases, the leaders had never met the person before. They'd never seen them in action. They had no proof of competence beyond what I relayed, but they placed a bet on talent because I used my influence to open a door and usher someone through it.

There have been many times I have shaped product, marketing, and communication strategies to include more dimensions of diversity with influence alone. Not power. Not resources. Just by asking pointed questions at the right time, which helped decision-makers see possibilities more expansively. In fact, I served in an ad-hoc role of "multicultural champion" at Hallmark, which led to the creation of the multicultural center of excellence. My sole responsibility was to help the company meet the needs of an increasingly diverse America with products, services, retail strategy, and marketing. The leaders on the receiving end of my questioning and guidance didn't report to me and certainly were not required to change course based on my point of view. They often did so because they trusted me and respected me.

Your influence as a leader, when people trust and respect you, can be used to create opportunities for others in very tangible ways. And you can start using that influence today. Ask your underrepresented colleagues who in their communities you should get to know. Then consider how you can use your influence to support them.

On Accountability

We'll talk about accountability a lot in this book, and for good reason. Our great ideas for making meaningful progress on diversity will remain exactly that—great ideas—if we don't hold ourselves accountable for implementing them. Diversifying our workforces is not something we will ever achieve naturally. We have our habits and cultural norms to thank for that, which have been designed for speed and efficiency. Unfortunately, as mentioned previously, speed and efficiency are safe havens for all types of biases. We don't think anymore. We just do. And when it comes to the pursuit of equity, unconscious doing is the enemy of progress.

I designed an inclusive leadership education session (which is really just leadership education without the qualifier) in which I share straightforward choices leaders can make and behaviors they can adopt to help people feel seen, respected, valued, and protected. This is where theory becomes practice and where realism shifts to responsibility. When it comes to helping people feel seen, listed below are choices you—as an individual—can make more mindfully and more regularly: (1) combat bias, (2) lean into potential, (3) rely upon diversity, and (4) be intentional.

1. Combat bias in talent search, identification, selection, and assessments.

The last few years have significantly elevated the implicit bias conversation, with many companies having deployed mandatory antibias training. I'm less interested in teaching a lesson on the many types of bias because the information is readily available, and we go deeper on the most problematic biases elsewhere in the book. I'm more interested in shedding light on when and how bias shows up day-to-day as you try to help people feel seen and in illuminating what you can do to interrupt it. Generally speaking, training ourselves to pause and ask new questions is an effective way to combat bias because it interrupts our unconscious thoughts and behaviors. Here are a few new questions to ask yourself and others to combat bias in key talent processes and activities that contribute to moments of visibility:

a. How do we know (what is the evidence)?

b. Where have we not looked (areas of the company, bodies of work)?

c. Who are we not talking about (unusual suspects)?

d. What information have we not yet gathered (feedback from multiple sources)?

e. Why do we believe this is the best person for this role, project, or promotion (results)?

f. Why *not* consider another person (forcing an alternate view)?

g. Which voices are we missing here (on this team, in this division, in our decision-making process)?

h. Who are we not seeing (on this team, project, candidate list, in these communications)?

Some leaders I've worked with have actually posted questions like these in plain view until they become second nature. There is nothing wrong with using prompts as you create new habits. We should use all the resources at our disposal on any learning journey, especially when our existing habits are so deeply ingrained.

2. Lean into potential; don't expect perfection.

Leaning into the potential of those who have been invisible to you will help you increase diversity, balance perspectives, and expand potential. We recognize and reward potential all the time, but we usually do so only for people we know and to whom we can relate. When we don't know someone or can't relate to them, we expect them to check every box before we elevate them or their work. As explored in the burden of proof concept, what we are really doing is seeking a level of certainty that minimizes or eliminates risk—to the business and to our own reputations. This behavior further marginalizes already marginalized talent. Waymakers see potential in everyone and shine a light wherever they find it so others can see it too. Turning potential into performance is one of the most compelling ways we pull people through the pipeline.

Here are a few ways to get more comfortable leaning into potential:

  a. Tap into passion: When people are passionate, they learn faster, are more self-directed, and generate more discretionary effort.
  b. Identify transferable skills: What has the person done in other roles that might lend itself to this new role? How can their past experience and success deliver value to your business?
  c. Expand the team: If you planned to have five people on a project, make it six, so you can increase visibility for more employees.
  d. Appreciate the value of a fresh perspective: You may be concerned about what someone doesn't know or what they've not done, but a fresh lens on a familiar problem can be of huge benefit to the work and help you avoid

costly mistakes. This leads me to the next behavior: rely upon diversity.

3. Rely upon diversity.

Staff teams with visible and invisible diversity, and partner with other people and groups (suppliers, for example) who can help you see beyond your own experience. This will help you create new opportunity and mitigate risk. I love the story of Richard Montanez, who was a janitor at PepsiCo when he created Flamin' Hot Cheetos, inspired by popular flavors in Mexican dishes. His innovation was a breakout success, and he later became a PepsiCo executive. In 2017, 2018, and 2019, Flamin' Hot Cheetos was hailed as America's favorite snack by Ad Age. Those leading product development at the time didn't have Montanez' unique life experience and, therefore, would not have seen the path to performance that he saw because of his lived perspective.

There are plenty of success stories, but there are also cautionary tales. Companies have made disastrous decisions because they didn't have diverse groups looking at a problem from multiple angles. Relying upon diversity is good business and also makes sure employees see themselves in your workforce and in all the ways you show up in the world.

Here are questions to ask when developing solutions for internal or external application:

a. Which life experiences are we representing or not representing? Consider gender, generation, race, ethnicity, ability, sexual orientation, types of families, etc.

b. Have we vetted our solutions with people who might see new things? Share concepts or strategies with diverse groups of employees who can point to strengths and weaknesses you might otherwise miss.

c. How can you leverage authenticity to drive credibility? Allow the diverse voices to not only contribute to your solutions but to also serve as ambassadors. Forget hierarchy—who are the best people to represent new ideas? Tap them. Prepare them. Propel them.

The last behavior, which is certainly not limited to enabling visibility and will come up again, is to be intentional.

4. Be intentional.

As we begin to envision how we might increase visibility for underrepresented talent—in our teams, our work, or any facet of our workplace experience—we must remember that intentionality is a powerful force for good. Instead of ruminating on all the reasons why it is hard to drive diversity or to increase visibility for people who have felt invisible for far too long, we should ask ourselves the following questions:

a. What do you have to believe, know, do, and monitor to increase visibility?
b. Who has to be involved or on board?
c. How will you know you're successfully helping more people feel seen?

I used to work for a really inspiring leader who had a reliable way of getting teams to move toward the possible. He believed anything was possible, really, and it was just a matter of knowing what must be true. This simple question broke us of our "but" habits—"but we

already tried that, but we don't have time, but it's too hard." Whenever he asked "What must be true," we immediately shifted into
problem-solving mode. When it comes to helping people feel seen
at work, there will always be excuses as to why we can't meet this
fundamental need. But if we develop a lens for what makes people
feel seen and commit to asking new questions and embracing new
behaviors, we can do it—and we will.

To Be Respected

The second need people have at work is to be respected. Of course,
it's not just at work. In everyday life, this means displaying common
courtesy, acknowledging a person's presence or voice, responding
to needs in ways others value and appreciate, and listening to their
advice when that advice is rooted in experience. It also looks like
honoring boundaries. In the workplace, respect is similar—a general
consideration for other people combined with a regard for who they
are and what they bring to the table.

Inclusion isn't possible without foundational respect. As mentioned earlier, we often reduce a complex set of ideas around inclusion and belonging to being welcoming. Yes, be welcoming—it's
the kind and human thing to do. But the conscious act of including,
which leads to belonging as an outcome, is rooted in respect. At work,
respect means appreciating a person for their unique perspectives
and abilities, trusting them to contribute to work in a meaningful way, and tapping into their expertise. Respect at work includes
consideration for the person, their values, what they know, what
they've done, and how they add value. Too many times, we bring
experienced people into our organizations and make them start
proving themselves as though their careers had just begun. Or we
bring talent in for their fresh perspectives and immediately expect

them to assimilate. When we do this, we are not respecting them. We are not including them. We are encouraging them to become someone else in order to succeed.

In our research, a Latino member of the LGBTQ+ community beautifully expressed how respect has manifested for him. After being a teacher for most of his life, he was working as a manager of a small microbrewery in Seattle. The brewery was about a mile from his home and had just opened, so it was a wonderful chance to get to know the neighbors and community. He fell in love with the job and took on more responsibility. One day, the company owner asked if he wanted to come on board as partial owner and earn yearly profits. He was basically asked to run the show. "I felt trusted and equal–like my hard work and passion were not only being recognized but also rewarded."

Notice this story is not about being nice. And it goes beyond asking for input and ideas, though that's important. It's about recognizing and respecting the contribution, the "hard work," and the dedication to excellence. Respecting employees and employee contribution leads to the kind of inclusion that breaks boundaries and builds teams. That's how we get to belonging.

Simply put, respect is an acknowledgment of an employee's capability and credibility. Our research found that we feel respected when we are asked to take on more responsibility or contribute on a larger scale. Respect makes us feel trusted by colleagues and leaders and helps us see ourselves as equal to others with whom we work, which ultimately affirms that we are in the right place and empowers us to perform at higher levels.

In the research, we found a few nuances between respondent groups that were really insightful. For Black employees, a theme of redemption emerged–being respected at work was like a sip of water after a long drought. Indigenous employees used the words *power* and *respect* interchangeably as tools of both agency and freedom. Latinx employees' stories of respect centered on situations in which they were able to demonstrate their worth–solving problems that would not have been solved without their intervention. South Asians felt respected when leaders cared about and respected them enough to provide feedback on their work performance. East Asians felt respected when they were viewed as experts or given an opportunity to take the lead. For LGBTQ+ employees, respect was experienced when they were tapped for guidance or advice, which made them feel their work was deemed credible. Interestingly, white cis-het employees, when we asked about times they felt respected, perceived respect as a natural outcome of their hard work and effort and were not surprised when they were shown respect. Respect in the workplace was unremarkable for them–a marked distinction from employees who exist on dimensions of difference.

As insightful as the stories about respect were to me, it's the stories of disrespect that I believe hold the most urgent watchouts for leaders. Disrespect is the embodiment of a hostile work environment. Moments of disrespect range from experiencing microaggressions, false accusations, and scapegoating to verbal and physical altercations. These hostile acts create an environment where we feel we are treated differently, which makes us feel unsafe.

In the stories where people felt disrespected, some harbored resentment toward the individual who disrespected them and felt disgust toward their workplace for allowing disrespectful behavior to go unchecked.

Moments of disrespect were described as moments of intentional discreditation. Unlike more passively aggressive moments, like instances that lead people to feel invisible, moments of disrespect are seen as conscious acts of humiliation that cause a targeted employee to feel "less than." More often than not, stories centered on disrespect were directly tied to an employee's race or gender. In these moments, they felt they were being judged by what they look like and not who they really are. And even when a comment or action was not directed to them individually but toward the group with which they identify, the employee felt invalidated. In general, when disrespect occurs, people worry they won't be able to live up to their full potential and that their growth will be limited. This worry fundamentally changes their relationship with their workplace.

Perhaps the most distressing outcome associated with disrespect is how damaging it is to one's psyche. We might dwell on how our aggressor got away with their comments or actions or question our choice to remain in a position where we are disrespected. We renegotiate with ourselves about how much we're willing to give to our companies, and we begin to separate–emotionally, if not physically–from our work and the organization. As you might imagine, there are distinct differences among groups in both how they perceive disrespect and how they respond to it.

In stories about disrespect, Black talent described a "go along to get along" mentality. Their life experience has taught them that disrespect is inevitable and unavoidable. In the more intense moments of disrespect, Black employees report suffering a loss of vigor and engagement. But because they anticipate disrespect in most professional settings and seldom have meaningful support to productively extricate themselves from these situations, Black employees often try to suppress the experience and avoid recurrence as a means of emotional survival.

Indigenous employees who rated their skin tone to be on the darker end of the spectrum, a question we asked to highlight how colorism might impact the employee experience, noted they often tempered their emotional reactions to disrespect so as to not seem combative or aggressive. For South Asian employees, a main form of disrespect is when colleagues mispronounce their names. Whether the mispronunciation is intentional or not, South Asian employees interpret this slight as colleagues not caring enough about them as individuals to learn their names correctly.

How do leaders show respect in the workplace? There are three leadership skills that help us demonstrate respect for others in ways that lead to genuine inclusion. They are relating, collaboration, and social responsibility.

On Relating

Being curious, open, and investing in new relationships is an important part of how we show respect for others. As leaders, we know that creating genuine connections with our team members helps accelerate the pace of doing business. We can speak more openly, guide more freely, adjust more rapidly, and challenge more productively when we foster true connections. When we do not consciously relate across differences, we fail to create enough familiarity to build and debate in flow, and we leave too many things unsaid. COVID-19 made finding time to relate to people even more difficult. One South Asian female shared a story about how her team made a conscious effort to make everyone feel included with weekly online team sessions in which they talked about their daily lives, not work. These intentional meetups have really helped her feel part of the team. Relating is a leadership gift that keeps giving.

On Collaboration

In a work setting, we show respect when we tap into others' experience and expertise. When we ask people for their opinions on business issues or invite them to contribute to an important project or work alongside them to solve problems, we demonstrate that we respect both their presence *and* their work. Collaboration is one of the most natural paths to relationships inside workplaces, since we learn to trust those who join us in the trenches. Those with whom you solve complex problems are the ones you will always want on your team, so it's important to be inclusive when seeking collaborators.

On Social Responsibility

Waymaking, to be clear, requires a giving mindset. It is rooted in the desire to make workplaces better for other people and the people who will come after them. I have found it really difficult to connect the dots for leaders who do not have an ounce of concern for how they impact people beyond their financial goals. It doesn't resonate. There is no compelling case for change, and all the "business case for diversity" conversations in the world won't penetrate. But when leaders begin with the intent to not only be good but to do good, they more readily accept the powerful role they can play in opening doors and holding them open, even if they won't directly benefit. (Usually, though, they do directly benefit. We all do.)

Four actions leaders can take that help cultivate belonging and make people feel respected as human beings and professionals are (1) facilitate connection, (2) amplify new voices, (3) include in decisions, and (4) partner on processes.

1. Facilitate connections on purpose.

We don't connect across boundaries naturally, and the last few years of political division, combined with a pandemic, have only sent us deeper into our safe places, which serve as echo chambers and strengthen our myopic views. Relating across boundaries must be a conscious act, and it starts with you—not the other person. I know because I hear it in my work every day that people are unsure of how to approach people who exist on dimensions of difference. No one wants to be accused of being inauthentic or insensitive or just plain inelegant. But as mentioned previously, connections across difference don't have to be overengineered. They do not have to be initiated on the basis of difference. Here are a few simple, low-stress ideas for inviting someone from a different background or lived experience to connect with you, which provides a path to cultivating belonging.

a. I know you're new to the team. Open to coffee (or online coffee)? Happy to share what I've learned/what I know.

b. I see we'll be working on this project together. It would be great to connect for thirty minutes or so to learn more about your work and your perspectives on the project.

c. I'm interested in learning more about your experience with X. Let me know if you're willing to share over tea/coffee.

d. Got 20 minutes next week to chat? We've not had an opportunity to learn much about each other, and I'd like to change that.

Connecting doesn't have to be deep or burdened with the weight of inequity. We are all people, after all. Let your shared humanity be a starting place.

2. Amplify new voices.

I remember when Barack Obama was president, and the women in his cabinet shared a story about how the team used the power of amplification to ensure all voices were heard. If a woman shared a perspective, others would repeat it. This practice helped guarantee their ideas were not lost and also that they received credit for those ideas. Such a simple concept but a really effective way to show respect. We can do this every day–amplify new voices and give credit where credit is due. One Black woman in our Waymakers study recounted how surprised she was that her boss gave her credit publicly for her hard work, which helped her establish her reputation with the management team.

People sometimes ask how they might do this for others and even for themselves when someone takes credit for their work and no one in the room speaks up. Here are a few simple phrases you can use to amplify others:

a. Tara made a great point. I agree and would add…

b. Tara, tell us more about that. It's an interesting perspective.

c. I think we need to better understand the point Tara just made. I don't want to miss anything important.

Simple phrases to help individuals advocate for their own work when someone repeats what they said or co-opts their idea in a room:

a. I'm glad you brought that up, Pete. I've been thinking more about it since our chat yesterday. I would also add…

b. Yes–great point. And as I shared earlier, it's also important that we realize…

c. Sounds like you agree–or is there a nuance I'm missing here?

Since we know that being ignored makes people feel invisible and being dismissed makes people feel disrespected, amplifying who gets heard and how is a simple step toward the inclusion we hope to achieve.

3. Include people in decisions.

An Indigenous woman, who is also a member of the LGBTQ+ community, shared a story about her colleagues discussing an important project. No one asked her for her input, even though she was heavily involved. She recalled feeling belittled and unheard. What's more, she felt unwanted and began questioning why she was even there.

When I bring people together for my Waymakers leadership training, I ask them to tell me which choices people make and behaviors they exhibit contribute to an inclusive culture. Inevitably, more than 25 percent of the responses point to including people in decisions. When we include people in decisions that directly affect them, we show respect for them as contributors of value. Consider bringing people into the loop. Ask them what they think about the proposed changes or choices. At the very least, it will make them feel respected. At most, it might shine a light on implications that may not have occurred to you.

4. Partner on processes.

While we tend to think of processes as unbiased, they are not. The ways in which we do things—share information, make decisions, engage with clients, manage talent, reward and recognize—are all places where bias can hide. Your underrepresented talent is likely to have invaluable perspectives on how these processes might improve to enable a more equitable workplace. Beyond the day-to-day, consider including a diverse group of talent—both visible and invisible diversity—in conversations about your processes. Ask key questions about each process that help you identify both what is working and not working, using the delights, frustrations, preferences, and concerns frame we discussed in chapter 2. Include people from various backgrounds and lived experiences in this conversation, so you don't miss important angles. As a reminder, the questions to ask are as follows:

a. What delights you about this process? What works well? What should we do more consistently or in more places?

b. What frustrates you about this process? What gets under your skin? What makes it hard to do your work?

c. What do you wish would happen during this process? If you had a magic wand, what would you do to change it?

d. What concerns you about how we manage this process? If we keep doing things the way we are today, what business and talent risks might we face in the future?

This way of partnering on processes is the very definition of benefiting from diversity. You are forcing a 360-degree view on an opportunity area through both the people you include and the lenses you assign to people. When you ask a homogenous group of leaders to solve a problem or improve a process, you always miss something. Including historically excluded talent in this work gets you double benefit—a broader, more textured lens on how to build systems of inclusion and the opportunity to show your underrepresented talent that you respect them enough to invite them to be part of the solution.

Remember, respect is a foundational need for all people, but not all people feel respected in the world or at work. It's not something we can afford to take for granted. We should cultivate it consciously and be aware of the immediate and long-term impact of disrespect, which, in our research, was most closely correlated to eventual separation between employees and their companies. I'll share more about how to interrupt overt and subtle harm later in this chapter when we cover how to protect people at work.

To Be Valued

The third fundamental need people have in a work setting is to be valued. One of my best clients invited me to be a guest on an equity-themed podcast series the company cohosted with Seneca Women on iHeartMedia. I said yes because I greatly respect this company's equity work and the leaders driving it.

We recorded the podcast. It was wonderful. I was grateful. That was that.

A month later I received an email from a member of the team, asking if they could pay me for my appearance. While I appreciated the gesture, I responded that it wasn't necessary, because I wanted to do the podcast and if I'd expected payment, I would have negotiated it up front. Shortly after, the person who initially extended the invite called me. In essence, she explained that she makes it a point to treat everyone equitably, and since she had paid others, she must also pay me. I will remember that conversation for a long time. In ten minutes, she reinforced an already trusting relationship. She demonstrated her regard for me as an experienced professional. And she insisted on equitable treatment, even when I didn't. What's more, I felt cared about. As a person.

According to the Waymakers research, receiving a promotion, raise, or bonus conveys that we and our work are valuable to our company. But while being valued includes tangible rewards like pay or promotion, it is about so much more than that. Value is also shown through acts of service and words of affirmation. Moments of value are elevating, legitimizing, and humanizing for us.

When we single people out for the right reasons, we communicate that they stand out in a positive way, which makes them feel appreciated and seen as capable of bringing a unique set of skills forward. Feeling valued fuels pride in one's work and in themselves. When employees feel they are a valuable and an integral piece of the puzzle, they report a higher intent to stay with their companies.

For Black employees, being valued appropriately frees them to do their best and helps them believe they'll be judged on merit. For both Latinx and white cis-het employees, feeling valued was triggered by unexpected acts of kindness or appreciation toward the employee, like a thank-you card or special note.

One East Asian woman told a story about how being publicly rewarded for a job well done made her feel she could achieve greater levels of success at her company and increased her loyalty. She stayed for fifteen years, continued to advance, and received more awards along the way.

To better understand how not feeling valued might impact the talent experience, we asked respondents to tell us about times they felt underappreciated. People who feel underappreciated feel their hard work is not acknowledged or recognized. They may have been passed over for a promotion, raise, or bonus. They may have colleagues or supervisors who do not think they are up for a particular task and who give work and credit to someone else. Being overlooked, to them, is being denied opportunities they should be able to compete for in a fair environment. Being denied strikes at the very heart of inequity.

People also defined underappreciation as feeling unsupported. Employees feel underappreciated when they believe their leaders don't care about them as people or when they feel taken advantage of by the company. They feel overworked or underpaid, they lack adequate work-life balance, they feel burned out without acknowledgment of the work they are doing, and they are sometimes denied the tools they need to do their jobs. When an employee feels their work is overlooked, unsupported, or underappreciated, they begin to feel defeated–like they are trapped in a role without benefit. They feel their efforts are worthless, and when this happens, their work loses meaning.

Black employees who experience underappreciation in the workplace see it as a more chronic condition, as in serial mistreatment and a consistent failure by leaders to recognize their accomplishments. Acute moments of underappreciation often just underscore years of struggle. More often than not, worth and appreciation were intertwined for Indigenous employees, who associated feeling underappreciated with being underpaid and having no power.

Responses from East Asian employees were unique. They felt caught between two perceptions. There is often an assumption that East Asian people do not speak up. Quiet people are sometimes criticized for not participating. At the same time, East Asian employees who consider themselves outspoken feel underrepresented and out of place at work–a feeling that is exacerbated when others expect them to be subdued. In both situations, respondents felt their work was not appreciated at the level of their colleagues. For East Asian employees, feeling taken for granted was most often their breaking point. These moments were cited as separation points–when they would decide it was time to leave a company.

One Indigenous man told us how, as the director of his finance department, he was responsible for preparing the financial forecast for his entire family of health care companies. The leadership had successfully turned the company around from near bankruptcy, and they sought out an entity to acquire their company and keep it intact. The night before the sale deadline, the department vice president, the chief financial officer, and the CEO watched over the director's shoulder while he finalized the five-year forecast for underwriters, which was submitted five minutes before their midnight deadline.

The sale was successfully completed and he received a one-time bonus for his efforts.

After new ownership took over, the vice president announced his retirement. Based on the director's recent performance, he expected to be promoted to the position. The vice president called him into his office to let him know that another person in the department, who had similar experience but hadn't been involved in the sale of the company, was being promoted instead. The director remained in his current position, working under a new vice president for the next five years. He recalls this as the lowest point in his career because he felt his hard work meant nothing–that politics would continue to supersede accomplishment. While he told his new boss he would help him succeed, he resolved to do the bare minimum. In his story, he wrote, "If they weren't going to reward me for my efforts, why should I go above and beyond for them? I would do what they asked and nothing more. I'd clock in, clock out, and go home."

Sound dramatic? Possibly. But stories like these are not uncommon. When hard work is overlooked and people are repeatedly passed over for pay and promotion, they lose steam. They question their potential in the company, which makes them lift their heads and look around for what else might be available. Opportunity denied. It's a moment of truth most recall easily and with great detail because like many other moments that matter it changes the very relationship between talent and companies.

A Latina told us she submitted an application for a promotion and wasn't even considered, although she had the requisite experience. Not only did her managers refuse to acknowledge her application but when she was denied, no one took the time to explain why. This severely impacted her morale and led her to look for another place to work.

Making people feel valued requires knowing what value means to them, individually, and being thoughtful about how you might support them in realizing that value. But it's also about using your power to open doors while removing roadblocks. Sometimes the roadblocks are gaps in knowledge or skill, but just as often they are gaps in others' knowledge of them. Here is where Waymakers play a role. You can get to know underrepresented talent, orchestrate high visibility assignments, then advocate for them with your peers. You can fight for them to be valued appropriately. You can set a new tone for how people are rewarded and recognized, inspiring others in your position to do the same. Three skills associated with making a way for equitable treatment and reward include negotiation, discipline, and coaching.

On Negotiation

I always reflect on talent-planning conversations I've participated in over the years and how deliberate I had to be about influencing equitable outcomes for others who were less known by decision-makers. I used to prepare for these conversations by checking in with underrepresented talent ahead of time to understand their aspirations, their journey to date, and the feedback they'd received on their potential and performance, which was sometimes lacking in depth and specificity. Once engaged in the talent discussion, I would bring up lesser-known or discussed talent and ask about perceptions, whether those perceptions were evidence based or assumptive and whether my peers were willing to place a bet on someone new. My approach showed up as curiosity in the moment, but it was very strategic, and that's exactly what it requires to interrupt our practiced rhythms.

We negotiate on behalf of talent constantly. Waymakers negotiate on behalf of people who do not have a voice—people whose names might never enter the room if not for your insistence. Waymakers clear a path for new stars to shine.

On Discipline

Waymaking is not easy. Anytime you push back on norms, ask people to slow down enough to ask new questions and consider new angles, or request that people expand their view before they make decisions (which can add time and complexity), people will bristle. Waymakers are undaunted by bristling. They recognize that changing habits is uncomfortable and will be met with resistance at first. We must stay the course in the face of opposition and push through the perceived complexity associated with leading equitably. Equitable leadership requires rewiring of both our processes and our brains. There are moments we will want to simplify–to rush through the work so we can check the box and call it finished. But transformation is as much about fortitude as it is about vision. The pursuit of equity asks us for both. There is no quick fix. We must be disciplined not only in our approach but in the ways we hold ourselves and others accountable for the outcomes we desire.

On Coaching

We already reviewed how bias hides in feedback in chapter 5, but I want to provide additional insight on how to think about framing and delivering it because it is a major leadership gap that we absolutely must fill to have a shot at creating a more equitable workplace. The ability and willingness to provide actionable, timely, and specific feedback on potential and performance is crucial to unlocking opportunity for underrepresented talent. I conducted an online survey that asked people about the nature and timing of feedback they receive. Eighty percent of respondents said they do not receive feedback on their performance until it becomes a barrier to advancement. Seventy percent said when they ask for feedback to help them grow, they are given feedback on their communication style. I expected to see dramatic differences between white respondents and respondents of color. I didn't. Basically, we are not great at growth-oriented coaching in general—not for women or men, for Black people or Brown people or white people. We have a lot of work to do.

Coaching is how we guide people toward their desired outcomes. I remember life before GPS mapping. Do you? If you didn't have a paper map or MapQuest directions, people would guide you using landmarks and street names. "Go about a mile down this road, turn right on Smith Street at the McDonald's..." If it were dark or a street sign were obscured, you could find yourself driving for miles, wondering if you drove too far in the wrong direction. Sometimes, your fears were realized.

When we don't coach people along the way, waiting instead for an annual download, we miss turns. We miss opportunities to correct people along the way and subsequently waste time, effort, and resources. We should think of coaching not as criticism but as directional support, since that's exactly what it is. And because we fear being perceived as racist or sexist or otherwise discriminatory, we do not offer it when it might make the most difference. Our coaching is either too ambiguous, too late, irrelevant, or disconnected from employees' goals.

Good coaching has the following characteristics:

1. It is specific.

Avoid giving feedback that sounds like a guessing game. When the person you're coaching has to keep offering you words and phrases to help you explain your feedback, you're doing it wrong. I've heard it all. The most egregious example I've heard is, "I'll let you know when you're ready." This is so disempowering. When we are not specific in our feedback, we leave talent to wonder how we define success.

The consequences of this approach are dire. Employees will start throwing darts at the board, hoping one might land near the center. When it doesn't, we blame the talent, without realizing the role we played in the failure.

I posted on LinkedIn about my favorite example—"developing executive presence," which is incredibly common and equally problematic. It reinforces our existing mental models of leadership, which again are based on white men, and prevents underrepresented talent from being themselves at work.[1]

There are better ways to help people build the skills you're thinking of when you use the term "executive presence." Instead of using this catch phrase, advise them to spend enough time with their material so they grow more confident in sharing it seamlessly. Share how important it is that they know what their audience needs and wants so they can shape solutions intentionally and create mutual benefit. Advise them to practice presentations out loud and listen closely for opportunities to strengthen their message and delivery. Ask them to invite others to listen to their position and give feedback. Encourage them to remember that they belong everywhere they are—and they should feel free to walk into spaces with their backs straight and heads held high. Remind them of their strengths and tell them to lead with them for more effective engagements with colleagues and clients. Encourage them to build their networks and help facilitate connections so they feel less alone in meetings and can enjoy a greater sense of safety. The above ideas paint a much clearer picture of success than any catch phrase ever could.

2. It is timely.

Don't wait until an annual review to provide performance or potential-based coaching. When you see something, say something. If you coach someone along the way, each coaching moment is less burdened. Both the giver and the receiver grow comfortable with regular, timely feedback through practice. If you wait until I'm one hundred miles out of the way to guide me, I'm going to be a lot more stressed and feel more defeated than if you tell me I'm about to take a wrong turn. No one should be surprised by feedback at performance time, ever. There should be nothing new in your reviews. Ideally, by the time you get to an annual review, every bit of positive and constructive feedback has been shared already and you are simply summarizing. I wish I could tell you all the Black and Brown people who have conveyed to me through the years that they do not get timely feedback—how they are blindsided by performance reviews full of problems they never heard about. Because of our own fears and lack of relationship across difference, we are robbing people of the opportunity to improve.

3. It is relevant.

A former colleague of mine once received secondhand feedback that eating her lunch during a meeting was unprofessional. In my view, having an opinion on someone needing to nourish their body is petty. And sharing that feedback with a direct report is unwise. The manager, when receiving this feedback about the direct report, should have asked whether the employee eating lunch compromised the outcome of the meeting. Were they not able to accomplish their goals? Did the lunch eating grind discussion and debate to a halt? As a leader, you don't have to coach people on everything someone brings to your attention. Instead, you can respond to irrelevant feedback by questioning the legitimacy of the input. This makes the reporter responsible for what may be a tendency to notice things that don't matter, which is often prompted by stereotypes, confirmation biases, or personal hang-ups. Remember my earlier question: Does it matter?

4. It is growth oriented.

I'm going to stick with this car analogy for a moment. Have you ever driven while a passenger tells you you're going too fast or too slow? Braking too hard? Not using your signal appropriately? If so, how do you respond? This is how it feels to receive coaching that is only corrective and not growth oriented. In this same scenario, growth-oriented coaching while driving—meaning coaching that will get you to your destination more efficiently and smoothly—would include shortcuts, taking highways that allow you to drive at a higher rate of speed, circumventing traffic delays, or avoiding traffic lights for more seamless travel. This is how we should think about coaching all our people. Where do they want to go, and what are the different ways they can get there?

The four behaviors that help both leaders and allies make people feel valued and usher in an equitable workplace have everything to do with contribution—eliciting contribution from new sources, leveraging that contribution, developing it with intention, and recognizing it—tangibly, and commensurate with impact.

1. Elicit contributions from new sources.

Be deliberate about seeking insight and participation from new voices. Remember you have rote ways of operating that build competence and confidence in the same people over time. Bring new people into important conversations so you can build new muscle and broaden the exposure of those who have been left out of the learning loop. People want to impact the business. That's how they define adding value and being valuable.

2. Leverage the contributions of others.

There is nothing so demeaning as when you gather your courage to share an idea and it gets smacked down without even a moment of consideration. When people share ideas, they are rooted in something—an experience, a preference, an insight. We have to remember it can be risky to share ideas that are different, and how we respond to new ideas from people who do not have power can either build them up or tear them down. Don't let dismissal be your first response. Be more curious and consider how you might apply ideas to business problems. At least, try to better understand where the idea comes from—it might point you in a constructive direction.

3. Develop people's contributions.

If someone's contribution has seeds of greatness but needs more thought, more evidence, more pressure testing, encourage them to do exactly that. (Remember, they need you to make a way, not simply judge the way.)

I share "the bridge to aspiration" with leaders to help them develop people toward their next opportunity. It's simple. First, the employee has to understand their current state of readiness. Then, they should give voice to, with your guidance, how they hope to be contributing on a given time horizon. The bridge is comprised of five dimensions of growth—skills (they need to build), behaviors (they need to demonstrate), knowledge (they need to acquire), experience (they need to gain), and relationships (they need to develop). I encourage both parties—leader and employee—to think through what stands between the employee and their aspiration, then develop an action plan to bridge the gap. Simple? Yes. But also specific, growth oriented, and time bound, which is the only way to get anywhere you are trying to go faster.

4. Recognize contributions.

The above behaviors will help talent develop on par with their peers. As mentioned in a previous chapter, we have not been making the best people for the job equitably. This requires mindfulness—an awareness that we all begin this professional journey from different places and with different tools. Helping all people use what they've been given to position themselves for greater opportunity is the role of a Waymaker, but the work doesn't stop there. We must reward their work and readiness with opportunity—pay, influence, and promotion. Tangible reward is how people know their efforts matter and that they are valuable to you and the organization. We pay for what we value in any other circumstance. Why would employees want anything different?

To Be Protected

The last and most profound talent need we must address is the need to be protected. If I've learned anything about truly inclusive workplaces, it's that they do not and cannot exist when people feel unsafe. This part of *The Waymakers* book is the "how" companion to the "lack of psychological safety" mountain we miss. When talent cannot share their ideas without fear of ridicule, when they can't challenge the status quo, when they can't defend themselves when faced with harm, when they can't ask for what they want or deserve, they will not feel part of the team. Protection at work may sound like a strange concept, but in an era in which political division has been at an all-time high, and people seem to be retreating into their corners, workplaces have become land mines for misunderstandings and missed opportunities.

When George Floyd was murdered, every Black American waited to see what their leaders would say to them—not only in a company statement but directly. Would they acknowledge the community pain? Would they express empathy? Would they offer a listening ear or seek to understand the emotional states of employees? Would they give grace when it became difficult to focus or deliver? Many leaders did show up for their Black talent, but far too many did not. This silence equaled complicity for many Black employees who needed to know whether their workplace was safe for them, whether their colleagues would honor their humanity.

I spoke to several white leaders who admitted they didn't know what to say or how to be supportive. They didn't want to say the wrong thing. I encouraged them to think not as a manager but as a person seeking to acknowledge and comfort another person. Sometimes, because we are in a work environment, we make compassion too complicated. We are so busy trying to be appropriate that we fail to be human.

In early 2021, when violence against Asians was on the rise, leaders asked the same questions and struggled with the same decisions—should I say anything? If so, what? Will it be overkill? Yet again, leaders missed the opportunity to show genuine concern for their Asian colleagues who were angry, confused, sad, and scared about the senseless violence emerging all over the country.

Then, when COVID-19 began ravaging India while other countries were trending in the right direction, Indian employees were devastated. They were worried for their families and friends. Many lost parents and siblings and cousins. What did their American leaders say? Some said nothing at all.

I get it. Leaders wonder how many times they should speak out on tragedies that affect various employee groups. They fear their compassion will lose impact if they speak up every time something tragic happens. But consider this: If a friend suffered a tragedy in January, then May, and then November, you wouldn't resist showing care in November because you had already done so twice. Wherever and whenever there is pain, compassion should show up. In the void, people make assumptions about you and your company.

Regarding police violence against Black people, they may assume you support that violence. In the case of the rising anti-Asian sentiment, they may feel you don't see them as worthy of your concern. With the situation in India, they may think you're not paying attention to them or what matters to them. In every case, people will feel unseen and undervalued, which will make them feel unsafe.

Our research found three primary dimensions of protection at work:

1. Protected from the threat of another or retroactively defended from physical or mental abuse. This looks like a manager or colleague (or human resources) intervening in the moment or helping the victim seek justice.
2. Protected from insecurity. This looks like a manager or organization keeping the employee and their job safe. (Many stories centered around COVID-19 where others were getting laid off or furloughed, but the respondent was protected.)
3. Feeling safe to speak the truth, use their voice, share their ideas. Stories often revolved around a manager encouraging someone to speak their mind or hold their ground in front of superiors. This is often a pivotal moment where people gain the confidence and self-esteem to believe they are worthy of their role, which leads them to feeling respected or valued or seen.

For almost all employees surveyed, feeling protected in the workplace was not the default. It was most often realized when a colleague came to their defense, such as when insensitive comments were made about the employees' race, gender, or sexual orientation. In those situations, employees were unsure how to react, but a colleague—often a superior—stood by their side and provided support.

One Black female retail worker recounted an unpleasant interaction with a customer return. Because the store policy required a receipt and the customer didn't have one, the employee denied the return. The customer responded aggressively, began hurling racial slurs, and asked for the manager. When the manager arrived, she told the customer that not only would the return not be accepted but her behavior would not be tolerated. The customer was then escorted out of the store. In this moment, when the employee was afraid, the manager had her back. She felt validated as a person and protected as an employee.

I'm frequently asked by leaders how to intervene when they observe racially motivated workplace harm in real time. They know they should show up for the person on the receiving end of harm, but they don't know what to say. I sometimes share three specific statements that help interrupt the harm and shift the responsibility to the perpetrator where it belongs.

If someone makes an offensive or inappropriate comment, you can say, "What do you mean by that?" This question forces the speaker to own their harmful words and shifts attention from the receiver to the bad actor. You can also say, "I don't know how your comment is relevant to this topic," which is a way to communicate disapproval without adding fuel to the fire. But if the remark is egregious—you must say so. If you tolerate bad behavior in front of you, it will continue, and you can guarantee it will get worse when you're not in the room.

We also offer protection when people do not feel pressured to be perfect. Respondents described these moments as being encouraged to contribute even if their ideas were not fully formed or went against the grain. Employees value opportunities where they feel unencumbered by the fear and anxiety associated with giving voice to divergent opinions or ideas. This makes them feel heard.

A South Asian woman told us, "I had a manager who always made me feel like my ideas mattered. He asked to meet with me once and mentioned that he hoped I would keep sharing my ideas, seeming to understand that I was shy and afraid others might judge me. After we met, I was more vocal in our team meetings and received a lot of support—a big change from a childhood that taught me to be subservient. That manager really empowered me to share my voice."

When it comes to feeling protected, trust and vulnerability are intertwined. Ultimately, we want to know that our colleagues can be trusted with our vulnerability. We want to take risks without having our motives or abilities questioned. We want to trust we will receive sufficient support when we are asked to do difficult things. When we spend more time working and less time worrying, we feel much more connected to our workplace.

If protection looks like support, the freedom to contribute without needing to be perfect, and intervention during moments of harm, what does a lack of protection look like? It takes shape as not showing up when people need you, but it also manifests as scrutiny. Scrutiny is the thread that compromises performance and potential and ultimately hampers equitable outcomes.

When employees experience scrutiny at work, they believe they are starting from behind. Instead of focusing on the good they have to give, they spend energy mitigating the negative thoughts and opinions of others. Often, due to various forms of bias, they have to answer to issues for which they are not responsible and are constantly working their way back to neutral. This is how people get stuck in place. Always pushing against the wind.

Scrutiny most often shows up through micromanagement. Employees who feel they are constantly being watched relayed a feeling of oppression–they are not free to be themselves and report "nit-picking," which eats away at their confidence and can change how they engage with others.

Scrutiny also diminishes an employee's ability to make their position their own. It shrinks their agency. Many described this as a "catch-22"–feeling the need to explain yourself, while feeling pressured to tell managers what they want to hear to balance existing mistrust. Ultimately, heightened scrutiny makes people feel excluded, like others are looking for ways to minimize or disable them. This leads to a feeling of futility, resulting in a lack of pride in their contribution and a general apathy that is difficult to unwind.

One woman shared how it felt to be micromanaged by her boss, who would criticize her for being two minutes late, ask why people were in her office, and even stand outside her door to listen to her conversations. She used the words *humiliating* and *debasing* to describe the feeling she lived with under that leader.

Every moment of harm or scrutiny experienced in the workplace creates distance between a company and everything good an employee has to give–trust, commitment, effort, talent, loyalty, and so on. While leaders have every right to expect greatness and to hold people accountable for business outcomes, *how* we do so matters.

Psychological safety is absolutely foundational to the talent paradigm and is connected to everything, including business results. From an individual leadership perspective, there are three skills associated with helping people feel protected at work and unlocking the creativity that comes with that protection. They are self-awareness, humility, and compassion.

On Self-Awareness

I've known too many successful business leaders with very low self-awareness. Often they don't feel the need to consider how they show up to others, because they are accustomed to others adapting to their preferences. When we lead unconsciously, we generate unintended consequences, and they are often most deeply felt by people who are already disenfranchised. The journey to self-awareness is one of the most important you can take on the road to Waymaking. There are assessments you can complete to understand whether your idea of you is similar to others' ideas of you. But there are also questions you can ask people close to you about simple behaviors, like how well you actively listen. Or whether you successfully adapt your tone and language to suit different people and situations. Or if you effectively exhibit self-control in times of stress. Knowing how you present to others, especially when stakes are high, will help you avoid compromising the psychological safety of peers and team members. Start by learning more about how you show up today, then consider how you might chart a course to a higher level of awareness.

On Humility

Recently, in the Transforming DEI Club on the audio app Clubhouse, a room I started and grew with other diversity, equity, and inclusion thought leaders to help new DEI professionals navigate the landscape, we hosted three disability experts for a conversation about why disability gets left out of DEI conversations and strategies.

Following the conversation, I wrote an article on LinkedIn titled "I'm Tara, and I Benefit from Ableism," which reads:

> I discovered more parallels with racism than I had given enough thought to, starting with the fact that I hadn't given enough thought to it. I've often said that most white people at work don't understand the complexities of race in America (and in

the world), because they don't have to contend with it in a real and present way. It doesn't affect them directly, and since many don't have personal relationships with people from other racial groups, they seldom have the kinds of conversations with Black or Brown people that might raise their awareness and inspire genuine concern and consideration.

In May of 2020, when George Floyd's murder rocked the nation, it also rocked well-meaning white people's worlds. It was an awakening of sorts—an undeniable case of institutionalized racism wrapped in abject disregard for Black life. While many Black people were perplexed by the revelatory response from white America (this has been going on for centuries), it was inarguably an awakening.

While not as dramatic, this is how yesterday's conversation landed on me. It woke me up to some of the ways I have benefited from ableism and how I have unconsciously left people with disabilities out of the conversation.

What is ableism?

"Ableism is the discrimination of and social prejudice against people with disabilities based on the belief that typical abilities are superior. At its heart, ableism is rooted in the assumption that disabled people require 'fixing' and defines people by their disability. Like racism and sexism, ableism classifies entire groups of people as 'less than,' and includes harmful stereotypes, misconceptions, and generalizations of people with disabilities."

You might be wondering why I say I've benefited from ableism, especially after reading this definition. I don't intentionally discriminate against people with disabilities, and I definitely do not believe they require fixing. I've never offered to pray for a disabled person I don't know, or used their mobility device as a resting place, or asked a stranger what happened to them, which was reinforced in the Clubhouse conversation as insanely intrusive. But I recognize the world and everything in it is built for abled people, which benefits me. I've also planned and facilitated events without asking whether anyone needed accommodations. I've held hundreds of conversations with executives about their DEI plans without probing into matters of accessibility and inclusion for disabled people. Unconsciously, I have behaved in ways that make a person's disability their "personal problem," without regard for how I can and should be more inclusive.

The big insight here? My lack of engagement in the disability conversation is not rooted in disdain or intentional disrespect. It is rooted in ignorance, lack of understanding about the role I should play as a leader and ally, and too few genuine relationships with disabled people who might evoke in me a personal commitment to better understand and mitigate the challenges disabled people experience every day.

Which is the same path to equity for Black and Brown people that I share with leaders: Realism (a clear picture of what marginalized communities are up against at work and in the world), Responsibility (knowledge of and a commitment to playing an active role in driving equity) and Relationship (genuine connections across difference that can serve as accelerators for change).

I don't consider myself ableist, but I benefit from ableism. If you are white, you may not consider yourself racist, but you benefit from racism. Clearly, privilege has layers.

I have a long way to go to feel confident speaking with authority about disability as a dimension of diversity, and by a long way, I mean I'm pretty much at the beginning of the journey. But since a journey of a thousand miles begins with a single step, I've decided to begin with educating myself and also making some new friends. It's the least I can do. And I know, based on the aforementioned parallels, that it can be a meaningful start.[2]

As you can see, as deeply entrenched as I am in this work, there are dimensions of diversity I am still learning about. I have work to do. We all do. There is no embracing realism and taking responsibility for equity without humility. We must first acknowledge what we do not know before we are willing to accept new insight as true and relevant.

When I first became a mother at twenty-five, someone gave me a quote on a tiny piece of paper by Jill Churchill that read, "There is no way to be a perfect mother and a million ways to be a good one." So poignant and so applicable to leading equitably. Waymaking is a walk, a path, a process. It means looking beyond what is right in front of us and assuming there is more to see, more to know, more to do than we realized. It's having enough faith in yourself to know that as obstacles to progress show up, you will have the courage and energy to overcome them. Leading in this way requires humility—an assumption that there is always more to learn about leading and a willingness to adjust along the way.

On Compassion

How do you define compassion? When Naomi Osaka withdrew from the French Open and I posted on LinkedIn about her honoring her mental health, someone commented, "Who cares? People call in sick all the time. Celebrating weakness is stupid." I clicked on the commenter's profile to see what he did for a living. (I usually try to ignore these types, but I was curious.) Turns out, he bills himself as an HR consultant who helps build corporate culture. Interesting.

You can't cultivate inclusion without compassion. You can't drive equity without desiring to better understand the plight of others who are not like you, who've not benefited from the same privileges you have. Caring about others' needs, hopes, and challenges is part of this work. Look for signs of it in the leaders you reward and recognize and point to it when appropriate. People pay attention to not only what you do but also what you pay attention to, which is another way to say they notice you, and they also notice what you notice (or don't).

Four behaviors that help create an environment that protects people are (1) opening doors to feedback, (2) establishing psychological contracts, (3) abiding by contracts, and (4) expecting compliance.

1.   Open doors to feedback.

I already touched on this briefly, but you can solicit feedback both formally and informally. If you ask for 360-degree feedback, make sure you prime your team by telling them you are genuinely interested in the ways you can be a more equitable and inclusive leader and that you hope they will be honest in any survey administered on your behalf. Once you receive feedback, you can reinforce that it is safe to be honest with you by bringing up something you're working on as a result of what you learned.

When I first became a manager at twenty-six, I received feedback on a 360-degree survey that by stating my opinions so strongly and poetically, I shut down conversations in my team meetings. This was never my intent. As a young, Black female leader at work, I always felt the need to be polished. Bulletproof. To not leave space for anyone to question whether I knew what I was talking about or had done my research. The unintended consequence of this learned behavior was that everything I said sounded final. Some of my team members didn't feel welcomed to share their opinions or ideas or to disagree with me. After I processed the feedback, I took it to my team. I shared what

I learned and expressed my intent, which was to benefit from their experience and insights. I told them I respected their points of view and that I would be more mindful of how I communicated moving forward. I also gave them permission to call me out if I resorted to old habits. Vulnerability works. Invitation too. As a leader, you are cocreating results with your team. Feedback in all directions supports both the work and the people.

You can also solicit feedback one-on-one anytime by simply asking what you can do differently to support a person or the team. "What can I do differently?" (versus "how am I doing?) is a pointed question that will make people feel safer to be constructive.

2. Establish psychological contracts.

Perhaps the most powerful tool I've used to create safety in my relationships and in my teams is the psychological contract. In one-on-one conversations, it means sharing your intent as a leader at the beginning of a new working relationship, expressing your desired outcomes for the relationship, then inviting the other person to let you know when your behaviors do not align with your intent. If you ask in advance, before conflicts arise, you will have set the stage for a mutual learning process, granting permission for team members or peers to say hard, but necessary, things to you.

3. Abide by contracts.

Once you establish contracts, it's absolutely crucial that you abide by them. If you don't, you will obliterate trust and unconsciously communicate that your team is a free-for-all. Without established and practiced norms, people will operate by their own, which could be rooted in not only bias but racism, sexism, homophobia, xenophobia, and so on, and your underrepresented talent, for whom psychological safety is not a given, will be subject to their whims. You have to model equitable leadership at all times. When you slip, they slip. And when they slip, people will fall.

4. Expect compliance.

It should go without saying, but do not tolerate "isms" (racism, sexism) or toxic behavior under any circumstances, and make sure you have mechanisms in place to understand what's really happening deep in your organization. Inspect what you expect through leadership evaluations, and if you find something unpalatable to you, deal with it immediately. When it happens publicly, address it publicly. You are not only holding people accountable but you are also sending signals to others about how seriously you take your own principles and priorities.

All the stories people shared with us in our Waymakers research study—both positive and negative—were so telling. Being able to discern the kinds of leadership choices and behaviors that make people feel seen, respected, valued, and protected or invisible, disrespected, underappreciated, and scrutinized across dimensions of difference revealed not only how uniquely people interpret their experiences but how distinctly they react to them. Clearly, there were many similarities. We are all human, after all. But the nuances were instructive too and are driven by cultural and societal norms, as well as personalities.

Beyond the stories themselves and the insights inherent in them, I was really curious about the relationships between and across the various emotional states. For instance, are some prerequisites for others? Are there tradeoffs—are some more important than others? Do any of these positive or negative states have more or less impact on how employees feel about their company or their ability to reach their aspirations? Are there differences across groups? Turns out, there are indeed interesting connections between the four talent needs, the degrees to which they are met or not met, and employee perceptions of their potential inside the companies where the experiences occurred.

How do emotional states impact people differently across groups?

Overall, Black and South Asian employees rated feeling *respected* as having a more positive impact on their professional aspirations than other emotional states. Indigenous and Latinx individuals rated moments of *visibility* as having the most positive impact. East Asian, LGBTQ-, and white cis-het people rated feeling *valued* as having the most positive impact.

All groups rated feeling disrespected as having the most negative impact on their professional aspirations, except for South Asian talent, for whom feeling underappreciated had the most negative impact.

Do some emotional states matter more than others? How do they differ?

Overall, being respected and valued seem to hold similar weight across all groups, with respect having the longest lasting impact on one's perception of self and their organization. Being visible seems to be a precursor to being respected and valued—if you don't see me, you can't respect or value me. Feeling protected is a foundational need.

Which of the experiences that result in the emotional states are acute versus chronic?

Positive moments shift in and out of time, but negative ones are either felt at a particular moment in time, or they build up over the course of time within a workplace. Feeling invisible, underappreciated, and scrutinized builds up in response to numerous and continued microaggressions. Feeling disrespected, however, is experienced immediately and strongly, and respondents were often able to recall the moment they were disrespected with more clarity than other negative experiences. Disrespect stays with people–at work and in life–and has the potential to irrevocably damage relationships. If no one intervenes to reconcile the damage, the relationship often breaks for good.

Which of these experiences are seen as more passive (unintentional) versus active (intentional)?

Positive moments can be felt both passively and actively. In moments of recognition, such as when employees are singled out for doing something good, they viewed it as another person purposely showing them that they are seen, respected, or valued. If these moments become commonplace, employees intrinsically know they are seen, respected, or valued without needing constant reassurance.

Negative moments, however, cannot shift between being active and passive without becoming something else entirely. Moments of invisibility and feeling underappreciated, for instance, were more often described as passive–not as intentional exclusion or purposeful lack of support. The exception, articulated most strongly by Asian employees, is when someone else takes credit for their work.

Moments of disrespect and scrutiny were described as intentional. As mentioned previously, people felt targeted, like someone wanted or expected them to fail.

How do leaders and peers contribute, specifically, to others feeling seen, respected, valued, and protected, or invisible, disrespected, underappreciated, and scrutinized?

How do leaders directly impact positive experiences?

Of the four positive emotional states, leaders have the most impact on making people feel visible, valued, and protected. The most commonly mentioned leader actions that contribute to these states are:

- Meaningful recognition in front of peers, especially when it is unexpected
- Solicitation of ideas and feedback, regardless of tenure/title
- Providing pathways to promotion
- Taking time to get to know team members on a personal level
- Giving an employee the benefit of the doubt
- Recognition of life events
- Providing a safe place to air grievances
- Equipping employees to perform their role
- Elevating voices that may get forgotten or spoken over

How do peers directly impact positive experiences?

Of the four positive emotional states, peers have as much impact on making people feel respected as leaders. The most commonly mentioned peer actions that contribute to the four states are:

- Acknowledging a peer's contribution of time and effort
- Recognizing someone's work publicly
- Defending a colleague by speaking up on their behalf when their security is threatened
- Creating moments of vulnerability through shared experience and deepening of the relationship

How do leaders directly impact negative experiences?

Of the four negative emotional states, leaders have the most impact on making people feel underappreciated and scrutinized. The most commonly mentioned leader actions that contribute to negative emotional states are:

- Taking credit for an employee's work
- Overlooking someone for a pay increase or promotion
- Singling out employees in front of others
- Allowing microaggressions to occur in the workplace with no corrective action
- Decision-making that doesn't involve team members
- Showing lack of trust
- Showing judgment
- Micromanaging
- Disregarding employee's contributions
- Setting lofty goals with no support
- Dismissing recommendations without consideration
- Not taking personal health or safety of employee into account
- Not recognizing contribution and achievements
- Criticizing employee's ideas
- Overworking employees

How do peers directly impact negative experiences?

Of the four negative emotional states, peers have as much impact on making people feel invisible and disrespected as leaders. The most commonly mentioned peer actions that contribute to negative emotional states are:

- Taking credit for a peer's work
- Actively singling out a peer in a negative way
- Ignoring a team member or leaving them off an invitation
- Speaking over a colleague
- Making ignorant comments that hurt or offend

At the end of the day, one thing is clear—equity is more than a destination and is most achievable when everyone is informed and equipped to lead with awareness and intent, regardless of title. Waymaking—a leadership state of mind that recognizes both minor and major opportunities to elevate others and removes barriers to performance and potential—is reinforced by our daily choices and behaviors. By the people we see and don't. How we show respect or fail to do so. The ways we value people for their perspectives and contributions. And how we create safe spaces within which others feel free to learn and lead.

If we remember that, among all our systems work and process transformation and strategic priorities, we lead human beings with fundamental needs, we will change our workplaces and the way historically excluded people experience them. And when people feel they work for an equitable and inclusive company, they will be more likely to stay and give their best effort to the company. Isn't that why we're all here?

CHAPTER 7

What Your Company Wants: Performance Drivers

The real competitive advantage in any business is one word only, which is people.
—Kamil Toume

A PROSPECTIVE CLIENT REACHED OUT to ask if I could help them build their business case for diversity. I said no. (I was nicer than that, but the end result was the same.) I don't help clients build a business case for diversity, because it is readily available to anyone who is even remotely interested in finding it. Leading researchers have produced reports making the case for decades. Recently they've acknowledged what many intuitively know: the "business case for diversity," while tempting to use as leverage, is difficult to prove. There are too many variables, and it's impossible to know which factors are driving which outcomes at any point in time.

According to Catalyst, one of the leading voices on the impact of diversity, managers are actually more likely to take action on social issues when they are presented in moral terms—aligning with the organization's values and mission—rather than in economic language.[1]

I am admittedly one of the experts who rolls my eyes when leaders ask their diversity, equity, and inclusion teams to build the business case for diversity. *For whom are they building it, exactly? And what are they waiting to discover that hasn't been written about already?*

What I've learned, though, is that some organizations have stakeholders whose love language is data. Hard data builds the confidence they need to move forward on issues they don't inherently understand. And clearly the highest levels of organizations are populated with people who do not inherently understand the realities associated with diversity, equity, and inclusion, because they've not been adversely impacted by these realities. When leaders who've yet to buy into diversity and inclusion are in powerful positions, those who *do* get it often feel held back—ready with ideas and plans for progress but unable to implement them until their peers or managers recognize the importance of the work. A dilemma for sure.

I decided to include my own spin on the business case for diversity in this book—not only as baseline knowledge for those who may not know but also as a tool for would-be Waymakers who must answer stakeholder questions before they can move beyond "business-case busyness." My intent here is to lay out business and culture outcomes companies can reasonably influence by unleashing talent—fully and fairly. These outcomes are (1) to attract talent, increase diversity; (2) to improve culture, cultivate belonging; (3) to support retention, ensure equity; and (4) drive innovation and unleash creativity by creating psychological safety. The strategies in this chapter are informed by firsthand experience, secondary data, and dozens of interviews with DEI experts whose collective experience spans more than six hundred years and over one hundred companies, most of which are in the Fortune 500.

To Attract Talent, Increase Diversity

An executive recruiter reached out to ask whether I knew any diverse candidates who could fill an internal role in her firm. She had been there awhile and was passionate about helping the firm make more progress on representation and inclusion. Before our first call, I searched the firm's website for photos of their leadership team. All white men. I then clicked through to the second leadership layer, which was comprised of mostly white men and a few white women. When we finally connected, she explained where the firm found itself on its DEI journey and was pretty transparent about some of the challenges they were facing. One of these challenges was the fact that her CEO did not believe in the work and was reticent to invest time or resources to support it.

I was honest with her. I told her I appreciated her dedication to making things better for her company, but I would not send any of my respected and experienced connections into an environment that would not see them, value them, respect them, or protect them. The lack of CEO belief and engagement is a nonstarter. I don't work with companies whose CEOs do not believe the work matters, because without their clear and vocal commitment, progress is nearly impossible (which was evidenced by their all-white leadership team).

Please hear me when I say that today's emerging workforce is playing no games when it comes to assessing whether or not a company is truly diverse and inclusive. Today's talent is on LinkedIn reading your posts and those of your leadership. They are checking your Twitter account for what you say and don't say during times of controversy. They are on Instagram scanning your imagery. They are searching the web for your leadership team and board members. They are on Glassdoor reading reviews. They are even finding other employees and sending direct messages to ask what it's *really* like working at your company. It is serious out here.

There are definitely benefits to diversifying your ranks, and while they manifest in better ideas when diverse perspectives are leveraged intentionally, they also help you attract talent. According to Catalyst, companies with higher levels of gender diversity *and* with HR policies and practices that focus on gender diversity are not only linked to lower levels of employee turnover—women are more likely to express interest in an organization and perceive it as fair when women are highly represented in top management positions.[2]

Beyond gender, Weber Shandwick and KRC Research partnered with the Institute for Public Relations in 2016 for a survey showing that 47 percent of millennials were actively looking for diversity and inclusion when sizing up potential employers.[3] I have to believe the number is even greater now and that Generation Z's expectations have only grown, seeing as how non-Hispanic whites are 52 percent of the Gen Z population—just a slim majority.[4]

The DEI experts we interviewed for the Waymakers shared valuable insight for companies seeking to increase diversity in their workforce. One idea I found especially compelling is "gatekeeper training." Talent gatekeepers are defined as anyone who recruits, selects, develops, or promotes talent. These are the people who have to *see people* unbiased, *position* unbiased, *select* unbiased, and *reward* unbiased. At every stage, there is opportunity to get it right and build on your momentum or get it wrong and dig a deeper hole. This is clearly a high bar, and in the absence of diversity among those making these critical choices, the gates will open for some and not for others. We must educate people whose roles determine our diversity success to recognize and deconstruct bias wherever they find it.

Pipeline development is something many leaders and recruiting teams are hyperfocused on, and for good reason. Even this work, though, requires a thoughtful and multifaceted approach. Should you invest in early talent programs, which might include internships or management rotation programs? Yes, you should. Should you build mutually beneficial relationships with targeted communities, schools, and organizations, such as historically Black colleges and universities or member organizations that boast large percentages of diverse talent? Absolutely. But you can't forget your internal talent. They have already committed to you and are working hard every day to earn their chance at bat. Identify unusual suspects with aspiration and potential and invest in them. This is equity work—equal access to opportunity.

On this note, it's important to evaluate our human resource processes for diversity enablement, especially when it comes to management positions. Are your job descriptions accessible to all? Do employees know and understand your promotion and performance criteria? Are they clear about what success looks like and which career options are available to them? If not, transparency is your friend. Information, unfortunately, is not equally accessible to all. As we've touched upon in previous chapters, it can be concentrated where the power is, while others have to beg for it or, worse, don't know to ask for it in the first place.

With early talent and experienced hires scanning for diversity at the highest levels of organizations, where representation is lowest, many companies are currently being cut by a double-edged sword. You need to bring talent in to increase your representation, but talent won't come on board because your representation is too low. What can you do? Which levers can you pull to increase representation at all levels of your organization, and how can you make progress visible so that your would-be employees (and existing ones, for that matter) recognize your efforts? According to the DEI experts we interviewed who have driven substantive change, there are a few primary levers you can pull to accelerate your diversity work and attract the talent you want. They include how we build candidate slates and interview panels, how we succession plan, how we form partnerships, and how we establish goals, metrics, and rewards.

On Candidate Slates and Interviewer Panels

Post all leadership roles instead of moving chess pieces behind the scenes, which only advantage people you already know and trust. This still happens in so many companies. We chart a course for the "favorites" through multiple roles before those jobs even become available. When a job does open, anyone we had not already considered starts from behind. This is such a clear intervention every company should adopt. Because they want to move quickly and confidently, managers will be frustrated. But standing your ground on this one process standard will open your eyes to new people and open pathways for them.

Require diverse slates for roles to broaden your lens. This is a numbers game. You can't select candidates who might bring diverse lenses to your work if they are not in the pool. I've seen leaders resist a diverse slate requirement, then be frustrated years later when they've still not made progress. That's what we call a predictable surprise.

Ensure interviewer panels are diverse to mitigate selection bias. Requiring slates to include diverse candidates who are then interviewed by all white men is the equivalent of inviting vegetarians to a barbecue. You had good intentions when you invited them, but they won't get fed. If you plan to open the playing field on the front end, you must make sure you keep it open on the back end.

Consider removing names from resumes. Business policy professors Judd Kessler and Corinne Low, along with doctoral student Colin Sullivan, conducted a study between 2016 and 2018 that found companies hiring for STEM roles rated candidates with female and minority names lower than candidates with white male names. On average, a female or minority candidate with a 4.0 GPA received the same rating as a white man with a 3.75 GPA. They didn't find a clear bias in other fields, but other studies have found this to be a more widespread phenomenon.

On Succession Planning

Focus on recent results. As we've discussed, bias hides in succession planning. If you rely on your "gut," you will not only be subject to your biases but you are also likely to be influenced by old tapes—information from years prior that may no longer be relevant but is stuck in your mind. Or worse, tapes someone else played for you. We often recall old information and convey it as truth—an unfair habit, since we all learn and grow.

Plan more time for discussion to avoid the bias speed trap. Don't ever shortchange talent discussions. You have people's careers in your hands. Handle with care.

Discuss unusual suspects, not only the chosen few. Be sure you review aspirations and results for people along various dimensions of diversity. They may not be ready now, but if they aspire to bigger roles, by characterizing the gap, you can be intentional about getting people ready.

Mind each other's business. Challenge your peers' assumptions about people and ask the questions listed in chapter 5, especially if you suspect bias is at play.

Share perceptions back with talent because often they don't know what leaders really think about their performance until their reputation has been solidified in the eyes of decision-makers. By then it's difficult to change minds, and they spend too much energy trying to dig out of a reputational hole.

Beware of the burden of proof. Are you expecting people who are not like you to prove their competence so they are more prepared, or are you doing it so you are more comfortable? Practice asking yourself why. "Why do I want this person to take on this assignment?" "What specifically am I looking for?" "Is it necessary or just preferable?"

Match people with projects to raise visibility to other leaders. The goal is to have very few, if any, "hidden figures" in your company. Position people on purpose–it will expand their opportunity and build their confidence too.

On Partnerships and Pathways

Develop genuine relationships with schools, associations, consultants, and consortiums that serve more diverse talent pools. I use the word *genuine* on purpose. Transactional relationships do not work. You have to invest time and care to learn what people value and to earn their trust, especially in this climate.

Identify internal and external ambassadors who can help you build reputation and trust with the talent pools you wish to attract. Invite them into your inner circle, share new ideas with them, equip them to represent you to their respective circles.

Offer wider pathways into your company by reconsidering job requirements versus skills and experiences that might be nice to have. We have begun building "bionic human" job descriptions that even hiring managers can't live up to! Someone who wanted to expand their candidate pool sent a job description to me recently, hoping I would share it with my network. I read it and responded, "So you're looking for Jesus?" (I was half-serious.)

On Goals, Metrics, and Rewards

Determine what great looks like for your organization/team first, then measure the proof points associated with your vision. For instance, if great looks like an increased sense of belonging, consider how people would think or behave differently if they felt they belonged. Would they be more productive? Would they respond to surveys at a higher rate and more favorably? Would they be more engaged in meetings and company events? Measure those sentiments and behaviors.

Measure leading signs of progress like number of people trained, diverse representation in succession plans, professional development plans completed, representation in externships/internships, mentorship programs, executive sponsor relationships, external professional development opportunities, diverse leadership partnerships, and so on as a way to sense movement on your goals.

Measure and track outcomes that take more time, like representation within every department/division and at every level, promotion rates, and retention to evaluate success.

One exercise I've found really helpful for people who want to check their own affinity bias—which as we've discussed is one of the most prevalent biases in the workplace and the one that challenges our diversity goals most profoundly—is what I call the "Go-to Crew" list.

Take a few minutes to write your answers to the following questions:

- *Who is on your team?* Do you have a diverse team? If not yet, do you seek diverse perspectives on the work at important times?
- *Who are your closest allies?* Who is in your trust circle? Does everyone look like you? Who else could you cultivate connection with?
- *Who do you choose to build with?* Who are your chosen collaborators on business problems and opportunities? Are you tapping new sources of inspiration on purpose?
- *Who do you call first?* When you have new information, who do you call first? Does everyone get the information they need when they need it?

What did you find? Are your lists diverse, or did you primarily write down people who are like you? When I ask people to engage in this exercise during workshops, it can be pretty telling. Black and Brown people usually have more diverse lists because lower representation forces a mixed go-to crew. White women usually have mostly white people on their lists, but a balance of men and women, except for their closest allies, who are mostly women. White men often have mostly white men on their lists and a few white women. Our preference for sameness is strong. We have to nurture a diversity mindset.

Driving diversity is an important part of any equity journey. It matters not only to the vitality of your business but also to the well-being of your culture and the talent that comprises it. It signals hope and possibility for those who do not represent the norm and tells potential employees they would be welcome at your company and can succeed in partnership with you.

To Improve Culture, Cultivate Belonging

When we bring new people into our companies or teams, are we prepared to be changed by them? Or do we expect them to read the cues and fall in line? Anecdotal evidence suggests the latter. During the hiring process, we usually look for our missing piece–the person who brings specific experience or perspective that fills a gap for us and enhances us somehow. When they arrive, we spend quite a bit of time orienting them to the way things work. Of course, helping people acclimate to a new work culture is part of how we help them succeed. Talent needs to understand the company, the business, the cadence of the business, key players, and more. At the same time, leaders need to delineate between cultural requirements and cultural preferences. Some company "ways" are in fact hindrances to belonging, erecting invisible walls that nurture some people and exclude others.

I believe we need to rethink both the acclimation process and our habits around leveraging talent. If you watched the Oprah interview with Meghan Markle in early 2021, you saw when Oprah asked Meghan if life in the Royal Family was "as it looked." She was asked if the family "welcomed" her.

> Meghan responded, "Everyone welcomed me. But I've learned over the last four years, that nothing is as it looks."[5]

This was such a powerful moment to me because it highlighted a key misperception about inclusion, which is that it is synonymous with being welcoming. As I touched on before, inclusion isn't about a warm welcome. It's not about being nice. It's about respect. True inclusion respects a person's values, selfhood, ideas, experience, expertise, and even boundaries. It requires that you truly see a person and respect them enough to make room for all the good they have to give. Again, people don't start careers to be welcomed. They start careers to fulfill their aspirations.

If you are nice to me when I walk into your house, but there is no chair for me to sit, I do not feel I belong. If you say hello but don't include me in the ongoing conversation, I do not feel I belong. If you cater dinner, but there isn't enough food to share, I do not feel I belong. If you let me stay for gift giving but are one gift short, I do not feel I belong.

When we welcome people into our workplaces, we show kindness on arrival. When we respect them and invite their contribution, we communicate that they do indeed belong.

There are several benefits to a truly inclusive culture. A 2020 diversity climate study by Oxford University Press found that organizations with strong "diversity climates" (defined by appreciation of individual differences and the adoption of practices to advance underrepresented groups) are likely to increase employees' job satisfaction and commitment to the company. Additionally, organizations with inclusive business cultures and practices are 58 percent more likely to improve their reputations, and employees who view their workplace as inclusive are also likely to consider their organization to have ethical value. Inclusive workplace cultures help mitigate harassment, increase trust and engagement, and improve absenteeism, adding nearly one day a year in work attendance per employee.

Perhaps most compelling is that inclusion is key to team performance. Catalyst released a 2019 white paper that pointed to overall inclusion as responsible for 49 percent of team problem-solving and 18 percent of employee innovation.[6]

The experts we interviewed shared what has worked to achieve a greater sense of workplace belonging for those who have traditionally been left out, including listening sessions where input is used to codevelop inclusion plans with goals, resources, timelines, and roles. Education also plays a part here, from foundations like unconscious bias and allyship education to more advanced workshops like shifting to a growth mindset. They also shared examples of shared accountability where everyone has DEI goals, from the CEO to individual contributors, which reinforces a universal commitment to a more inclusive culture. A few measurement ideas like participation in empathy experiences or employee resource group engagement were mentioned as signs of progress, and measures like brand health and net promoter scores are good examples of desired outcomes. Measurement matters in all of this work. As one expert so eloquently stated, "We measure what we treasure."

A few systemic levers you can pull to help cultivate belonging in your company are idea funnels, advisory groups, and bridging sessions.

On Idea/Decision Funnels

Create mechanisms to gather ideas from new people, like suggestion boxes or innovation sprints. These mechanisms communicate that the culture itself is open and inclusive, beyond any one individual leader who might be getting it right. Reward great ideas in important meetings or with an opportunity to continue building the ideas toward execution.

Establish think tanks to solve real business problems. This will not only make your solutions better but will also provide greater visibility to diverse talent. Have executives meet with think-tank members periodically to share business insight or answer questions.

Ensure feedback loops. When you try something new, make sure you perform an after-action review to find out whether you achieved what you set out to achieve—not only from a business standpoint but also from a cultural one. We should learn how to effectively impact inclusion with as much rigor as we do our business goals.

On Advisory Groups

Invite colleagues to co-own your culture. I had a manager several years ago who tapped approximately twenty employees from deep in her organization and met with them monthly. She would order lunch and invite them to her big, beautiful conference room to talk. She asked questions about how they were doing, whether she could do anything differently or better, how they thought the rest of the organization was doing. She would rotate people occasionally, providing more employees with the chance to spend time with her and share their perspectives. I thought this was brilliant. It is no surprise that she always seemed to "feel" her organization—their hopes, their fears, their frustrations. She was intuitive, but she was also very strategic about how she led.

This "advisory group" idea is one I think every leader should adopt. It shows respect, builds trusting relationships, forms new connections, and helps leaders keep their ears to the ground.

On Bridging Sessions

Bring teams together across differences for important conversations to build empathy, trust, and coalitions of the willing.

I developed "Building Bridges," a training course to help leaders facilitate emotionally sensitive conversations across difference, in response to the rise in discussions about race at work. This session has served me and countless other leaders well since it was designed. It starts with establishing a clear purpose, then exploring the various truths represented in the room, imagining a preferred future together, and finally, discussing individual needs and commitments. The client I originally designed the session for asked me to think about how I might help leaders respond to "lightning rod" comments–those charged statements people sometimes make that threaten to derail already tenuous conversations. I created the "Will and Skill: Managing the Dialogue" grid as a tool to help facilitators understand the various positions people might be speaking from and respond appropriately based on both how open the speaker is and how knowledgeable they are about the topic. I've included the grid here, in case it helps you too.

The Will and the Skill Explained

The *confident contributor* is a person with high openness and high knowledge of the subject. They have done their own research and have at least a fundamental grasp on the topic. They will often engage with both humility and transparency because they realize they are on a learning journey. Their comments are often instructive and insightful. I usually amplify these voices to further the conversation.

Inelegant curiosity is exactly that and describes those who are open to learning but have low knowledge of the subject. They may ask questions that make them sound awkward or ill-informed (because they are). We should reward the openness that gives way to inelegant curiosity because the majority of people are in this quadrant, and many are attempting to become more knowledgeable about topics they've not had to think much about.

Misguided conjecture is a term I coined to explain the contributions of people who feel confident in their assertions about a topic but have already made up their minds about it. Their opinions are often incomplete or biased. When facilitating, you can ask questions to better understand where they're coming from while inviting them to think more critically and broadly about their positions.

Last, we have *disrespectful disruptors*–people who don't know much about the topic and don't want to. They may resent being in the conversation in the first place and intend to dismiss or disregard others' needs or concerns. In these cases, it is best to diffuse the negative energy and, if that doesn't work, dismiss the individual or risk compromising your purpose and the psychological safety of others in the space.

MANAGING THE DIALOGUE: THE WILL AND THE SKILL

	WILL = OPENNESS +	
INELEGANT CURIOSITY		**CONFIDENT CONTRIBUTION**
"Does talking about it make it worse?"		*"I recognize the privileges I have."*
FILL IN THE GAPS...		**AMPLIFY...**
-Clarify the question		-Thank the contributor
-Thank the person for speaking up		-Ask others what they think
-Ask if others can help fill in the blanks		about the contribution
-Confirm understanding		-Go back to that person when helpful

– SKILL = KNOWLEDGE +

DISRESPECTFUL DISRUPTION		**MISGUIDED CONJECTURE**
"Racism is just an excuse."		*"We all have the same chance to succeed."*
DIFFUSE OR DISMISS...		**QUESTION...**
-Refer to ground rules		-What have you seen/experienced
-Refer to purpose		that makes you believe that?
(Is this getting us closer or		-How committed are you to
further away?)		the belief?
-Remove the person from the space		-What else could it be?

©TJF CAREER MODELING LLC 2021

To Support Retention, Ensure Equity

There are very clear links between equity (both equal pay and equal access to opportunity) and talent retention. As mentioned previously, our Waymakers respondents directly link value–the degree to which they feel valued and receive tangible value–to an intent to stay. It's important to be overt about this because we oversimplify retention by focusing on belonging or having a good manager. We've all heard the phrase, "People don't leave companies; they leave managers." This may be true, but the important question is why? Why does a person leave their manager? If employees feel unseen or devalued by their manager and cannot see a way out from under that manager's control, they will exit the organization.

Several years ago, I observed an executive disenfranchise an entire group of employees who had previously enjoyed long track records of success. He was relatively new to the company and brought valuable experience to a role designed to build and grow a new line of business. It was immediately clear that the leader's style was different from what employees were accustomed to, but initially it seemed like that might be a good thing. Until it wasn't. He threw temper tantrums, expected people to work unreasonable hours and be at his beck and call, and had an obvious handful of favorites who felt challenged and highly valued. The rest of his organization felt used and abused. I kept wondering when someone would put a stop to his toxic behavior. His superiors knew he was creating an unhealthy climate, but for reasons that remain unclear, they allowed his behavior to continue until he either fired those who did not meet his unrealistic expectations or they fired themselves as a rebellious act of self-care. The worst part about this story is that he not only failed at leveraging the talent in his charge—he also failed to grow the business. A lot was lost during those years, including the trust of many who watched the unraveling.

I remember hearing that he believed those who left did so because they couldn't handle a high-pressure business. He saw them as unwilling to put in the hard work it took to win. This was not the case. What they *were* unwilling to do was give their all without any appreciation or reward. They felt overworked and undervalued—a combination that only leads to one place: a dead end.

As we've explored, value takes many forms. Better Buys conducted a survey that investigated the effect of professional development opportunities on retention and found there's a 34 percent higher retention rate for those who have development opportunities compared to those without. Seventy-five percent of employees with opportunities said they are likely to stay at their companies another five years versus 56 percent of employees without opportunities who said the same. Where low engagement was a factor, there was an 87 percent higher rate of retention for those with opportunities over those without. So even when engagement is lacking, professional development opportunities can make a significant impact on retention. Inclusion is contextually important to ensuring a productive and enjoyable employee experience, but appropriately valuing people is the power play.

A few levers you can pull to help ensure equitable outcomes are pay and opportunity reconciliation, talent-planning transformation, leadership development, and advocacy.

On Pay and Opportunity Reconciliation

Conduct a pay audit and reconcile disparities. You have the data—use it, and don't give yourself too much time to rectify it. Women lose hundreds of thousands of dollars over a forty-year career because of pay inequality, and for women of color it's closer to $1 million. Every year you wait to reconcile pay, the lifetime wage gap increases.

Regarding opportunity reconciliation, conduct performance-review audits for style feedback. Many underrepresented employees tend to receive more style feedback than majority employees. Realize that reputations may have been adversely impacted over time as a result of style bias. If you notice troubling patterns, educate your managers but also take steps to reconcile reputations.

On Talent Planning

Know every employee's aspirations and strengths (self-defined and identified by others). This is not hard—many companies have a talent development process that includes this data. (You may be surprised to know that many do not.) At the very least, ask your employee what they aspire to and capture their goals so you can develop people toward them. Conduct 360-degree surveys as a rule, not the exception, to keep growth-oriented feedback flowing.

Collaborate on career migration maps toward future roles and opportunities. Earlier, we covered the bridge to aspiration. But talent cannot build a bridge to aspiration if they don't understand the universe of opportunities available to them. Help people define the opportunity landscape and help them build multiple avenues to growth.

Ensure movement and continuous learning. Don't let people get stuck. We often measure promotion data, but as covered in chapter 2, we should also measure movement data. Movement—whether to a different project or team or leader—supports the learning process, which enables people to expand their capability.

On Leadership Development

Develop employees in cohorts. Leadership development programs for women or other dimensions of diversity can be very enabling if they are designed with purpose. Remember the power-core example and ensure insight, access, and opportunity are built into the development experience. This is what marginalized talent is missing. Provide insight on business challenges and priorities and create a forum for questions and answers. Provide access to executives through panel conversations and happy hours or mentor pairs. Create opportunity by curating visibility through real-world problem-solving projects that allow for demonstration of skill. I am a big proponent of cohort leadership experiences and have designed many over the last several years. Sometimes you have to make major investments to accelerate your equity goals—it's like a shot in the arm. If you don't intervene with accelerants, your progress will be slow, and you'll risk losing steam.

On Advocacy

Launch an advocacy program. The importance of sponsors cannot be overestimated. In fact, a sponsor is the very definition of a Waymaker—one who uses power and position to make a way for others by not only guiding them but actively creating opportunity for them to advance. Some companies require that every member of its executive team sponsor two people, at least one of whom is not their same gender or racial/ethnic background.

Assign mentors to every new person who enters your workforce. Assign one from their affinity group (whether it be race, gender, disability, sexual orientation, or situational, like working mothers), and assign them one who is outside their circle of affinity. If we create a diverse circle of support right away, we will build capacity to meaningfully connect across differences from the start.

As discussed previously, affinity bias is such a powerful force in almost any context where people are doling out benefits. When it comes to ensuring equal access to opportunity, there are three ways to mitigate it. One, by driving diversity at the top of the house so that everyone benefits from affinity bias equally. (Human nature will do its thing, and the benefits will trickle down.) Two, by engineering your processes to be more objective and instituting more checkpoints. And three, by becoming familiar with people and their work across differences, which creates exposure and genuine insight about the strengths and abilities of others who are not like you.

The affinity chart shows how affinity bias actually works in practice, with the highest advantage going to those who share an affinity with a leader who also knows their work. The next highest advantage actually goes to people who share affinity with the leader, even if their work is not known. And the lowest advantage goes to the one who shares no affinity with the leader and whose work is not known. I shared this chart with a group of leaders recently, and one admitted he was skeptical, then said he thought about it and realized how many times it had played out in his own decision-making. For him, the affinity was the army. For another, it might be the school you graduated from or the company you were hired from. For others, most unconsciously and most problematically, it is race or gender. The call to action here is for you to get to know your team members and become familiar with their work, starting with those with whom you do not share an affinity.

AFFINITY

MEDIUM ADVANTAGE	HIGH ADVANTAGE
Affinity bias can trump evidence in many established workplace cultures - a version of *"it's not what you know, but who you know."*	Evidence plus affinity creates the best advantage for any employee, which is why it's important to check our affinity bias while building relationships across differences.

EVIDENCE

NO ADVANTAGE	LOW ADVANTAGE
An employee who has no affinity with talent leaders where the leader has little awareness of their accomplishments has little to no chance of growth.	Even when leaders have strong evidence of contributions, low affinity can cause leaders to require more proof of their competence, compromising opportunity and building resentment.

©TJF CAREER MODELING LLC 2021

Our DEI experts shared sage advice about what is required to drive equity in the workplace, and that is to remember that equity is a nuanced, individualized approach to everything. It's about giving each individual what they need to succeed. As one well-respected expert who works at a large retailer stated, "Equity isn't a handout;

it's a leveler." Above all, it's really important to do what you say, as perfectly summed up by DEI expert Deb Elam: "Without accountability, it's all performative. Nothing will truly change."[7]

Equity strikes at the heart of DEI work and directly challenges power dynamics. It stands to reason that it would be the hardest to realize, but if you want a return on your talent investment, it is perhaps the most important.

To Drive Innovation, Unleash Creativity by Creating Psychological Safety

When a Boston Consulting Group study found that companies with more diverse management teams have 19 percent higher revenues due to innovation, I found myself reflecting on why that might be the case.[8] As mentioned previously, my hypothesis is that this outcome is about more than the diversity itself. I believe that the psychological safety created when people are not the only ones like them in a room (or one of the only) frees those people to contribute more fully and creatively, which fuels innovative ideas and better business results.

According to Catalyst, when companies establish inclusive business cultures and policies, they report an increase in creativity, innovation, and openness and a better assessment of consumer interest and demand to the tune of an almost 40 percent advantage.[9] As we learned in our Waymakers research, contribution is unleashed when people feel seen, respected, valued, and protected, but protection is both foundational to and also an outcome of visibility, respect, and being valued.

Beyond the previously shared ideas that any individual leader can implement, how do we create psychological safety on a systems level? You must define your company culture—from the top down—with clear operating principles, make sure people know what those principles look like in action, and determine how you will reinforce them long term.

Almost anyone can craft beautiful statements. But you need insight about who you are today as a company and clarity about who you want to be to know which principles will serve you best. You also need to articulate your principles as actionable guidance—as choices and behaviors and even responses to actions that may be counter to your culture. And ultimately, you need the discipline to abide by your principles and the courage to call people out in real time when they forget about or dismiss them. This is how we shape culture—with vision and clarity. With courage and consistency. Intentionally and over time.

Define Culture

At the highest level, define the culture you want to cultivate. Culture principles might relate to values, beliefs, policies, decision-making, behaviors, competition, outcomes, conflict resolution, processes, learning, relationships, justice, talent, and community. If you need inspiration as you seek to define your unique culture, go back to the "what has to be true" question. It's a great place from which to understand the principles that will get you closer to your ideal state.

Open Doors

Elevate open and honest feedback to a principle. Even if you thoroughly define your company culture, it will not always be honored. To temper any adverse impact that might result from those who ignore or dismiss your principles, set the stage for "open doors" as a way of life (more than a choice and beyond a behavior), and provide alternate avenues for employees to relay important and potentially sensitive feedback when necessary.

Evaluate Leaders

Ensure regular feedback mechanisms for all leaders, regardless of level. Many companies are losing the talent they work so hard to acquire because some leaders are ill-equipped to develop talent or do not know how to organize talent for maximum impact. Being promoted into a leadership position should not prevent professionals from seeking and receiving constructive feedback on their performance. When companies implement feedback mechanisms for all leaders, it helps them reinforce or correct behaviors in a timely fashion.

Equip leaders to lead inclusively. As a follow-up to evaluating all leaders, we should admit that leading people is not second nature to everyone with a title. You will have leaders who need support to lead inclusively. They should be educated about how to meet talent needs genuinely and consistently. Whether you connect them with reading materials, like this book, or expose them to experiential learning, leading inclusively is a muscle that must be developed.

Create company-wide rewards for leaders who embody your principles. Publicly reward leaders who model your desired behaviors and who achieve success defined by your equity and inclusion goals. Some companies have annual diversity and inclusion awards, or they build awards into annual leadership conferences. Public recognition of this kind makes leaders feel good about their investment in the culture and shows other leaders there are real benefits for living up to a higher standard of leadership.

Psychological safety can be hard to cultivate because we move through the day unaware of the many land mines that might exist. Additionally, we may not know how our words and behaviors unconsciously contribute to an unsafe environment. This is, in part, why *The Waymakers* exists, to help well-meaning leaders understand what it looks like to make a way for others. Remember, mistakes will be made. Admit them and do better next time.

The commitment cycle is a tool I have used with teams for well over a decade. It is such a simple process but very effective. Essentially, it asks a team to define their preferred culture in words and phrases, declare the actions and behaviors required to realize that culture, then individually state what they need in order to behave in new ways and what they're willing to commit. It relies on collaboration and strategic thinking in steps one and two, then taps into vulnerability and personal accountability in steps three and four. Such a powerful circle, resulting in a shared vision of what great looks like and an anchor teams can return to when they find themselves back in the wilderness.

COMMITMENT CYCLE

COMMITMENTS

Ask each person to state out loud what they are willing to commit in service of their shared aspiration.

ASPIRATION

Ask the group to share words and phrases that describe the kind of team culture they hope to achieve. Write everything down where all can see.

NEEDS

Ask each person to state out loud what they need from others in order to behave in the new ways declared by the group.

BEHAVIORS

Ask the team to name behaviors they might need to adopt or practice more consistently in order to realize their stated aspiration. Write it down.

©TJF CAREER MODELING LLC 2021

The conversations I had with experts as *The Waymakers* was coming to life were truly enlightening. Even with work under way in corporations all over the world, there remain elements of DEI that get short shrift. Accountability is not standard, for example. And while the principles in this book are relevant across most dimensions of difference, we must all get better at understanding and responding to the needs of disabled employees with both visible and invisible disabilities. There are nuances here that matter to the lived experiences of our disabled team members and colleagues. Add the intersections of race and gender, and the challenges can feel insurmountable.

In the spring of 2021, we all watched tennis champion Naomi Osaka withdraw from the French Open after being threatened with expulsion for refusing to participate in press conferences. She suffers from anxiety and depressive episodes, and the conferences triggered her anxiety. While many were compassionate, others criticized her harshly, citing unprofessionalism and entitlement. If a twenty-three-year-old renowned champion is not believed or supported as she seeks to manage her health, what do we think happens to those who are not famous? The burden is undoubtedly great.

Other missed opportunities: We seldom embed DEI principles in our existing work, which can make our efforts feel bolted on and optional. This is one of the reasons why so many teams are still fighting for resources.

I also want to call out the need for companies to better support their DEI practitioners. This is painfully harrowing work. As one expert poignantly shared, "You wake up every day knowing you are going to fail." That comment really struck me. Working on something that feels as expansive as world hunger and as impossible as swallowing an elephant is a heavy burden for DEI leaders to bear, and if executives expect one person or a small team to carry the weight of culture change *for* them instead of *with* them, we will all fail.

Being a Waymaker means recognizing the work of equity and inclusion as your work. It belongs to every person in the company but especially to you. Because you are the only person you can control.

CHAPTER *8*

When Waymaking Matters Most: Defining Moments

Life was always a matter
of waiting for the right moment to act.
—Paulo Coelho

EARLY IN MY HALLMARK CAREER, I was invited to participate in a marketing innovation effort. Guided by a consultant, we
were hoping to see the brand through new eyes so we could better
represent people's relationship needs and expand our role in their
emotional lives. To this point, growth conversations usually revolved
around the big seasonal drive periods, which were Christmas, Val-
entine's Day, and Mother's Day. This approach had all the makings
of a straightforward strategic effort: a defined calendar window
(set number of selling weeks), historical success measures (year-
over-year trends), demographic data (how many people were likely
to celebrate the occasion and where), and time-tested iconography
and messaging. What we learned in the research phase of this effort,

though, transformed the way many of us thought about the brand and its power. It wasn't the big holidays that created people's emotional story arc. It was the more intimate, life-changing inflection points. Having a baby. Getting married. Falling ill. Losing a loved one. These were the real moments of truth, and being there with and for someone in the midst of them built trust, deepened connections, and increased loyalty. These were the moments that mattered, and they were also the ones people remembered.

When you spend twenty-one years of your professional life thinking about moments that matter, you start to see every journey as having exclamation points.

In the talent journey, there are pivotal experiences that can either draw an employee closer to a company or push them further away. When leaders begin thinking about creating an equitable and inclusive workplace culture, they usually go to the "big rocks" first. Recruiting. Hiring. Retention. Promotions. These elements are extremely important, but they tend to hinge on company processes, not on human experience.

Put yourself in the shoes of a person who just got a great job offer. If I ask how the hiring process is going, you'd have to translate that question into emotion, then access it to get deeper than "fine" or "difficult." But if I ask how you feel about starting something new, having worked hard for it, you'd be able to access those feelings immediately, along with the circumstances driving the emotion.

"Hiring" doesn't mean much to a person. Retention doesn't either. The more you aim to see the journey through the eyes of your employees, the more insightful you will become. And that insight holds important clues to making the workplace better for all people.

There are defining moments in the talent journey when employees really need Waymakers–to help them navigate when they are starting something new, define the opportunity landscape when they're chasing their dreams, provide air cover when the stakes are high and patience is low, or be an anchor during times of major change. How leaders show up (or don't) during these crucial moments can mark the difference between inclusion and exclusion, loyalty and detachment. These moments challenge our beliefs about who we are as leaders. If we lead consciously, we can use them to become the leaders we aspire to be.

Doing Something New

I will never forget my official start at Hallmark as a newly minted greeting card writer. My early days were thoughtfully curated with support at every turn. I entered with a group of creative people who had also just graduated from college. We'd been together the summer before—over a dozen interns from diverse backgrounds and experiences, hired to infuse the creative division with new lenses and fresh ideas. Together we were a vibrant group of designers, illustrators, lettering artists, sculptors, and writers who were white, Black, Asian, Hispanic, male, female, gay, and straight, from the West Coast, the East Coast, the South, and the Midwest. It was like Nirvana—we all landed roles at our dream company to do dreamy work and were learning to navigate together.

Our group was assigned mentors from prior internship classes who invited us to hang out after hours, and there were full-time employees who also took an interest in making sure we had a good experience. We also had individual mentors. Our managers were poised to not only train us but to also shepherd us.

We shadowed experienced writers and artists who invited us into buzzing spaces where they made all kinds of cool things—paintings and storyboards and cards and ornaments and fabric pieces and wood carvings and packaging. Our onboarding process included far more than beliefs and values and policies and tours. And the messages we received went far beyond "You are welcome here." By the end of the first few months of employment, we felt *necessary*. We believed we were hired explicitly for our unique talents and worldviews and that the creative division was a better place because we were there. That's what they said, that's how they behaved, and that's what we bought into. I think back to the leader of the creative division at the time and the many others whose influence shaped our daily experiences. They cared about our individual and collective success, and they believed in our potential.

As I listen to stories of employees entering the workforce today, I can't help but long for the days when we spent *time* on people processes. In some ways, we have defaulted to "sink or swim" workplace norms, and because safety nets and value networks can be harder to build when you stand out or stand alone, many Black and Brown people find themselves either sinking or treading water. One will take you out, and the other will exhaust you while you get absolutely nowhere.

I would not have been as successful at Hallmark so early in my career if not for the village of people who surrounded me with their advice, their support, their generosity of spirit, and their willingness to teach as much as I wanted to learn. The Hallmark creative culture in the mid-1990s was a Waymaking culture. I learned to create there—to make products and design services and meet customer demands and build businesses. But I also learned to lead because in a company where creativity is king, creatives—the people—are the kingdom.

I'm grateful for that experience, and I believe everyone deserves to have one just like it. The bad news? Our need to "streamline" every activity we don't see as mission critical has watered down the onboarding process in many companies, sucking the magic out of it. We can recreate that special something by remembering this simple universal truth: new hires, whether new to a company or just to a role, need help navigating when their circumstances change. Some of the need is about the work itself, and some is about how the work gets done.

If you, as a new employee, are on the outside looking in or otherwise different from your colleagues, you are likely to take extra care with your learning approach. You may overthink the questions you ask and of whom (Will they think I should already know?), when and where you seek clarity (Maybe it will become clear if I just wait?), and the risks you are willing to take (How will it affect others' confidence in me if I make a mistake?).

In this fragile time of "getting up to speed," Waymakers are navigators. They demystify cultures, processes, and even people. They take the guesswork out of how success is defined and assessed and by whom. They point out the mile markers and are honest about when people are getting close to the marker and when they're going too far or too fast.

When I was first promoted into executive management, the person who promoted me sat me down and gave me the "look here" speech. Everyone needs the "look here" speech—watchouts and success factors no one writes down, but not everyone gets it. It includes things like how key stakeholders like to communicate or receive information—data or story? Or how to get them to buy into your ideas—make them think it's their idea or bring them in early so they can "help"? Cultures are filled with unwritten rules, which disadvantage underrepresented talent, because as we've covered, they're often not in the circles where the rules are disseminated.

A good friend—a Black man—told me how when he first entered college at a well-respected technological institution a couple of decades ago he struggled to get his work done. He caught wind of the "underground" system the white fraternity boys had created. This system was well organized—binders filled with answers to every test, sample papers, intelligence on professors, and so on. They essentially created a cheat code, and only the white fraternity boys had access to it. This made their success easier, their work faster, and their headaches fewer.

I often reflect on that story and think about the parallel—not only to corporate America but to society at large. There are cheat codes just about everywhere. If you aren't in the right circles at the right time, everything is more difficult. And I do mean everything. There are only two ways to mitigate the risk of disadvantage in these situations. We can demand that entities be more transparent about what it takes to succeed. Or we can be the ones who spill the secrets.

Chasing Dreams

The role of a Waymaker, when employees are chasing dreams, is to help define the landscape of opportunity and broker relationships.

Defining the landscape means offering a broader view of what's possible. This often looks like inquiring about the person's aspirations, passions, and skills and providing insight on existing divisions and roles, how they work together, while sharing business strategies that might lead to emerging bodies of work. Waymakers help employees translate their aspirations into tangible goals they can work toward.

They also assist employees in thinking through what it will take to cross the bridge from where they are to where they want to be. This bridge to aspiration, which I explained in a previous chapter, hinges on the aforementioned categories. As a reminder, they are:

- **Experiences**—What kinds of experiences does the employee need to get to their desired outcome, and how might you help position them?

- **Skills**–Are there distinct skills that need to be developed to be successful in the preferred position, and where can they learn and practice those skills?
- **Knowledge**–What do they need to know about the business, a function, a division, or the competitive landscape in order to be successful? Where can they find this knowledge?
- **Behaviors**–Which behaviors will next-level leaders be expected to exhibit? Is there specific feedback you or others can provide or leadership capacity building options available, like a coach?
- **Relationships**–This is the last category and perhaps the most important. Which relationships does the person need to build to achieve their goals? Here's where you become the broker. If relevant hiring managers don't know someone is interested or what might be uniquely valuable about their abilities, they will never make the list of successors for roles.

The challenging part of all this is, even when someone is skilled up and experienced, bias can creep in and obstruct the path to opportunity. I can't tell you how many conversations I've had with women, especially Black and Brown women, who graduated with honors (sometimes with multiple degrees), exceed job expectations, and help others at work be successful, only to be continually denied opportunities to advance for reasons the denier can't clearly articulate or validate. When someone doesn't look, speak, or engage how we think leaders should, we find reasons upon reasons to hold them back.

One of our survey respondents, a Black woman, was a top coordinator at a medical research firm. Most of the doctors would ask for her assistance, and she was assigned to support the research efforts of all the fellows and residents. A managerial position she really wanted opened in her department, but she was told the position wasn't posted yet. She'd been in her role for years and had the most experience in this particular area of study. The hiring manager decided to hire someone from outside the company who had never worked in the field or with the relevant population. When she asked about the position and why she didn't get a chance to at least apply, they gave her the runaround, and she was asked to train the person they hired. She quit shortly after. She felt disrespected. She was hurt, upset, annoyed. She couldn't help but feel that her race was a factor in their decision process—all the managers were white, and she was the only Black coordinator. All the doctors she worked for were shocked, wondering why she didn't get the position. There was no real answer. The role of a Waymaker here is crucial for those who are striving to grow and fulfill their aspirations but keep running into invisible obstacles.

What can you do? When someone has demonstrated skill—so much so that you trust them to train others—instead of asking "Why them?" ask "Why not them?" If a peer is passing someone over that you believe is worth placing a bet on, say so. Is their rationale sound? Meaning, are the reasons they won't promote specific (not a feeling), relevant (not old tapes or something that has nothing to do with performance), and actionable (stated in a way that an employee can actually do something about)? If not, push back. Challenge your peers. Stop minding your own business.

High Risks and Short Fuses

Recently a young white man shot and killed eight people in Atlanta, Georgia, six of whom were Asian women, across three separate locations. A captain in the Atlanta police department found himself under fire for saying the twenty-one-year-old man "had a really bad day." With this characterization, the officer minimized the heinous act, assuming the best about a young man he didn't even know. Why did he do that?

The internet exploded with posts from people recounting their worst days, none of which led to them killing eight people. Others were angry (but not surprised) that the killer was apprehended "without incident," knowing that so many Black men and women have been murdered on assumption of guilt, only to be cleared of wrongdoing when facts were revealed. Why am I sharing this? When situations get tense, those who represent the majority are often assumed to be blameless. Those who don't are assumed to be at fault and treated accordingly. Waymakers have the opportunity and responsibility to provide air cover.

When our second youngest son was in seventh grade, the counselor called to let me know he would be spending the afternoon in detention for a classroom disturbance because he "yelled at a fellow student." When our son got home, we asked what happened. He told us they were having a conversation, and the classmate called our son a monkey. Our son yelled, "Don't call me that!" Of course, the teacher heard him raise his voice and admonished him.

My husband and I scheduled an appointment with the administrators the next day. We sat side by side as they calmly explained why our son had to go to detention. I asked whether they knew why our son yelled, and they responded that the boys were "just arguing." I looked the administrator in the eye and said, "He called my son a monkey."

They were taken aback. They hadn't asked our son why he responded angrily or raised his voice—they simply assumed he was being difficult and punished him. I told them I found it unrealistic that they would expect my twelve-year-old child to respond to a racialized insult more calmly than I would, in my midforties, if one of them had called me that on the street.

When there are disagreements between majority employees and underrepresented employees in the workplace, anecdotal evidence suggests leaders are more likely to believe the white person's account of the experience than the Black or Brown person's account. Sometimes it's confirmation bias–if you believe people of color are difficult or volatile, a reported disagreement might cause you to subconsciously place blame in alignment with your bias.

I have a friend who worked at a company for more than fifteen years and had always had productive working relationships until she was moved under a manager with whom she struggled to connect. The friend exceeded her business objectives, received great feedback from partners about being responsive, thorough, and organized, and generally got along with peers. But the manager always found something to complain about. In a relatively short period of time, she was labeled as "difficult." This "difficult" label followed her every time she tried to get out from under that manager into a part of the business where she could do her job without heightened scrutiny. Other managers wanted her to reconcile with the existing boss before they felt comfortable promoting her and moving her elsewhere.

When an otherwise successful and productive employee is suddenly "difficult," peer leaders should be more curious. It's not always the fault of the employee. There are racist or sexist or xenophobic or homophobic managers who see the worst in people no matter what they do. There are others whose biases may be more latent–they just know an employee "rubs them the wrong way" but can't explain why.

In both cases, marginalized employees need Waymakers to provide air cover. Recognize that one manager's opinion of a person, especially if they are of a different race or gender, is not sufficient evidence to sideline talent when they have been successful in the past.

Gather more information. And never require someone to convince one leader to accept them in order for their careers to progress, because if that leader doesn't like them, for whatever reason, you are condemning them to stagnation. This reminds me of the scripture I shared earlier, Isaiah 43:2, which reads, "When you pass through the waters, I will be with you; and when you pass through the rivers, they will not sweep over you. When you walk through the fire, you will not be burned; the flames will not set you ablaze." In the workplace, Waymakers offer protection from personal and reputational risk.

During Transformation

A talented Black woman I know worked at a company for almost twenty-five years. She grew up there. She had garnered the respect of her colleagues, held leadership roles in various divisions, been trusted to lead breakthrough projects, and was seen as a beacon for other Black women in the company. Within weeks of a CEO and human resources leadership change, her position was eliminated. The new CEO had a different vision in mind for how the work would get done and who should do it. I could tell, from conversations she and I had in the weeks leading up to this news, she expected her work might change. But after having reported to the former CEO for just under a year, she didn't expect to not be offered another role. She didn't expect to be terminated without so much as a discussion. And she certainly didn't expect to be escorted out of the building. After twenty-five years of service.

The decision sent shock waves through the organization. Not only because she was loved and respected by many but because for other Black women she was a safe harbor—the person they relied on to help them through the maze and the one they reached out to when they needed emotional support. At this point, she was their *only* safe harbor. In the aftermath of this decision, things fell apart. Feeling isolated and unprotected, Black women began searching for external opportunities and exiting the organization. Because the trust was broken, those who remained shifted from marginal engagement toward an even more debilitating box-checking mindset. The company had to effectively start over with Black women and with Black talent in general.

In this scenario and others in which organizational change can completely disrupt what was once certain, what can Waymakers do? Simply be an anchor in the storm. Stand against the current or the tendency to rush into consequential decisions. Hold firm, or plead with colleagues to hold firm, until you explore the options. Assess the possibilities before your company loses proven talent and the invisible value–and the credibility–you sometimes lose with them.

We all need people to help us navigate new terrain, expand our vision, avoid pitfalls or recover from them, and to be an anchor in the storm. This is what great leaders do. The better we understand the many ways underrepresented employees can get lost along the way, the more responsive we will be to their needs, enabling us to keep the talent in the pipeline and grow our people and our businesses.

CHAPTER 9

Be the Way:
Model for Results

I'm no longer accepting the things I cannot change.
I'm changing the things I cannot accept.
—Angela Davis

WHEN IT COMES TO EQUITY at work, we spend too much time mulling and not enough time modeling. It helps to remember that no one is getting everything right, and waiting for the perfect vision with a lock-tight strategy and aligned tactics and communication plans is not the way we guarantee progress. It is how we delay impact. Our need to know everything before we start is how we get stuck, because there is no one repository that will answer all your questions. There is also no person or book or process that will offer you what you really want—the assurance that you will not make mistakes. Let me help you. You will make mistakes.

This is not to say you shouldn't be thoughtful and planful and disciplined—we have talked about all these things, and they are important.

But Waymaking takes stepping into it. You have to think before you know. You have to look before you see. You have to walk before you run. And you have to try before you change.

When companies were releasing statements in the wake of George Floyd's murder, I found myself cringing over a few of them. CEOs and the communication teams have an incredible responsibility to all their stakeholders, including employees and the communities they serve. They wanted to lay it all out and preemptively answer any question someone may ask about what they stood for and how they planned to stand for it. I celebrate a well-laid plan. But I also know this was not a moment for perfection. It was a moment for progress, and progress is sometimes messy but always purposeful. This work is less about avoiding mistakes and more about moving in the direction of your dreams. If you are clear about what you stand for, intentional about how you stand for it and what you expect as a result, consistent in how you show up as a leader, and bold in your choices and decisions, you will get increasingly closer to the equitable workplace we deserve. And you may even establish a new high bar.

Be Clear

When I deliver my Race at Work sessions, I talk about leadership expectations as one of the doors to walk through on the way to the equitable workplace. We can set representation targets and refine recruiting strategies and implement development programs. If, however, we fail to clearly define the role of leaders in transforming our cultures, we will not realize our equity goals. Clarifying your expectations of leaders is to DEI work what customer relationship management is to retail sales strategy. There are people who stand between you and your DEI aspirations. They are called managers, and the ones in the middle impact your outcomes the most profoundly.

One expert we interviewed called out that executives must invest in the middle because it is this layer that has the most to lose. Many of your leaders want to do their part to help others succeed, but they are still trying to figure out what success looks like. Be clear about your definition, complete with behaviors that embody it. Give everyone a fair opportunity to rise to the occasion by making it easy to understand how to move forward and show them—every day—by how you show up and engage with your people.

Recently I was in a session with a division leader where he announced to everyone present that no customer or business goal was as important to him as the safety and well-being of his multicultural talent. In this moment, he didn't have to tell his leaders what his priorities were. He stated plainly that he would protect his people at all costs, and this very declaration set the tone for how his leaders were to respond should they discover their talent has been compromised. This kind of clarity is what culture shifts are made of. Define it, communicate it, but also model it.

Be Intentional

I understand why companies are hesitant to set diversity and equity targets. I really do. There have been countless instances of targets driving bad behavior, simply to check a box. Some organizations have experienced backlash from their majority populations, citing reverse discrimination. I've actually heard tales of hiring managers bringing underqualified minority talent on board, knowing they lacked the requisite experience, to prove a point and undermine the very idea of driving accountability around diversity and inclusion.

Ultimately, we can't say diversity is a business imperative and not establish a business goal. You would not expect to meet customer demands without setting a retail sales increase (RSI) target. You would not expect to drive margin on product sales without establishing cost of product (COP) guidelines. You would not expect to meet your safety requirements without defining "safety" for your company and quantifying acceptable risk. In the safety example, you would assess your risk along multiple dimensions and devise a plan to minimize or eliminate it. Occupational Safety and Health Administration (OSHA) promoted a process for workplace health and safety that includes seven facets: management leadership, worker participation, hazard identification and assessment, hazard prevention and control, education and training, program evaluation and improvement, and coordination and communication on multiemployer worksites.[1] Basically, achieving a physically healthy and safe workplace requires a systemic approach. Creating and nurturing an inclusive environment requires the same.

Be Consistent

My husband and I have six children together, four of whom are teenage boys. My husband is very good about establishing rules and holding our children accountable to those rules. Before we got married, in the window after my divorce from my first husband, the two sons I brought to the party would frequently test me. Because I lacked consistency in my parenting tactics, I would often fail the test. I'd get caught up in simple things. I'd say they couldn't eat in my car, but I let them do so when rushing from one place to another. I established a bedtime, but I broke it occasionally when I got a late start on the nighttime routine. Sometimes, though, I would fail more important tests, like the degree of respect I demanded from them, which I thought was clear. But on those days when I was tired from doing everything myself at home while working as a corporate executive, I didn't correct certain behaviors with enough speed or intensity. If I'm being honest, it was sometimes easier to let things slide. But it was never *better* to do so. In fact, when I "let things slide" out of momentary convenience—to avoid a meltdown or a time suck—it created confusion, brought about more drama in the long run, and took even more time to make right.

My unwillingness to do the hard things in the moment, every time, gave way to a Wild West of sorts—children doing what they wanted to do, when they wanted to do it. My children were not bad. They were merely children following my lead. It wasn't until we blended families and I watched my husband establish new norms and "inspect what he expected" without fail that I realized where I went wrong. I had strong morals and values. I was clear about how I wanted my household to run. But because I was inconsistent, my sons knew they could get away with deciding when they would or would not abide by my rules.

While I don't love comparing leadership to parenting, there are undeniable similarities, and creating a healthy workplace culture fits the bill. Several of the old adages apply: It's what you do, not what you say. You have to set a good example. And yes, consistency is key.

During a recent fireside chat with a client, the moderator asked me about holding others accountable for how they lead. I shared with him that executives have to define what it means to lead at their company—values and behaviors—and hold every single leader to that expectation. And when a leader behaves in ways that are counter to the expressed expectation, you have to act. He asked me outright, "Are you saying we should fire people who don't abide by our leadership expectations?"

The simple answer is yes. There is, however, a "but." There are many leaders learning how to lead inclusively, and they will make mistakes. We cannot fire people for making mistakes. But blatant racist or sexist or homophobic or xenophobic or ableist commentary or acts should not be tolerated. And we must avoid the tendency to prove that someone who behaves in overtly racist ways is in fact a racist before we take action. Companies want to find patterns of racism or wait for the leader to establish a racist pattern. How ridiculous does this sound? When a leader who is supposed to model excellence for a company intentionally misuses the corporate charge card once, they are let go immediately. If a leader's negligence causes significant harm to the business, they will be fired. But if a leader publicly behaves in a way that harms marginalized employees, we want to prove it before we take action. Which harms people even more.

The best way to avoid this is to be crystal clear about your leadership expectations, do not make exceptions to these rules, and apply both rewards and consequences consistently. When you say you have zero tolerance for certain behaviors, have zero tolerance. When someone resists your expectations in any way, have a process by which you communicate the implications of resisting and respond accordingly. If you have different strokes for different folks because some are more valuable to you than others or you don't want to be inconvenienced or it might take time and money or it might bring attention to the problem, you are working against your stated culture and allowing toxicity to thrive. If would-be bad actors know the rules do not apply to them or at least that they may have a way out of suffering the consequences of their harmful actions, they are not likely to shift behaviors to accommodate the culture or the people. And whenever there is toxic leadership anywhere in an organization, those on the margins are harmed most acutely.

Be Bold

Since the pandemic, I've been privy to many conversations about the intersection of driving diversity and remote work. It's come up in casual conversations with my husband, who leads a large global team and in innovation workshops with client teams when I invite them to imagine bold goals for the future, name the barriers that might get in the way of achieving those goals, and come up with brave actions that might overcome the barriers. The talent war is now being waged on fronts company leaders have been warned about for years. What seemed like a future concern is real and present, and companies are having to rethink their long-held beliefs if they want to be competitive.

I was fortunate to participate in an innovation initiative at Hallmark several years ago, during which I learned new ways to think about familiar problems. Many of the ideation tools I use in my DEI work are inspired by this experience, which serves as an enhancement to my product-development expertise. One of the concepts we learned about is orthodoxies or long-held beliefs and rules that are so deeply entrenched in company cultures and processes that we no longer question them. You can usually identify orthodoxies based on how they're referenced. When you hear, "this is the company way" or "that's just how we do things around here" or "it's always been this way," there's often an orthodoxy hiding there.

The marketplace has changed dramatically over the last few years, and companies have been forced to reconsider their consumer, competitive, and operational orthodoxies in order to survive. The bricks to clicks pendulum swing is probably the most obvious. If you held an orthodoxy that your brand is tied to a physical retail experience, even after years of watching competitors go digital, your business has likely suffered. Enter a global pandemic, your business may have even died. Orthodoxies keep our lenses narrow, our vision blurry, and our possibilities limited. They are protected by both longevity and systemic support, since value chains are sometimes built around them, which include partners, assets, processes, skills, technologies, and the like. Challenging them is no small thing. But in a business world where the only thing we can count on is change, the ability to interrogate whether and how they still serve you is not only advantageous—it is necessary to your survival.

On the issue of remote work, as an example, many large corporations are resisting the idea of allowing talent to work from afar indefinitely, even as the pandemic has proven it can work, with some companies driving significant revenue growth and maximizing profits thanks to lower expenses. Some reasons for this resistance include difficulty building culture and connectedness, concerns about long-term productivity, or impact to collaboration.

The orthodoxy for some companies might be that *physical collocation builds culture, increases productivity, and enhances collaboration.*

There are two ways to use an orthodoxy when you want to innovate. One is to lean into it and the other is to flip it. If you lean into it, you might ask yourself:

"If it is true that physical collocation builds culture, increases productivity, and enhances collaboration, how might we evolve the way we collocate to better build culture, increase productivity, and enhance collaboration?"

By asking this question, you might decide to collocate somewhere even more desirable or where there is more diverse talent available to you. You might decide to invest in that collocation with state-of-the-art technology and amenities that are proven to increase productivity, like childcare or a café or a gym on-site. You might create collaborative spaces and bring in creative tools that are even more inspiring. All of which would set you apart as an employer and make you more competitive in the talent market.

If you decided to flip this orthodoxy, you might restate it to say:

"A primarily remote workforce would allow us to attract the best talent wherever they are, increase profitability by saving on capital expenditures and travel, and make us more agile as an organization."

By restating it in this way, you might rework your employer brand to position yourself as the best place to work (from any place), effectively eliminating location barriers to hiring and retention. You might sell or lease space and improve your financial position. You would indeed become more agile because you are no longer attached to a physical space but also because you would invest in building your digital competence, which would undoubtedly position you for less disruption in the future.

Remote work is just an example of how challenging long-held beliefs or rules can support your diversity, equity, and inclusion progress. But challenge them we must if you want to shift culture and make a way for new people in your company with distinct voices and experiences. Orthodoxies don't change on their own. You will either be the one to boldly tackle them head on, or the market will do it for you, as we have seen time and again. Be bold and know that today's talent is not abiding by yesterday's rules. It is barreling forward, full force, and will completely remake how we work together whether you come along or not.

Be Accountable

I have a long-standing partnership with a $100 billion multinational conglomerate that has almost two hundred thousand employees. One of my most transformational projects during 2020 was facilitating a series of educational sessions on race in America, otherness at work, and the ways leaders must engage to enable progress. Between the CEO, his executive team, their executive teams, and their larger leadership community, well over five hundred executives participated. Both by the CEO's declaration during our first conversation and also in the multiple executive discussions afterward, it was clear that this leadership team was serious about impact. I believe the CEO's words to me and his team were, "When we decide to do something, we do it. So that's it."

In fact, during a meeting months later for a related project, one of the C-suite leaders revealed a provocative data point about the company's diversity goals and recommended actions. He shared that in order to meet their commitments, seven out of ten future hires would be from an underrepresented group. I was blown away, not by the aggressive target (which was pretty profound). Instead, it was the matter-of-factness with which he stated the target that hit me. He did not say, "If we want to do x, we will have to do y." It was more of a "We are going to do x, so we have to do y." For me, that one moment was further evidence of their intentionality. The leadership team was rapidly developing their diversity consciousness and, while I already had high hopes for them based on our engagement to date, my hope was turning into confidence.

The bottom line: You can't say diversity is a business imperative and not establish a business goal. As one leading voice whose expertise spans global food and marketing industries passionately stated, this work requires 100 percent intentionality. "Business impact is the accelerator. Tie everything to the bottom line—everything—and hold leaders accountable for their results. To do this, you have to be able to call a thing a thing."[2]

Modeling equitable and inclusive leadership is the way we signal to others, who are also trying to figure out how to adapt to new ideas, that the journey toward an equitable workplace is worthwhile. When we show up as clear, intentional, consistent, bold, and accountable, we demonstrate to other leaders and colleagues that this work matters to us. We say to them, without words, that we believe in equity, and we want them to believe in it too.

CHAPTER *10*

Bring People Along: Model for Momentum

If you want to go fast, go alone.
If you want to go far, go together.
—African Proverb

IT WASN'T UNTIL ALMOST ONE year into the pandemic and America's racial reconciliation that leaders began to realize the racism education they'd been investing in, while insightful, was leaving the putt short. I should have seen it coming, but I was in the moment with them—bringing them along from total ignorance toward awareness, then understanding, then buy-in. But when it came time to internalize and embed what they had learned, everyone got stuck. I quickly saw that many leaders who had come to understand the importance of leading equitably didn't know how to translate that understanding into daily choices and behaviors. This is where the Waymakers Leadership Model (a leadership framework that ties skills, levers, and behaviors to talent outcomes) was born—out of the growing chasm between knowing and doing. Leaders are smart. They grasp concepts quickly and connect dots between what they learn and what they've witnessed or experienced, but it's not easy to insert yourself in the story without development and support.

There are five leadership choices that help bring the idea of Waymaking to life inside companies. These choices are (1) be available–present and accessible, (2) be transparent–honest and communicative, (3) be collaborative–open and team oriented, (4) be the change–lead out in front, and (5) be humble–maintain a learning posture.

Be Available

Those who need it can't get to workplace equity without talent leaders, many of whom still reflect the majority. As we've explored, if you are leading people or desire to do so one day, you are or will be a necessary part of this journey. While an obvious point, how to engage across difference in a way that truly moves the ball isn't always obvious. In the large majority of American companies, the path to fairness for underrepresented talent will be traveled in partnership with white men and women or not at all. As Soraya Chemaly so eloquently states in her book *Rage Becomes Her*, "We can't 'self-help' our way to equality."

So how do you show up–day-to-day–for someone who doesn't look like you? How do you learn what matters to them? Show empathy? Connect on a deeper level? Let them know you care and support them and their journey? All without saying too much or coming across as trying too hard? These are the questions I often receive from well-meaning people who, when they're being honest, tell me they are afraid to say the wrong thing. Fear is, in my opinion, one of the greatest obstacles to connecting across differences. It's not easy, but if we want to create more equitable workplaces, we have to "do it afraid." Here are a few important communication tips as you seek to be more professionally and personally available for those with whom you work.

Tip 1: Listen to understand, not to defend.

If you really want to know what Black and Brown people are experiencing at your company, ask. Then listen. Check for understanding by playing back what you think you heard. Keep checking until you get it right. Don't go into this conversation with the hope to feel better about your current state (or to feel better about yourself). If you do, you are likely to distort what you hear to fit a narrative you can tolerate. You are gathering information—that's it. Gather it objectively.

Tip 2: Empathize. Don't make it about you.

Don't work too hard to relate. You may be able to naturally, but then again, you may not. We often seek common ground in these conversations to help us feel connected. This is not the time to equate your struggle with another person's struggle. Do empathize by putting yourself in the other person's shoes. How would you feel if your repeated requests for promotion were denied (or ignored) without explanation? If you didn't receive timely career-altering feedback? If people marginalized your input or contributions? Probably frustrated and helpless. Sadly, this is a familiar state of mind for many people at work. Simply acknowledge the other person's truth and try to understand how they must feel. Respond accordingly.

Tip 3: Learn what inclusion looks like for the people with whom you work.

You don't have to guess what would make a work experience more fulfilling for the employees on your team. You can ask. *What does inclusion look like for you? When have you felt most included? What were the circumstances? When have you felt excluded? What were the circumstances? What do you wish were true about your opportunities here? What is most helpful for you as you seek to grow in this company?* Be more curious. Determine what you can control or heavily influence. Then act.

Tip 4: Grant permission for two-way feedback.

Sometimes our best intentions fall flat. Establish a psychological contract up front. Express your intent to the person (or people) on the other side of the table. Then grant permission to let you know when your actions are out of line with your expressed intent. If and when they take you up on your offer, thank them for telling you the truth. The more open you are to receiving difficult feedback, the more you will learn about leading inclusively. People will tell you exactly how they feel and what they need if they believe you truly care to know.

Tip 5: Don't take missteps personally—we all misstep when we do hard things.

Leading across boundaries is a very emotional thing to get wrong. When we do, we tend to retreat. No one wants to feel like a bad person—ignorant at best and racist or sexist at worst. That's why leading equitably takes courage—deep, personal, abiding courage. If it were easy, more people would do it, and we would have made more progress by now. Accept that you will make mistakes. Find a safe space to work out your frustration but don't give up.

Tip 6: Don't perpetuate racialized or gen-
der-biased feedback and decision-making.

Raise your consciousness regarding feedback that is rooted in exclusionary thought and cut it off at the pass. If you're in a talent review and someone says a woman of any race might not want a promotion because she just had a baby, intervene with, "How is childbirth relevant to this conversation?" If someone says a person of color doesn't have executive presence, ask them to be specific. If their specifics aren't connected to business enablement, ask for business-relevant examples. If they don't have any, reiterate the importance of focusing on business outcomes.

Tip 7: Don't go it alone.

If there are significant and far-reaching issues in your company around race and gender, find out who else in your company cares about this issue as much as you do. It may be worthwhile to create a "coalition of the willing," where several leaders come together to better understand the challenges at hand and commit to collaborating on real solutions. One individual can't create an exclusionary culture. And one person can't unwind it. Get yourself a crew of influencers and band together for progress.

Tip 8: Take heart.

If you truly aim to be a Waymaker, you have already begun. Wanting to use your agency on others' behalf is an important first step. There is no handbook, really. You will get it right sometimes. Other times, you will fall on your face. Realize that we, the professionals who stand to benefit from your advocacy, understand this feeling. For many of us, our entire careers have been a series of tries unacknowledged, accomplishments uncelebrated, risks unrewarded. It has made us stronger in many cases. If you persist, it will make you stronger too.

Together we can make it easier on everyone.

Be Transparent

The second leadership choice aspiring Waymakers must embrace is the choice to be transparent. There are so many unknowns for people who have been historically excluded.

I was the first person in my immediate family to attend a four-year college immediately following high school and the first in my extended family to hold a corporate job. Recently, at dinner with a client, I found myself explaining one of the lesser-discussed gaps for many Black and Brown people in corporate America. There is no one to tell us the rules of the road. For those of us of a certain age, there is no "office politics" guru in our household. We don't know people who know people. We had to navigate this invisible obstacle course alone, knowing there was a playbook but not having access to it or to the people who could crack it open for us. Many of us are first generation corporate players, which has many real-life consequences.

As previously discussed, marginalized employees need insight into unwritten rules and access to important information, like business strategies or customer intelligence or simply where to find the resources they need to do their jobs. Here's where you can make a way by opening the playbook. You can share business-critical information with your teams and peers more uniformly instead of at the impromptu meeting you have with a friend in the hallway. You can be generous with your guidance and lessons learned.

By favoring transparency, speed, and structure in both knowledge transfer practices and in ongoing communications, you increase the chances of enabling equitable insight and avoid leaning on your instincts to know what to say, whom to say it to, and when to say it. When we rely on our instincts and remove the rigor from our communication processes, our affinity bias creeps in and we make assumptions about what people know or don't know. We judge what's important to communicate in the moment through our personal lenses. We share information, sometimes at the tail end of conversations, about completely different topics. In so doing, we unconsciously advantage some and disadvantage others. Inside corporate walls, knowledge is everything—what you know, when you know it, and how well you know it can make the difference between barely performing and setting the world on fire.

Be equitably transparent with your employees and your peers and realize that some may even need an information booster out of the gate. If they grew up in a family like mine, they are starting with an insight deficit.

Be Collaborative

The third choice leaders can make is to be collaborative. It was in my first succession-planning meeting as an executive that I realized there was such a thing as "the usual suspects." The usual suspects were a handful of people who were first in line for everything. They were the first in line for promotions. For special projects. For meetings with the C-suite. To present in front of important customers. To benefit from awards and recognition. They were the chosen ones, and every time something amazing was available that would help someone grow, be seen, earn more money, or otherwise benefit, this same handful of people were tapped. In the years since my firsthand realization, I have heard about and seen countless examples of this tendency to rely on a small group of "trusted" colleagues to get big things done, which leads to professional advantage for those we trust.

Every time you invite an employee into a learning loop, you offer them exactly what they need to grow—new knowledge, new relationships, new skills, and the opportunity to demonstrate expanded leadership competence. When you continually pass over other employees in your group, you deny them these same benefits. It stands to reason that when we unconsciously submit to this cycle, we are better equipping some people for leadership than others. The most prepared and pressure-tested team members are better equipped for big roles because we intentionally equipped them, not always because they are more capable. Thanks to affinity bias, those we equip are usually like us. The cycle continues.

Waymakers take care to tap new sources for growth opportunities. And they start early. Leaders should see every important project or emerging business problem as an opportunity to skill build and should scan teams for unusual suspects. We tend to tap the people we know and who can get things done fast, which is understandable, but this merely perpetuates the cycle of sameness. If you must, expand the circle. It is our role as leaders to develop talent, and it is the role of a Waymaker to do so equitably. What's more, as the landscape rapidly evolves, you should want new and different eyes on your business problems. You may have people you trust to get the work done quickly, but what if the work gets done *better* with more perspectives? As we've covered, diversity is tied to innovation performance. Cultivate new sources. Grow new leaders. Make more people "the best person for the job."

Be the Change

In early 2021, I decided to hire a life coach. I felt, in my spirit, that it was time to push through my self-imposed barriers to be even more bold in how I make a way for others. I had been using all the tools at my disposal, but I felt like I needed more tools, more partners, more platforms to bring *The Waymakers* vision to life. No one makes it alone.

My coach invited me to watch *The Black Godfather* on Netflix, a documentary about Clarence Avant—an entertainment executive and relationship guru who has created opportunity for some of the most legendary Black leaders in the history of America. Too many musicians and producers and actors and politicians have been changed by Avant to name them here, and I'm sure the film only scratched the surface. Just know there have been dozens, if not more, self-described "children of Clarence" who have broken records of their own and gone on to change others' careers. As the first Black man to enter many of the decision-making rooms he ultimately made home, Clarence Avant created a domino effect of the very best kind.

I know why Tim asked me to watch the documentary. Clarence Avant is the ultimate Waymaker. I watched it twice in twenty-four hours, completely transfixed by his journey. His friends described him as fearless. He described himself as a numbers guy—someone who was "serious about his money." But he never charged those he served. In the film, he simply says, "If I like them and they need help, I help them." When asked why he served others in this way, he answered that he helped Black people move forward because he grew up so poor. But I have to believe that a life as consequential as Clarence Avant's has to be fueled by more than difficult life experience. There is an intentionality and boldness that characterizes everything he has done for as long as he has been doing it. Every choice made, every act of support offered, every network facilitated, every friendship built was built upon the purpose of progress. Not only for himself but for his community. A purpose of progress. Purpose. Progress.

Are you purposed for progress? If so, whose progress are you purposed for beyond your own? I remember Eileen Drummond, a Hallmark mentor whose leadership position I would inherit, telling me how executive leadership was like being in a fishbowl. Every move you make is magnified. It's true. When you reach a high level of influence in any organization, people receive everything you do, and don't do, as a sign. They watch your facial expressions and body language when others are speaking for hints of approval or displeasure. They read your tone of voice when you speak and imbue every word you choose with the meaning of their making. If you arrive late to a meeting, they assume it's not important to you. If you leave early, they are convinced you did so because you are unhappy. Leaders must be hyperconscious of how they show up every day because like it or not you are sending messages to your organization.

When it comes to diversity, equity, and inclusion, employees are watching for the same signs. When your employees tell you they are hurting and you do nothing to address their pain, they notice. When you speak out against anti-Black violence but not anti-Asian violence, they notice. When you find out that one of your leaders is behaving badly but you promote him because he is "good at his job," they notice. Every decision you make, person you protect, risk you tolerate, issue you ignore sends a signal to those watching you about who and what you value and teaches them whether and to what degree to trust you with their loyalty and contribution. This is why Waymakers must realize that we are modeling both the beliefs and the behaviors we want people to adhere to.

Be Humble

As leaders, we are encouraged to begin a new role with a learning posture, but not to maintain one. We are taught to do our research, gather intelligence, and ascertain "the success formula," so we can succeed repeatedly. We are taught to get up to speed quickly, take calculated risks, and avoid pitfalls. Leading equitably and inclusively flies in the face of all of that because to do it well means to slow down and accept that we will likely encounter a land mine or two or three. Waymakers know that while there are success principles, there is no success formula. What works for employees is as unique as the employees themselves. Leading for *all people* is work–personal and vulnerable work that asks us to set aside our "agile and competitive" ways for something much harder to practice and impossible to measure–humility.

How do we learn, on the individual level, what our people need to succeed? How do we grow our awareness, build our understanding, and embed new ways of engaging people that will make them feel seen, respected, valued, and protected? We connect and communicate, yes, but how? When I first started sharing really tactical advice on LinkedIn, I thought colleagues might come after me for being condescending. The opposite happened. I've learned in the years since that the gap between theory and outcomes is significant. Sometimes, it helps to make it plain. Here are four conversation starters for different types of leaders who want to lean into learning about what true support looks like for the people in their charge whose life experience is not like theirs or who may have suffered over the last few years because of world and national events. I wrote these shortly after George Floyd was murdered and corporate America was turning itself inside out to connect with Black employees, but the approaches are timeless and universal.

Type 1: The Compassionate Connector

"Tara, I'm coming to realize that these last few months of racial unrest in America are just the tip of an iceberg you've been living with your whole life. I want to better understand your experiences, especially here at (company). If and when it works for you, I'd like to set up time to get a better feel for how things are *really* going and to hear what you need from me to be successful."

Key messages: I care. I'm open to learning. You are worth my time.

Type 2: The Bold Bridge

"Tara, I've made a personal commitment to step up and be the advocate you deserve at this company. I want to set up time to better understand your career aspirations and what I can do to help you achieve them. Do you have time this week or next?"

Key messages: I am committed. I'm ready and willing to help you get ahead. This is urgent to me.

Type 3: The Truth Teller

"Tara, what's been going on in America and in our company is not okay. I'm honestly embarrassed that I never took the time to have this conversation with you before. That's not the kind of leader I want to be. But when you know better, you do better. I want to do better. Please help me understand what support and enablement look like in your eyes–for you, personally, and for others who may share similar experiences."

Key messages: I won't make excuses. I've been disengaged, but that changes now. What can I do?

Type 4: The Supportive Seeker

"I need to be a better ally to you and our Black colleagues. I'm not asking you to solve this for me, but if you have specific feedback, I'm all ears. Some of my questions are, "What should I stop doing? What should I start doing? What can I be doing better or differently?"

Key messages: I must do more. What kind of action is valuable? I want your feedback.

At the end of the day, being an inclusive leader is about leading with humanity. Not strategy. Not suspicion. Not precedent or policy or rules. Just curiosity, care, and compassion.

Leadership today is as much about shaping norms as it is driving business. In the workplace, leaders are the potters, and the culture is the clay. Every day—with every choice we make and every person we support—we form our culture into a living, breathing entity that will either feed talent or starve it. The choice is ours to make, and we must make it consciously.

CONCLUSION

A New Thing: The Waymaker Life

See, I am doing a new thing!
Now it springs up; do you not perceive it?
I am making a way in the wilderness
and streams in the wasteland.
   —Isaiah 43:19

WHEN I FIRST STARTED WRITING this book, I wanted to make it easier and faster for high-level executives to get DEI efforts right by offering a clear and well-researched playbook for creating more equitable workplaces. If you have ever written a book or tried to, you know that where you start is not always where you finish. Because I continued to consult while writing, I started paying closer attention to the kinds of information and experiences that seemed most compelling and that drove results most consistently.

I began experiencing my client engagements on two levels. First, on the purpose and objectives level, meaning I focused on what we were there to accomplish. But also on the investigative level, which is to say I would shift into insight mode, asking myself a series of questions: Which concepts are leaders responding to most favorably? Which are harder to understand or embrace? What questions are they asking?

What are their concerns? How are they thinking about the problems their companies are facing? When we talk about solutions, where does their energy increase? How confident and competent are they with the language and principles of diversity, equity, and inclusion work? What's their tolerance for the learning journey? Through it all, I kept asking the big question: Beyond systems and policies and expectations, what really removes barriers and ushers underrepresented talent through to higher levels of contribution and achievement?

This greater awareness changed how I thought about *The Waymakers*. This book is not so much the answer to inequity, as it is a carefully constructed framing of new ways to think about achieving and sustaining equity. In my mind, it is a response to every need, hope, goal, question, point of confusion, and fear-based barrier I've personally experienced, observed, or helped clients reconcile.

It provides guidance, but it's not the playbook I originally set out to write.

It illuminates a path to change, but it's not a road map.

It shares best practices, but it's not a manual.

It's validated by research, but it's not a white paper.

In my heart, it is an invitation. An invitation to every leader, at every level, who is willing to make a way through the wilderness for people who, historically, have not been given the tools, resources, or guidance to do it for themselves or others like them. The success of those who need Waymakers relies on the unwritten being written and the unspoken being spoken. They don't need a handout, but they do need an outstretched hand–someone who will shine the light, open the door, and guide them through the terrain. When we fix our systems and invite the most disadvantaged onto the playing field, we fix the systems for and invite everyone.

Which takes me back to my big question:

"Beyond systems and policies and expectations, what really

removes barriers and ushers underrepresented talent through to higher levels of contribution and achievement?"

The answer, without question, is you.

Heal the Body

Until 2020, racism was not a conversation we had at work, at least not like we are now. I entered the workforce knowing there were three things you shouldn't talk about: race, politics, and religion. One of the reasons why Black and Brown talent continue to be among the least represented in leadership positions relative to their presence in entry levels is that while there have been movements to level the playing field, like affirmative action, they didn't advantage Black and Brown people at work. Instead, they advantaged white women. And one of the reasons race-based discrimination has not been rooted out is because we couldn't talk about race at work. Now that we're talking about it openly, there are increasing numbers of white professionals growing concerned that they might be now disadvantaged. Teresa Sande, author of *Find Your Fierce*, used the term "Blacklash" to describe this phenomenon on a LinkedIn post of mine in which I was lamenting this rising challenge to a growing equity consciousness.

It is very uncommon to lead a session on equity these days without a white leader asking how they should respond to their white male colleagues who express genuine concern that they may somehow be left behind. The first time I was asked, it caught me off guard. But it's pretty common now. First, I help them pressure test the concern by asking what percentage of their entry-level workforce is white and male. The answer is usually somewhere around 35 percent, which reflects the national average, according to McKinsey & Company's 2020 Women in the Workplace data. I then ask them what percentage of their top executive positions are white and male. This number was as high as 90 percent for one partner company, which is much higher than the McKinsey national average of 60–65 percent.[1] I then state the obvious: "You can tell them what your data suggests: that the odds are in their favor." This usually lightens the mood. But I also help them reframe the concern. As I mentioned in a previous chapter, the idea that someone will take an opportunity away assumes the opportunity belongs to someone, and opportunities belong to no one. They simply exist—no assumptions, no biases—just waiting for someone to seize them.

The goal here is to not disadvantage anyone. What we want is to provide all people equal access to opportunity. Equity acknowledges that you can't expect two people to arrive at a finish line at the same time when one is wearing running shoes and the other is wearing sandals. And even if they are both wearing running shoes, if one runs his race on a windless day and the other in a storm—there is no equity. Equity makes sure both people have running shoes and are running in similar conditions—and *then* makes room for them to compete.

Lastly, I share an analogy that seems to really help people see how equity work helps everyone, not just marginalized talent—when you heal the deepest wound, you heal the body. Treating symptoms of illness will make you more comfortable. But when something is really broken in a complex system like the human body, the goal is to better understand the root of the most significant injury and treat that. In doing so, we often eliminate secondary issues that we didn't even know were connected. In our workplaces, the people who are most different from those in power have the hardest time fulfilling their promise.

I conducted a survey in early 2021 about microaggressions and other experiences closely associated with workplace equity and leadership effectiveness. I received a total of one thousand responses from people of all races, genders, industries, and levels. Here's what

I learned: While Black people and Hispanics and Asians are having truly difficult experiences at work when it comes to feeling seen, respected, valued, and protected, they are not alone. For instance, in regard to the statement "I don't really know what executive leadership thinks of my potential," 83 percent of Asian employees, 76 percent of Black people, and 89 percent of Hispanics agreed. But 73 percent of non-Hispanic whites agreed with this statement too. Similarly, with the statement "I don't believe anyone with influence over whether or not I achieve my career aspirations knows what I have accomplished," 60 percent of Asians, 63 percent of Black people, and 50 percent of Hispanics agreed. Sixty-two percent of non-Hispanic whites agreed. For the statement "I have been talked over in a meeting or ignored," 81 percent of Asian respondents agreed, 87 percent of Hispanics, and 84 percent of non-Hispanic whites. Black respondents were actually less likely to report having had this experience than others but still reported high at 76 percent. There were similar trends for statements about timing and specificity of feedback, clarity on what it takes to grow in an organization, and continually needing to validate one's presence and perspectives.

It is very clear to me, not only thanks to surveys like this but also based on conversations I've had with countless groups of employees who are engaged in inclusion work, that if we make the system work better for marginalized talent, we make it work better for everyone. The opportunities to enhance our cultures and systems are endless.

No More Excuses

It's time to get into the arena. Not them. You.

As you've learned throughout this book, a human problem requires a human solution. The inability to create and sustain cultures of inclusion in which people have equal opportunity to thrive does not hinge on policy. It's how leaders interpret and implement policies–through narrow lenses and without understanding of or regard for other people's lived experiences and unique needs–that prevents companies from realizing their cultural aspirations.

I can't recall the number of times I've heard how difficult it is to diversify workforces and drive equity: It's complicated. It takes too much time and effort. It detracts from running the business. I've heard them all. Ray Dalio's book *Principles* again comes to mind. He says, in a chapter about how to make good decisions, that we should consider first, second, and third order consequences with equal weight, but we don't. We usually overemphasize first order consequences.

He uses physical exercise as an example. The first order consequence of exercising is discomfort and inconvenience and a sacrifice of time. The second would be a stronger heart and body. The third would be health and longevity. When we put too much weight on the first order consequence, we forgo exercise. It's too hard or takes too long. But if we considered the long-term benefits and the value of those benefits, we would likely choose to push past the first consequence to enjoy the second and third.[2]

When it comes to equity and inclusion, the same thinking applies. First order consequences are time, effort, and discomfort. Second order consequences are more ideas, holistic problem-solving, and stronger teams. Third order consequences would be sustainability. We have to stop thinking about diversity, equity, and inclusion as more "things to do," and start seeing it for what it is: limitless potential through more trusting and respectful relationships.

A strong relationship between an employee and a company is like any strong relationship–built on trust and reciprocity and the ability to be your best within it. If any one of these foundational needs goes unmet for too long, the relationship breaks. I wish I could say corporate America has broken its bond with many Black, Latinx, Asian, and Indigenous employees, but in many cases a genuine relationship was never formed in the first place.

You can change that. This is your work. The reason we remain stuck is that we keep waiting for other people to do it. There is no "they"—only you, with your genuine desire to make a difference in your workplace, the insight you gain every time you engage with people who are not like you or read books like these, and the courage you tap into with each bold goal you set, each barrier you name, and each brave action you embrace to overcome those barriers. You are the answer you've been waiting for.

Now

I wish I'd thought to track every story I've heard from a Black or Brown woman at work who said they were trying to "stick it out," hoping their boss would warm up to them or their company would make more substantial culture changes or their countless "proving" attempts would pay off. There have been so many. Some of these women stuck it out for years, only to be unceremoniously let go. Time does not heal all brokenness. Some things actually get more broken with time, and that's exactly what happens in the case of workplace inequity and, if we're being honest, in our personal relationships too.

While Tim and I were talking about *The Waymakers*, he pointed out the power of the "shift" and asked me to read John 2 in the Bible, where Jesus first reveals His glory. While at the wedding at Cana in Galilee, Jesus' mother turns to Jesus and says, "They have no more wine." Jesus responds, "Woman, what does this have to do with me? My hour has not yet come." Mary turns to the servants and advises them to do what Jesus tells them to do. He instructs them to fill six stone jars with water, draw some out, then take it to the master of the banquet. They did so, and when the master of the banquet tasted the water, it had been turned into wine.[3] Jesus had not planned to reveal His glory on that day. In fact, he was resistant at first. But He was needed. At that moment and with the miracle only He could perform. I believe this is also true for us. This is our collective moment as leaders—to stand up and deliver the shift in our workplaces and in the leadership realm. Our time is now.

Waymakers are not bench sitters. They are on the court, taking chances they know won't all land, looking to see who's open, passing the ball, and working with others to put points on the board. Waymaking is an individual commitment, but culture change is a team sport. And if you want to accelerate change, that game starts now. You can win it by facing your current reality, taking responsibility for leading in new ways, and building the cross-boundary relationships necessary to grow your business in partnership with your employees instead of at their expense.

The Workplace We Deserve

Meritocracy is a myth. We do not all have an equal opportunity to succeed.

Racism is alive and well. We are not in a post-racial era. We are, sadly, still embroiled in racism and all its manifestations.

Gender discrimination exists. Women are still carrying more water at work and in life and getting less to drink.

We are not all starting from the same place, with the same tools, in the same conditions. Headwinds abound. Roadblocks are erected. And even when we arrive at the same time, the clocks are sometimes reset.

People still say, with all the evidence in the public domain, that we do not see what we see or hear what we hear. That we do not experience what we experience. But we do. And it is not only a drag on our careers but on our very lives, our liberty, and our pursuit of happiness. We, Black and Brown people in America, have been alienated from our inalienable rights.

I've been thinking a lot about why I'm here—on this earth and in this position. I never considered myself an activist in the traditional sense of the word. But I have come to realize there are many kinds of activists—people who choose their weapons of change and wield them in an arena of their choosing for a higher and common good. These people cross rivers, climb mountains, and overcome obstacles to arrive at their destination, as Dr. Maya Angelou wrote about love, "full of hope." Waymakers are, in their own way, activists for the equitable workplace we deserve.

My weapon is my voice. That voice is shaped by both experiences and expertise.

My arena is the professional workplace, which impacts millions of lives and societies with its power and position. It is where I have learned and led and where I now advise others to do the same.

My higher and common good is equity. Equity is the goal. Not equality but equal access with consideration for the numerous ways we must compensate for imbalanced systems.

The obstacles I overcome are antiquated ideas and norms—our ways of operating that have become so second nature we no longer pause to consider whether and how they're serving people in the ways we want them to.

And my destination? Fulfillment. It's something I want every leader—every person—to enjoy. I hope every individual has the chance to do what they came here to do—to use the gifts they've been given to make a difference in the world and in the lives of other people. That's what Waymakers do. They gather what they have—power and position—and walk boldly into the thick of inequity, not knowing exactly what awaits them but willing to confront resistance if it means clearing the path for others to travel. If you're still here, you have the heart and mind of a Waymaker . And with intentionality and practice, you will soon have the hands of one too.

Thank you for walking with me. I invite you to continue your Waymaker journey from here, using the strategies and tools in this book. They are proven–not only by me but by the dozens of workplace equity experts who were kind enough to share their insight and experience and by hundreds of employees across race and gender and sexual orientation and ability who have lived in the margins and stand ready to fulfill their potential.

When strategies are taking too long and tools are not at your fingertips, lean into the Waymaker principles. Build empathy by being more curious. Be fair when it is easier to go fast. Be courageous in the work, even when it's inconvenient or risky–especially when it's inconvenient or risky. Own the choices you make (or don't make) and the culture you create. And above all, have integrity. Be who you say you are–in all things and at all times. Keep walking the talk toward the equitable workplace we all deserve–one step, one choice, one way at a time. I'll meet you there.

Acknowledgments

THE INSIGHTS AND STRATEGIES FOUND in this book are not only substantiated by my own professional experience, both as a corporate executive and C-suite consultant, but also by secondary research (thank you, Katie McAuliffe!), interviews with thirty equity and inclusion experts from Fortune 500 companies and leading consultancies, and by a proprietary study conducted in partnership with Brandtrust, a research and strategy firm that utilizes applied social and behavioral sciences to solve complex business challenges. When I first reached out to the founder and CEO of Brandtrust to participate in this project, I was prepared to invest heavily in ensuring *The Waymakers* would shed new light on the underexplored challenges to equity. I wanted to uncover where bias is hiding in our systems and where it fails underrepresented talent so leaders would be more insightful about and equipped to make a way for others. It took one phone call for him to tell me that he wanted to field this research not for me but with me. I didn't find a vendor, after all. I found a partner who believes, as I do, that we must all do our part to create more equitable workplaces and, by extension, a more equitable world.

Thank you, Daryl Travis and the Brandtrust team (Lindsey, Carmie, Alyssa, and Annalisa), for partnering with me to inspire and prepare more Waymakers and for bringing your expertise to my vision. And thanks to Dave Mihanovic for your early guidance and for introducing us.

Thank you to Teresa Barnhill for your interviewing and expert insight translation skills and to the thirty diversity, equity, and inclusion experts who allowed us to learn from you, including but not limited to Keith Wyche, Subha Barry, Tamika Curry-Smith, Kenya Thacker Pierre, Dr. Westina Matthews, Dr. Sheila Robinson, Roz Houston, Deb Elam, Pete Burney, Nzinga Shaw, Michelle P. Wimes, Gerri Mason Hall, Millette Granville, Michele Meyer-Shipp, Esq., Celeste Warren, Shona Pinnock, Susan Johnson, Tasha Gilroy, Monika Pierce, Sequoya Mungo, Ezinne Okoro, Deanna Bass, Erby Foster, Merary Simeon, Suezette Robotham, Sonia Cargan, Virginia Hardy, and Kellie McElhaney. Your collective experience spans more than one hundred organizations (most of which are Fortune 500 companies and leading consultancies) and over six hundred years of know-how. Your knowledge about what it takes to achieve true equity at work added a critical dimension to this book and helped me clarify the requirements and strategies necessary for sustainable progress.

Thank you to each person who, when I reached out to ask if you would write a testimonial for this book, said yes without hesitation: Amy C. Edmondson, Tom Hayes, Mike Hyter, Latriece Watkins, Nzinga Shaw, Anré Williams, Michele C. Meyer-Shipp, Esq., Beth Andrix Monaghan, Soraya Chemaly, Dantaya Williams, Minda Harts, Sarah Alter, Wendy Davidson, James Rhee, D. Keith Pigues, Kevin Samuelson, Dolly Chugh, and Shelly McNamara. A special shout-out to Dr. Amy Edmonson—your work on psychological safety is paramount to progress. And much love and gratitude to Steve Pemberton, who has inspired me with his leadership and compassion since I was a fourteen-year-old student and he was my Upward Bound director. Thank you for writing a foreword that surpassed my highest hopes.

Thank you to Tara Mohr and Soraya Chemaly for nudging me toward authenticity and letting me know I could shed the "burden of proof." Thanks to Lisa DiMona and Lauren Carsley of the Writer's House for coaching me toward a better book and for uncovering this fantastic title I'd hidden in my writing. Thanks to Delia Berrigan Fakis and Jacqueline Fletcher Johnson for holding my hand through the early proposal days and the latter days of big decisions.

Thanks to the Amplify Publishing team. You helped me get a timely book into the hands of leaders who need it now. Naren Aryal, Jess Cohn, Claire Pask, Sophia Wilhelm, Caitlin Smith, and every other "amplifier" who read, touched, and refined this work–I am grateful. You have blessed me with your passion and urgency and commitment to excellence.

Thanks to my Waymakers–Kim C., who convinced an uncertain leadership team to hire me into Hallmark. She embraced my passion. Lois, who insisted I succeed her as creative director. She positioned me. Eileen, who shared the unwritten rules of executive leadership. She prepared me. Teri Ann, who trusted me to lead "the heart of Hallmark." She promoted me. Pete, who told me the truth and defended my occasional flub. He protected me. Mike, who spoke well of me in rooms I wasn't in. He propelled me. Don and Dave, who believed in my unique perspectives. They partnered with me to make a difference. Marquetta, who showed me who I was and could be. She schooled me. And Jen and Lindsey, whose love and friendship have been constants in a sea of change.

Thank you, also, to my personal support crew:

My husband, John–my most present and consistent Waymaker. You are all the things. Loving and being loved by you is the greatest gift of my life. None of this happens without your relentless support of me and belief in my ability to inspire meaningful change. With you, no dream stays a dream—each one becomes real and expands. Me and you (and the dogs), forever.

To our beloved children—Alexandria, Kasim, Ilijah, Jordan, Ian, and Jaden—my inspiration. May you not have to fight as hard for what you desire or deserve.

My parents (John and Marlene Centeio and John and Linda Frank)—my safe harbor. Your love and wisdom keep me sane, and your faith propels me. I also want to thank my siblings for being awesome—Todd, Jon, and Keilana.

Machelle Selbe—my right arm. I would suck at life without you.

Em, Mike U., and Sade—thank you for using your creativity and talent to help me birth this vision and show up in my very best light.

D. Keith Pigues—my mirror. You help me see what's possible and challenge me to go after it.

Leilani Brown—my Virgo sister. You remind me to have fun.

Melissa, Brenda, Kim P., Kim N., and Malea—you are home base. You were there "when," and you're there now. Thank you for supporting me through it all. I love you.

My Spelman sisters—Joslyn "Chae," Tara, Toiya, Jonica, Tracie, and Susan—my shipmates. We sailed into adulthood together. You keep me tethered to our sisterhood.

Tim Storey—my coach. You helped usher in the revelation that changed everything. When I stopped being scared, the sky opened up. You reminded me of what I already knew—God is at work. Always. And in all ways.

I also want to thank a few other Waymakers in my life who passed a baton or recommended me early in my consulting career when no one knew who I was or whether they should trust what I have to say. Trudy Bourgeois, Subriana Pierce, Mike Hyter, Eileen Tarjan, Kathy Bayert, Shanda Hinton, and Monica Turner—you are the real

MVPs. And to my LinkedIn family—our bond is real! I am glad to know you.

A big thank-you to my clients. You may have invited me into your companies and teams to guide and teach, but I have learned so much. You give me hope and an opportunity to make a difference in the world. I'm grateful.

I also want to thank the many aspiring professionals whose journeys move me to find better ways to change hearts and minds. You deserve an equitable workplace. You deserve equal access to opportunity and equal pay and a seat at the table and your own tables. You deserve to be rewarded for your hard work—to not have to "hustle and grind" in perpetuity with uneven results. This book is for you.

Last, I want to thank Dr. Maya Angelou. You are no longer on this earth, but the ten years I spent working alongside you planted seeds in me that continue to blossom. When you transitioned, I promised myself I would never again be afraid to walk through any open door. This is me, walking—with my head held high. I will never forget you or the lessons you taught me.

Endnotes

Introduction

1   Isa 43:2 (English Standard Version).

2   Siofra Brennan, "Not long to go! Pregnant Kate tenderly cradles her baby bump while wrapping up her royal duties ahead of maternity leave– and William confirms she's due 'any minute now,'" *Daily Mail*, March 21, 2018, dailymail.co.uk/femail/article-5526339/Pregnant-Kate-looks-blooming-green.

3   "Why can't Meghan Markle keep her hands off her bump? Experts tackle the question that has got the nation talking: Is it pride, vanity, acting - or a new age bonding technique?" *Daily Mail*, January 26, 2019, dailymail.co.uk/news/article-6636233/Why-Meghan-Markle-hands-bump-Experts-tackle-question.

Chapter 1

1   Naomi Murakawa, *The First Civil Right: How Liberals Built Prison America* (New York: Oxford University Press, 2014).

2   Phillip A. Goff et al., "The Essence of Innocence: Consequences of Dehumanizing Black Children," *Journal of Personality and Social Psychology* 106, no. 4 (2014): 526–45, https://doi.org/10.1037/a0035663.

3   Neil Bhutta, Andrew C. Chang, Lisa J. Dettling, and Joanne W. Hsu, "Disparities in Wealth by Race and Ethnicity in the 2019 Survey of Consumer Finances," *FEDS Notes*, Federal Reserve, September 28, 2020, federalreserve.gov/econres/notes/feds-notes/disparities-in-wealth-by-race-and-ethnicity-in-the-2019-survey-of-consumer-finances-20200928.htm.

4   Lachlan Cartwright and Maxwell Tani, "Ex-NY Times Reporter Finally Speaks Out, Disputes Student Claims, Calls Himself 'Jackal Circled by Jackals,'" *The Daily Beast*, March 1, 2021, thedailybeast.com/ex-ny-times-star-reporter-donald-mcneil-finally-speaks-out-calls-himself-a-jackal-circled-by-jackals.

5   Martin Luther King, Jr. Encyclopedia, "Birmingham Campaign," accessed July 29, 2021. kinginstitute.stanford.edu/encyclopedia/birmingham-campaign.

6   Martin Luther King, Jr., "Letter from Birmingham Jail," *The Christian Century: An Ecumenical Weekly*, June 12, 1963, 767-773, in *TeachingAmericanHistory*, teachingamericanhistory.org/library/document/letter-from-birmingham-city-jail-excerpts, accessed July 29, 2021.

7   Martin Luther King, Jr., "Letter from Birmingham Jail," *The Christian Century: An Ecumenical Weekly*, June 12, 1963, 767-773, in *TeachingAmericanHistory*, teachingamericanhistory.org/library/document/letter-from-birmingham-city-jail-excerpts, accessed July 29, 2021.

8   "Women in the Workplace, 2020," McKinsey & Company.

9   John Dewey, *How We Think* (New York: Dover, 2003), p.78.

Chapter 2

1   Jim Carter, "Historic Drop in Employee Engagement Follows Record Rise,"
     Gallup, July 2, 2020, gallup.com/workplace/313313/historic-drop-em-
     ployee-engagement-follows-record-rise.aspx.

Chapter 3

1   Nikole Hannah-Jones, et. al. "The 1619 Project," *The New York Times
     Magazine*, accessed July 29, 2021, nytimes.com/interactive/2019/08/14/
     magazine/1619-america-slavery.html.

2   Frank E. Lockwood, "Bill by Sen. Tom Cotton targets curriculum on
     slavery," *The Arkansas Democrat-Gazette*, July 26, 2020, arkansasonline.
     com/news/2020/jul/26/bill-by-cotton-targets-curriculum-on-slavery.

3   Tara J. Frank, "Why We Can't Just 'Move On,'" *LinkedIn*, July 27, 2020,
     linkedin.com/pulse/why-we-cant-just-move-tara-jaye-frank.

4   Malcolm Gladwell, *The Tipping Point: How Little Things Can Make a
     Big Difference* (Boston: Little, Brown, 2000).

5   Martin Luther King, Jr., "Letter from Birmingham Jail," *The Christian
     Century: An Ecumenical Weekly*, June 12, 1963, 767-773, in *Teachin-
     gAmericanHistory*, teachingamericanhistory.org/library/document/
     letter-from-birmingham-city-jail-excerpts, accessed July 29, 2021.

6   Susan Annunzio, *eLeadership: Proven Techniques for Creating an Envi-
     ronment of Speed and Flexibility in the Digital Economy* (New York: Free
     Press, 2001).

7   Kevin Kruse, "The 80/20 Rule and How it Can Change Your Life," *Forbes*,
     March 7, 2016, forbes.com/sites/kevinkruse/2016/03/07/80-20-rule
     /?sh=28dd98023814.

8   Michelle P. Wimes, interview with author, April 2021.

9   "The Sponsor Dividend," *Coqual*, 2019, https://coqual.org/wp-content/
     uploads/2020/09/CoqualTheSponsorDividend_KeyFindingsCom-
     bined090720.pdf.

Chapter 4

1   Jeremy Sutton, "Developing Empathy: 8 Strategies and Worksheets for Becoming More Empathetic, *PositivePsychology*, December 10, 2020, positivepsychology.com/empathy-worksheets.

2   [[cite]]

Chapter 5

1   Katie Reilly, "Here Are All the Times Donald Trump Insulted Mexico," *Time*, August 31, 2016, time.com/4473972/donald-trump-mexico-meeting-insult.

2   Brad Brooks, "Victims of Anti-Latino Hate Crimes Soar in US: FBI Report," *Reuters*, November 12, 2019, reuters.com/article/us-hatecrimes-report/victims-of-anti-latino-hate-crimes-soar-in-u-s-fbi-report-idUSKBN1X-M2OQ.

3   Kuang Keng Kuek Ser, "Data: Hate Crimes Against Muslims Increased After 9/11," *The World*, September 12, 2016, pri.org/stories/2016-09-12/data-hate-crimes-against-muslims-increased-after-911.

4   M. L. Frazier et al., "Psychological Safety: A Meta-Analytic Review and Extension," *Management Faculty Publications* 13 (2017), https://digitalcommons.odu.edu/management_fac_pubs/13.

5   Amy Edmondson, "Psychological Safety and Learning Behavior in Work Teams," *Administrative Science Quarterly* 44, no. 2 (June 1999): 350–83, https://doi.org/10.2307/2666999.

6   Dnika J. Travis and Jennifer Thorpe-Moscon, "Day-to-Day Experiences of Emotional Tax Among Women and Men of Color in the Workplace," *Catalyst*, 2019, catalyst.org/wp-content/uploads/2019/02/emotionaltax.pdf.

7   Dnika J. Travis and Jennifer Thorpe-Moscon, "Day-to-Day Experiences
     of Emotional Tax Among Women and Men of Color in the Workplace,"
     Catalyst, 2019, catalyst.org/wp-content/uploads/2019/02/emotionaltax.
     pdf.

8   Dnika J. Travis and Jennifer Thorpe-Moscon, "Day-to-Day Experiences
     of Emotional Tax Among Women and Men of Color in the Workplace,"
     Catalyst, 2019, catalyst.org/wp-content/uploads/2019/02/emotionaltax.
     pdf.

9   Rocío Lorenzo et al., "The Mix That Matters: Innovation Through Diversity,"
     Boston Consulting Group, April 26, 2017, bcg.com/publications/2017/
     people-organization-leadership-talent-innovation-through-diversi-
     ty-mix-that-matters.

10   Dnika J. Travis and Jennifer Thorpe-Moscon, "Day-to-Day Experiences
     of Emotional Tax Among Women and Men of Color in the Workplace,"
     Catalyst, 2019, catalyst.org/wp-content/uploads/2019/02/emotionaltax.
     pdf.

11   Derald Wing Sue, et al. "Racial Microaggressions in Everyday Life: Im-
     plications for Clinical Practice," *American Psychologist* 62, no. 4 (2007):
     271–286, doi: 10.1037/0003-066X.62.4.271.

12   Women in the Workplace, 2020," McKinsey & Company.

13   Women in the Workplace, 2020," McKinsey & Company.

14   Women in the Workplace, 2020," McKinsey & Company.

15   Laura Wronski, "CNBC/SurveyMonkey Poll: International Women's
     Day 2020," *SurveyMonkey*, accessed July 29, 2021, surveymonkey.com/
     curiosity/cnbc-international-womens-day-2020.

16   Neil Bhutta, Andrew C. Chang, Lisa J. Dettling, and Joanne W. Hsu,
     "Disparities in Wealth by Race and Ethnicity in the 2019 Survey of
     Consumer Finances," *FEDS Notes*, Federal Reserve, September 28, 2020,
     federalreserve.gov/econres/notes/feds-notes/disparities-in-wealth-by-
     race-and-ethnicity-in-the-2019-survey-of-consumer-finances-20200928.
     htm.

17 Ibid.

18 Carol S. Dweck, PhD, *Mindset: The New Psychology of Success* (New York: Random House, 2006).

19 David S. Pedulla and Devah Pager, "Race and Networks in the Job Search Process," *American Sociological Review* 84, no. 6 (December 2019): 983–1012, doi.org/10.1177/0003122419883255.

20 "Women in the Workplace, 2020," McKinsey *&* Company.

21 Ibid.

Chapter 6

1 Tara Jaye Frank, "Stop telling people they need to develop executive presence. It's a farce." *LinkedIn*, February 2021, linkedin.com/posts/tarajayefrank_respect-inclusion-belonging-activity-6770108722522968064-ZMaV.

2 Tara Jaye Frank, "I'm Tara, and I Benefit from Ableism," *LinkedIn*, May 25, 2021, linkedin.com/pulse/im-tara-i-benefit-from-ableism-tara-jaye-frank.

Chapter 7

1 Why Diversity and Inclusion Matter (Quick Take)," *Catalyst*, June 24, 2020, catalyst.org/research/why-diversity-and-inclusion-matter/.

2 Why Diversity and Inclusion Matter (Quick Take)," *Catalyst*, June 24, 2020, catalyst.org/research/why-diversity-and-inclusion-matter/.

3 "Millennials@Work: Perspectives on Diversity *&* Inclusion," *Institute for Public Relations*, accessed July 29, 2021, instituteforpr.org/millennialswork-perspectives-diversity-inclusion.

4   Kim Parker and Ruth Igielnik, "On the Cusp of Adulthood and Facing an Uncertain Future: What We Know About Gen Z So Far," *Pew Research Center*, May 14, 2020, pewresearch.org/social-trends/2020/05/14/on-the-cusp-of-adulthood-and-facing-an-uncertain-future-what-we-know-about-gen-z-so-far-2.

5   Prince Harry and Meghan Markle, interview by Oprah, *The National*, CBS News, March 7, 2021.

6   "Why Diversity and Inclusion Matter (Quick Take)," *Catalyst*, June 24, 2020, catalyst.org/research/why-diversity-and-inclusion-matter.

7   Interviews conducted by author, April 2021.

8   Rocío Lorenzo et al., "How Diverse Leadership Teams Boost Innovation," *Boston Consulting Group*, January 23, 2018, bcg.com/en-us/publications/2018/how-diverse-leadership-teams-boost-innovation.

9   Why Diversity and Inclusion Matter (Quick Take)," *Catalyst*, June 24, 2020, catalyst.org/research/why-diversity-and-inclusion-matter/.

Chapter 9

1   "Recommended Practices for Safety and Health Programs," Occupational Safety and Health Administration, accessed July 29, 2021, https://www.osha.gov/safety-management.

2   Interview conducted by author, April 2021.

Conclusion

1   Women in the Workplace, 2020," McKinsey & Company.

2   Ray Dalio, *Principles: Life and Work* (New York: Simon & Schuster, 2017).

3   John 2 (ESV).

MODERN NOVELISTS

General Editor: Norman Page

MODERN NOVELISTS

Published titles

MARGARET ATWOOD   Coral Ann Howells
SAUL BELLOW   Peter Hyland
ALBERT CAMUS   Philip Thody
FYODOR DOSTOEVSKY   Peter Conradi
GEORGE ELIOT   Alan W. Bellringer
WILLIAM FAULKNER   David Dowling
GUSTAVE FLAUBERT   David Roe
E. M. FORSTER   Norman Page
ANDRÉ GIDE   David Walker
WILLIAM GOLDING   James Gindin
GRAHAM GREENE   Neil McEwan
ERNEST HEMINGWAY   Peter Messent
CHRISTOPHER ISHERWOOD   Stephen Wade
HENRY JAMES   Alan W. Bellringer
JAMES JOYCE   Richard Brown
D. H. LAWRENCE   G. M. Hyde
ROSAMOND LEHMANN   Judy Simons
DORIS LESSING   Ruth Whittaker
MALCOLM LOWRY   Tony Bareham
NORMAN MAILER   Michael K. Glenday
THOMAS MANN   Martin Travers
GABRIEL GARCÍA MÁRQUEZ   Michael Bell
TONI MORRISON   Linden Peach
IRIS MURDOCH   Hilda D. Spear
VLADIMIR NABOKOV   David Rampton
V. S. NAIPAUL   Bruce King
GEORGE ORWELL   Valerie Meyers
ANTHONY POWELL   Neil McEwan
MARCEL PROUST   Philip Thody
BARBARA PYM   Michael Costell
JEAN-PAUL SARTRE   Philip Thody
MURIEL SPARK   Norman Page
MARK TWAIN   Peter Messent
JOHN UPDIKE   Judie Newman
EVELYN WAUGH   Jacqueline McDonnell
H. G. WELLS   Michael Draper
PATRICK WHITE   Mark Williams
VIRGINIA WOOLF   Edward Bishop
SIX WOMEN NOVELISTS   Merryn Williams

Forthcoming titles

IVY COMPTON-BURNETT   Janet Godden
JOSEPH CONRAD   Owen Knowles
JOHN FOWLES   James Acheson
FRANZ KAFKA   Ronald Spiers and Beatrice Sandberg
SALMAN RUSHDIE   D. C. R. A. Goonetilleke
ALICE WALKER   Maria Lauret

MODERN NOVELISTS

MARK TWAIN

Peter Messent

St. Martin's Press
New York

St. Martin's Press, Scholarly and Reference Division,
175 Fifth Avenue, New York, N.Y. 10010

First published in the United States of America in 1997

This book is printed on paper suitable for recycling and
made from fully managed and sustained forest sources.

Printed in Hong Kong

ISBN 0–312–16479–3

Library of Congress Cataloging-in-Publication Data
Messent, Peter B.
Mark Twain / Peter Messent.
p.   cm. — (Modern novelists)
Includes bibliographical references (p.   ) and index.
ISBN 0–312–16479–3
1. Twain, Mark, 1835–1910—Criticism and interpretation.
I. Title. II. Series.
PS1338.M47   1997
818'.409—dc20   96–9831
                                                      CIP

Contents

Acknowledgements   vi

General Editor's Preface   viii

1   Keeping Both Eyes Open: 'The Stolen White Elephant'   1

2   Old World Travel: *The Innocents Abroad*   22

3   *Roughing It* and the American West   44

4   *Tom Sawyer* and American Cultural Life: Anxieties and
     Accommodations   65

5   Racial Politics in *Huckleberry Finn*   86

6   Fantasy and *A Connecticut Yankee in King Arthur's Court*   110

7   Severed Connections: *Puddn'head Wilson and Those
     Extraordinary Twins*   134

8   The Late Works: Incompletion, Instability, Contradiction   157

Notes   177

Select Bibliography   228

Index   232

Acknowledgements

Mark Twain wrote in *Following the Equator* that 'Man is the only animal that blushes. Or needs to.' I have been spared many blushes by the friends and colleagues who were good enough to read parts of this manuscript, and who corrected my mistakes, suggested new avenues to pursue, and helped put me right when I had gone (often badly) wrong. So, my grateful thanks to Lou Budd, Chris Gair, Colin Harrison, Richard King, Peter Ling, Christine MacLeod, Scott Michaelsen, Peter Stoneley and Tim Youngs. And especially to Dave Murray for reading the completed manuscript. His comments provided, at this late stage, just the help I needed to make some important final revisions and readjustments. All those mentioned above helped to make this a much better book than it would otherwise have been. Any faults it still has are down to me alone. My thanks to Douglas Tallack, my Head of Department, for his encouragement and support in this project. My thanks, too, to my very patient and helpful editor, Margaret Bartley. I acknowledge my debt to the British Academy: without its grant, which doubled the sabbatical time available to me, this book would not be finished now, or, I suspect, for some considerable time. The Mark Twain Circle of America contains the most unusual collection of academics I have come across. Its members genuinely enjoy each other's company, are unselfish in their support of those working on Twain, and have a great deal of fun too. I have benefited greatly from my membership. My family and friends gave me all the support I could hope for as I wrote this. My dear father, John Messent (1912–1996), died soon after I had completed the manuscript. The example of his life and love will stay with me. As I worked on the book, my son and daughter, William and Alice, bore all with patience and even with interest. Ella and Leah, my two step-daughters, got used to my continual time at the computer, even though it meant, for Leah, that 'Jill of the Jungle' had to go unplayed. Carin, my wife, read parts of the manuscript for me, phoned every day from work to make sure I was still sane and stable, and (whichever the condition) kept me going with her encouragement and love. I dedicate this book to her with all my love.

Nottingham   PETER MESSENT
February 1996

General Editor's Preface

The death of the novel has often been announced, and part of the secret of its obstinate vitality must be its capacity for growth, adaptation, self-renewal and self-transformation: like some vigorous organism in a speeded up Darwinian ecosystem, it adapts itself quickly to a changing world. War and revolution, economic crisis and social change, radically new ideologies such as Marxism and Freudianism, have made this century unprecedented in human history in the speed and extent of change, but the novel has shown an extraordinary capacity to find new forms and techniques and to accommodate new ideas and conceptions of human nature and human experience, and even to take up new positions on the nature of fiction itself.

In the generations immediately preceding and following 1914, the novel underwent a radical redefinition of its nature and possibilities. The present series of monographs is devoted to the novelists who created the modern novel and to those who, in their turn, either continued and extended, or reacted against and rejected, the traditions established during that period of intense exploration and experiment. It includes a number of those who lived and wrote in the nineteenth century but whose innovative contribution to the art of fiction makes it impossible to ignore them in any account of the modern novel; it also includes the so-called 'modernists' and those who in the mid- and late twentieth century have emerged as outstanding practitioners of this genre. The scope is, inevitably, international; not only, in the migratory and exile-haunted world of our century, do writers refuse to heed national boundaries – 'English' literature lays claim to Conrad the Pole, Henry James the American, and Joyce the Irishman – but geniuses such as Flaubert,

Dostoevsky and Kafka have had an influence on the fiction of many nations.

Each volume in the series is intended to provide an introduction to the fiction of the writer concerned, both for those approaching him or her for the first time and for those who are already familiar with some parts of the achievement in question and now wish to place it in the context of the total *oeuvre*. Although essential information relating to the writer's life and times is given, usually in an opening chapter, the approach is primarily critical and the emphasis is not upon 'background' or generalisations but upon close examination of important texts. Where an author is notably prolific, major texts have been made to convey, more summarily, a sense of the nature and quality of the author's work as a whole. Those who want to read further will find suggestions in the select bibliography included in each volume. Many novelists are, of course, not only novelists but also poets, essayists, biographers, dramatists, travel writers and so forth; many have practised shorter forms of fiction; and many have written letters or kept diaries that constitute a significant part of their literary output. A brief study cannot hope to deal with all of these in detail, but where the shorter fiction and non-fictional writings, private and public, have an important relationship to the novels, some space has been devoted to them.

NORMAN PAGE

1

Keeping Both Eyes Open: 'The Stolen White Elephant'

When detectives called for a drink, the would-be facetious bar-keeper resurrected an obsolete form of expression, and said, 'Will you have an eye-opener?' All the air was thick with sarcasms.

('The Stolen White Elephant')[1]

I

In this opening chapter, I look closely at one of Twain's most puzzling short stories, 'The Stolen White Elephant', to identify how, in this specific case, the narrative works, and where its comic effects lie. Although my general approach in this book will be chronological, I begin with a text written in 1878, two years after the publication of *The Adventures of Tom Sawyer* (1876).[2] It might seem perverse to disrupt my main organising principle so early. I do so because 'The Stolen White Elephant' provides a particularly appropriate introduction to my analysis of Twain's work as a whole, and the problems involved in such a task.

The sheer size of an elephant, and its incongruity in an American setting, would make it unmissable. Yet, in Twain's story, it has been stolen; has disappeared from view. The detective looks for clues to find the elephant, but it is barging chaotically around the landscape as he does so. The relationship here between the obvious and the hidden is peculiarly unstable. I would argue that the stress in this text on such instability, incongruity, and shifting perspective, provides a paradigm for Twain's work as a whole. 'The Stolen White Elephant', despite its undoubted celebrity, has had comparatively little written about it; a result, perhaps, of its enigmatic quality. I start my book by giving it, to adapt a phrase from 'Jim Smiley and His Jumping Frog', my own little critical punch behind.[3] Then, in the final section of the chapter, I widen my scope to suggest the relevance of this analysis to my larger argument.

'The Stolen White Elephant' is a narrative that appears to be 'pointedly pointless'.[4] Though the specific comic techniques Twain uses can be identified, the story as a whole, like so much of Twain's work, seems not quite to add up. The reader is left with a peculiar sense of not having got the joke. This sense of puzzlement, the struggle to interpret satisfactorily a problematic text, is (self-reflexively) signalled as a subject of narrative concern when Inspector Blunt, the chief of the detectives employed to recover the stolen goods, places an advertisement in the morning papers to open negotiations with the thief. His message remains a form of gibberish for both the narrator and the reader (though their response to it implicitly differs). Shared codes break down as both are left on the outside, as it were; the point of the communication completely blunted. The detective's cryptogram is impenetrable: 'A.—xwblv. 242 N. Tjnd—fz328wmlg. Ozpo,—; 2 m ! ogw. Mum.' (p. 25).

The reader has a similar feeling of being left stranded at the conclusion of Twain's story. The enigmatic nature of the text as a whole, however, takes a different form than that of Blunt's brief message. The language of 'The Stolen White Elephant' is straightforward enough. Its cryptic element does not lie in any inability to understand the individual phrase or sentence. Rather, it is the overall humorous intent which remains obscure and causes the sense of frustrated expectation[5] already noted.

I would suggest, however, that it is in this very sense of readerly frustration and disorientation that the comic ends of the narrative (uncomfortably) lie. The story's apparent pointlessness *is* its point. A type of double effect operates here, for it is only as our initial sense of puzzlement is explored, or so I would contend,[6] that another level of humour becomes apparent. We then discover a comedy of estrangement that speaks to the very condition of the modern – a form of humour that operates at an epistemological level. The story, as I see it, finally operates as a form of anti-narrative 'programmed to go nowhere'[7] and it is here that its deeper 'joke' is to be found.

It is at this point that I need to add a note of hesitation and qualification concerning the nature of my own critical activity. An indication of Twain's mastery of the comic form is that to try to interpret or explain his humour is to risk falling, figuratively, flat on one's face. When I do so, I always have the sinking feeling I may be missing the point entirely, may be ending up as the victim of Twain's joke. The gap, in 'The Stolen White Elephant', between the myopic logic of the detectives and the elephant's random force is the main incongruity round which the story pivots. The former are burlesqued for their 'pompous assumption of infallibility and ridiculous inappropriate procedures'.[8] As I do my own critical detective work, here and in the rest of the book, trying to pin down and explain the incongruities and shifting effects in Twain's work, I hope at least to avoid a similar fate.

II

On first reading 'The Stolen White Elephant', clear parallels emerge with Twain's other humorous sketches, particularly in the use of narrative frames and of a central deadpan narrator. The title of the story is followed by a footnote attributed to the author (M.T.). This note both gives the provenance of the sketch and immediately foregrounds the potentially problematic relationship of the real to the fictitious: 'Left out of *A Tramp Abroad*, because it was feared that some of the particulars had been exaggerated, and that others were not true. Before these suspicions had been proven groundless, the book had gone to press'. A first narrator (presumably the same M.T.) then briefly introduces the teller of the main tale as 'a chance railway acquaintance . . . a gentleman more than seventy years of age . . . [whose] good and gentle face and earnest and sincere manner imprinted the unmistakable stamp of truth upon every statement which fell from his lips' (p. 1). The latter's tale is then told, in the first-person voice, with no return made to the initial narrator. The immediate sense of possible contradiction, as the reference to suspected exaggeration gives way, first to its dismissal, and then to the deep earnestness of the central narrative voice, strongly indicates to any Twain reader that the story will work as a hoax: the literary form with which he was identified from the early Virginia City *Territorial Enterprise* days onward.

Susan Gillman sees Twain's use of such a form as 'responding to an insatiable appetite, both on popular and literary levels of culture, for the hoax and the stunt, often in the form of the sensational . . . "true crime" report'. She links Twain, in this use, to the figure of P. T. Barnum[9] whose career 'exploited the national appetite for fraud'.[10] Barnum himself figures in Twain's tale, cutting a deal with Blunt, as a telegram reports, for 'exclusive privilege of using elephant as travelling advertising medium from now till detectives find him. Wants to paste circus-posters on him' (p. 18). Barnum's presence, and the comic rupture in narrative expectation and logic which has the elephant then 'plastered over with circus-bills' (p. 20) just three hours after Barnum's original despatch, while large numbers of detectives continue unsuccessfully in its pursuit, all confirm – if it needs to be confirmed – the nature of the literary form Twain is using.

Any of Twain's contemporaries reading with even one metaphorical eye open would probably have made the connection between the subject of Twain's story and the frontier expression 'seeing the Elephant'. Forrest G. Robinson speaks of Twain's own predisposition during his years in the Far West (described in *Roughing It*) to 'fall lock, stock and barrel for the practical joke that the mining frontier amounted to'. To see the Elephant, in this mining context, was to be aware of this joke, to see through the hoax. For behind western illusions of wealth and success lay mainly 'the Elephant of gross self-deception and inevitable failure'. Robinson comments further on the way Twain's art relates to the hoax that the frontier turned out to be, when he writes that 'having seen the Elephant, [Twain] would plant a whole herd'.[11] In the title and subject matter of this sketch is the clear acknowledgement of one such (individual) literary planting.

When Marcel Gutwirth describes comic surprise in terms of 'the good laugh at [one's] own expense' that follows 'the joyous sense of having been had – in no very material sense, however – and having got over it',[12] he might have had the hoax in mind. Twain was a master of the deadpan and his earlier famous sketch, 'Jim Smiley and his Jumping Frog', foregrounds the difficulty of penetrating narrative imposture: 'because Simon Wheeler never breaks his own deadpan presentation, we never know exactly who is the duper and who is the duped'.[13] The question of the identity of the hoaxer is also a central one in 'The Stolen White Elephant'. Its main narrator, the aged gentleman, is unflinchingly deadpan throughout the story, but there is little evidence of any hoax being played on his part. His deadpan appears not to conceal anything. It would seem, rather, to be a way of representing both his naivety and gullibility. For the narrative ends with an affirmation of his 'undimmed . . . admiration' for Inspector Blunt as 'the greatest detective the world has ever produced' (p. 28), despite all the evidence both of the detective's ineptitude and of the narrator's own duping.

It is the first narrator (M.T.?) whose deadpan in this story seems to conceal the hoax.[14] He is the one who vouches for the truth of a story which contains so many patent absurdities, and who speaks of the possibility of exaggeration only to deny it. If the hoax is being perpetrated on the reader as he or she follows the plot of a detective story to its (generically) unsatisfactory ending, it is none the less of an odd kind. For two different aspects of the narrative work against each other here, and any attempt to foreground either one at the expense of the (overlooked) other cannot succeed. As I proceed, this will become a recurrent motif in my analysis of Twain's work.

Here, the comic incongruities in 'The Stolen White Elephant' make it clear that the detective story genre is being undermined. They also alert us to the fact that a 'swindle' is occurring: that the whole story is a comic fabrication. Indeed, such incongruities put us in the position of detector rather than victim of this swindle. At the same time though, as readers, we are caught up in the detective plot, and *cannot help* but follow it to its strange and elliptic conclusion. Blunt places his coded advertisement, the meaning of which remains obscure. He then leaves his client (who is also the main narrator) supposedly to meet with the criminals at midnight. Both client and reader are left ignorant of what then occurs and are left to puzzle over a series of unanswered questions. *Are* there any criminals actually involved? Does a meeting take place? Is the detective duping his client? Finally Blunt literally stumbles over the rotting corpse of the stolen elephant – if it ever *was* stolen – with no further detail given of the clues or information which led him there. The detective is then celebrated as a hero for recovering the elephant, the death of which renders that act of recovery pointless. These joint strands of the narrative ending operate in antithetical relationship to that logical clarity with which detective stories, and their closures, are conventionally associated.

Twain's comedy might be explained as operating precisely in the gap between his story's two narrative strands. The reader is aware of all the incongruities of the tale which render its status as a detective story absurd. Yet, he or she is none the less involuntarily caught within the fictional system which has been engaged; is made to follow that detective story through to its frustrating – as far as the conventions of the genre are concerned – conclusion. This may be where at least one element of the hoax lies: on a reader who has been caught between variant ways of reading and responding to a text; who is led to read a story in two ways, and ends up stalled between them. 'That is what a joke is', according to Max Eastman, 'getting somebody going and then leaving him up in the air.'[15] Twain makes us aware of having been trapped between two narrative positions. The hoax occurs in catching us mentally off guard. We realise that our minds have been 'briefly taken in'[16] as, having placed ourselves in a superior position to the main narrator, and aware (unlike him) that everything in this story tells us not to take it seriously, we nonetheless fall into the trap of puzzlement or frustration at the detective story's unsatisfactory end. We end up looking for readerly satisfaction in a form of narrative that has already been subjected to parody and which we have been thus warned not to take seriously.[17] These two readerly responses cannot be squared, and recognising that we have been left up in the air, all we can do is acknowledge our awareness that we have been taken in by this narrative joke.

III

I retrace my steps here to explore the ways in which we come to know that this narrative is a comic fabrication as we read it, and not a detective story to be taken seriously. If humour can be associated with 'the playful character of contradictory signals that come at [consciousness] simultaneously',[18] then 'The Stolen White Elephant' complies with comic expectation from the first. A gift from the King of Siam to the Queen of England, the white elephant of the title is stolen from the main narrator, a member of the Indian civil service who is responsible for conveying the present from the one country to the other. This theft occurs in Jersey City. Although there is an explanation given for the presence of the elephant in that last location – the journey has been broken in New York and the animal is in need of recuperation – some sense of (potentially playful) disconnection and of the anomalous has already entered the narrative. This occurs in different ways: in the range of geographical locations introduced; and in the presence of an exotic beast, a 'transcendentally royal . . . token of gratitude', of specifically 'Oriental' nature (p. 2), in a modernised and urban, western and republican, setting. It comes, most of all, in the mental and visual play that is released with the idea of an elephant, the epitome of loud enormity,[19] now become the proverbial needle in the haystack, the hidden object which must be found. The problematic quality of the relationship between what is obvious and what is not is placed right at the centre of the text.

The process of detection itself is parodied as Blunt proceeds to ascertain the facts of the case. The humorous nature of the narrative becomes overt as he first asks a set of routine questions which apply to missing persons, and then responds to the elephant's disappearance in the manner routine to burglary cases. From the fact that the two reactions are mutually inconsistent, and that neither is appropriate to this stolen animal, comes something of the sense of comic contradiction which now plays through the text:

'Now – name of the elephant?'
'Hassan Ben Ali Ben Selim Abdullah Mohammed Moise Alhammal Jamsetjejeebhoy Dhuleep Sultan Ebu Bhudpoor.'
'Very Well. Given Name?'
'Jumbo.'[20] . . .
'Parents Living?'
'No – dead.' . . .
'Very well. . . . Now please describe the elephant, and leave out no particular, however insignificant' . . .
[Blunt takes down this description and reads it back to the narrator]

'Height, 19 feet . . . ; length of trunk, 16 feet . . . ; footprint
resembles the mark when one up-ends a barrel in the snow . . . ;
limps slightly with his right hand leg, and has a small scar in his
left armpit caused by a former boil. . . . ' (pp. 4–5)

The comic effect stems from the obtuseness of the detective as he
applies his 'strict and minute method' (p. 3) to the case in hand, as
he keeps making the category mistakes on which humour thrives.
Thus he has, for example, fifty thousand copies of the elephant's
description 'mailed to every . . . pawnbroker's shop on the
continent' (p. 5). This is the humour of incongruity – what Marcel
Gutwirth calls 'a derogation . . . from that which holds together in
the mind as fitting'[21] – though to put it that way is to diminish
Twain's individual comic instance in the pursuit of the general rule.

Gutwirth's further description of humour in terms of the 'clash
of levels' that occurs as the playful and logical sides of the self
collide is, however, much more apt in helping to explain the specific
effect Twain produces in this story, taken as a whole. He analyses
the comic move from the one side of the self to the other, and the
rupture that occurs with an awareness of the resulting incongruity,
in terms of a type of 'joke played by our irresponsible, our ebullient
selves upon our sober-sides logical selves trudging glumly in the
inescapable tracks of purposive existence'.[22] These words can be
reapplied to the nature of the comic charge in 'The Stolen White
Elephant', which operates in the gap, and relationship, between the
figure of the detective as Twain constructs him, with his logical and
myopic approach to existence (both eyes open but seeing in a very
limited manner), and the ebullient and random force of the white
elephant on the loose. This is to suggest a widening of Gutwirth's
frame of reference from internal to external reality, from the grounds
of self to that of the represented world. A similar comic effect is then
produced in the move between the high seriousness of the attempt
to order and control reality and an (alternative) acceptance of its
unwieldy and dislocating nature, mocking any human urge to
exercise control over it. The detective here, to use an amended
version of the earlier quotation, purposefully trudges in the tracks
of an eruptive and uncontainable presence. He sticks to his grounds,
and to his conventional operating procedures, while the elephant, a
paradigm of irresponsible ebullience, leaves complete havoc in its
wake.

IV

In first discussing the theft of the elephant, I compared the search for its hidden presence to that for a needle in a haystack. Such a comparison is, of course, metaphorically inept. It does, however, fit a version of the world which accords with the sober-sides Blunt methodically searching for the 'good clues' (p. 8) that will eventually enable him and his fellow 'experts' (p. 9) to find the vanished object.[23] As Blunt persists with his fixed routines, comedy continues to emerge both in the wholly inappropriate nature of his measures to the case at hand, and in the disparity between cause and effect, between the assumed difficulty of detection and the obviousness of the 'evidence', which follows. Among the measures he takes is the 'search of all suspicious persons' in the railway and ferry depots and other exit points from Jersey City. Once put into effect, Blunt turns to the narrator confidently (and comically) to state: 'I am not given to boasting, it is not my habit; but – we shall find the elephant' (pp. 9–10).

If the elephant does turn out initially to be as elusive as that needle, it is nothing like as invisible. It crashes through the local environment causing mayhem. It is reported 'dispersing a funeral . . . and diminishing the mourners by two' (p. 19) in Bolivia, New York, and '[breaking] up a revival' at Baxter Centre, 'striking down and damaging many who were on the point of entering a better life'. The elephant, now momentarily captured, also brains Detective Brown ('that is, head crushed and destroyed, though nothing issued from the debris' – p. 20) when the latter tries to identify it by looking for the boil scar under its armpit, before it once more escapes on the loose.

Gutwirth associates laughter with 'the threat of uncontained disorder', referring to 'the anarchic potential of an outburst that is apt to occur in any context'. He speaks of comedy as 'a field of force-on-the-loose'.[24] Language like this prompts me, given the way Twain represents his elephant, to a (tentative) figurative reading of it. Certainly this elephant comes to signify disruption and disorder in the text as the 'glaring headlines' of the newspapers clearly indicate. The narrator gives an example of their general tone:

THE WHITE ELEPHANT AT LARGE! HE MOVES UPON HIS FATAL MARCH! WHOLE VILLAGES DESERTED BY THEIR

FRIGHT-STRICKEN OCCUPANTS! PALE TERROR GOES
BEFORE, DEATH AND DEVASTATION FOLLOW AFTER!
AFTER THESE, THE DETECTIVES. BARNS DESTROYED,
FACTORIES GUTTED, HARVESTS DEVOURED, PUBLIC
ASSEMBLAGES DISPERSED, ACCOMPANIED BY SCENES OF
CARNAGE IMPOSSIBLE TO DESCRIBE! (p. 21)

The rituals of religion and its accessories (the elephant eats Bibles),
the forms of community, the means of sustenance, the patterns of
work: all these things are disrupted by the elephant. The closeness
of the fit between Gutwirth's theorising language and the
description of the elephant suggests an allegorical relation[25]
between the elephant and the comic principle itself, with Twain
representing comedy as a potentially anarchic force; a threat to the
established social order and all the codes and conventions on which
it depends.

I am aware of treading on thin ground here, but it does seem that
such an allegorical reading can, once made, then bear further
development. For a common analysis of the way humour works is
to show how it can be associated with misrule and lawlessness,
'chaos celebrated in relief from the oppressiveness of order . . . a
release of (demonic?) energies pent up under rule'. The other side
to the same definitional coin, however, is that it is also subject to
containment, a force which can function only briefly as the normal
authorities are temporarily disrupted, challenged, and even
overthrown. If, in Gutwirth's words, 'laughter preserves the
equilibrium of a culture as it does that of a group by the timely
release of an outburst that dissipates animosities', then this disorder
must shortly be brought under control. Laughter, in such a view, is
an 'aid in maintaining whole our allegiance to an orderly existence'.
Or, to put it another way, comedy is subject to a peculiar form of
social policing. Seen like this, the 'disorder' of laughter is accepted
in the 'well-regulated state' as a healthy part of the social process.
It contributes to 'the creation and maintenance of a living order'.[26]
If humour threatens and disrupts authority, the challenge it presents
to the established system is always temporary (that, however, is not
to say it cannot effect changes in that system) for it is to the accepted
forms and norms that a return is soon to be made.

My heavy use of Gutwirth at this point suggests how closely I am
following his analysis of what he calls the 'socio-integrative

approach' to humour.[27] However, we might wonder, as we return to Twain, if his view of comedy accepts its hegemonic incorporation in the way that such an analysis suggests. For, to continue with an allegorical reading, the disruptive force of the elephant, once it gets out of control and commits its 'red crimes' (p. 21), is not allowed free (or even limited) run, but is subject to immediate challenge by the dominant society. It is shot at with small cannon-balls by the citizens of Bolivia, New York, and pursued by the detectives – the next best thing to the police – until it is dead, its rotting corpse found in the recesses of the very room in which the detectives sleep. The detectives regain their authority at the cost of the elephant's life. When the central narrator uses a rather odd and unexpected phrase and speaks of the elephant as his 'irresponsible agent' (p. 21) at exactly the point at which its anarchic power is most evident, might we shift the referent and read this (and thus the story as a whole) in terms of Twain's ambivalent response to his own comic art? To do so is, from one point of view, to see the white elephant as 'transcendently royal', and signifying great value: a positive agency which acts as a powerful subversive and anarchic force, and which can only be held in check by the representatives of a repressive society which constitutes it as a type of feared other ('the dread creature' – p. 22). From a different perspective, the value of the elephant is cancelled out once it runs unchecked. For its force is now identified only with negative forms of destruction, and has necessarily to be contained by the social body if that body is to continue to function properly.

If there is a veiled allegory at work in this narrative, then it is this last reading – that humour unchecked (and the humorist unchecked?) should be seen as a dangerously irresponsible counter to conventional social existence – which might seem initially the more convincing. The violence done by the elephant in the course of the narrative, the people killed and maimed, appear to endorse such a view. However, it is at this point we step back to remind ourselves that this is just a comic sketch and *not* a direct representation of reality. Humour may have the power to fundamentally disrupt social convention. So Twain will write, in *The Mysterious Stranger* manuscripts, that 'against the assault of Laughter nothing can stand'.[28] It is, though, essentially a form of 'nonviolent dissent'. The humorous treatment of both death and violence in 'The Stolen White Elephant' can only endorse our

knowledge of their essentially *unreal* quality. Detective Hawes
reports that 'Elephant . . . killed a horse; have secured a piece of
it for a clue. Killed it with his trunk; from style of blow, think he
struck it left-handed' (p. 15). This is an absurdist and cartoon
violence, any aggressive quality modified by 'the consciousness of
inconsequentiality',[29] our knowledge that real pain is not at issue
here.

In short, there is no simple reading available here concerning the
relationship of the elephant (the comic?) to social convention. Those
who represent the social in the tale are themselves associated with
violence, as the maiming of the elephant with cannon-balls shows.
The justice and the health of the order being maintained is also open
to question, for the chief detective uses the elephant on the loose to
buttress his own prestige and financial position. Moreover, the
violence of the elephant, contained within the comic frame of the
story, can be contrasted with the *actual* violence associated with the
figure of the detective in the period when Twain is writing. To move
from Twain's text to its framing historical context is to be made
aware of the detective's role as a violently repressive social agent.
Pinkerton agent, James McParland, for instance, was accused of
playing the part of *agent provocateur* in the Molly Maguires case of
the late 1870s, acting on behalf of powerful business interests; part
of an hegemonic order which was to sustain its position by legalised
violence (the hanging of the twenty Irish coal miners).[30] Later, the
Pinkertons' role in the 1892 Homestead Steel Strike would confirm
the nature of such a reactionary social role in trumps.

If, then, 'The Stolen White Elephant' is an allegory about the
comic, the relationship between the power of humour and its
hegemonic containment is presented in ambivalent and unresolved
terms. The anarchic potential of comedy can be read in two
contrasting ways: as a beneficial, and potentially revolutionary,
counter to a dull, authoritarian and repressive social order, or
(unless properly harnessed within strict boundaries of acceptability)
as a negative and destructive force which disrupts our necessary
social routines and systems. The story can also be interpreted in
terms of its juxtaposition of two contrasting types of violence – that
associated with comedy, in its aggressive mode, and that wielded
by the socio-political establishment: the physically violent means by
which it exercises its power. If, in the relationship between the
elephant and the comic, a one-to-one allegorical frame can be

identified, the allegory only develops so far. Its point and purpose, the clarity which underlies the allegorical form, finally gets lost, to borrow metaphorically from the text, in a type of foggy indeterminacy. This may suggest Twain's own ambivalence about his comic art.

V

Whether it was his conscious intention or not, Twain's use of the white elephant at the centre of this story does encourage a figurative reading. Indeed the elephant starts off, in the text's own terms, as the ground for one such reading: its physical presence a sign or token of gratitude and propitiation. A straightforward account of the value of the white elephant is given at the start of the sketch: 'You know in what reverence the royal white elephant of Siam is held by people of that country. You know it is sacred to kings . . . even superior to kings' (p. 1). Such an account, though, does raise problems concerning figurative or representational value, for though such a creature might signify the 'transcendently royal' and the holy in Siam, that is not to say it signifies equally in the American context of the narrative. More, the question of whether we can trust our narrator's interpretive account is also at stake here. He is, after all, to be depicted in the story to come as both naive and uncritical in his reading of the events which affect him.

A white elephant is both a 'rarity in nature . . . considered sacred and precious', but also (and this is the more common meaning today) something you cannot get rid of, 'an unwanted possession' now 'up for sale'. The latter meaning, indeed, evidently derives from 'the story of a Siamese king who used to make a present of a white elephant to courtiers he wished to ruin'.[31] This might lead us to think again as to the exact nature of those 'Oriental ideas' (p. 2) motivating the King of Siam as he sends his gift to the Queen of England. And we should remember that Twain's comic fictions repeatedly play around the relativistic shift in value centres, especially regarding assumptions of cultural superiority. The question of what the white elephant might figuratively connote runs right through Twain's text as the reader puzzles over precisely what it is doing there: whether it is just a literal presence (a very unusual animal); whether the first-given figurative meaning (the sign of the transcendentally royal) is relevant; or whether the elephant signifies some other concept(s) or term(s). I would suggest that we cannot help but speculate on this last possibility. We know anyway that this is a phrase that carries a heavy figurative charge; indeed that normally we would *only* use it in a figurative sense.[32]

Marcel Gutwirth discusses the changing relationship between figure and ground as constitutive of humour itself. He quotes Gregory Bateson: 'The joke may be thought of as involving a shift between the figure and the ground, where the figure is altered or the ground is reconstituted or a reversal of the figure-ground is taking place.' This sounds complicated, but the example which follows helps to clarify. Referring (via E. H. Gombrich) to those trick figures which can be read, depending on the angle or way of looking, as either (for instance) a duck or a rabbit, Gutwirth continues:

> The mystery of illusion resides in the impossibility of capturing both views simultaneously. . . . Is laughter then the apprehension of that inability? Do we not in the art of raising a laugh voluntarily expose the single-track character of a mental apparatus incapable of focusing at once on the figure and the ground?[33]

This becomes doubly interesting when applied to Twain's story. If the elephant in its animal literalness is the ground, what then is the figure we can read onto it? Is that elephant a metaphor for the sacred and the valuable? For the principle of the unexpected and the alien (a type of mysterious stranger figure but taking animal form) which disrupts everyday logic and routine and which may suggest unknown determining influences (the intentionally malevolent gift)? For the comic spirit itself? And does the humour of the narrative arise from our confusion as readers – and from our awareness that that confusion is being cleverly manipulated by Twain – as we try and fit a 'straightforward' narrative of an elephant on the loose with a variety of clashing figurative possibilities?

What makes for the doubling of the interest is that there appears to be a self-conscious play on the relationship between figure and ground as Twain's narrative develops. His elephant, now taking the part of the figure, much as in Gutwirth's rabbit/duck example, literally disappears into the (back)ground toward the story's end. The descent of a dense fog which closes the second part of the narrative means that 'all trace of the elephant [is] lost'. The sighting of a 'dim vast mass [at] the most absurdly distant points' (p. 22) becomes just a confirmation of the confusion now reigning as the white elephant disappears into the fog; a confirmation of the fact that figure and ground have become more or less indistinguishable.

This takes me circuitously back to the relationship between figure and ground in comic theory. Gutwirth states that the 'laughter [of what he calls "frank amusement"], to come into being, has to be sure of its ground', and has to be based on a sense of the self which is 'utterly secure'. If (to use again the duck/rabbit example given previously as an analogy of the way the comic perception might be seen to function) it is the awareness of our 'single-track' mental apparatus that produces laughter, then this laughter comes from a position of mental strength. We are sure of ourselves, of our sanity and normality, and know that the mental confusion that has occurred is merely momentary. The 'pleasurable helplessness'[34] we briefly feel as our minds are taken in by that 'shift between figure and ground' depends on a more fundamental sense of being absolutely sure of our (larger) ground: the sense of our own firm mental grounding and stable relationship to the reality which surrounds us.

It is exactly such security, such a sense of ourselves, that Twain brings into question in 'The Stolen White Elephant', where the relationship between figure and ground collapses in on itself. At the narrative point I have described (to be followed only by the final turn of the illogical and elliptic ending), the sense of the relation of figure to ground – which is the white elephant and which the fog – has become completely blurred. This suggests, to me, the reason why the clash of figurative possibilities in this narrative does not function in any direct sense, as Gutwirth suggests that it theoretically might, as a source of humour. As readers, we end up half-aware of such possibilities (that the elephant is to be read figuratively) but unclear about the relationship between figure and ground. We are uncertain which of these metaphoric readings apply, or of how we decide which one applies, or indeed whether we should be trying to read this narrative in such a figurative manner at all: quite *what* level we should be taking it at. Twain dislocates his readers here: leaves us unsure of the base from which we are meant to be operating – unsure of *our* ground. Just as the elephant merges with the fog toward the end of the tale, so too are its readers unable (metaphorically) to see the elephant: to see the point of the story; the point of the joke. We can find immediate humour in the parody of the detective story, in the individual comic incident and incongruity within that story, in the burlesque of the detective business itself. We find further humour at a second and deeper level in the way we are caught between two sets of readerly responses to the narrative. But we are still left puzzled by the sense that we still have not penetrated to the core of the narrative or its comic intention: that there is some kind of further level yet, or larger meaning, which continues to remain enigmatic. We are left with the odd sense of being (like the narrator?) victims of a further hoax which we do not really understand.

VI

This brings me finally back to the 'pointedly pointless' aspect of this narrative with which I began. If Gutwirth discusses '*uneasy laughter* [as being] utterly incompatible with mirth',[35] and sees such laughter as a form of humour where we are *not* sure of our readerly ground, then 'The Stolen White Elephant' seems paradigmatic of such a form. Indeed, I would suggest that much of Twain's humour, and indeed, many of his narratives, work in this way. The theme of disorientation is a major one in this story. It is a product of the (unanswerable) questions we are led to ask about the enigmatic qualities of the narrative – *has* this elephant, for example, actually been stolen at all and, if so, by whom and for what possible purpose? It is produced, too, by the use of a narrative form where an illogicality and a lack of connectiveness are apparent, and where spatial dislocations predominate. For a geographical tracing of the movement of the elephant (exactly what Blunt does) suggests a principle of both randomness and uncertainty at work in terms of where it is going to go next, and how one can tell. In the course of a single night and early morning, it is reported as being in Long Island, New Jersey, and New York (pp. 13–14); though, alternatively, it might be in none of these places, and the reports of its presence false. The elephant certainly 'does move around' (p. 14). References to the directions it takes tend to leave the reader unmoored: 'some say he went east, some say west, some north, some south – but all say they did not wait to notice particularly' (p. 15). Further unmooring occurs as elephant and fog merge. The more the text continues, the more we lose any firm sense of our general ground. At the text's conclusion we are not quite sure what has happened nor why. The more our eyes should be opened to what exactly is the case, and to what is the narrative intent, the less we actually see. The comedy in the story is built on a base of radical uncertainty.

Twain's humour, then, from an early stage of his career, is that of epistemological uncertainty.[36] To be human in a world which lacks logic, sense, even meaning, is to be unsure of one's bearings. To get the joke, to see the elephant, is to acknowledge such a fact. The references to the illogical and the absurd within the text ('"That is perfectly absurd!" I exclaimed' – p. 18) might be extended beyond its margin to speak of the condition of the modern – note all the references to the factory, to photography, to telegrams, steamships, omnibuses and railroads in the story – where all that we can know is just how little we know; all we know of the ground on which we stand is just how uncertain it is. Indeed, in later chapters of the book, I extend my analysis of how closely Twain's work relates to an America in the process of rapid modernisation, and the anxieties associated with such a process.

But it is the sense of shifting perspective and uncertain ground in 'The Stolen White Elephant' which prompts me to use it to introduce my discussion of Twain's writing. That sense is exemplified in the unstable relationship between the hidden and the obvious which both structures the story, and suggests a quality of constant undecidability to Twain's work as a whole. In 'The Stolen White Elephant', the elephant crashes its way to the textual foreground. An uncontrollable and alien force, it stands out, in an anomalous and unsettling way, from the described background. But it also disappears into this background, leaving only traces of its presence, as the focus switches to the detective seeking his clues. Foreground becomes background, and vice versa, depending on the textual moment and on the perspective taken.

The detective is associated, at least in theory, with rational analysis, and the impulse to gain logical control over a confused narrative. But in 'The Stolen White Elephant', the elephant (and the principle of narrative chaos it symbolises) gets equal attention:

turning up unexpectedly and randomly, and disrupting all ordered
sequence. A similar sense of incongruity pervades all Twain's texts,
destabilised as they are by conflicting elements, changes of focus,
shifts of perspective, generic disconnections, and disruptive comic
effects. What at one textual moment is hidden or at the margins of
the narrative, will, at the next, become a bulky and central presence
that frustrates its smooth development. And if Twain thematises
epistemological uncertainty in this story (and recurrently), his
reader too ends up, as often as not, unmoored; unsure of her or
his ground, uncertain in which direction the various textual figures
are going.

In all of Twain's narratives the hidden and the obvious exist in
unstable relation to one another. This is not just a matter of the way
various elements are represented within his texts but affects the very
way we read them. Thus, at an internal textual level, *Puddn'head
Wilson and Those Extraordinary Twins* (1894) features another of
Twain's fictional detectives. What his detective work reveals,
however, is what should have been obvious all along: that in a
society where race is determined on fractions of blood, 'black' and
'white' have become indistinguishable from one another. Indeed it
is Puddn'head who makes explicit, at the beginning of the book,
that without their clothes Tom could be taken for Valet, and vice
versa. He already has, too, from the time of the boys' infancy, the
fingerprints that clearly show a switch has occurred. But when
Wilson finally exposes this switch, he also reveals the blindness of
a whole society. For its members still fail to see the joke: that the
absurd nature of their own racial assumptions has allowed them to
be fooled. The detective himself appears also to overlook this
(glaring) fact at the novel's end.

The instability of this relationship between the hidden and the
obvious also carries over to the reading of Twain's texts. It is difficult
to decide if the meanings of his books exist below the surface, and
need to be uncovered by the detective reader, or are rather in plain
view – like the elephant – and staring that reader in the face. For
what critics detect in Twain's work is always, in one sense, already
apparent. Recent interpretations of the ending of *Adventures of
Huckleberry Finn* (1885) uncover an allegory of post-Reconstruction
racial politics. This is partly because of the particular (new
historicist) interests of today's community of readers. It is also,
though, because of something already present in the book, and

something that Twain may have intended his reader to notice. The textual elements which produce that reading have been openly available, and on view, from the time he first wrote the novel.

I am saying, in other words, that Twain's texts (like the reports of the elephant's comings and goings) move in different directions, and, as they do so, contradictions and conflicting meanings appear. We can never be quite sure what he is deliberately thematising, which elements are meant to be foregrounded and which not, or to what degree the meanings of the text emerge despite its author. Twain's role as a comic writer, and one, moreover, who ended up writing just fragments of texts, is relevant here. His humour depends on incongruity and tends to resist the type of analysis which works in terms of direct authorial intent and unambiguous meaning. Indeed 'The Stolen White Elephant' can be taken as a comic story of ambiguity about the comic, which ends with the reader not sure of the joke on any level. Humour took Twain into uncomfortable places. One of its defining qualities is the ability to express what we would normally suppress and censor, often in an unintentional and double-edged way. Twain himself, even thirty years after the event, could not quite decide whether the speech he made at the Whittier birthday dinner in 1877, where he burlesqued aging members of the New England literary establishment (Henry Wadsworth Longfellow, Ralph Waldo Emerson and Oliver Wendell Holmes) as drunken roughs, was a disrespectful snipe at his cultural superiors, or just innocent fun.[37] At the time, he thought it the latter, and was mortified to find it taken as the former. The cultural analysis and criticism in Twain's work can easily be missed by the reader. It is quite possible, as I argue in my chapter on *A Connecticut Yankee in King Arthur's Court* (1889), that he missed it too.

Among the subjects I discuss in this study are the generic instabilities in Twain's texts, the anxieties about the status of the self in his writing, and (a related subject) the way in which this writing engages the cultural dialogues of its times. I follow Steven Mailloux in looking to show how the literary text can be sited in the larger context of cultural history.[38] I pay particular attention to Twain's representation of race, of capitalist processes and assumptions, and of the larger impact of modernisation. In the last analysis, I sideline the matter of authorial intention. As I proceed, however, I suggest that Twain's awareness of what he was doing was both shifting and multi-levelled. Twain is a particularly difficult writer to pin down.

'The Stolen White Elephant' can be read as an allegory about humour itself, and its uncomfortable relation to the dominant social order. But it can also be read as a type of pointless, but comic, hoax. Or it can be read as thematising interpretative indeterminacy itself. But we cannot know how much of this Twain intended as he wrote. I may be seeing here what is precisely obvious, the very point of Twain's story, or I may be uncovering something deeply hidden, of which he himself was unaware. His texts are marked by undecidability.

This is again to raise the question of the hidden and the obvious. Allegory itself, indeed, complicates the relationship between these terms, relying on concealed meanings but also (usually) overtly flagging their presence. For allegory implies signalled intentionality, with explicit textual signs that trigger our awareness of a further narrative level. When I use the term in the context of Twain's work, I am aware, however, that the allegory may be unintentional, seen neither by Twain nor by many of his readers, but obvious to myself and other later readers due to the nature of the interpretive communities to which we belong, and the critical apparatus and frameworks we use. But the very presence of the elements that signal such a reading raises the possibility, nonetheless, of direct intentionity. Thus, when I discuss *Huckleberry Finn*, I sugggest – on the basis of a certain amount of knowledge of Twain's position in regard to post-Civil War racial debates – that his allegorical critique of contemporary treatment of the African-American may be deliberate, and argue that the novel is ultimately a powerful anti-racist text. Other critics, though, disagree: reading the end of the book as non-ironic racial and racist farce, with Jim as the inconsequential butt of Tom and Huck's games. There is no way of finally deciding which meaning is the more obvious one, but also if the obvious one is the one 'authorised' by Twain.

It may be that Twain's role as a humorist, and his own ambivalent attitude to the dominant American values of his time, led him to write texts that move in multiple directions, and where any social critique is placed in incongruous relation to other and contradictory textual elements. It may be that his texts interrogate dominant cultural assumptions despite himself: that he remained blind to many of the incongruities, ambiguities, and disruptive elements that, like the elephant in his story, barged their way into his narratives. I want to keep both my critical eyes open, and to recognise all the curious movements of his texts. Any implied authorial intention, or the lack of it, in the chapters that follow take second place to my analysis of the contradictions and divisions of Twain's writing, the shifts of perspective within it, and the 'cultural work'[39] his texts do as a result. I argue that the anxieties about fictional form, and about the status of the self, the workings of society, and the patternings of history, which his texts reveal, make his writing – and the direction it came to take – central to any consideration of his period.

2

Old World Travel:
The Innocents Abroad

*Dan told to gather all manner of statistics, reports that brandy
is 8 cents a drink, & cigars 3-pence. . . .
Then came to NAZARETH, where Christ lived & carpentered
till 30 year of age. . . .
Got some pieces of the old Temple.*

(*Mark Twain's Notebooks & Journals*)[1]

I

The Innocents Abroad, or The New Pilgrim's Progress (1869) was
Twain's first full-length book. Funded by the San Francisco *Daily
Alta California*, he sailed from New York in June 1867, on board the
Quaker City, for Europe and the Holy Land. *The Innocents Abroad*,
written on his return to America, was the revised and expanded
version of the newspaper reports he had sent back on this 'great
Pleasure Excursion'.[2]

The symbolic resonances, both of this voyage and of 'Mark
Twain's' role (as the quasi-fictional narrator/protagonist'[3]) in the
book that describes it, are clear. For the *Quaker City* expedition was
'the first large-scale pleasure voyage of its kind in American
history',[4] and, as such, helped to usher in a new pattern of
relationships between the New World and the Old. 'American travel
abroad seemed to explode after 1865',[5] a result of a dramatic
improvement in transatlantic transportation, and the changes in

22

both economic conditions and attitudes that followed the Civil War.[6]
A new American mood of self-assertion and confidence[7] was
reflected in the 'changing tone' of travel in the period. William W.
Stowe suggests the different expectations of post-bellum Americans
abroad to those of the early nineteenth-century travellers, who saw
themselves 'primarily as learners and appreciators', when he writes
that:

> By the time of Twain's Innocents . . . the chief purpose of many
> travelers was not to submit to Old World influences but to acquire
> choice bits of culture and experience at a good price. Education
> was all very well, and a little polish never hurt anyone, but
> the new American travelers . . . were not about to purchase
> these European commodities on any terms but their own. These
> successful capitalists and their wives . . . were no longer
> diffidently, painfully aware of their shortcomings, but proud
> of their own and their country's new-found economic power
> and eager to experience the very best that their hard-earned
> money could buy.[8]

I suggest, in this chapter, that Twain's attitude to his Old World
materials is more complicated than Stowe implies here. But in *The
Innocents Abroad* he did begin to provide the literary measure of this
new American spirit. Twain's announcement of the 'purpose' of his
book makes it clear that he saw himself as representative of his
countrymen,[9] and of a new way of approaching Old World
materials. For he wants, he says, 'to suggest to the reader how *he*
would be likely to see Europe and the East if he looked at them with
his own eyes instead of the eyes of those who travelled in those
countries before him' (p. 3). Twain stands in for his audience in
sounding 'a new American voice'.[10] And where better to sound its
representative and legitimising note than on a tourist trip (for Twain,
whatever his other motives, was 'willy-nilly, a tourist'[11]) back to the
Old World, the traditional centre of civilisation, culture and
tradition, and in the reversal of longstanding relationships of
dominance and subordination which occurs there?

Travel writing tells us as much about the country travelled from
as about the country travelled to. Twain, in 1867, spoke on behalf
of a mass American audience, with considerable financial power,
starting to redefine the Old World according to a new set of cultural

needs and values. Something of this is suggested by Bruce Michelson when he writes:

> The *Quaker City* contained the vanguard of the largest and richest invasion of wandering pleasure-seekers in history. The Americans were coming to turn Europe into one vast amusement park, to transform every gallery, palace, cathedral . . . into a hometown sideshow, to gape at the 'foreigners' and have themselves a good time. The millions back home waited to hear of the great national pleasure adventure from someone who had gone along in the proper spirit. . . . Mark Twain had no better choice than to assume the role of the American gone out to play.[12]

Though *The Innocents Abroad* was not altogether original in what it did, Twain's ability to combine the themes and techniques of earlier writers, the particular voice(s) he created, and his synthesis of comedy with travel chronicle, helps to explain both its short- and long-term importance.[13] Certainly much of the book's success lies in the 'cultural comedy' it dramatises,[14] as conventional assumptions about Europe, its traditions, and the value of its artistic heritage are subjected to the apparently 'innocent' and iconoclastic eye of Mark Twain, the playful and 'free-talking American frankly sizing up the Old World'.[15]

My argument, though, is that Twain's text is not as straightforward as it may at first seem. In fact, *The Innocents Abroad* signals a recurrent pattern in his major works in the *contradictions* that it contains. The more closely the book is examined, the more apparent its complications and internal tensions are. The narrative is both a playful account of a pleasure trip *and* a more serious description of a cultural and spiritual pilgrimage,[16] and the gap between these two very different motivating impulses cannot be bridged. This helps to explain the textual swings between iconoclastic mockery and standard travelogue, and between comic irreverence and conventional piety. If Twain's task in this book is a representative one, to 'describe for a new mass audience what had been an elite-identified experience',[17] his position as a narrator and protagonist is far from unified or consistent.

This introduces another central concern, both here and in my critical study as a whole. For the interest Twain shows in *The Innocents Abroad* with the shifting, self-divided and uncertain status of the self is continued throughout his writing career. The instabilities of voice and identity in *The Innocents Abroad* do not, though, simply relate to Twain's response to his Old World subject matter. They result, also, from his divided attitude to America. Twain's humour in *The Innocents Abroad* cuts two ways as he both represents his nation and criticises it. Celebrating American innocence and frankness, he is also aware of the naivety, shallowness and blinkered nationalism that these qualities can imply. There is a further complication here, too. For Twain's text reveals that the Americans about whom, and for whom, he writes, are not a homogeneous group. As he separates American 'pilgrims' from 'sinners' in his text, so he recognises the divisions and differences that the concept of a fixed national identity disguises. In doing so, he tends to destabilise the clear-cut nature of the opposition between Old World and New on which so much of the narrative rests.

Twain's first full-length book, then, is marked by contradiction and shifts of perspective. I focus here on two other features of Twain's writing, both of which are also central to my developing analysis of his work as a whole. The first is the sense of epistemological uncertainty in *The Innocents Abroad*. For its instabilities of identity and voice indicate a deep uncertainty about the position of the subject and his ability to interpret experience in an accurate and authoritative manner. William Stowe discusses tourism as a way of 'coming to know and hence to dominate the world', with the tourist as the *sightseer* whose 'subjugating gaze reduces individuals, institutions, art-works, and landscapes to bits of knowledge and elevates the tourists and their class, race, gender, and nation to the position of the authoritative knower'.[18] If Twain, as confident American iconoclast, seems to adopt exactly this role, it is by no means on a full or permanent basis. For the very possibility of such knowledge tends to disappear in a type of 'vertigo',[19] sometimes comic, sometimes not, that repeatedly undermines any fixed and determinate reading of reality in the text. I earlier describe how the ground tends to disappear from under the reader's feet as he or she reads 'The Stolen White Elephant'. I briefly suggest, at the end of my third section, how a similar sense of unmooring inhabits this book.

I am also interested here in Twain's use of genre. As my book proceeds, I show how the thematic contradictions and instabilities in his work relate to his formal practice: the organisation of his texts and the generic shifts within and between them. *The Innocents Abroad* and *Roughing It* (1872), the next book I discuss, are travel narratives, and this form particularly suited Twain's artistic methods. For the travel book has a shape imposed on it, but one that is extremely flexible: alternating the linear description of the ongoing journey with the pauses along the way, where the writer can insert a dramatic scene,[20] a description (of people, of scenery or an event), a joke or story, a thought or associative digression.

Richard Bridgman's discussion of Twain's travel writing makes a number of perceptive remarks on the author's use of this form. He notes the way Twain's imagination was so often 'liberated' by the 'mechanisms of association': how, within the developing narrative, one subject will trigger the move to another apparently unrelated one. While such 'associative bridge[s]' often occur, both in *The Innocents Abroad* and his other travel books, the changes of topic and direction they bring are, though, by no means formally disruptive: 'for the travel account proved capable of absorbing any improvisation he might conceive'.[21] Bridgman explores the analogy between newspaper reporting, where Twain got his training as a writer, and travel narratives. 'A newspaper', he says:

provides . . . a cornucopia of facts, stories, and commentaries, minimally linked at best and without any synthesising conclusion. In a travel account, though, Twain could rely on the sequence of the journey itself to provide at least a simulacrum of coherence for his materials.[22]

If Twain is given less credit here for the consistent development of a number of themes and subject positions than he deserves, none the less, these comments on his use of the travel book genre are suggestive. For the contradictions in *The Innocents Abroad*, Twain's moves from one narrative role to another, and the shifts in attitude and perspective that accompany such moves can, despite their inconsistency, be easily contained within the baggy limits of the genre. When Twain turned to fiction, such containment would often prove rather more of a problem.

II

The Innocents Abroad can be read as a confident assertion of American nationalism.[23] I begin my analysis of the text from this perspective, putting other complications temporarily to the side. The initial popularity of *The Innocents Abroad* undoubtedly had much to do with its use of a comic irreverence and mocking wit based on an assumption of American cultural superiority. That assumption rested in turn on an American ability to spend freely on a world stage. The rapid increase in tourism to Europe – from about 30,000 a year in the 1840s to more than 100,000 by the 1890s[24] – provides one indicator of that spending power in a market where, as Twain makes clear, a favourable rate of exchange applied. Calling for 'unstinted champagne' for himself, Dan and the doctor in the Grand Casino in Marseilles, Twain comments that 'it is so easy to be bloated aristocrats where it costs nothing of consequence!' (p. 78).[25]

Financial power, of course, brings other forms of authority in its wake.[26] Twain's description, on arriving at Tangier, of 'a tribe of stalwart Moors . . . wading into the sea to carry us ashore on their backs from the small boats' (p. 60), is a pertinent example of the inequalities permeating relations between the tourist and the populations he (in this case) comes to exploit. The apparent lack of any ironic intent (though the judging of tone is often a problematic matter in this text) allows us to see economic mastery unconsciously allegorised here in terms of bodily relations, with the native Moor represented, reductively, only by his brief physical function in the travellers' onward progress. 'Drifting with the tide of a great popular movement' (p. 24), Twain, and those fellow Americans for whom he spoke, were engaged, at least in part, on a commercial mission to the Old World, to buy (if they chose) into its culture, and to spend on sightseeing, enjoyment and souvenirs: 'In Smyrna we picked up camel's hair shawls and other dressy things from Persia' (p. 517).[27] 'We came, we saw, we spent' would be one way of describing their trip. The patriotic cheer that greets the sight of the Stars and Stripes in a foreign land (p. 51) acts, moreover, as a subliminal reminder of the link between mass tourism and the quest for new and expanded markets then taking place on the part of the nation as a whole. This stress on economic power and purchase is, as I suggest in the final section of the chapter, perhaps the one unifying feature in Twain's representation of American national identity.

Robert Regan, in 'Huck Finn in the Wake of the *Quaker City*', examines the way Twain's texts invoke one another, focusing on the connections between *The Innocents Abroad* and *Huckleberry Finn*. Mark Twain and 'the boys', like Huck, 'travel light, bookless, and see and feel for themselves', casting off the 'cumbersome baggage' of prior (often genteel) 'respected author-authorities' who would 'impress free Americans into involuntary servitude'. Thus 'the "boys" of *The Innocents Abroad* defend their spontaneity by feigning ignorance of Old World culture and history, by pretending to recall no discourse anterior to their own'.[28] An alternative tactic here is to directly debunk that prior discourse, together with the piety and religious credulity that is seen to accompany it (as in the 'heart of St Philip Neri' episode – p. 234).

Alfred Kazin relates the cockiness and bumptious quality of *The Innocents Abroad* to 'the solidly good opinion that Americans held of themselves at a time when they believed themselves to have all the virtues of the English as a race and none of the defects of the English as a society'.[29] Edward Said writes that 'self-definition' is 'one of the activities practised by all cultures: it has a rhetoric, a set of occasions, and authorities (national feasts, for example, times of crisis, founding fathers, basic texts, and so on) and a familiarity all its own'.[30] Twain's book works in more than one way. In part, it questions both the unity of American culture and its absolute difference from that of Europe. Yet, contradictorily, it helped to define the distinctiveness of American identity at a time of crisis, when internal division had threatened permanently to tear the country apart.

In its account of travel abroad, *The Innocents Abroad* promotes a type of historical amnesia concerning very recent American history. The Civil War is mentioned in the section on the Azores but only as evidence of Portuguese ignorance of the larger world, when 'a Portuguese of average intelligence inquired if our civil war was over?' (p. 45). This is, significantly, immediately followed by a reference to American technological progress, a source of national pride: the completion of the Atlantic cable of 1866. Apart from descriptions of the muleteers in the Azores 'singing "John Brown's Body" in ruinous English' (p. 48),[31] and of an engraving in an American paper of Jefferson Davis 'signing a secession act or some such document', haunted by the spectre of Washington 'in warning attitude' behind (p. 154), the Civil War stands itself as a silent presence ghosting the book's strong note of national self-assertion.[32] The patriotic references that do occasionally enter the text also speak of an American unity now constructed in the face of former sectional difference. Thus, granted audience with the Emperor of Russia, Twain writes that 'our party . . . felt . . . they were representing the people of America. . . . [W]e felt a national pride in the warm cordiality of that reception' (pp. 316–17).[33]

The Innocents Abroad works in part, then, both to debunk European cultural authority and, simultaneously, to define America's own cultural identity. If such self-definitions have much to do with founding fathers and national occasions, then Twain's use of one of the most highly charged and symbolic events in the history of European–American relationships, Columbus's discovery, is of especial interest here. The influence of the European founder and father is metaphorically cast off in an episode which can be read in terms of a necessary tactical act performed as part of an explicitly nationalistic agenda. The guide in Genoa, rechristened 'Ferguson' by 'the boys' after their usual ethnocentric manner, shows mementoes of Columbus, expecting them to respond like most Americans, with 'wonder . . . sentiment and emotion' (pp. 229–30):

> 'Ah, genteelmen, you come wis me! I show you beautiful, O, magnificent bust Christopher Colombo! – splendid, grand, magnificent!' . . .
> The doctor put up his eye-glass – procured for such occasions:
> 'Ah – what did you say this gentleman's name was?'
> 'Christopher Colombo! – ze great Christopher Colombo!'
> 'Christopher Colombo – the great Christopher Colombo. Well, what did *he* do?'
> 'Discover America! – discover America, Oh, ze devil!'
> 'Discover America. No – that statement will hardly wash. We are just from America ourselves. We heard nothing about it. Christopher Colombo – pleasant name – is – is he dead?'
> 'Oh, corpo di Baccho! – three hundred year!'
> 'What did he die of?'
> 'I do not know! – I can not tell.'
> 'Small-pox, think?'
> 'I do not know, genteelmen! – I do not know *what* he die of!'

'Measles, likely?'
'May be – may be – I do *not* know – I think he die of somethings.'
'Parents living?'
'Im-posseeble!'
'Ah – which is the bust and which is the pedestal?'   (pp. 230–1)

The European discovery of America, thus implicitly the whole process of colonisation, is met with pretended ignorance. The 'is he dead?' joke (taken from Artemus Ward[34]) reinforces the fact that these 'self-reliant Americans' (p. 411), like Huck Finn, 'don't take no stock in dead people'.[35] Twain and his friends, representatives of a young and confident nation, are conspicuously *not* 'genteelmen', beholden to, and respectful of, tradition. Rather they relentlessly undercut the pious assumptions of their puzzled guide with deadpan humour and broadscale, and finally explosively absurd, jokes. Not only have these Americans got out from under the European heritage, cast off the burden of this past, but the journey of discovery itself is now reversed. Twain and the boys' discovery of Europe, their journey to see what it has to offer them and the benefits to be gained there blot out the traces of Columbus's earlier voyage.[36]

The end of Twain's journey, here and elsewhere in the text, is a confident assertion of American 'innocence' and newness, a rejection of Old World culture as lacking interest and value to clear-sighted American eyes. Such a stance is by no means consistent. It is, however, one that informs much of the humour and best-remembered incidents in the book. This assertiveness takes a slightly different form when Twain sees the original of Da Vinci's *The Last Supper*, which fails, for him, to have that special aura associated with the authenticity and uniqueness of the great work of art. He straightaway sets his voice against the inherited weight of reverence and opinion when he says, scandalously, that the multiple reproductions of the picture he sees being painted are, to his 'inexperienced' but implicitly honest eye, 'superior . . . to the original' (pp. 150–1). He is careful to base this opinion on the poor and faded condition of Da Vinci's painting, but none the less this is, to any traditionalist, cultural heresy. Twain then repeats it shortly after when he judges the 'copies of all the celebrated sculptures in Europe' found in the shops of Florence much more 'enchanting to the eye' than 'the dingy petrified nightmares they are the portraits of' (p. 194). This partly results from Twain's role as mass tourist, doing all the things that the tourist did ('he did all these things one after another. And he did them faster and faster by aid of improving transport'[37]), and preferring, here at least, the shops to the galleries. But such responses result too from the function of the art object in the process of cultural self-definition and the question of aesthetic judgement that goes with it.[38] Twain's preference of copy to original might again be read metaphorically as an assertive gesture on the part of the formerly subservient cultural dependant. To say the copy is brighter, fresher, more lustrous and lively than the original is not, in this case, to dismiss the forming influence of the latter. It is, though, to suggest that the American nation, far from being a pale imitation of that Europe from which her customs, beliefs and settlers originally came, has come rather to outshine and better the original 'dingy' and 'petrified' place of origin.[39]

Twain evidences a combative sense of American cultural identity in such episodes. Traditional notions of a civilised Old and uncivilised New World are revised as the narrator reports back on Europe and the Near East. The Portuguese of the Azores are described as 'shiftless' and 'lazy'. That they raise their corn 'just as their great-great-great grandfathers did' (p. 44) distinguishes them from Twain's Americans who, it is implied, know when to reject the influence of the ancestor. The Moors in Tangier are 'savages' (p. 70). Italians are identified in terms of their 'garlic-exterminating mouth[s]' (p.145). 'Educated to enmity toward every thing that is Catholic' (p. 479), Twain's American Protestant consciousness has no time for an Italy 'which has groped in the midnight of priestly superstition for sixteen hundred years' (p. 201). The Arabs of the Valley of Lebanon 'never invent any thing, never learn any thing' (p. 352). The Fountain of Figia in Syria is surrounded by a 'wretched nest of human vermin' (p. 358). The Old World is repeatedly represented in terms of a type of an alien backwardness.

Indeed, as the book proceeds, and as the protagonist moves beyond European limits, so the narrator's dismissal of the representatives of other cultures becomes more hostile.[40] So too a refusal of dialogue with such people, which has appeared as an earlier textual motif, becomes increasingly rigid. As Mark Twain and his colleagues travel through this foreign world, they constantly 'translate' it into familiar conceptual and linguistic moulds, renaming their guides as 'Ferguson', an Arab village as 'Jonesborough' (p. 370). Twain describes Arab speech as a 'disagreeable jabbering in unknown tongues' (p. 433). Jerusalem is, we are told, a polyglot community, but the only word that Twain hears is 'the eternal "bucksheesh"' (p. 446), just as (in a way) the only word he speaks is 'dollar'. Mark Twain's assertive American voice drowns out and ignores the voices of the inhabitants of the countries through which he travels, his dollars the sign both of his authority and his self-proclaimed superiority.

III

I start at this point to explore both the 'slipperiness'[41] of Mark Twain's identity in *The Innocents Abroad* and the contradictory nature of the text. Descriptions of the Old World in terms of alien backwardness (the Portuguese in the Azores) are, as far as one can tell, absolutely serious. The views put forward are apparently those of the author. However, at other points, a gap appears between the author and the fictional persona he constructs. For the ethnocentric assumptions of the latter are, as the final examples above begin to suggest, associated with an ignorance and a form of linguistic arrogance that is clearly subject to satiric attack. Indeed, the claim at the text's end that 'travel is fatal to prejudice, bigotry and narrow-mindedness' (p. 521) is countered by the clearly xenophobic strain that runs through the whole book.[42] The relation between the civilised and the uncivilised gets thoroughly tangled up in the process.

If the phrase 'soap and civilisation' denotes the bringing of progress to primitive societies,[43] then the absence of soap in Europe – a repeated complaint of Twain and his travelling companions – implies a lack of civilisation too. But when this sign of backwardness becomes a central issue (in the Milan bath-house episode), it does not work to validate the superior nature of Twain and his fellow Americans, but rather is used to satirise what David Sewell calls their 'insistent monolinguism': a 'linguistic imperialism' which is but another 'form of [their] cultural assertion'.[44]

Twain and the doctor's early attempts in Marseilles to try out their French meet blank incomprehension, and, from that point, any effort 'the boys' make to communicate in native languages is minimal. So, here:

After we were stripped . . . we discovered that haunting atrocity
that has embittered our lives in so many cities and villages of Italy
and France – there was no soap . . .
Dan's voice rose on the air:
   'Oh, bring some soap, why don't you?'
The reply was Italian. Dan resumed:
   'Soap, you know – soap. That is what I want – soap. S-o-a-p,
soap; s-o-p-e, soap; s-o-u-p, soap. Hurry up! I don't know how
you Irish spell it, but I want it. Spell it to suit yourself, but fetch
it. I'm freezing.'
I heard the doctor say, impressively:
   'Dan, how often have we told you that these foreigners can not
understand English? Why will you not depend upon us? Why
will you not tell *us* what you want, and let us ask for it in the
language of the country? . . . I will address this person in his
mother tongue: 'Here, cospetto! corpo di Bacco! Sacramento!
Solferino! – Soap, you son of a gun!'   (pp. 147–8)

Whatever the doctor's pretensions, his ability to communicate in
Italian (or his version of it) is no better than that of Dan, who never
tries. No dialogue takes place here, only a one-way conversation
with the Americans quick to insult and xenophobically abuse those
in a relation of economic dependency to them, whose living
depends (here, at any rate) on the tourist trade. If gold is the
universal language of financial exchange,[45] then English (once the
poor attempts to speak French or Italian have failed) is the only
speech system Twain and 'the boys' will use to complete that
exchange. Dan acts on the principle that if, when you speak to a
foreigner, you repeat something often enough, spell it enough
different ways, assume idiocy on their part, and use enough forms
of command, you will get what you want. The doctor adds a
smattering of misplaced Italian and the odd inappropriate (but
Italian-sounding) word, but operates from a similar stance.
   This is the comedy of cultural aggression. Mark Twain, the tourist,
gets what he wants through his money, and refuses dialogue with
the inhabitants of the countries through which he travels.[46] Unequal
relationships of economic power are paralleled by a dismissive
impatience with the uncivilised and stereotyped foreign 'other'.
Here, however, Twain (as author rather than character) clearly holds
his naive and ignorant protagonist at an ironic remove; that

protagonist's assertive American know-nothing, monolinguistic and ethnocentric attitudes a source of satire rather than of celebration. But the innocence of this protagonist, as I have suggested, does not always connote ignorance. It is also associated with a clear-eyed way of seeing, a casting-off of traditional values and cultural reverence, with which the reader is encouraged to empathise. The gap between the narrative persona and the authorial voice varies as these different positions are adopted. The assertion of American superiority is both endorsed and criticised in the text, and a curiously unstable effect in thereby created.

Our sense of our readerly ground starts to give way here. Are we meant to identify with the American nationalism with which the narrator is identified or are we meant to hold it at arm's length, seeing it as an uninformed and shallow prejudice? When do innocence and ignorance become the same thing? There are no simple answers to these questions. Twain shuttles his reader between positions, makes her or him aware both of the strengths of the way of reading the Old World of his (representative American) narrator, and of its absurd limits. The gap between a serious authorial voice, an adopted voice which echoes or may echo the author's values, and an adopted voice which is the subject of satiric undermining, but yet may or may not represent a certain element in the authorial identity, constantly and disconcertingly opens and closes as the text proceeds.

This is a contradictory and destabilising text in other ways too. Certainly, the combative sense of American identity constructed in *The Innocents Abroad* cannot be denied. The series of contrasts, implicit and explicit, made between Europe and America, seem to leave the reader clear where Twain's sympathies lie. America, unlike the Old World, is free from aristocratic forms, every man (at least in theory) a king. Twain describes his '*roy*al summer flight across [the American] continent in a stage-coach' (p. 87, my emphasis) – a scenario to which he returns in *Roughing It* – and the scanning of 'the blue distances of a world that knew no lords but us' (p. 86). The various superstitions alluded to in Europe (Galileo's scientific discoveries judged as heresy by the Church – p. 192), and its cruel, repressive and autocratic forms of political authority (which underlie the descriptions of the Castle d'If, pp. 82–4; the Bastille, p. 90; the Medicis, p. 193), also function as a reminder of American democratic difference. Nature may imitate art in the open spaces and grandeur of the western American landscape, with its 'mimic cities . . . pinnacled cathedrals . . . massive fortresses, counterfeited in the eternal rocks' (p. 86). As it does so, however, it implicitly provides a healthy contrast with the cultural sights of Europe, and the extremes of wealth and poverty, the aristocratic or religious privilege, associated with its real cities, cathedrals and fortresses.

But if this is so, Twain can neither celebrate his own country nor denigrate the Old World completely. Angles of vision both shift and clash in *The Innocents Abroad,* undercut each other, as Twain moves between narrative positions, and this movement renders any unitary reading of his materials impossible. Thus an attack on Rome, its lack of open government, its superstition and backwardness, from the perspective of American democratic difference, has its comparative foundation removed as Twain suddenly shifts to criticise plutocratic corruption in public life back home (pp. 210–11). Accordingly, we 'glimpse the very American face of Mark Twain, disillusioned observer of postbellum venality and future co-author of *The Gilded Age*'.[47]

Similarly, the negative picture of the Old World, and the perspective that frames it, drops away in a countering recognition of its attractions. Alfred Kazin talks of 'the sound of breathless respect for Old Europe in which so much has *happened*' that runs alongside the 'disdain for backwardness and ignorance' in the book.[48] The irreverence of Twain's narrator is matched elsewhere, in direct contrast, by cultural reverence. The 'noble' and 'beautiful' Milan cathedral, with the 'beautiful marble statues' on its roof, is described (in notably undemocratic terms) as 'surely . . . the princeliest creation that ever brain of man conceived' (pp. 136–8). To be in Venice is, attractively, to be 'in a half-waking dream . . . drifting back, back, back, into the solemn past, and looking upon the scenes and mingling with the people of a remote antiquity' (p. 186).[49]

The contradictory and clashing nature of Twain's responses to the Old World in *The Innocents Abroad* can, in part, be explained by the sense of epistemological provisionality which he explicitly dramatises in the book. For the reading of reality, and its interpretation, depends on the position of the subject, and this is a relative, not a fixed, thing. In the Pallavicini garden, near Genoa, Twain draws conscious attention to the problems and limits of representation, with his awareness that 'the carefully contrived accident of a framework' determines the 'entrancing beauty' of the view, excluding 'all unattractive features' from it (p. 416). The version of reality you give depends, in other words, either on the chosen or the determined point from which you give it. When Twain discusses art and its interpretation, moreover, he shows two things: one, how the nationality (subject position and ideology) of the painter affects his representation of his subject (pp. 153–4); and two, how the reading of an expression or painting varies according to the individual, and does not necessarily bear any relation to an original meaning or truth (pp. 152–3). Again, in other words, our ways of depicting reality vary according to our particular circumstances, and our ability to interpret what we see is profoundly unreliable. In this series of comments, Twain self-reflexively prepares the ground for the instabilities and shifting perspectives that all his books reveal. His subject inhabits multiple positions, and the experience he represents is multiform.

IV

The lack of respect for tradition and the exposure, both comic and serious, of Old World humbug is just one of the viewpoints Twain projects in *The Innocents Abroad*, to question the worth, and cast off the weight, of Old World cultural forms and traditions. But quite another position is taken too. For the narrator cannot ignore anterior discourses,[50] completely escape the influence of tradition, or of the guidebooks that provide the 'prior textual and cultural framework' for its reception.[51] Not only guidebooks but what we might call the huge library of Europeanism,[52] all the prior descriptions of, and attitudes to Europe, its cultural monuments and artefacts, shape, in however mediated a form, his consciousness.

This helps to account for some of the contradictions, switches of tone and perspective in *The Innocents Abroad*. The revisionary impulse operates, and can only operate, sporadically. The narrative voice may at times indulge in broad satire and burlesque at the expense of tradition, but this stance is not consistent, for preformed cultural assumptions and ways of reading Europe (and the Orient) have their effect too. The voice of the iconoclastic comic persona comes and goes, but so too does a more serious and conventional one. For this was a pilgrimage as well as a pleasure trip, and if amusement encouraged an irreverent step outside prior ways of responding to the Old World, the more established and ritualistic aspects of Twain's journey made a more conservative response to his experience inevitable.

Thus, in the Roman section of the book, the narrator finds himself unable to escape earlier established versions of, and knowledge about, the city. When he comes to St Peter's he says, 'I prefer not to describe St Peter's. It has been done before' (p. 217). Before saying this, however, he has already felt bound to give a long description of the building. His response to the Coliseum is similar. Twain commences by saying that *'every body knows* the picture of the Coliseum; *every body recognizes at once* that "looped and windowed" band-box with a side bitten out' (p. 218, my emphasis). He does what he can to get a fresh angle on this well-described material by his use here of contemporary metaphor, and, more successfully, by his 'translation' of the contests that once took place at the Coliseum, first into American play-bill (pp. 220–1), and then into journalistic form ('the *Roman Daily Battle-Ax'* – p. 221). His earlier description, though, is one which stalely echoes any number of similar prior descriptions:

> [T]he monarch of all European ruins, the Coliseum, maintains that reserve and that royal seclusion which is proper to majesty. Weeds and flowers spring from its massive arches and its circling seats, and vines hang their fringes from its lofty walls. An impressive silence broods. . . . More vividly than all the written histories, the Coliseum tells the story of Rome's grandeur and Rome's decay. (p. 218)

The language used here and the assumptions of cultural value made are entirely conventional. Similarly, Twain's reaction to the Etruscan tear-jug (pp. 197–8) would seem to illustrate the strong influence of the sentimental tradition, and its attitude to the past, on him.[53] Different aspects of the narrator's perspective on the Old World clash more or less head-on here, with the inevitable sense of instability and contradiction that ensues.

When Twain moves beyond European boundaries, the gap between any kind of comic and irreverent response to his material and the pressure of conventional frameworks which condition the view of the countries through which he travels becomes even more noticeable. This might be explained partly by the fact that the earlier lively engagement with the central paradox of the American–European relationship (that to be an American is to be attracted to, and to share an identity with, Europe, as well as to insist upon the fact of cultural difference) no longer drives the text. But it is also a result of at least three different frameworks which now limit Twain's narrative: the general effect of Orientalist stereotypes, the prior conventions of pilgrimage literature, and the nature of the religious material with which he now has to deal.

For, first, when Twain writes about the 'otherness' of the East, he does little more than repeat the stereotypes and tropes which have conventionally been used in western descriptions of the Orient. These, in Edward Said's words, operate around assumptions of 'the ineradicable distinction between Western superiority and Oriental inferiority'.[54] Thus references to Oriental timelessness and exoticism suffuse Twain's descriptions. Constantinople has from a distance 'the quaint Oriental aspect one dreams of when he reads books of eastern travel' (p. 283), and 'to see a camel train laden with the spices of Arabia' coming through the narrow passages of the bazaar in Smyrna 'is a genuine revelation of the Orient. The picture lacks nothing. . . . [A]gain you dream over the wonders of the Arabian Nights' (p. 326).

The 'picture' Twain gives us here is composed of a culturally inherited discourse and set of fixed images. He gives his reader an Arabian Nights world in terms of picturesque setting, but one which on closer view reveals backwardness, cruelty, squalid degeneracy and heresy. Both of these elements are different, but equally powerful, parts of the Orientalist stereotype. Thus, when he describes a group of 'picturesque Arabs' in the Holy Land, the initial reference to 'a grand Oriental picture which I had worshiped [*sic*] a thousand times in soft, rich steel engravings' gives way to a closer focus on the 'desolation . . . dirt . . . rags . . . fleas' and the 'besotted ignorance in the countenances' (p. 433). The Arab guard on the journey onward from Galilee is described as an 'infamous star-spangled scum of the desert' (p. 411). The narrator swings here between two versions of a stereotype in describing these Eastern scenes and peoples, but the same move from remote charm to direct repulsion is recurrent.

When Twain comes to describe the sacred places on his Holy Land

itinerary, he has similar difficulties in consistently avoiding the
'basic repertoire of images'[55] already associated with the region. But
he is now also caught within the accepted parameters and examples
of pilgrimage literature, and by the sensitive nature of his religious
subject matter. He ironically recognises the former of these limits
when he says of the 'pilgrims' in his party that, 'I can almost tell,
in set phrase, what they will say when they see . . . Nazareth, Jericho
and Jerusalem – *because I have the books they will "smouch" their ideas
from*' (p. 406). The religious nature of the repertoire of images he
works with, too, inhibits both spontaneity and humour. For the
trajectory of the narrative (with Jerusalem as the expected climax)
is fixed. And the sensibilities of his audience discourage anything
but stereotyped language and reaction.

The constraints imposed on Twain by the prior conventions of
pilgrimage literature are everywhere evident. The panorama visible
from the high ground above Lake Galilee is 'so crowded with
historical interest' that all Twain seems able to do (despite his doubts
as to whether these are the actual sites of the traditions ascribed) is
to list the places and their associations:

> Bethsaida; the supposed scenes of the Sermon on the Mount . . . ;
> the declivity down which the swine ran to the sea . . . ; part of
> the battle-field of Hattin, where the knightly Crusaders fought
> their last fight, and in a blaze of glory passed from the stage . . . ;
> Mount Tabor, the traditional scene of the Lord's Transfiguration.
> (p. 412)

A description of prickly pears 'like hams' (p. 413) which follows,
shows Twain attempting a vernacular intervention, but he is soon
back smouching *his* ideas from travel books, and consciously
acknowledging the fact (see, for instance, p. 413).

Twain is trapped here, too, if not by the nature of his own religious
beliefs, then certainly by the knowledge that comedy at the expense
of Christianity would both risk alienating a sizeable part of his
audience and prejudice his own acceptance into the more
respectable American circles.[56] The irreverence of humour and
hegemonic religious values are not capable of reconciliation.[57] When
Twain finally reaches Jerusalem, he shows a sharp Protestant eye

for the religious trappings and manufactured mementos which abound in the Church of the Holy Sepulchre. But, despite an awareness of the ironies of the religious disputes that have raged round the sacred sites, a pious reverence, similar to that of any number of pilgrims who precede and follow him, overwhelms any other response at the site of the crucifixion itself:

> I . . . looked upon the place where the true cross once stood, with a far more absorbing interest than I had ever felt in anything earthly before. . . . And so I close my chapter on the Church of the Holy Sepulchre . . . the most illustrious edifice in Christendom. With all its clap-trap side-shows and unseemly imposture of every kind, it is still grand, reverend, venerable – for a god died there; for fifteen hundred years its shrines have been wet with the tears of pilgrims. . . . History is full of this old Church of the Holy Sepulchre – full of blood that was shed because of the respect and the veneration in which men held the last resting-place of the meek and lowly, the mild and gentle, Prince of Peace! (pp. 456–7)

There are some subjects Twain finds it hard to joke about, or/and where the weight of inherited response tends to bury much of the distinctive quality of his voice and point of view.

He does, however, manage to escape this stifling reverence obliquely, when he introduces, just previously, another voice and another perspective. For he burlesques many of the qualities endorsed in the Holy Sepulchre scene – piety, the sentimental response to history and tradition, and the value and importance of cultural and spiritual places of origin – when he reaches the supposed site of Adam's tomb in Jerusalem to find it a complete fraud, and completely marginal to his own concerns or needs (pp. 451–2). The burlesque here invades, if only by suggestion, the piety of the Holy Sepulchre scene. The contradiction between iconoclastic humour and fresh response and the weight of the religious subject matter at the centre of this section of the narrative can only, though, be (partially) overcome by such indirect means. For the most part, the distinctive comic nature of Twain's voice recedes to the very fringes of the text till Jerusalem is safely passed.

V

My analysis of *The Innocents Abroad* to this point has been largely based on its opposition between America and the Old World. Much of my reading has rested on the assumption of a unitary national identity: that to be an American is to be defined in terms of New World–Old World difference. But Twain's narrative is more complicated than this, as many of my previous comments have implied. The opposition between the New and the Old World which Twain constructs is destabilised as he (also) treats his national and international materials from another perspective; as he shows the deep cultural influence Europe and the Holy Land have on American identity; and as he upsets, to a large degree, the notion that this latter identity is coherent and homogeneous.

It is Twain's exposure of cultural differences within America, as well as those between America and the foreign 'other', on which I focus here. As this occurs, so the boundaries of the New–Old World binary are inevitably complicated and blurred. Twain describes two different types of American, 'saints' and 'sinners', on the excursion. The strong nationalistic tone completely disappears when the narrator refers to the 'pilgrims' (the pious, genteel, respectable, sober and self-righteous members of the *Quaker City* company) and their abuse of the Arab mosque at Nain. Instead, a relativist cultural stance takes its place:

> We entered, and the pilgrims broke specimens from the foundation walls, though they had to touch, and even step, upon the 'praying carpets' to do it. . . . To step rudely upon the sacred praying mats, with booted feet . . . was to inflict pain upon men who had not offended us in any way. Suppose a party of armed foreigners were to enter a village church in America and break ornaments from the altar railings for curiosities. . . . (p. 432)

As the contrast between alternative types of American is developed, it is the narrator and his fellow sinners who are represented as clear-sighted, straight-speaking, companionable, non-conformist and spontaneous truth-tellers, while the pilgrims are seen as hypocrites, 'credulous and guide-book-clutching, indoctrinated with the received attitude of reverence toward the wonders of the past . . . unquestioning [in their] conformity'.[58] Twain attacks the pilgrims'

lack of charity and compassion (pp. 355–6). He criticises their
mean-mindedness, bickerings, hypocrisies and their desire for
self-advantage (see, for instance, pp. 393–4). The 'vandalism' of the
group is scorned repeatedly: 'They broke off fragments from Noah's
tomb; from the exquisite sculptures of the temples of Baalbec. . . .
Heaven protect the Sepulchre when this tribe invades Jerusalem!'
(p. 373).[59]

Twain stresses the contrast between pilgrims and sinners much
more than their shared attributes.[60] At first glance this seems to
endorse the opposition between the New and the Old World in the
text, for the pilgrims are generally associated with a reverence
for the culture of the past and its values. In the Holy Land they
borrow their words and ideas from guide books, and 'revere,
almost . . . worship, the holy places' (p. 393) they see. The sense of
American–Old World difference modifies here into a contrast
between types of American: the genteel, pious and self-righteous
(see the clearly allegorical representation of 'the "Pilgrim" bird' in
Marseilles Zoo – pp. 78–9) and their opposite. The internal conflicts
of the Civil War (and its South–North divide) are here drawn up
along different (East–West) lines; the representatives of 'America's
official culture' opposed by 'an uncouth deflating, philistine bunch
of vernacular figures'.[61] The nationalistic qualities of Twain's book
are, however, complicated and compromised by the fact that the
Americans who *officially* represent their country are both ridiculed
and closely linked to the Old World and its values.

One could argue with this conclusion, however, by suggesting
that for Twain 'real' Americanism implied a necessary cultural
transformation – the shucking off of the genteel and the celebration
of the vernacular. But if this is the case, then the contrasts between
the New and the Old World based on cultural differences that
apparently *already* exist (the stress on an American rejection of past
models, for instance) begin to look problematic. At the very least,
they need further explanation in terms of the one particular version
of American identity which is being endorsed. But I have already
suggested that the narrator is himself implicated in the 'pilgrim'
values he would appear, with his criticisms, to deny. Twain might
set himself against his fellow American pilgrims, but in his sub-title,
'The New Pilgrim's Progress', in his description of his own
'pilgrimage' to Versailles (p. 122), in the cultural solemnities he, too,
variously mouths, and in his occasional use of the first person

plural, he blurs the boundaries between himself and this other group. In describing Moslems as 'trespassing on *our* holy ground' (p. 466), for instance, his narrow piety seems but a variant of theirs.

When, moreover, the narrator does distance himself from the 'fantastic mob of green-spectacled Yanks' with their green cotton umbrellas, who intrude into 'the scenery of the Bible' (p. 369), his own *single* refusal to equip himself similarly collapses earlier structures of differences among the different groups of tourists (pilgrims *or* sinners). For it is Twain against the rest here. No single perspective or subject position is complete in itself in *The Innocents Abroad*. Twain's view of American identity and of Old World–New World difference lacks stability and contains contradictions.

The various Americans (pilgrims and sinners) of *The Innocents Abroad* do, however, have one thing in common. I have described the American economic power of the period, and the confident sense of national self-assertion as the 'invasion' of the Old World took place. I quoted, too, William W. Stowe, who linked travel abroad in Twain's period with American capitalist enterprise and expectation. When Twain describes the 'vandalism' of the invading tribe of pilgrims in the Holy Land, he conveniently omits the fact that he himself was not above such vandalism. The editors of his *Notebooks* mention 'a small marble head' taken on his trip to the Acropolis,[62] while Twain's own reference to getting 'pieces of the old Temple' (see the prefacing quotes to this chapter) comes as he describes the Mosque of Omar in his journal. For there is *one* constant in American identity as Twain represents it; one important connection between these sheep and goats (saints and sinners). For both are linked in their expansionist and acquisitive drive. It is in this, and this alone, that the word 'American' comes to take on a unified meaning. Twain may downplay, foreground only sporadically, the economic power of a fast developing capitalist society and its influence on the events, places and people he describes. But that influence haunts this text, as it did the majority of Twain's works. In *Roughing It*, the theme of capitalist expansionism makes its strong return, this time, though, in the geographical and historical context of the American westward movement.

3

Roughing It and the American West

It's a Great Country, Ma.

(*Mark Twain's Letters*)[1]

This perennial rebirth, this fluidity of American life, this expansion westward . . . furnish the forces dominating American character. . . . The frontier is the line of most rapid and effective Americanization. . . . The fact is, that here is a new product that is American.

(Frederick Jackson Turner)[2]

I

The West that Mark Twain described in *Roughing It* (1872) was a confused and confusing region. In a letter to his mother from Carson City, written on 25 October 1861, he spoke of the country as:

> fabulously rich in gold, silver, copper, lead, coal, iron, quicksilver, marble, granite, chalk, plaster of Paris, (gypsum,) thieves, murderers, desperadoes, ladies, children, lawyers, Christians, Indians, Chinamen, Spaniards, gamblers, sharpers, cuyotes (pronounced ki-yo-ties,) . . . poets, preachers, and jackass rabbits.[3]

Stephen Fender notes the 'jumbling of categories' here, and comments, more generally, that the letters of this period 'bristled

44

with unresolved contrasts'.[4] Such an analysis can be usefully extended and applied to the version of the West represented in *Roughing It*.

The historian Frederick Jackson Turner, in 1893, famously located American cultural rebirth in the 'new field of opportunity' offered by the western 'wilderness'. The contrasts, evolutionary discourse and metaphors of rebirth and 'steady growth' under frontier conditions, which Turner used to support his argument[5] had, though, already been deconstructed twenty years earlier by Twain. They appear one-dimensional and reductive in comparison to Twain's account of the chaotic aspects of western life in *Roughing It*. If Twain seems at first to tell a similar story to Turner, he quickly complicates and undermines it.

The description of the 'practical joke' played by the inhabitants of Carson City on the newly arrived US Attorney, General Buncombe, suggests something of what I mean. Buncombe is duped into involvement in 'The Great Landslide Case'. Accordingly, he agrees to represent the interests of a local rancher, Dick Hyde, against Tom Morgan, who owns the land on the mountainside immediately above

> the trouble was, that one of those hated and dreaded land-slides had come and slid Morgan's ranch, fences, cabins, cattle, barns and everything down on *his* [Hyde's] ranch and exactly covered up every single vestige of his property, to a depth of about thirty-eight feet. Morgan was in possession and refused to vacate the premises – said he was occupying his own cabin and not interfering with anybody else's – and said the cabin was standing on the same dirt and the same ranch it had always stood on.
>
> (p. 253)

Buncombe's spirited defence of his client fails, but, on personal appeal, ex-Governor Roop, who is hearing the case, modifies his verdict:

> at last his face lit up happily and he told Buncombe it had occurred to him that the ranch underneath the new Morgan ranch still belonged to Hyde, that his title to the ground was just as good as it had been, and therefore he was of opinion that Hyde had a right to dig it out from under there and – (p. 257)

This, of course, is a hoax, one of the favourite forms of western humour.[6] It operates round a repeated motif in the book: the taking in of the eastern greenhorn by the western community. But the content of the episode has additional interest. The conflicts over property and title described, the social and legal confusion that occurs as one layer of land covers up another, and the comic chaos suggested in the idea of digging one ranch out from beneath the other, implicitly interrogates the neat and ordered process Turner implied in the 'law of continuity and development' he proposed for western history.[7]

The idea of an evolutionary shape to history can accommodate temporary confusion along its way. Twain, however, unlike Turner, consistently and repeatedly focuses on the unresolved contradictions and multiplicities of the West. He stresses, too, the difficulty of interpreting this disorienting western world; of gaining any firm and reliable knowledge about it. For the sense of epistemological uncertainty identified in *The Innocents Abroad* recurs here, but with greater emphasis. Any authoritative reading of this ever-shifting reality proves unattainable. Twain uses the motif of the 'blind lead' recurrently in *Roughing It*. The career his protagonist takes, and the narrative he tells, keep running into dead ends. The form of the book is meandering and digressive, with 'bizarre jump[s] from one narrative stance into another'.[8] A repeated sense of instability and inconclusiveness defines the text.

Twain does, however, suggest one source of continuity and shape, not just to western American history, but to the history of the nation as a whole. The focus on the regional myths of the West, and its representation as a place of conflicting accounts and indeterminate meanings, runs alongside – and is in tension with – a larger theme. Martha Banta, in a revealing phrase, refers to Twain's work as a whole in terms of a 'capitalist historiography'.[9] In my final comments on *The Innocents Abroad*, I suggested that the one thing linking the different types of Americans he depicts is the way they are jointly identified with the expansive and acquisitive drives of an emergent capitalism. In *Roughing It*, the stress on western distinctiveness exists alongside another story which undermines, and replaces it. Twain identifies a constant element to American historical development as a whole: the driving force of commerce, business and the market, which erases regional difference in its path, and affects every stage of national expansion in the period of which he writes. This problematises any reading of the westward move that sees it, as Turner does, as a journey into the 'wilderness'; as a healthy regression 'into the simplicity of primitive conditions'.[10] For heterogeneity and difference (all that makes the West what it is) and homogeneity (the development of a national economic system, and the uniform effects of this process) exist – and especially in this place and at this time – in considerable tension with one another. Twain's focus on the western education (or lack of it) of his first-person protagonist, on regional conflict, and on the anecdotes, persons and incidents that exemplify the unique features of the West, tends to cut against his other, and larger national, story of the inevitable spread of capitalist enterprise and its values. The western characteristics Twain identifies cannot, in the long term, co-exist with the capitalist expansionism which he also describes.

Roughing It, then, is marked by a sense of narrative tension and ambiguity which results from the shifts of focus and perspective in the text. As my study continues, I draw increasing attention to Twain's unease about the direction of American history and the dominant values of his time. These are already beginning to be apparent in this book. Twain, though, neither consistently foregrounds, nor explicitly comments on, the incompatibilities between the two (regional and national) stories he tells here. His stress on immediate experience (much of it comic) filtered through the first person voice, tends to resist serious and sustained historical analysis. As in *The Innocents Abroad*, his use of the travel narrative allows him to shift narrative direction and to change tone and register almost at will. The associative method Twain developed[11] works against tight textual unity. Indeed, in a book where the author admits openly that 'I digress constantly anyhow' (p. 359), the sense of internal contradiction and of jumbled categories becomes – as I suggest in my final section – no artistic disadvantage, but rather part of the very fabric of what is an accomplished comic textual performance.

II

At first glance, Twain's language and the shape he gives his narrative in *Roughing It*, would both seem to confirm, rather than contradict, Turner's frontier thesis and its description of significant western difference. The 'exhilarating sense of emancipation' the narrator and his fellow travellers feel as they leave 'the States' behind them[12] mirrors Turner's description of the 'buoyancy and exuberance which comes with freedom' on the frontier.[13] The historian's celebration of 'perennial rebirth' in the move west, similarly, is suggested in Twain's use of metaphor: the overland coach in which his protagonist travels is described as 'an imposing cradle on wheels' (p. 54). The figurative link is then reinforced as he strips to his underclothes, not quite naked but nearly so, to increase comfort in the womb-like interior of the vehicle: 'as "dark as the inside of a cow," as the conductor phrased it in his picturesque way' (pp. 65–6).

Roughing It, then, initially appears to be structured round the idea of the restorative return to the primitive. Jeffrey Steinbrink, accordingly, describes the first stages of the trip West as 'a flight from civilization to conditions more . . . rudimentary, . . . from the rules of decorum and the forms of polite address to the unrestraint of practical usage and the vigor of colloquial language, from the tame to the wild'.[14] The clothing (swallow-tail coats and white kid gloves) of genteel respectability is discarded with other 'baggage' at St Joseph to conform with the weight restrictions on the overland coach (p. 52). New modes of dress take its place, and by the time the narrator has reached Carson City he has 'grown well accustomed to wearing a damaged slouch hat, blue woolen shirt, and pants crammed into boot-tops', glories 'in the absence of coat, vest and braces', and feels 'rowdyish and bully' (p. 186) as a consequence. These are not quite the 'hunting shirt and the moccasin' Turner associates with effective Americanisation on the frontier. But certainly 'the garments of civilization', the styles of dress and customs identified with effete European influence, are here also, to use the historian's trope, stripped off by the wilderness.[15]

The 'freshness' and 'breeziness' of the new frontier landscape entered by Twain's protagonist and the sense of emancipation associated with it (p. 54) are initially reflected by a narrative that fairly rattles along. Twain's growth in literary confidence since *The Innocents Abroad* is seen in his increased technical command: the gap he establishes between the 'young and ignorant' (p. 49) first person semi-fictional[16] narrator-protagonist and a more experienced, and retrospective, narrative voice, both shapes the text and allows a dual perspective on its materials from the first.[17]

It soon becomes apparent, however, that Twain's representation of the West is by no means as straightforward as the above parallels with Turner might suggest. The West, for Twain, is a place of contradictions. *Roughing It* tells a more complex story than anyone versed in the historian's later narrative of the rise of individual liberty and democracy on the frontier, and aware of the clear oppositions which structure that narrative, might expect.

Twain's attitude to the American Indian is a case in point. For Turner, the Indian and the untamed wilderness stand in one-to-one relationship to each other, joint components of a 'savage' West which the frontiersman (the bringer of a 'new order of Americanism') will civilise and settle.[18] It is, indeed, exactly such a view of the Indian, depending on a clear savage–civilised binary, which informs Twain's description of the Goshoot (a pun on Gosiute) Indian. A repeated pattern in the book is replayed here as the naive and romantic expectations of the greenhorn protagonist are shown to be illusions. Cooper's 'Noble Red Men' turn out 'paint and tinsel' creations, a product of 'the mellow moonshine of romance'. Twain uses evolutionary discourse (on which Turner, too, will rely) to claim that the members of 'this silent, sneaking, treacherous-looking race' are descended from 'the self-same gorilla, or kangeroo, or Norway rat, whichever animal-Adam the Darwinians trace them to' (pp. 166–8).[19] He launches a swingeing attack on the Gosiutes as 'the wretchedest type of mankind I have ever seen' (p. 166), equating their particular tribe with every other Indian as he does so.[20]

But the opposition between savage and civilised is far from stable in the book. Twain's earlier story of the 'town-dog' futilely chasing the despised 'spiritless and cowardly' coyote and being taken in by the deceptive speed of this swindling stranger (pp. 75–8) has conventionally been read as an allegory of the tenderfoot gaining knowledge from the western veteran, as he works his way through his various humiliations toward 'the superior maturity and sophistication of the old-timer'. As such, it has been taken as a paradigm for one of the narrative's basic patterns.[21] But Twain repeatedly (three times) links the coyote to the Indian as he tells this story, and says that they are connected in 'blood kinship' (p. 79). And Coyote is, of course, the Indian trickster, an intelligent but duplicitous shape-changer and prankster, 'perhaps the most conspicuous figure in the oral literature of the Native American peoples' in the western United States.[22] Turner's narrative of 'the disintegration of savagery'[23] takes an unexpected twist as a note of relativistic uncertainty appears here. For the 'title' (to return to the Buncombe case) to superior knowledge, if we are to read the episode allegorically, is held not by the western veteran but by the supposedly 'savage' – but in fact culturally different – Indian. It is the Indian too who knows more than the white inhabitants of the region when the flash flood descends; who has that gift of prophecy that the narrator never gains (p. 317).

The frontier in *Roughing It* becomes, in other words, not a place of clear meanings and well-structured contrasts, but of instability and complexity. This can be seen, too, in Twain's representation of the opposition between eastern genteel and western vernacular forms of language, and the social difference it signifies. For any tendency to endorse 'the vigor of colloquial language' and to consequently dismiss eastern 'forms of polite address' is, similarly, undermined in Twain's description of Buck Fanshawe's funeral.

The battle over language enacted here is foreshadowed in the early symbolic emphasis Twain places on the weight of the Unabridged Dictionary which (together with the United States statutes) he and his brother carry West. This 'uneasy Dictionary' is thrown about as the stagecoach passes through the new and hilly landscape, and 'assault[s]' and 'damage[s]' the passengers within (p. 66). On reaching Carson City, it is placed in the 'government fire-proof safe' in the narrator's room (p. 180). Just what worth this linguistic tool will have for Twain, the apprentice westerner and apprentice writer, remains (as in the case of the law book as legal tool) ambiguous. Its value, indeed, is almost at once put in question with the introduction, via 'the Sphinx', of vernacular and regional forms of speech – 'danged', 'sot', 'a-bust'n' – which appear in no dictionary of the time, and which correspond to no written grammatical rules (p. 56).[24]

In the chapter on Buck Fanshawe's funeral, Twain directly contrasts vernacular and genteel forms of language. The meeting between Scotty Briggs, the 'stalwart rough' with 'flaming red flannel shirt, patent leather belt with spanner and revolver attached, . . . and pants stuffed into boot tops', and the minister, 'a fragile, gentle, spirituel [*sic*] new fledgling from an Eastern theological seminary . . . unacquainted with the ways of the mines' (pp. 337–8) repeats a recurrent textual motif: the encounter of, and difference between, old-timer and tenderfoot. It does not, though, bring the usual result. Briggs and the parson (whom Briggs wants to conduct Fanshawe's funeral service) represent for Kenneth Lynn 'two utterly different conceptions of what American life should be'[25] and speak two utterly different languages. However, no one form of speech (and way of thought) triumphs here. Rather a thoroughgoing relativisation of discourse occurs as the two languages engage with one another on different, but intersecting, planes.

David Sewell describes Twain's representation of Briggs's voice as creating 'a tour de force of Western slang'.[26] Briggs's attempt at dialogue with the representative of a genteel and decorous culture is initially jammed by the difference in register of their different forms of speech. Scotty uses a predominantly 'low' discourse, informed by experiences of the gambling table, the mining camp and popular forms of entertainment. The minister, in contrast, uses the 'high' language appropriate to his religious sensibility and membership of an educated élite: one of considerable grammatical and verbal sophistication and complexity. So a sample of their interchange, starting with Scotty's words, runs as follows:

'Why you see we are in a bit of trouble, and the boys thought maybe you would give us a lift, if we'd tackle you – that is, if I've got the rights of it and you are the head clerk of the doxology-works next door.'

'I am the shepherd in charge of the flock whose fold is next door.'

'The which?'

'The spiritual adviser of the little company of believers whose sanctuary adjoins these premises.'

'You ruther hold over me, pard. I reckon I can't call that hand. Ante and pass the buck.'

'How? I beg pardon. What did I understand you to say?'

'Well, you've ruther got the bulge on me. Or maybe we've both got the bulge, somehow. You don't smoke me and I don't smoke you. You see, one of the boys has passed in his checks and we want to give him a good send-off, and so the thing I'm on now is to roust out somebody to jerk a little chin-music for us and waltz him through handsome.'

'My friend, I seem to grow more and more bewildered. Your

observations are wholly incomprehensible to me. Cannot you not simplify them in some way? At first I thought perhaps I understood you, but I grope now. Would it not expedite matters if you restricted yourself to categorical statements of fact unencumbered with obstructing accumulations of metaphor and allegory?'

Another pause, and more reflection. Then, said Scotty:

'I'll have to pass, I judge.'

'How?'

'You've raised me out, pard.'

'I still fail to catch your meaning.'

'Why, that last lead of yourn is too many for me – that's the idea. I can't neither trump nor follow suit.'

The clergyman sank back in his chair perplexed. (p. 339)

Two 'complete and separate ways of knowing the world'[27] collide here. Class, regional and experiential difference is reflected in the instability of language, as meaning fails to emerge in what Bakhtin calls 'a single intentional whole'.[28] Eventually the two men start, if only briefly, to understand each other, as the parson is able to 'translate' – an activity which itself points to the provisional nature, and competing claims, of differing idiolects – Scotty's 'kicked the bucket' as 'departed to that mysterious country from whose bourne no traveler returns', and as Scotty, still trying to make linguistic contact, answers 'why pard, he's *dead*'. The parson can then, for once in the whole episode, reply that 'Yes, I understand' (p. 340). The narrative voice seems to act as a neutral medium once the dialogue between the two men has started, thus illustrating the more effectively the 'outright impasse' that, for the most part, occurs.[29]

There is no favouring of western language and value here. A rejection of genteel forms of language is implied in the failure of its rhetorical forms and elaborate but well-worn turns of phrase adequately to connect with the facts of western life.[30] But vernacular forms of language are not thereby rendered fully admirable. Scotty Briggs asserts his liking for the minister by saying, 'I think you're white', and closes the funeral sermon with the words, 'AMEN. No Irish need apply' (p. 344). The limited register of his discourse, and its xenophobic, racist and violent aspects, prevent the reader from taking such a language (and ideology) as a preferred model.

III

Twain's attitude to his western materials, then, is complex and contradictory. He endorses a celebratory version of frontier experience – the evolutionary replacement of a worthless and depraved savagery, and the triumph of untamed and exuberant vernacular values over inherited formal and genteel cultural patterns – only also to undermine it. Moreover, the sense of buoyant adventure and emancipation repeatedly associated with the West in *Roughing It* is countered by the unmooring of the narrator: his confusion at the lack of sense to be made of his experiences there.

This confusion relates both to the dislocating paradoxes of the region and to the repeated dead-ends that mark the protagonist's experience there. These go together with, and in part explain, the sense of epistemological uncertainty in the text: the difficulty the narrator has finding his bearings in this alien western world. The West is represented as a place of illogical and conflicting detail, as the account of the outlaw Slade (a figure who fascinates the narrator) suggests. Slade is the epitome of the 'Rocky Mountain desperado' (p. 104), an 'actual ogre who, in fights and brawls and various ways, *had taken the lives of twenty-six human beings*' (p. 110). He is a man marked by his savagery, cutting the ears from one of his slaughtered enemies and carrying them 'in his vest pocket . . . with great satisfaction' (p. 110). But he is also associated with the efficiencies and rationalisations of western development. A division agent for the Overland stage company, it is his 'energetic administration [that] had restored peace and order to one of the worst divisions of the road'. In an area with 'absolutely no semblance of the law' (p. 106), Slade acts as 'supreme judge . . . jury and executioner' (p. 107), protecting the private property both of his employers and of passing emigrants. Twain, stopping at a stage post, finds himself sitting down to breakfast with Slade, whose 'quiet and affable' behaviour just cannot square with the 'raw-head-and-bloody-bones the nursing mothers of the mountains terrified their children with' (p. 110). A vigilante hanged by a vigilance committee, 'an outlaw among outlaws and yet their relentless scourge . . . at once the most bloody, the most dangerous and the most valuable citizen' (p. 103) of the area, Slade does not, for Twain, add up. As Lee Clark Mitchell puts it, 'with Slade as with so much else in the West, all that remains are conflicting accounts'.[31]

A number of critics have focused on the metaphoric qualities of the 'blind lead' episode in *Roughing It* (pp. 286–99). Thus John E. Bassett, for instance, examines the book's gaps and contradictions to argue that 'Twain provides as many false leads and missed leads as do the silver mines' themselves.[32] The narrative itself, and the life of the protagonist it describes, keep running into dead ends. They (both) then start up again up in new, but generally unsatisfactory, directions. The narrator's early occupational moves (private secretary, miner, mill operative) only raise the question of 'what to do next?' (p. 300). His stint as a journalist in Virginia City is followed by restlessness and dissatisfaction (p. 398).[33] The moves to San Francisco, to and from the Tuolomne mining camps, seem yet another series of false leads. The logic of the narrator's life, and of the narrative itself, repeatedly stalls.

One of Twain's repeated tactics as a writer, and a distinguishing mark of his humour, is the plumbing of misleading, and usually romantic, surface to reveal its illusory quality. Thus the naive narrator's 'unmarred ecstasy' at apparently discovering a gold mine is undercut by the experienced Mr Ballou, who informs him that the 'deposit of shining yellow scales' he sees is no more than 'nasty glittering mica' (pp. 222–4).[34] Such a stripping away of romantic veneer is typical of a realist aesthetic. Right from the start of Twain's career, though, the epistemological confidence conventionally associated with this aesthetic – a privileged access to the nature of the real – is denied. Though the stripping away of false surface can reveal essential truth (as in the fool's gold incident), it is as often as not a negative one; that what was thought valuable has no worth. More commonly, all such unmaskings (and other such explorations of reality) reveal is a sense of bewilderment, an awareness that our readings and constructions of the world are both partial and unsatisfactory.

This bewilderment results from the puzzling aspects both of the western materials which the narrator attempts to interpret, and of the resources available to help him. The phrase 'Three Sides to all Questions' (p. 38), which refers to Twain's chapter about the 'Mountain Meadows Massacre', suggests the impossibility of discovering any clear interpretive way through the varying accounts of the West he is given. For the increasing amount of information Twain gains about the Mormons and their activities is matched by an accompanying inability to know 'what portion of it was reliable and what was not' (p. 157). Thus one version of the story has the Indians bearing major responsibility for the massacre in question; another blames the Mormons; yet another shares responsibility between both parties. And even when the narrator finds out that the Mormons '*were* the assassins' (p. 157), this still does not allow him a unified perspective on Mormonism as a larger whole: in the first two appendices to the book – one 'essentially sympathetic' to Mormon history and achievement; the other, in its immediate focus on Mountain Meadows, not – Twain conveys 'ambiguous feelings about the Mormons, which he could not otherwise synthesize into a single characterization'.[35] He both starts and ends here stuck between conflicting versions of the truth, his excavation of it – at least in part – stalled. Again, the metaphor of the blind lead seems an appropriate one.

The sense of uncertainty and provisionality in *Roughing It* also comes from the unstable and problematic nature of the relationship between the individual figure (the narrating subject) and the ground he explores. As the narrator keeps, literally and metaphorically, losing his bearings, so the possibility of his giving any firm or authoritative reading of reality is interrogated. Any such reading, given by a subject positioned *within* the disorienting world he describes, can only be relative, provisional and unreliable. The loss of bearings acts as a repeated motif in the text, and works to self-reflexive and allegorical ends. The Overland stage loses its way in the rainy midnight gloom, 'wandering about a plain with gaping gullies in it' (p. 126), missing disaster by inches. Lost in a snowstorm, Twain and two companions circle round in their own tracks, the 'mental compass' of their leader awry, the search for a known, familiar and well-marked path frustrated by the 'white oblivion' (p. 242) all around. Such episodes take on clear figurative significance. The regular patterns of the sage bushes convey an impression of 'a distinctly defined avenue' leading 'in *any* direction that you proceeded' (p. 243). This means that, once the snow has fallen and the men, individually, attempt to find 'proof' that they are on the right track (the road that leads to safety), the regularity of the landscape convinces each 'that *he* had found the true road, and that the others had found only false ones' (p. 244). Knowledge is relative and unreliable here, a product of the relationship between the individual subject and the reading he constructs of the confusing reality around him, with no guarantee of truth or coherence available.

Relativistic uncertainty about the position of the subject, as he attempts to negotiate a confusing and pathless (or many-pathed) ground, is resolved comically here. The three men renounce their vices, respectively throw away whisky bottle, playing cards and pipe, to accept the inevitability of freezing to death. They wake the next morning, though, to find themselves safe beside a stage station, shamefacedly seek out their discarded possessions, and abandon their various reforms. The 'painfully ridiculous and humiliating' nature of all this is acknowledged, but it is the clownish aspect of the men's behaviour that is foregrounded. Thus Ballou openly acknowledges his foolishness by saying, 'Will some gentleman be so good as to kick me behind?' (p. 249). A parable of epistemological uncertainty – and of the self-deluding attempts of the human subject to understand his own motivations, to respond rationally to surrounding events, and to control in any but the most minimal way the patterns of those events – has, accordingly, its most serious implications deflected in the move to farce that occurs.[36]

But any such deflection can only be temporary, for the incident fits, too, in the larger context of the narrative's overall pattern. Twain's protagonist is continually, literally and metaphorically, losing his way, but the fundamental structure of *Roughing It* remains fixed: that of the continuing journey West, and the sense of adventure and possibility associated with it. This is the path repeatedly recovered. In the last analysis, though, the whole shape and point of this underlying process is put in doubt. Twain replays his earlier representation of the westward move in the Sandwich Isles section of the book. Critics have tended to dismiss this whole late sequence as 'detachable',[37] but to do so is to miss the underlying thematic unity of the text.[38]

If Hawaii is the last stage of the westward move of the protagonist, the utopian connotations of the journey – the promise of freedom and rebirth – continue to be presented in a highly ambivalent way. When (earlier) the narrator first heads West, he finds 'happiness' (p. 161), and then, in Nevada, an emotion close to 'unmarred ecstasy' (p. 221) as his fortune seems to beckon. San Francisco is then, though, described as 'Paradise' in contrast to the Washoe alkali deserts and sage brush (p. 418).[39] But Honolulu, in its turn, has 'a Summer calm as tranquil as dawn in the Garden of

Eden', and is explicitly contrasted with San Francisco's 'noisy confusion' (p. 454). This last dreamy climax is then, itself, immediately interrupted by a scorpion bite. Before this happens, and completely unexpectedly, the narrator has praised the rich and varied *eastern* American landscape, when compared to California, as 'a vision of Paradise itself' (p. 408). The utopian quest, in other words, is continually displaced and decentred. Twain ends up, in at least one stage of his narrative, desiring the place he first left. The westward movement which structures the whole book turns out itself to be something of a blind lead.

IV

Twain starts *Roughing It* by 'tapping into and . . . extending the myth of the West'.[40] But the independence, and the move back into nature and beyond civilising restraints, associated with that myth prove half-truths at best. I have focused until now on the contradictory aspects of Twain's representation of the West as he both acknowledges the distinctive qualities of the region, but undermines any unified or simple (mythic) reading of it. I have shown, too, the interpretative indeterminacy that confronts the narrator as he tries to make sense of this western world. But there is a different, and contrasting, strand to Twain's book – a clear sense of history, unmuddied by any sense of interpretive disablement – in the story of American capitalist development it tells. This story both threatens to displace the (alternative) stress on the conflicting aspects of the West, and to collapse the contrast between regions on which the book is structured. The full implications of this element in the text, and its uneasy relation to the material around it, however, go relatively unexplored, and are developed in an inconsistent way. It may be, indeed, that Twain was not aware, or only half-aware, of them.

Alan Trachtenberg shows the effect that 'the script of industrial progress' was to have on America in the post Civil-War period, saying that:

the logic of events in the 1870's and 1880's disclosed . . . not an agrarian but an industrial capitalist scenario. Penetrating the West with government encouragement, the railroad and the telegraph opened the vast spaces to production. Following the lead of the railroads, commercial and industrial businesses conceived of themselves as having the entire national space at their disposal: from raw materials for processing to goods for marketing.[41]

Twain, writing in the 1870s, is aware of the shift in temporal–spatial coordinates that modernisation (here taking the shape of railroad penetration of the West) has brought. The three hundred mile journey from Omaha to the North Platte crossing, he reports, now takes just fifteen hours and forty minutes, in luxurious circumstances. Thus the time of the overland coach journey – the only practical mode of travel available to the protagonist of *Roughing It* – is cut by almost two complete days (pp. 73–4). But other references, to the laying of the telegraph for example (p. 135), illustrate that the type of incorporation Trachtenberg describes was already well under way in the 1860s too.[42] No space exists beyond business and the marketplace in the West that Twain describes.

It is this underlying historical process – toward advanced capitalism[43] – which silently undermines, but at the same time explains, many of the contradictions in the West that Twain represents in *Roughing It*. Howard Horwitz's analysis of *Life on the Mississippi* (1883) deconstructs the opposition Twain established between the romantic independence of riverboat piloting and the institutional hierarchies and economic constraints of a developing corporate system. Horwitz comments, revealingly, that what ended with the Civil War was not, as Twain suggested, the glory days of steamboating. Its decline had in fact started earlier with the growth of the railroads. Rather, what had died was 'in fact, only the mythological independent self, a notion already an exercise in nostalgia in the 1850s'.[44] This is entirely relevant to *Roughing It*. For Twain's romantic celebration of individual autonomy and of the majesty of an untamed nature, both synonymous with the mythic idea of the West, exists in uneasy and contradictory relation with the historical awareness that the region is already no separate space, and that the idea of independent selfhood is fast under erasure. In the 1860s, the practices of industrial capitalism were already and inevitably, as Twain's book reveals, part and parcel of westward expansionism.

Thus the idea of individual retreat from the complexities of civilisation toward a pure space of nature (a standard part of the western myth) is replayed in Twain's book, but also interrogated, in the ambiguities of his representations of Lake Tahoe. Twain's admiration for the lake's beauty was often repeated, both in his books and in his private correspondence. He speaks of it in the language of regressive wonder, stressing its distance from the world of men and action. Tahoe becomes variously 'the Fountain of Youth' and the 'beautiful relic of fairy-land forgotten and left asleep in the snowy Sierras when the little elves fled from their ancient haunts and quitted the earth'.[45] In *Roughing It*, Twain and his companion breathe the air 'angels breathe' (p. 188) at Tahoe. In a landscape subject to 'Nature's mood' (p. 191) and away from all other human presence, their main 'business' is 'drifting around in the boat', enjoying 'the luxurious rest and indolence' (p. 192) found there.

The conversion of the language of the work ethic to playful ends, and the idyllic mood and Edenic aspects of the scene, however, cannot hide the fact that no pure retreat from culture into nature exists.[46] The interrelated quality of these terms is suggested as Twain moves from the Carson City world to this apparently untainted space, only immediately and destructively to affect it. The ordinary domestic routine with which man announces his presence (lighting a fire to cook) brings 'devastation' as the dry lakeside mountain is transformed into 'a tossing, blinding tempest of flame' (p. 194).[47]

The impossibility of separating out wilderness world from historical event (in the form of commercial enterprise) has been solidly established earlier in the sequence. For Twain has other 'business' here, and now the word is used in its normative sense. He wants to become a 'land-owner' (p. 190), to fence in the wilderness, establish a timber ranch, and 'become wealthy' (p. 187).[48] The hum of similar enterprise is already evident even as the two men enter what appears to be this natural paradise, with the sawmill and workmen only three miles away (p. 188). Twain's references, following the forest fire, to the fact that he and his companion carried 'no insurance' (p. 195), and to the 'payment of damages' (p. 196) for their raid on the provisions of others, reinforces the fact that there is no move available here beyond the market; beyond the institutional matrices and contractual codes of (national) business practice.

Ideas of autonomy, emancipation and unspoiled nature are, then, in paradoxical relationship here to capitalist processes and assumptions. That the latter, in historical fact, provide the dominant ongoing narrative of the West is clear in *The Big Bonanza* (1876), the story of the Comstock Load written by Dan de Quille (William Wright), Twain's colleague on the Virginia City *Territorial Enterprise*. Just fourteen years after Twain's first trip to Tahoe and four years after his writing of *Roughing It*, De Quille would report how the mining industry, with its incessant need for timber, had made Tahoe a primary resource for its industrial needs and, in doing so, had wrought considerable environmental damage:

> The Comstock lode may truthfully be said to be the tomb of the forests of the Sierras. Millions on millions of feet of lumber are annually buried in the mines. . . . For a distance of fifty or sixty miles all the hills of the eastern slope of the Sierras have been to a great extent denuded of trees of every kind . . . Yerington, Bliss, & Co., one of the heaviest lumbering firms in the Sierra Nevada Mountains, have built a narrow-gauge railroad from their sawmills on the shore of Lake Tahoe. . . . Logs are rafted across Lake Tahoe to the mills from all points . . . This is all very well for the company . . . but it is going to make sad work, ere long, of the picturesque hills surrounding Lake Tahoe . . . But timber and lumber are imperatively demanded.[49]

Twain's own entry to Tahoe's lakeside paradise was part and parcel of its swift commercial development and despoilation. Natural resources, on the mining frontier, were subject to the 'imperative demands' of an emergent capitalist economy, and seen in 'business' terms from the moment of the mines' first discovery.

Twain's narrative again moves in several and contradictory ways in his descriptions of his Nevada experiences. The hum of commercial enterprise provides the continuing background noise against which a more romantic story of the West (of uniqueness, adventure and individualism) is told.[50] It is this noise, too, which is in the process of rendering that latter story defunct. Twain's realisation of the impact of economics on western history does not mean that he abandons an (alternative) representation of the region based on individualism, freedom, male camaraderie and the possibility of fresh starts. But the stress on money-making in the book undermines the notion of any escape from what Banta calls 'late capitalist procedures'.[51] If the unresolved contrasts of Twain's narrative are a sign of his own ambiguous attitudes and responses to such issues, they could only, historically, be resolved in one way.

The Tahoe trip, then, describes incompatible activities, for the retreat to nature is, at the same time, the beginning of a commercial enterprise. So, too, do analogous contradictions appear in Twain's other descriptions of the silver- and gold-rush West. Thus mining is associated, in its earlier Californian gold-rush phase, with:

> a driving, vigorous, restless population . . . stalwart, muscular, dauntless young braves . . . royally endowed with every attribute that goes up to make a peerless and magnificent manhood . . . – none but erect, bright-eyed, quick-moving, strong-handed young giants. . . . It was a wild, free, disorderly, grotesque society!
>
> (pp. 414–15)

The move into a new western community is defined here by its freedom of opportunity and assertive, even anarchic, individualism (images recurrently endorsed by Twain in his text, not just in this nostalgic note). Again, though, the history of mining, at least in the period when Twain was in the West, tells an increasingly different story. In actuality, and as Twain sporadically suggests, East and West, metropolis and frontier, were symbiotically bound together. Nevada mining practices, in Twain's account of them, come almost to parody the speculative enterprises of the wider commercial market and of the commodities exchanges (developing rapidly in the post-Civil War years).[52] The type of futures trading he describes – the salting of mines, the shady assaying practices, the feverish buying and exchange of stock – mirrors the activity in the nation's financial capitals. Walter Benn Michaels describes the 'fictitious dealings' of the commodities markets in terms that fit Twain's mining context equally well: 'the mechanism of the futures contract was simple: it allowed the producer of a commodity to sell the commodity on an exchange for future delivery; it allowed him, in other words, to sell a product that he did not yet have'.[53]

East and West, city and country, in other words, could not in economic terms be separated in an incorporated age. The opening and exploitation of the Comstock Lode 'gave renewed impetus to the growth of San Francisco as a financial and industrial center, stimulated the development of new mining and metallurgical technologies, and elevated mining into the company of America's biggest businesses'.[54] Twain refers in *Roughing It* to the 'energetic San Francisco capitalists' who run the Sheba mine (p. 213), and to the 'New York capital' enlisted for further mining development (p. 424). As the silver rush continued, the Nevada mines were increasingly controlled by 'capitalists in San Francisco, Portland and the East'.[55]

Mining in Nevada was, in Earl Pomeroy's words, 'unmistakeably an industry rather than a treasure hunt', with the miners coming 'less as refugees from advancing urbanism than as its exponents'.[56] Twain's dream of 'pick[ing] up . . . nuggets of gold and silver on the hill-side' (p. 49) bore little relation to actual mining conditions, with the complicated technology and considerable finance needed to reach, refine and process the majority of the ore. Some fortunes were made, and the 'blind lead' incident Twain reports (when 'I was absolutely and unquestionably worth a million dollars . . . for ten days' – p. 299) did evidently have its basis in truth.[57] For the most part, though, the hierarchies of labour and capital in Nevada mining reflected those elsewhere. The description of Virginia City and the other 'busy city under it, down in the bowels of the earth', with the superintendents above ground conveying orders by signal bells to the population working in the 'dismal drifts and tunnels' beneath (pp. 380–1), reads like an allegory of relationships between management and production in the broader industrial economy. Twain's account of his own 'dreary and laborious' (p. 262) work in the quartz mill, and its 'exceeding hardness' (p. 267) is another reminder that 'on the Comstock Lode free-lance prospectors disappeared quickly and were replaced by thousands of wage laborers employed by corporations with headquarters in San Francisco and New York'.[58]

As Twain, then, describes the difference between the East and 'the curious new world' (p. 49) of the West, and illustrates the specific regional traits of the latter (its geography, its social forms, its humour), so at the same time the reader comes to realise that the two regions are impenetrably connected: that western difference can only remain an eccentric or marginal exception to dominant national business practice, and cannot be described outside its parameters. Twain travels to a West associated with manly independence and freedom, and such notions are not altogether disappointed. But he also finds himself working (however briefly) as a wage slave in a mining industry which itself underpins the monetary base on which the national economy rests. And it is this part of the present that points the way to the American future.

Twain's remark, concerning difficulties in establishing the new Territorial government in Carson City, that 'greenbacks had gone down to forty cents on the dollar' (p. 206), and the statement that 'paper money has never come into use on the Pacific coast' (p. 313), act as a reminder of the importance of gold and silver (until the latter's demonetarisation in 1871) to the entire American financial system at the time. The belief in the 'intrinsic' value of money, and the corresponding distrust of 'paper money' (greenbacks) then prevalent, are evident in Twain's words. Confidence in the gold and silver standard, and the corresponding trust in the 'natural' value of such metals (that the face value of the coin was equal to its actual and 'universal purchasing power'), meant accordingly that the more such metal in circulation, the more wealthy the nation.[59] The workings of the Nevada mines and the financial health of the nation were thus, for many of Twain's contemporaries, directly linked. Again, Twain writes his way into the West, only to reveal (in however partial a manner) that he has written himself back into the economic and social complexities that his younger self had thought to escape. For the West is already incorporated, or fast becoming incorporated, part and parcel of an emergent capitalist nation

V

Roughing It ends with Twain's return from the Sandwich Isles, where he found the same contradictions and unresolved contrasts he discovered elsewhere in the West. When he gets back to California, it is to start his career as a successful comic lecturer. In terms of its account of the narrator's changes of profession, this is how the book ends. Lecturing, here, can be taken as a symbolic displacement for writing. Despite their difference, both activities mark Twain's own recognition, as a businessman *and* artist, of the way that the multiplicities, comedies and contradictions of his own western experience could be reshaped artistically and used to entertain a wider audience.[60] Twain's first lecture was first given in San Francisco, but soon he would be lecturing countrywide. And it is clear that his written text, *Roughing It*, was directed to a national audience from the first.[61]

The importance and centrality of this national market is a theme of *Roughing It*, but it is also what motivated Twain as he wrote. He used the flexible formal structure of the travel narrative (which paralleled the baggy quality of his lectures) successfully to contain all the various and inconclusive aspects of his western subject matter. From one point of view, *Roughing It* seems little more than a bricolage. Its episodic structure is predicated on the basis of the repeated dead end rather than that of evolutionary growth and gradual education. It represents the experience of the West as a loose rag-bag of different materials, filtered through a variety of tones,[62] which continually escape the confines of a single narrative position or perspective. But, from another angle, what Twain does here is to mine literary gold from such heterogeneity.

Lee Clark Mitchell points out the analogy between Twain's description of 'pocket mining' (the sporadic discovery of small nests of gold), and his techniques in *Roughing It*, similarly scattering 'tall tales and humorous anecdotes . . . amid long stretches of dull facts and boring details extracted from scholarly sources'.[63] Twain represents the random and paradoxical qualities of western experience, accepts the wandering and diverse quality of his text as apposite to such material, and gives his America readers gold (as well as garners it) in the clusters of jokes, descriptions and comic stories he tells. As a businessman as well as an artist, he makes his own success out of the contrasts, blind leads, misdirected dreams and failed enterprises that he describes.

4

Tom Sawyer and American Cultural Life: Anxieties and Accommodations

What's the politically correct term for whitewash?
(*Time* review of *Panther*)[1]

I

It seems, in retrospect, no coincidence that *The Adventures of Tom Sawyer* was published in 1876, the year the United States celebrated the centennial of its nationhood. For the book 'lays claim to being America's most popular novel', and its title character has the status of a 'national icon'[2] – pictured (along with whitewashed fence) on bicentennial stamps, recalled in Disneyland at Tom Sawyer's Island,[3] the repeated subject of films, musicals and other representations. If Tom Sawyer occupies 'the perfect place . . . in our national literature and consciousness',[4] the boy cannot be divorced from his background. For Twain's book has come to stand for a wider 'glorification of life in small-town America',[5] an expression of longing for an earlier time and a simpler society, when the tensions that marked Twain's own period, and – in more extreme form – our own, did not exist. 'Twain', in Louis J. Budd's words, 'charms millions as the magic flutist of nostalgia for childhood in a simpler, nicer time'.[6]

Such forms of cultural nostalgia generally cover over the fact that authenticity, wholeness, innocence and security retreat endlessly before the search for them. Twain knew this, and, as Cynthia Griffin Wolff points out in referring to the 'darker side' of the novel (the 'ominous air of violence' that suffuses it), 'every one of [the] sentimental evocations' of *Tom Sawyer* as 'exuding the security of childhood-as-it-ought-to-be in small-town America . . . is false to the original'.[7] Twain's reconstruction of community life in a Missouri riverbank town of the 1830s or 1840s ('thirty or forty years ago'[8]) is not the simple exercise in antimodernism for which it is so often taken. Rather, the ambiguities and contradictions of the book reveal cultural tensions both of the time of the novel's setting and of its writing.

Tom Sawyer relates both to Twain's American present and its past. It was just one of a spate of 'boy books' written in the period between the end of the Civil War and the early twentieth century, but set in the ante-bellum period. The long period of the genre's popularity testifies, for Marcia Jacobson, 'to the fact that it spoke to persistent and apparently insoluble needs on the part of Americans' in a period of 'massive, disruptive social change'. Jacobson sees the boy book as offering a 'vicarious escape from . . . the culture that produced it'.[9] The vicarious escape offered by Twain's novel, however, is not into a world which differs completely from that of the 1870s. Undoubtedly the social patterns, forms of economic activity and institutional frameworks represented in his fictional St Petersburg are simpler, and allow room for the type of individual freedom of action and movement that would later disappear. The nostalgic quality of the book stems in part from this. But though modernisation increased remarkably in speed and intensity in the post-bellum period, what occurred was a series of developments *within* an existing process, and no sudden transformation. The social critique in *Tom Sawyer* is directed not just at Gilded Age America but at the conditions of Jacksonian America too. The escape that it offers has more to do with the *boy* than the place: one who functions at the margins of the normal social rules and constraints, and who is associated with charisma, heroic individualism and the spirit of play.

But the forms of escape associated with Tom are always, in turn, compromised by pressures toward cultural conformity. There is a peculiar double movement to Twain's text that has already been prefigured in *Roughing It*, and on which I focus in this chapter.

Tom Sawyer is both a rebellious *and* a socially respectable, even representative, figure. He is given the authority and agency of the free individual *and* made subject to the pressures of a determining environment. Twain both resists and accepts the historical logic of American capitalism; of American cultural life. His novel reveals anxieties about the direction and development of that culture, and the tensions it contains, but also acts to suppress them – acts, to paraphrase Jacobson, to further its dominant ends.[10] In the matter of race relations, in particular, Twain whitewashes the uncomfortable socio-historical facts of American life to massage (however unconsciously) the sensibilities of his audience. The reasons for the novel's enduring popularity may lie not just in its nostalgic appeal, but in its very ambiguities and paradoxes: the way it both resists and accommodates itself to changing American social and economic patterns.[11] It is this double process I examine here.

Ante-bellum St Petersburg is the fictional equivalent of Hannibal, Missouri,[12] the small town on the Mississippi where Twain spent most of his childhood. The reasons for Twain's turn to fiction, and to the time and region that was to serve as the subject matter for some of his best known and most accomplished writing – *Life on the Mississippi*, *The Adventures of Huckleberry Finn* and *Puddn'head Wilson* all return to this setting – must remain a matter for speculation.[13] One explanation, though, might be found in the influence and impact of the other boy books appearing at the time, and especially Thomas Bailey Aldrich's *The Story of a Bad Boy* (1869). For it was his reading of the latter which, according to Alan Gribben, 'apparently prompted Mark Twain to value at last the wealth of literary materials lying unclaimed in the recollections of prewar Hannibal'. Such influence may also have prompted the change in narrative mode from the earlier travel books. *Tom Sawyer* (and particularly its early stages) shares the same flexible move between autobiography and fiction of those prior narratives. But its fictional form and reliance on an omniscient and retrospective narrative voice may have been triggered both by the reading Twain was doing and the stimulus to his own memory it spurred.[14]

Twain's turn to the novel, however, did not bring taut formal unity with it. For here, too, Twain contains his various materials only loosely. The developing narrative of Tom's boyhood life, which gives its own shape to the narrative, proceeds far from consistently.[15] Twain's use of satire, burlesque and sentimentality often run in uneasy relationship to one another.[16] There is a logic to the book's ending, shaped both by the melodramic plot of Tom, 'Injun Joe' and the buried treasure, and the success narrative it climaxes. Twain's formal unease is, though, even then textually overt: 'So endeth this chronicle. . . . When one writes . . . of juveniles, he must stop where he best can' (p. 221). I do not concentrate on literary structure in this chapter. It is worth noting in the light of my later argument, however, that Twain is here able to contain the various thematic tensions and ambiguities of his book within the one formal frame. The cultural anxieties he traces are always kept in textual check: apparent here, but balanced by the social accommodations made; partly covered over by the use of conventions of mystery, adventure and romance (formulating Tom's financial and community success within these generic bounds); and disguised in the return to an apparently unproblematic boyhood world. As Twain's writing career progressed, his doubts both about the status of the individual and the direction of the society in which he or she lived increased. So, accordingly, did his problems in containing conflicting themes within a unified narrative form. The developing story of my book lies, in part, in the tracing of these doubts and problems.

II

The moves between boyhood and adulthood, and between a pre- and post-Civil War world, which *Tom Sawyer* makes, and the complex and ambiguous attitude to the developing patterns of American cultural life the novel reveals, are the immediate focus of my analysis. I begin with the whitewashing episode, for if there is one scene that most readers remember from the book, and which has gathered considerable iconographic significance, it is this. The whitewashed fence was illustrated by True Williams in the first edition as having four horizontal boards with equally wide gaps between, supported by well spaced-out vertical posts of approxi- mately Tom's shoulder height. That fence has come, nostalgically, to signify the securities and clean orderliness of small-town America, even despite the problematic nature of Twain's representation of that locale. We are, though, immediately aware of boundaries being staked out here (and the boundary metaphor is a repeated one in the novel). Wayne Fields puts it rather nicely:

[Tom Sawyer's] nightly forays and adventures depend upon the St Petersburg fences. In climbing over them, as he presumes to leave the commonplace behind and imagines himself escaping all the constraints of authority while playing at the lawlessness of pirate and outlaw, the fences serve as tangible – though ironic – evidence that he has 'gotten away,' crossed some significant boundary, in a necessary prerequisite for adventure. But just as important is the return in which the enclosures [of orderliness, parental and civil authority], no longer cause for claustrophobia, provide respite and security. Without fences there would be no appropriate barriers over which adventurous boys could crawl. Without fences there would be no safe retreats when the adventure is over or when it threatens to become too real.[17]

Williams's depiction of the fence (repeated in similar form in other representations of the scene) departs considerably from Twain's original description. The fence is not nearly as easy to cross as the illustration suggests. The barrier between what is kept in and kept out is a significant 'thirty yards of broad fence nine feet high' (p. 15). In Neil Schmitz's words, 'the fence, after all, is a brutal affair, almost a wall, so long and so high you can't see over it or around it'.[18]

The conventional (*OED*) definition of 'whitewash' in the context used here is of a 'solution of . . . whiting and size for brushing over walls . . . etc., to give clean appearance'. But it can also mean 'to cover up, conceal, or gloss over the faults and blemishes of'. It is easy for the reader to gloss over Tom's faults and blemishes, the ambiguities in his presentation, in this scene. For the initial motive behind his actions is undoubtedly attractive, as he looks for spontaneity, play and 'pure freedom' (p. 16) rather than 'the misery of profitless convict labor, the end of which is a vast thirty yards distant'.[19] Tom is identified with the play principle, as he is so often throughout the novel,[20] always seen yearning for 'seductive outside summer scenes' (p. 37) rather than domestic or institutional confinement. Here, he is already outside, but the idea of seduction has been cancelled out, his 'captivity at hard labor' (p. 14) a result of Aunt Polly's domestic disciplines (he is being punished for playing 'hookey,' p. 8). Cardiff Hill, 'a Delectable Land, dreamy, reposeful and inviting' (p. 15), lies close to the village boundaries, but the invitation is closed to Tom. 'When all the boys is having holiday' (p. 8)[21] and 'skylarking' (p. 15), he is tied to his set work, and work is something 'he hates . . . more than he hates anything else' (p. 8).

The reader is encouraged to empathise with Tom and his commitment to childhood play. He manages his escape ('Mayn't I go and play now, Aunt?' – p. 20), is 'over the fence and gone' beyond the reach of 'capture and punishment' (p. 21), through his own imaginative ability to convert work to play for his fellow boys. The fence metaphorically separates the arena of social discipline from that of adventure and romance. Thus a make-believe battle, and then the first sight of Becky Thatcher, follows Tom's move beyond his aunt's domestic enclosure. Tom, at the spatial point where these two sets of values intersect, manages to fudge their difference. For though Ben Rogers and the other boys 'fagged themselves out' as they 'worked and sweated in the sun' (p. 19), Tom has succeeded in transforming their perception of this activity, in whitewashing hard labour into apparent play. As the narrator comments, naming the principle that Tom exploits, 'work consists of whatever a body is obliged to do, and . . . play consists of whatever a body is not obliged to do' (pp. 19–20).

Before commenting further on Tom's role here, I focus on the opposition between work and play which is constructed; one already, in fact, partially undone by the verbs used to describe the boys' activity as they paint. Play, in other words, is highly contaminated by work here. The relation between these two terms, and the way it was culturally understood at the time of Twain's writing, can be analysed to show both the impact of modern disciplinary practices[22] (with leisure and playfulness rationed out according to the primary needs of a workplace world) and, further, to illustrate how Tom Sawyer himself – contrary to initial impressions – is deeply implicated in the capitalist system he would seem to reject.

This is complicated material, and I proceed slowly. At the time Twain wrote *Tom Sawyer*, the cultural perception of the relation between play and work (like that between the savage and the civilised) was rooted in the idea of a child–man divide. This perception was, indeed, already becoming established in the pre-war period of the novel's setting. Michael Oriard looks back to 1830s America to see the start of a pattern that became more evident as the Industrial Revolution advanced: the 'uncomfortable awareness that perhaps leisure, not labor, offered the best possibilities for human fulfilment'. He shows how the play impulse was harnessed to the new industrial order as the nineteenth century progressed. Recognising the 'labor/leisure dualism at the heart of industrial capitalism', and its corollary, that 'play embodied a countercultural desire for work-oriented men' in Gilded Age America, Oriard shows how the boy (and girl) book provided a way of containing and disguising such tensions.[23] These books helped to smooth over the divide between labour and leisure in their celebration of 'work and play as two halves of the ideal life', with childhood represented as 'the time for play'. This allowed for the creation of a series of 'idealized figures on whom middle-class America projected its desires and fantasies, but without jeopardising its ultimate commitment to work'.[24]

Twain's book, however, complicates this pattern. For *Tom Sawyer* never quite works as the story of a merely playful boy. Rather, Twain implicates Tom in the business ethic from which childhood, supposedly, provided an alternative and escape. The partial unravelling of the work–play opposition in the whitewashing scene, as the play of childhood overlaps with work, points to the ambiguities in Tom's representation in the novel. He is associated both with 'boyhood's free spirit'[25] and with proto-capitalist attitudes and practices.[26] He is nostalgically linked throughout the novel with adventure, imagination and the escape from the responsible adult world, but also depicted as an entrepreneur, an emergent businessman, finally rewarded by the status, praise and fortune which symbolise complete social acceptance and success. The peculiar double effects here do not add up. The gap between labour and leisure differs from the model Oriard suggests,[27] for Tom is simultaneously both playful boy and apprentice businessman. Twain appears, moreover, to criticise capitalist attitudes and values in his description of the methods Tom uses to achieve his profitable ends, and his suggestion of what is being sacrificed in the process. But if ambivalences appear here about the values associated with the world of labour which are, in the boy book, normally covered over, Twain has his own way of (partially) disguising them. The criticism of business values remains implicit rather than overt;

suppressed, to considerable degree, by the *confusion* of work and play, by the nostalgic tone of the book, and by Tom's central, and often heroic, role in the success story it enacts. To start to unpack the contradictions in Tom's representation and the divisions in his performance is, though, to suggest the cultural tensions it masks. A strong note of ambiguity concerning his activities runs right the way through the novel.

Tom's first fortune results from his whitewashing scam, which leaves him 'literally rolling in wealth' (p. 19). If to whitewash is to 'cover up and conceal', Tom conceals rather a lot in the victory he wins at the expense both of Aunt Polly and his friends. Later, when Becky is threatened with punishment following her accidental tearing of the schoolteacher's *Anatomy* book, Tom says that 'girls' faces always tell on them' (p. 132). Here, he disguises his intentions behind a false face, 'took up his brush and went tranquilly to work' (p. 16) once he decides on his plan to whitewash his friends; to con them out of their possessions. For Jesse Bier is not alone in seeing Tom as a 'con man'.[28] Tom tricks his friends into doing his work for him, and relieves them of their wealth, whatever its form ('twelve marbles . . . a tin soldier . . . a kitten with only one eye' – p. 19) into the bargain. Unearned increment is too modest a term to describe the capital Tom accumulates out of nothing but Aunt Polly's raw materials and his wits alone.

In *Confidence Men and Painted Women: A Study of Middle-class Culture in America, 1830–1870*, Karen Halttunen identifies the figure of the confidence man as standing at 'the center of anxieties that advice manuals expressed about American youth' in the period. These anxieties focused on the move, on the part of young men in particular, 'far beyond the surveillance of their families, their towns, and their churches' as they responded to ante-bellum social change and sought work 'in the booming cities of industrializing America'. The confidence man, she continues, became a figure representing all that was threatening in 'the growing confusion and anonymity of urban living'. Charisma was likely to replace established social authority in such conditions, and 'fluid self-aggrandisement' easily resulted from the hypocrisy and duplicity – beneath the mask of perfect sincerity – of such trickster figures.[29]

This fearful scenario was already becoming established in the Jacksonian period about which Twain wrote. In one very obvious sense, however, Tom Sawyer cannot be associated with such anxieties, firmly bound as he is to the relatively self-contained small-town world of St Petersburg (referred to variously as both town and village). One might, however, see here both a hint of the fears of that period, and an anxiety about the types of changes (and the figures who would symbolise them) altering America, both before and after the Civil War.[30] For the processes of social trans-formation in the period were continuous ones. Twain represents Tom not only as a proto-capitalist but as a confidence man into the bargain. In doing so he taps into anxieties not only about business values but about social status too: anxieties first apparent in Jacksonian times but present in more persistent and stronger form in Gilded Age America.[31]

Tom Sawyer is a junior version of the confidence man or 'man of confidence', the 'man-on-the make' adept at 'manipulating surface impressions for selfish gain'. His 'highly theatrical attention to the presentation of self' is, by and large, extremely effective in this village society and prefigures forms of behaviour that would flourish in a rapidly changing Jacksonian (and post-Jacksonian) America, when 'everything [was] up for grabs: wealth and status to be won by enterprise not birth, an entire social order to be decided by wit and opportunism'.[32] Tom consistently turns traditional forms of social power upside down. He directs the pirate play world on Jackson's Island beyond the scan of family authority. He disrupts the rituals of both church and school. These 'rebellions' are, though, ultimately safely contained within the fabric of ongoing village life, and the sentimental frame of the boy book which represents it.

But there are signs of a more fundamental change in the social order here, too. Tom is associated, as these occur, not with a childhood disruption of established authority, but with the establish-ment of new patterns of social authority and success. Here, in other words (and in contrast to his former role), he actually represents the dominant values of an emergent capitalist culture. The tensions within the book are clear as such a representation clashes with Tom's position as a figure of anti-modernist wish-fulfilment: the playful child who cannot be pinned down by society's fixed routines and disciplines, and who can temporarily escape its authority adventuring on Jackson's Island or Cardiff Hill.

Tom can certainly be read in terms of an emerging enterprise culture. In *Tom Sawyer: A Play* (commenced in 1875–6, finished in 1883–4), Tom's business acumen in the whitewash scene becomes even more obvious, as he tells the other boys, 'Come, pay in *advance*! We don't *trust*, here. Pay up, pay up before you *begin*.'[33] A confidence man who has no confidence in others, Tom trades his way to the prizes available in St Petersburg by duplicitous means.[34] 'A wily fraud', Tom none the less has 'the certified checks' to gain possession of the forty-cent Bible at Sunday school: the tickets that vouch for the 'industry and . . . application' (p. 30) needed to memorise two thousand of its verses. These checks, too, are 'good for their face' (p. 34), despite the lack of knowledge, on Tom's part, normally expected to underwrite them.

Such forms of language repeatedly suggest the connection between Tom's dealings and the financial market. Worldly wealth, security and profitable exchange certainly consume Tom's interest. Almost straightaway, in the sequence when he sees Huck's captured tick, Tom will ask, 'What'll you take for him?' (p. 49). And while Huck plans to spend his share of any discovered treasure on 'a pie and a glass of soda every day, and [a trip] to every circus that comes along', Tom, as his dialogue with Huck indicates, has more serious things in mind:

'Well, ain't you going to save any of it?'
'Save it? What for?'
'Why, so as to have something to live on by-and-by.' (p. 155)

When Indian Joe discovers the buried fortune in the haunted house, Tom's response is to 'Find him! Track the money!' (p. 169) and plan to 'snatch that box' (p. 173) containing it. This, one might argue, would constitute theft, as opposed to Indian Joe's act of legitimate discovery. When the boys do eventually get the treasure, any attention to their ethical position conveniently dissipates due to Joe's prior death. But this death is a direct result, however unintentional, of Tom's actions: all that leads to the boy's entombment in the cave; and its sealing following his escape.

The use of the resurrection motif is recurrent in *Tom Sawyer*. It commences with two 'resurrectionists' (for so nineteenth-century grave-robbers were known) raising the dead for medical purposes. It concludes with Tom and Becky's return to the daylight world, and to the community, after three days and nights buried in the cave. Joe, the socially terrifying figure whose initial transgression of Christian ritual started this cycle, ends symbolically buried in place of the children. There is a peculiar twinning between Joe and Tom here,[35] and one that again partly works to suggest something rather dubious about Tom's financial activities. Scott Michaelsen, in fact, notes Tom's linked association with both robber and entrepreneur as conforming to a standard trope in the representation of the capitalist in Gilded Age literature.[36]

As *Tom Sawyer* ends, Tom's money is out 'at six-per-cent' and his income is 'prodigious' (p. 216). He is, then, certainly shown as, in some degree, an apprentice version of the 'man-on-the-make' whose charisma, enterprise and eye for the main chance together bring him success. This script addresses (in however veiled a manner) anxieties about social and economic change in the Jacksonian period about which Twain was writing, but also in Gilded Age America too. The social order Twain describes in the novel is one in transition, with (or so it is implied) the introduction of new patterns of wealth based on enterprise[37] rather than birth. The final sequences of *Tom Sawyer* indicate a dramatic change in social and status hierarchies that complements Tom and Huck's new wealth: the two boys earn as much hard cash, in interest on their money, as the minister gets in a good week, and their twelve thousand dollars 'was more than anyone present [at its counting] had ever seen at one time before, though several persons were there who were worth considerable more than that in property' (p. 216). New ways of measuring wealth, and of determining social hierarchy and authority, are readily apparent here.

This, though, is a lop-sided reading of the novel. Undoubtedly anxieties about money, class and social change, and their effect (both before and after the Civil War) on American culture are evident in *Tom Sawyer*. But it is easy to read the book, as I did at the start of this section, as about childhood skylarking and adventure, and the escape from the adult world of responsibility and business success, rather than seeing the representation of Tom as a site for social critique. Indeed, to recognise Tom's business side is not necessarily to see Twain as attacking capitalist values; for his enterprise and material gain, both legitimised by the traditional American success ethos, are expected components of the popular genres (adventure and romance) on which Twain relies. Moreover, though the narrating voice might at times adopt a tone open to ironic interpretation in describing the way Tom accrues wealth, and his accompanying actions, it would be difficult to read the novel (and especially its final sequences) consistently in terms of such a deliberate intent. If the boy book genre generally recalled past cultural vitality and authenticity,[38] then it is Tom's opposition to the 'frowsy hum of study' (p. 50) in the schoolplace, his subversion of day-to-day institutional and social rituals, and his imaginative efforts to escape these boundaries into a world of heroic individualism and romantic adventure which undoubtedly helped (and helps) to account for *Tom Sawyer's* success. In other words, and again, cultural tensions are both revealed and masked here. Tom is shown both as boy businessman (the child as father of the man) and as romantic rebel at one and the same time. Anxieties about the growth and direction of an entrepreneurial and materialist society are balanced, on one side, by an implied acceptance of its norms, on the other, by a return to an apparently unproblematic ante-bellum world of childhood play.

III

Anxieties about the direction of American cultural life in *Tom Sawyer* are also evident in its representation of the individual subject: Tom's freedom of action and romantic self-expression are contrasted with, and run alongside, a quite different type of passive determinism. The resulting tension indicates a concern with the question of subjective agency which was to haunt Twain throughout his career, and especially in the major novels following *Tom Sawyer*. The relationship between individual autonomy and the effect of social conditioning became, increasingly, a crucial area of debate for nineteenth-century Americans. Twain joins that debate here, but tends finally to evade its more disconcerting aspects.

It is clear that on the most obvious textual level, Tom Sawyer acts as the hero in a romance. He is a central character, and leading actor, in the life of St Petersburg, dominating the various spaces he inhabits. An early review indicated that the appeal of the book lay (and still lies) in its story of 'certain bold and restless youths who, finding every-day life very monotonous, went in for living like outlaws in the woods, exploring for hidden treasures, and other romantic adventures'.[39] The whole village is composed of performance artists: 'Mr Walters fell to "showing off". . . . The librarian "showed off". . . . The young lady teachers "showed off"' (p. 33). But it is Tom, with his quick imagination, leadership and flair for adventure, who is the figure centre stage. 'Theatrical gorgeousness' appeals 'strongly to his nature' (p. 104), and Tom is nowhere happier than when he can indulge his flair for the dramatic, whether in arranging to attend his own funeral service (p. 118) or in pouring gold coins in a heap before a startled audience (p. 215). His success is measured in terms of the role of 'glittering hero' (p. 151) he assumes, 'thronged' by an excited population 'roaring huzza after huzza!' (p. 200). For Tom, nothing could be better than making, over and over again, 'a mighty stir' (p. 216).

Tom Sawyer, then, is the charismatic centre of the novel. Adventure, mystery and romance dominate his life, and in all three realms he plays the lead part, whether as 'Tom Sawyer the Pirate! The Black Avenger of the Spanish Main!' (p. 61), the detective who tracks down the dangerous Injun Joe's money, or as the lover 'swimming in bliss' as he sweet-talks Becky Thatcher ('Do you love rats?', p. 56) into becoming his fiancée. He sets up performances which rival and outdo those available from more traditional sources, and exposes the boredoms and familiarities of the minister's Sunday sermon in the alternative entertainment which he (in this case, unintentionally) instigates, when a poodle sits on the pinch-bug he has released:

Then there was a wild yelp of agony, and the poodle went sailing up the aisle; the yelps continued, and so did the dog. . . . By this time the whole church was red-faced and suffocating with suppressed laughter, and the sermon had come to a dead standstill. (pp. 41–2)

Jackson Lears discusses the late-Victorian image of the innocent child in the context of 'a world where selfhood had become problematic'.[40] Twain's return to ante-bellum boyhood in *Tom Sawyer*, and the active and heroic nature of the main protagonist's role, implies similar anxieties even in the mid-1870s. Indeed, Eric Sundquist looks further back, to the ante-bellum period, to discover concerns which were to become more and more prominent as the century progressed. He sees even then, in *Moby Dick* (1851) and *Life in the Iron Mills* (1861), a focus on 'the material and technological details of American life' and a measuring of 'the distance between the sovereign territory of the individual self and the powers of social or political community that surround and create individual destiny'.[41] It is exactly this same tension between different conceptions of the self that is an underlying motif in Twain's novel. For, as Fred G. See says, putting this in a slightly altered way:

> There is a contradiction in Clemens' work between the self caught in sequence and measurement and the self freely expressed in fantasy and play. These are the two linked and opposing ways of ordering reality that lay claim to Tom Sawyer, and he is the border between them.[42]

We can start to see this tension between the free expression of the self and the determining influence of environmental forces in the repeated use of insect metaphors in the novel. Tom Sawyer is given a type of god-like authority, not only in his ability to loose the pinch-bug from 'the percussion-cap box' (p. 40) in which he keeps it, but also in his later control over the tick that takes its place as captive there. Tom releases the tick onto his school desk, and Joe joins him in 'exercising the prisoner' (p. 54). The boys use pins to direct the insect, playing a game of 'crossing the equator'[43] as each tries to keep it on his side of the desk:

> At last luck seemed to settle and abide with Joe. The tick tried this, that, and the other course, and got as excited and anxious as the boys themselves, but time and again, just as he would have victory in his very grasp so to speak, and Tom's fingers would be twitching to begin, Joe's pin would deftly head him off and keep possession. At last Tom could stand it no longer. The temptation was too strong. So he reached out and lent a hand with his pin. (p. 55).

The stress on power and manipulation, on anxious but unsuccessful attempts to escape their limits, and on boundaries being crossed, prepares us for the shift in perspective and position which then occurs. For the schoolteacher comes down with 'a tremendous whack . . . on Tom's shoulders, and its duplicate on Joe's' (p. 55), to remind the boys both of his superior power and of their relative lack of autonomy in his presence.

This metaphoric shift where Tom becomes the captive insect, and the relativising of the relation between authority and subjection that it enacts, is repeated and played out in different ways throughout *Tom Sawyer*. The book starts with Aunt Polly turning around 'just in time to seize a small boy [Tom] by the slack of his roundabout and arrest his flight' (p. 7). Tom is repeatedly, too, subject to switchings and floggings by Mr. Dobbins, 'the potency of the masculine "muscle" . . . used with . . . consistent vindictiveness and violence'[44] to keep the mischievous boy in check. The town librarian is associated with 'insect authority' (p. 33), a phrase which cuts two ways in suggesting both the further levels of authority which lie beyond his own, but also in implying the low and powerless status of those in his charge. When Tom, burdened by his secret knowledge of Joe's crime, hears a great storm at night, he takes it as a direct response by 'the powers above', and sees 'nothing incongruous about the getting up of such an expensive storm as this to knock the turf from under an insect like himself' (p. 144). If Tom continually 'insists on the exciting apparatus of action,' there is a constant awareness of the social and institutional forces which restrain and hold him in check: that 'another authority always comes first, whatever he is doing'.[45] Elizabeth G. Peck, in fact, goes so far as to suggest that, in this respect, Tom's characterisation foreshadows 'the environmental determinism of *The Tragedy of Pudd'nhead Wilson*'.[46]

The impact of the determining forces – social, religious, legal and moral – on Tom's development and the way in which they compromise a sense of his autonomy can, however, easily be overlooked in the novel. Tom's fracturings of the social rules are always temporary and *depend* on the safe return to society. His 'play' ultimately conforms to the values of respectable society; all his effects are finally predicated on the approval and indulgence of his elders. His 'rebellions' are sanctioned ones.[47] Joe's words, when Tom describes the delights of swimming on Jackson's Island, are no more than an overt admission of Tom's own underlying attitudes: 'swimming's no good; I don't seem to care for it, somehow, when there ain't anybody to say I shan't go in. I mean to go home' (p. 108). Individual expression and social conformity are variously represented *both* as oppositional and as complementary in this novel. If Tom's final actions are heroic, they work to the benefit of the community. He ends up fully contained within its boundaries, the protector both of justice (that is, as this community recognises it) and of weak womanhood, his social success assured. The opposition between subjective desire and social regulation and convention is covered over. The whitewashing that is being done here, concerning the nature of individual agency and its limits is, however, implicit in the description of Huck Finn's initial separation from the community, and in his status as 'forbidden society'. For he does what Tom will never want – or be allowed – to do:[48]

> Huckleberry came and went at his own free will . . . ; he did not have to go to school or to church, or call any being master, or obey anybody. . . . In a word, everything that goes to make life precious, that boy had. . . . Tom hailed the romantic outcast.
>
> (p. 46)

Full self-expression is described, in Huck's case, as entirely at odds with community membership, and the social conditioning that accompanies it. Though Twain fails to develop the implications of this in any depth, and indeed ends the novel by pulling Huck (uneasily) into the community alongside Tom, such a tension would not, in his work, stay buried for very long. Indeed, as *Tom Sawyer* comes to its close, so the alternative possibilities contained in Huck's person and voice start, disruptively, to emerge.[49]

IV

Tom Sawyer's representation, as I have shown, is complex and ambiguous. He ends up socially successful, contained (symbolically) by the whitewashed fence, within the boundaries of what, nostalgically, can be constructed as the attractive, peaceful and well-ordered haven of American small-town life. But his position here is at odds with other aspects of his characterisation. Cynthia Griffin Wolff points out that Tom has common traits, too, with the most aggressively antisocial figure in the novel, Injun Joe, whom she sees as his 'shadow self'.[50] She suggests that the 'carefully constructed rituals of devastation' in which Tom participates in the safety of his 'own fictional world' are sublimated versions of 'the rebellion and rage that never fully surface in his dealings with Aunt Polly and the other figures of authority in this matriarchal world', a rebellion and rage that Joe overtly represents. For Wolff, the death of the 'ruthless predator', Joe's 'summary banishment', is 'an ending with no resolution at all'. For he is banished from sight, mind and text, as 'all too dangerous to traffic with'.[51] Tom's resurrection from the underground cave (with all its symbolic connotations) is consequently presented as prelude to the start of a useful adult career, all fears about his antisocial impulses carefully put below ground with Joe's dead body. Judge Thatcher then pronounces on Tom's socialised future, saying 'he meant to look to it that Tom should be admitted to the National Military Academy, and afterward trained in the best law-school in the country' (p. 217).

The anxieties evident here, and the textual patterns of threat and containment revealed, can be taken, though, in a rather different direction. For what *Tom Sawyer* reveals, but only in turn firmly to suppress, is a highly uncomfortable attitude to the history of American race relations. In the matter of race particularly, the reader of Twain's boy book is finally left with a whitewashed version of Mississippi village life, all anxieties about its prejudices and injustices pushed firmly, but not completely, under cover. The novel hints at this subject, only then *almost* wholly to conceal ugly social and political realities pertaining both to the time when the book is set, and when it is being written. Part of the book's cultural significance may lie in the readiness of its (adult) audience to collude in such a whitewash.

First, to connect with Wolff's argument, it is noticeable how sexual anxieties in the novel are, by and large, taken beyond the borders of St Petersburg village life to settle on the figure of Joe, the social and racial outsider. If the innocent patterns of Tom and Becky's pre-adolescent romance reflect the genteel courtship rituals and conventional gender relations of their immediate community, their behaviour is directly contrasted with (and yet peculiarly linked to) the sexual threat contained in Injun Joe. For, as John Seelye suggests, there are sexual undercurrents to Joe's plan to 'tie the widow to her bed' and then 'slit her nostrils . . . notch her ears like a sow's' (p. 180).[52] Tom generally seems pre-sexual, but he is associated with a type of 'secret sexual knowledge'[53] in the Anatomy book incident, where he first surprises Becky as she looks at the 'handsomely engraved and coloured frontispiece – a human figure, stark naked',[54] then takes the punishment for the torn page that results. Forrest Robinson suggests the implicit connections being made in a Tom–Becky–Joe triangle, as he discusses Becky's failure to face Joe in the cave sequence. Saying that 'as Tom well knows, Injun Joe is quite literally beyond Becky's ken', he continues:

> Becky's carefully guarded ignorance about Joe's appearance in the cave is culturally of a piece with her carefully preserved ignorance in the matter of the anatomy book. Tom knows immediately and for a certainty that knowledge about Indian Joe, in anything like its full range of implication, is incompatible with Becky's culturally defined 'innocence'.[55]

Joe appears as Tom's shadow self here too, his sexual presence and threat testifying to a quality necessarily repressed on the boy hero's part. The racial and social outcast is identified with a violent and dangerous sexuality that cannot be contained by normal village life. Anxieties about adult sexuality, and the social violence it can wreak, are here dumped on Joe's symbolic figure.

One last meaning of whitewash (for my purposes here) is that given in *Webster's Dictionary* (1858 edition): 'a wash for making the skin fair'. Certainly, the notion of 'community' in St Petersburg takes on a distinctively European-American cast. Twain is writing in the Reconstruction period about an ante-bellum slave-holding society, but little hint of social criticism concerning the subject of race enters his text. Slavery appears not to be an issue, and the stable and fixed nature of racial hierarchies is repeatedly confirmed. This American small town is run for, and by, its white citizenry. No sign of racial tension between white and black is apparent here.

Jim, in *Tom Sawyer*, is a 'small coloured boy' (pp. 8–9). Thus, by necessity, the metaphorical equation of slave with child that characterised the Southern family romance,[56] and which *Huckleberry Finn* would shortly challenge, cannot be subjected to critical interrogation. No African-American is seen – and this is only to be expected given the social world Twain describes – in church, school or at formal social occasions. There are, however, occasional textual signs, if very quickly passed over, of the racial problems which were, in fact, so crucially to alter the shape of Southern (and American) history. Indian Joe puts himself ahead of the African-American in the social hierarchy when he says that the Widow Douglas's former husband had him 'horse-whipped . . . like a nigger' (p. 180). The hint here is of 'white injustice and mistreatment',[57] not just toward

Joe, but also toward the slaves with whom he compares himself; of a brutal treatment of those who are considered social and racial inferiors. If this theme remains undeveloped, it certainly briefly disturbs the surface of the text, and serves to indicate a shadow on, or stain beneath, the St Petersburg whitewash.

A similar brief disturbance occurs in the footnote pointing to the shades of difference in this community between the ownership of a slave and a dog. Thus the naming of a dog, Bull Harbison, is followed by the note that 'if Mr. Harbison had owned a slave named Bull, Tom would have spoken of him as "Harbison's Bull"; but a son or dog of that name was "Bull Harbison"' (p. 75). This analogy, and marginal distinction, between slave and dog, foreshadows a central motif of *Puddn'head Wilson*. There is no sign here, however, of the irony of the later text. The very presence of this apparently uninflected note (one of only two footnotes in the whole book) does, though, stop the reader short; make her or him wonder if the contemporary critics who saw Twain's naming of St Petersburg as a deliberate reference to a 'Republican freedom from class prejudices' lacking in its Russian counterpart,[58] had read the novel entirely correctly. St Petersburg can pass for an easygoing, free and equal society, a model of the American democratic ideal, but only by ignoring *racial* difference. The very few references to black–white relations that can be considered troubling, and the complete lack of their development, can (to speculate) suggest one reason for *Tom Sawyer's* long-term popularity. On the surface, at any rate, it nostalgically projects an idyllic version of white (whitewashed?) small-town America, where the racial issues that were to plague the country both before and after the Civil War are unproblematised, pushed to the margins of the text. In this respect, Twain's boy book looks back, as the genre so often encouraged, to a trouble-free world, and one all the more attractive to its audience for so being. It is just the odd passage in the book which suggests something different; reveals anxieties that never completely disappear beneath the textual surface.

A related argument can be made about Injun Joe's role in the book. Injun Joe, unlike his fellow marginal man, the African-American slave, does unsettle the community of St Petersburg. But, positioned so clearly within a melodramatic frame, and defined so overtly as racial and moral 'other', the threat he poses is always subject to his expected final textual containment (indeed obliteration). Joe's half-breed status is repeatedly foregrounded, and this accordingly raises the threat of racial contamination. If Twain is writing about a period when Andrew Jackson 'as the President of the United States responsible for Indian removal . . . developed a philosophical explanation which transformed Indian deaths into moral inevitability',[59] he is writing in a period of continued hostilities between the US Government and the Indian (Custer's Last Stand took place in the centennial year too) which were only to close, much later in 1890, with 'the symbolic end of Indian freedom'[60] at Wounded Knee.

Injun Joe is, in *Tom Sawyer*, unmistakably other, the repository of all the traits that St Petersburg and its dominant white citizenry would deny and reject. His spring from the courtroom window, tearing 'his way through all opposers' (p. 151), shows him violently breaking the boundaries that limit small-town life (Tom, too, repeatedly crosses the symbolic boundary of the window; one more thing they have in common). Sexually cruel, criminally and unnecessarily violent, and powerfully and antisocially disruptive, Injun Joe is a demonic figure, described variously as 'that murderin' half-breed' (even before he kills Dr Robinson – p. 68), 'Injun devil' (p. 73), a 'stony-hearted liar [who] had sold himself to Satan' (p. 81), and as 'half-breed devil' (p. 147). Joe himself puts his own desire for vengeance on Dr. Robinson down to his 'Injun blood' (p. 69). Twain's story dramatically projects the extinction of this savage and racially different other as necessary for the continued safety and good order of small-town life. As Robert Tracy puts it, Joe is:

> in Whitman's phrase a 'dusky demon and brother,' whose brotherhood is denied and whose demonhood is exaggerated. . . . [At the novel's end] the Indian dies and the treasure disappears into a bank – a neat and accurate symbol of the fate of the trans-Mississippi frontier. Civilization's progress exorcises the devils, exterminates the Indians, and banks the proceeds.[61]

Anxieties about racial injustice are raised in *Tom Sawyer*, and the oblique suggestion is made that Joe 'was the victim of white society before he was its villain'.[62] Such anxieties have their base, if we take Joe's case as paradigmatic, in historical fact: the whitewashing of America, in the case of white–Indian relations, covered up considerable injustice and violence by the dominant racial group.

But these textual tensions are undeveloped, the cultural uncertainties they indicate suppressed almost as soon as raised. The demonisation and extermination of Joe, and his role as melodramatic agent of evil, suggest how firmly – hysterically, one might almost say – uncomfortable socio-historical facts are being covered up as they appear in this fictional form.

The Adventures of Tom Sawyer, then, presents us with an American village world[63] where divergent racial elements (and the cultural heterogeneity they might suggest) are, for the most part, marginalised or suppressed.[64] If metaphorically, 'all those buckets of whitewash [are necessary] to St Petersburg's security and self-confidence',[65] perhaps they have been necessary to the security and self-confidence of many of the readers of Twain's book too. For one *can* read this fictional world as one where the pressures of modernisation do not apply, where boys (tolerated by adults) can play their pranks and indulge in antisocial behaviour with no lasting effects,[66] and where social hierarchies (and especially those constructed on the basis of race) are, finally, entirely stable. To do so would not be entirely inaccurate, but would deny the complexities and ambiguities which closer study of the novel reveals.

5

Racial Politics in *Huckleberry Finn*

> *'Now, old Jim, you're a free man again, and I bet you won't ever be a slave no more.'*
>
> (*The Adventures of Huckleberry Finn*)[1]

I

Adventures of Huckleberry Finn (1884–5) is the best-known novel in America's literary history. Sales figures have been estimated at over 20 million worldwide.[2] Hemingway said that 'All modern American literature comes from . . . *Huckleberry Finn*'. T. S. Eliot called it a masterpiece.[3] It is one of the few American novels where new academic scholarship or dispute consistently stimulates wider public interest, as in the case of the 1991 discovery of the first two-fifths of the handwritten manuscript of the novel. 'Jim and the Dead Man', a previously unknown passage found here (edited out prior to the book's original publication), received considerable attention when it appeared in the *New Yorker* in 1995, placed alongside the comments of five contemporary American writers reflecting on 'Twain's novel and our most persistent moral dilemma'. The exact nature of this dilemma is not specified. William Styron, though, indicates its implied grounds in writing that Huck and Jim, 'with their confused and incalculable feelings for each other, remain symbols of our racial confusion'.[4]

In this chapter, my focus too is on race. I thus necessarily downplay other important aspects of the book that stands as a 'vital critical centre'[5] in any discussion of the American literary tradition. Thus, for instance, the importance of Twain's use of the vernacular voice, a type of 'verbal outlawry',[6] cannot be overestimated. In having Huck tell his own story, he overturned all the novelistic conventions of his time concerning the use of formal or standard English, and set the American novel on a new course. Twain also interrogates the whole nineteenth-century sentimental tradition here. If right action is grounded, as Huck's is, in feeling alone, the issue that remains is what authority one person's right feeling has over anyone else's, and how such judgements are made.[7] I sideline, too, the important question of individual agency and identity and their relation to the social and institutional environment, to nature and to political belief (a democratic ideology). *Huckleberry Finn* works, first and foremost, as a comic novel, but I do not examine Twain's use of different forms of humour, and I only touch on his use of genre in the text. These are just some of the issues which have made the book such a rich arena for critical explication and debate, and have helped to contribute to its status as an American 'classic'. The production of books and articles on *Huckleberry Finn* is so profuse that the reader who wishes to explore in more detail its other aspects will have no difficulty in finding a series of excellent critical guides available.[8]

The subject of race is generally muted in *Tom Sawyer*. In *Huckleberry Finn*, though, it becomes a matter of central concern. I use Huck and Jim's conflict over the meaning of the word 'freedom' to illustrate how their two stories diverge, and how the marginalisation of Jim's voice affects our readerly knowledge of his role and status. I then argue that *despite* the differences between Huck and Jim, Twain also (and alternatively) shows how their stories come together to complement one another, and represents their relationship on the raft as idyllic. In doing so, his novel enters, however indirectly, into the public debate about race in 1880s' America, and suggests a new model of interracial relationships. This idyll necessarily comes to nothing within the narrative frame within which Twain works, but nonetheless gives the book a powerful and polemic social and political charge which the frustrating nature of its ending (for this is how I read it here) cannot entirely defuse.

I suggest that, like *Tom Sawyer*, *Huckleberry Finn* is not just about the ante-bellum past in which it is set, but also reveals anxieties about social problems in Twain's contemporary America. In the former novel, Twain's use of the boy book provides him with a generic form[9] which helps to disguise ambiguous attitudes to American social and historical development. So too, here, the particular setting of the novel, its different narrative strands, its use of a child protagonist, and of the comic mode, make for a text that can be read in a number of different ways: as one which both responds critically to immediate social issues but also diverts attention from them. In this chapter, and exceptionally in my book, I focus on the former process alone – to stress how the novel can be read as an allegorical commentary on, and positive response to, discriminatory racial practice in a post-Reconstruction America.

This is not, however, to deny the way *Huckleberry Finn* disguises its engagement with Twain's American present, nor that it contains ambiguous and contradictory elements. It is perfectly possible to read the book, as others have and still do, as both racist, in its representation of Jim, and disappointingly conservative, in its return to comedy and to a modified version of the social status quo at the story's end. Twain's use of the first person voice and of the picaresque hold his novel together in formal terms, but there are clear hints of the type of narrative tensions that would become more evident in later works. The novel pulls in two directions. In the late evasion sequence (when Tom Sawyer reappears to help 'free' Jim), an extravagant and farcical humour clashes with what (on another level) is a serious and contentious social theme. One narrative sequence and literary mode – Jim and Huck's raft journey as idyll – is abandoned, or rather, left incomplete, as another story of boyish excitement, high jinks, and convenient plot resolution finally replaces it. But while I recognise the various formal and generic manoeuvres of *Huckleberry Finn*, and the strains and cracks in artistic vision which they signify, I choose here to emphasise a dimension of Twain's book which has been unrecognised, despite the textual indicators, until quite recently: the challenge it offered to the racial assumptions of its time.

If modern readers recognise race as a (perhaps the) central subject of *Huckleberry Finn*, what now seems extraordinary is that Twain's contemporaries, as far as we can tell, did not read the book in those terms. Steven Mailloux speaks of the 'perplexing silence on the novel's attitude toward racism' at its time of publication. This may have been because a more obvious cultural debate concerning

juvenile delinquency and 'the bad-boy boom'[10] engaged the
audience's attention; one certainly less disturbing in terms of its
moral and intellectual self-regard.

Race did, however, figure strongly in the twentieth-century
critical reception of the novel, and, by 1950, T. S. Eliot's comment
on the 'kinship of mind and the sympathy between the boy outcast
from society and the negro fugitive from the injustice of society'[11]
reads as a commonplace. While the majority of critics of that time
focused on the moral abuses of slavery and the failures of Southern
society in the ante-bellum years of the novel's setting, very few saw
something more pressing and barbed in the satiric attack it
contained on post-bellum racial practice. Thus the novel still had
some of its sharpest historical teeth drawn. From a present-day
perspective we might reformulate Huck's resonant question about
why Tom Sawyer should 'bother to set a free nigger free' (p. 366) to
interrogate Twain's artistic intentions: why should he write about
slavery, and the moral and social anxieties that went with it, when
it was over and done with? Any answer to this question must
remain provisional, and it may be that Twain was unaware, or only
part aware, of the contemporary relevance of his narrative (though
there is some evidence to suggest otherwise). But, whatever the
authorial intention, to read *Huckleberry Finn* with the racial
circumstances of its time of writing in critical mind, is to discover
how clearly it engages such a social and historical context. Indeed,
to read it as a straightforward representation of pre-Civil War
America is to wipe the novel of much of its significance; to divert
from ongoing historical process (the war is over and the slave is free
at the time that Twain writes) and to focus instead on personality:
Huck's bonding with Jim, his struggle with his conscience, his
conflict with the surrounding public world. This easily slips into an
ahistorical and mythic opposition between innate goodness, good
heart and free self, and the corrupt society against which they
together stand. Such versions of the novel became normal,
particularly in the 1950s and 1960s.[12]

Recent years, though, have seen increasing critical emphasis on
how Twain's book is involved in the debate over racial status in
post-Reconstruction America. This coincides with a developing
historicist critical turn, and an interest in the way that literature
engages in the cultural dialogues of its day. The ending of
Huckleberry Finn (the evasion sequence and its conclusion) offers a

bleak, if indirect, commentary on the compromised nature not just of Jim's final 'freedom' but of that of the recently emancipated slave in the 1880s' South. When Jim is re-enslaved at the Phelps's,[13] Twain's use of apparently comic incident has a disturbing effect. Thus Tom, at one point, plans to saw Jim's leg off, only abandoning the idea because 'Jim's a nigger and wouldn't understand the reasons for it' (p. 312). Jim is returned to the category of imbecile here as Tom, however briefly, threatens his selfhood with literal deconstruction. The play between history (the failure of Reconstruction signalled by the 1876 election and the collapse of the Republican party) and fiction (Jim's projected *de*construction; his role as passive African-American victim of white authority) is more than coincidental. And Twain may well have known exactly what he was doing here. Shelley Fisher Fishkin notes that from the early 1870s onward he was collecting press clippings concerning Klan activities and other brutal treatment of the African-American in the South.[14] R. J. Ellis, too, notes the recurrent 'unease about the situation of the post-bellum Southern African-American' in *Life on the Mississippi* (1883), the travel book intimately related to, and (partly) written alongside, *Huckleberry Finn*.[15]

Most critics now agree that *Huckleberry Finn* engages the explosive question of race relations in post-Reconstruction America, but in an indirect and ironic way. Twain's contemporary audience, and later ones, may not have read the text from this perspective, but the question then raised is of artistic method and interpretative community quite as much as whether Twain had 'a sharp sense of history' or not.[16] Steven Mailloux, discussing Twain's contemporary readership, points out that George W. Cable set *The Grandissimes*, written in 1880, among Louisiana Creoles in 1804 but that reviewers still 'easily interpreted the novel as a parable of 1880's race problems'. Twain was publicly associated with Cable on lecture tour in the winter of 1884–5. *Huckleberry Finn* came out then, and so did Cable's 'The Freedman's Case in Equity': a 'polemical attempt to reopen the debate on the race question' published in *Century Magazine*. The passages from his novel that Twain most often read on this tour were, too, 'those that most directly involved his humorous critique of white supremacist ideology'.[17] If this provides further evidence of Twain's intentions, certainly his reading audience appear not to have put two and two together, and to have identified his novel with that same contemporary debate.

II

Toni Morrison argues that a 'dark, abiding, signing Africanist presence' haunts the 'hearts and texts of American literature'.[18] This idea of a black ghost in the American literary machine (part of a more general reaccentuation of the literary landscape in the direction of cultural heterogeneity) directly informs Shelley Fisher Fishkin's *Was Huck Black?*. Fishkin contends that Twain owed a profound debt to African-American cultural forms in his writing of *Huckleberry Finn*; that the novel was a product of 'mixed literary bloodlines', and that Huck's own distinctive voice may well have been modelled, in actuality, on an African-American source. She traces the possible genesis of this voice to a short newspaper piece, 'Sociable Jimmy', where an African-American child – in Twain's words, 'the most artless, sociable, and exhaustless talker I ever came across' – takes charge of the brief narrative. This, Fishkin suggests, was 'a model for the voice with which Twain would change the shape of American literature'.[19] In other words, the book that has been celebrated for its representation of a distinctively American colloquial style has, both in terms of its general content and its particular syntax, African-American roots.

Fishkin argues, valuably and convincingly, for 'cultural syncretism', seeing American lives and literature as a 'tissue of cross-cultural influences'.[20] Her central thesis, however, might be modified by putting more stress on the code-switching that went on at an everyday level between Black English and both standard American English and other non-standard dialects[21] in the South that Twain knew, and less on the 'Sociable Jimmy' piece. What remains unresolved, though, is the nature of the relationship between Huck's voice and Jim's. For if Huck's speech is influenced by, and borrows from, African-American syntax and forms of expression,[22] it is none the less clearly differentiated from that of the black man, Jim. They just do not speak in the same way. This can be seen when, for example, Huck's 'But hang it, Jim, you've clean missed the point – blame it, you've missed it a thousand mile' is answered by Jim's 'Who? Me? Go 'long. Doan' talk to *me* 'bout yo' pints. I reck'n I knows sense when I sees it; en dey ain' no sense in sich doin's as dat' (p. 134).

Indeed, for much of the early sections of the novel focusing on Huck's relation with Jim, their voices and stories diverge from one another, are in strong competition. Fishkin tends to play down this divergence in her analysis, though she does show Jim's voice to be a 'diminished' one.[23] Huck's voice may contain black elements, but Jim (who *is* black) clashes with Huck in terms of his role, his use of language and his values; is clearly marked off from Huck in his African-American distinctiveness and difference.

Huck's voice contains Jim's in the literal sense that Huck chooses when and how (directly or indirectly) to report his companion's words, but his control over Jim is often precarious. According to Mikhail Bakhtin, language is the site of 'opposition and struggle',[24] a register of social and historical diversity, of power relations and hierarchies, in any given culture. To focus on the competing nature of Huck and Jim's languages and stories in *Huckleberry Finn* is, almost automatically, to call attention to their different uses of the word 'freedom', a heavily overdetermined word both in the text and in American political culture generally.[25] My analysis of the use of this term serves as paradigm of the textual conflict between Huck and Jim. It also, though, prepares the way for the later stage in my argument when I examine how their two voices and narratives overlap and *complement* each other as well as differ.

'Freedom' signifies differently for Huck than it does for Jim. On the raft Huck speaks as one who is 'free and easy and comfortable' (p. 176), words shot through with a specific set of meanings: the product of his situation now in comparison to his former one. He is comfortable because he can laze about all day. He is free of Pap's violence, of Tom's games which never quite make sense to him, of a hierarchical and repressive social structure personified by the Widow Douglas and Miss Watson. He is easy since he has no firm plans for the future. The three words – free, easy, comfortable – act synonymously for Huck since, on the raft, desire is no longer displaced. The language (and values) of Southern riverbank society are challenged by his stress on drift, nakedness and ease rather then decency, regularity and respectability. As Neil Schmitz comments: 'the raft is for Huck the end of his journey, the place where his "free and easy" river world is regained'.[26] Huck's description of the way he and Jim run the raft, 'we let her alone, and let her float wherever the current wanted her to' (p. 178), is suggestive of his own unforced and relaxed preferred mode of behaviour.

Huck's needs and interests are restricted at every turn by dominant social codes and those who would enforce them. Desire and social pressure are generally at odds. Huck is floating on the fringes of the body politic, the body social. Freedom for Huck lies outside the normal boundaries of society, and indeed what he would call freedom, society would call license, moral irresponsibility, a fracture of the social charter. Huck is thus left necessarily compromised, even divided, able to function only by siting himself within the social (and ideological) networks available to him, but needing at the same time to reject, as far as he is able, such networks; finding them oppressive and diminishing in terms of his sense – one he could never put into words – of mental, physical and moral agency. Huck, in other words, cannot escape the language and values of the surrounding society, even as they stick in his craw. His voice and value scheme, to put this very differently, can never, in this Southern world, be entirely congruent with Jim's.

The word 'freedom' certainly has a different meaning for Jim than it does for Huck: it signifies the removal of the internal and external oppressions associated with the institution of slavery.[27] The change in Jim, once he has run off, is first measured on Jackson's Island, where he tells Huck, 'I owns mysef, en I's wuth eight hund'd dollars' (p. 100). This is a fascinating sentence. Jim judges his own worth as property in the dehumanising terms of economic exchange. In doing so, he shows how far the language and values of the white masters of this society have influenced his own way of thinking and speaking; he is unable to break fully free from his slave self. Yet, if he remains (to use Harriet Jacobs's term) 'human stock' in his own mind, he also becomes, as he asserts self-ownership, master of his own fate with 'the right to do what he likes with his own property', his own body. If 'according to Southern laws, a slave, *being* property, can *hold* no property',[28] Jim starts to change his sense of self in closing the gap between possession and possessor.[29] The right to autonomy he expresses signals a profound mental shift from his prior status as owned slave.

At this stage in the novel it is clear what Jim is escaping *from*, but no clear statement has been made as to what he is running *toward*. When Jim does come to speak more directly of his intended actions, it is noticeable that his words are given in indirect discourse, with Huck acting as the mediating narrator. It is also noticeable that a gap between Huck and Jim's joint interests, and Jim's self-interest, is being drawn. It is Huck who first spells out the plans that will take Jim north to 'freedom' (now clearly positioned as a positive other to slavery) when he says that 'what we was after' was to get to Cairo,[30] the point where the Ohio and the Mississippi rivers join, for then 'we would sell the raft and get on a steamboat and go way up the Ohio among the free States, and then be out of trouble' (p. 137). Jim echoes this sense of shared narrative intention when he interprets his 'dream' of fog and tow-heads: 'he said . . . if we minded our business . . . we would pull through and get out . . . into the clear river, which was the free States, and wouldn't have no trouble' (p. 142). Huck and Jim's plans are mutually identified here, as their use of pronouns shows.

As Cairo comes close, the relation between the two voices becomes more problematic. I focus on the pronoun activity that occurs in the text at this point to suggest the developing sense of conflict between them. Jim has not been associated with the plain use of the word 'free' until Chapter 15 of the novel, when Cairo is near, and, for the first time, escape to the north opens up as a practical possibility. In the following chapter, with Cairo apparently directly at hand, Jim's excitement, as he literally dances around, is accompanied by a sudden increase in his sounding of the words 'free' and 'freedom' – six times in the first three pages (pp. 144–6). Now, for the first time, the full extent of Jim's plans become known: to get to a free State, save up money, buy his wife and then buy (or steal) his children out of slavery. It is here, too, that pronouns start shifting about as Jim starts to distance himself from Huck. First the 'we' that Jim has used earlier modulates, as Huck reports his speech, to the singular 'he': 'Jim said . . . he'd be a free man the minute he seen [Cairo]' (p. 144). Then that third person singular gives way, not to the first person plural, but to its third person variant as Huck begins to disappear from Jim's picture of the future. A gap appears between Huck and Jim's joint plan, formulated earlier, of going 'way up [together] . . . among the free States' (p. 137), and the further plans now revealed. For once '*he* got to a free State' and had earned enough to buy his wife, Jim intends that '*they* [he and his wife] would both work' to buy their children's liberty, and 'if their master wouldn't sell them, *they*'d get an Ab'litionist to go and steal them' (p. 146, my emphases). Huck becomes here a friend and companion in the present, or at least one who is treated as such (the implications of this phrase become clear shortly), but one who has no future role. When Jim's voice is then heard speaking directly, later in this same sequence, he swiftly jumps from the remaking of a plural identification of interest with Huck ('We's safe, Huck, we's safe!') to the first-person expression of self-assertion: 'I'm a free man' (p. 146).[31]

Two related issues emerge in the way the relationship between Huck and Jim is represented in the novel. The first is the dynamic tension of Jim's 'freedom-talk'[32] with Huck's own interests, and accordingly with Huck's narrative freedom of expression; his textual power. One story cuts against the other here. Huck's narrative of 'freedom', leisure and good companionship on the raft (one which depends on Jim for its value) conflicts with Jim's slave narrative. For the latter contains a version of freedom which is, in Laurence B. Holland's words, 'antithetical' to Huck's, centring as it does on Jim's desire 'to escape from slavery and enter *into* the civilization that chafes Huck'.[33] Huck and Jim's languages, their words and plans, to varying degree, conflict. Freedom for Jim means, to borrow from Frederick Douglass, to 'clear himself from the chains and fetters of slavery'.[34] When Jim says that a raft 'doan' *make* no track' (p. 97), he is thinking of how best to evade the dogs and men who would hunt him down as a fugitive slave. When Cairo approaches and Huck is faced with Jim's words running in a direction counter to his own, is threatened with what amounts to abandonment, he immediately slips back into the language of the dominant culture. This is his way of retaining a measure of control over the situation. Now, instead of mutually (and mistakenly) identifying himself with Jim as an escapee ('Git up and hump yourself Jim! . . . They're after *us!*' – p. 117, my emphasis), he reconstructs Jim as property, '[Miss Watson's] nigger' and one who has run off from his 'rightful owner' (p. 145). And he responds to Jim's escape plans in a way fully sanctioned by the slave-holding culture of his region – with racist slur: 'give a nigger an inch and he'll take an ell' (p. 146). Huck reacts exasperatedly to Jim ruining his narrative, disrupting his script.[35] He takes over the hegemonic language as a way of gaining power over Jim; denying the validity of, and the needs revealed in, his words. He reduces him to a stereotype who, if he will not go easily along with Huck's definitions of freedom, with Huck's words and Huck's plot, can simply be handed back to his former 'owners'.[36]

Huck would much prefer to stay on the raft while Jim wants to get off it. For Huck, the very meaning of the raft – freedom, ease, safety, 'home' – is conditional on Jim's presence. The 'we're all right, now' that Huck sings out with 'joy' (p. 279), when he reaches the raft after escaping from the King and the Duke in Pikesville, gives way to tears when he discovers that Jim is gone. His use of the first-person plural carries the implication that Huck (first-person singular) will be far from 'all right' if he continues his journey alone. Huck gets 'sort of lonesome' (p. 91) or 'mournful' (p. 288) very quickly by himself. He survives, but without much 'joy'. The worth of Huck's river story depends on Jim being there to share it.

It is noticeable that once Cairo is passed, Jim's voice is increasingly silenced in all but its most passive aspects. Any practical way for Jim to escape slavery has by now faded as an option, and, what is more, both his and Huck's plans are increasingly disrupted by circumstance or co-opted by others. The notion of Jim as *agent* of his own liberation fades from view. The 'determined and clear-headed adult'[37] in him is killed off as his status changes: as he becomes subject to the King and the Duke's authority on board the raft, and then to Tom Sawyer's command[38] (with Huck acting as his subordinate double) on the shore. Jim's voice ends up marginalised, almost unheard. Following the Cairo episode, there is just one brief scene on the raft (pp. 177–80) where Huck and Jim are shown in harmonious relation to each other before the King and the Duke take over. Attention then switches to the latter pair, the meanwhile Jim is first tied 'hand and foot with a rope' (p. 195), and then made up to impersonate a 'sick Arab'; looking, with his face painted blue, not 'only . . . like he was dead . . . [but] considerable more than that' (pp. 220–1).[39] If Jim is subject, to borrow a later linked word, to 'mortification' (p. 291), with its twinned meaning of humiliation and devitalisation, on the raft, things are not much better, with Tom and Huck, on shore. Again, he ends up as a passive target for the thoughtless manipulation of others, his 'linguistic agency . . . a major part of the novel's verbal wealth' now thoroughly sapped.[40]

There is sharp irony in the evasion sequence in the correspondence between play and selfish and gratuitous abuse, as Jim's position is re-established as 'socially constituted fiction': the black man as docile, unintelligent and subhuman inferior.[41] Jim, in alien territory, imprisoned, in trouble, now falls back into the habitual responses of an earlier stage in the text. Twain unsettles his reader as he links his series of what are, superficially, comic effects, to the dehumanisation of Jim that now occurs. For Jim acts the largely silent butt to Tom and Huck's new plot: 'he couldn't see no sense in the most of it, but he allowed we was white folks and knowed better then him' (p. 321). His status becomes that of victim for practices that verge on the sadistic: 'Tom shoved a piece of candlestick into the middle of a corn-pone . . . and it worked just noble; when Jim bit into it it most mashed all his teeth out' (p. 322). His role now is that of the preposterous black body shaped at will to the humorous pleasure of the white manipulator, spectator and superior.[42] Twain takes us back, perhaps inevitably given the social situation he describes, to a Jim pinioned firmly within stereotyped representations, and able to do little more than to accept them: his voice and narrative more or less effectively silenced once the brief interlude alone with Huck is ended.

A second issue emerges from my analysis of Huck and Jim's relationship. This concerns Jim's overall role in the novel and how Twain represents him. Huck's textual freedom of speech directly counters his social powerlessness.[43] Jim though remains doubly constrained, not just by the social (his lack of civil rights[44]) but also by the textual, for this is someone else's narrative. His voice sounds powerfully and independently (in direct discourse) only fitfully. Indeed, this containment of Jim's voice – the fact that his story is necessarily placed in the context of, and subordinate to, Huck's own[45] – can account for many of the critical debates over his characterisation.

Commentators have argued over the text's racial discourse as a whole. Thus, for instance, while John H. Wallace calls the book 'racist trash', David L. Smith argues that it takes an 'explicitly anti-racist stance'.[46] Similar problems surface in discussion of Jim's characterisation, for while some critics see him as 'frozen within the conventions of the minstrel darky', others would agree with Smith in describing him as 'an intelligent, sensitive, wily, and considerate individual' who shows in his behaviour that 'race provides no useful index of character'.[47] What is at issue here is our knowledge (and ignorance) of Jim's *consciousness*. For though we are often given Jim's words, we are never allowed direct access to his thoughts. Even my earlier reading, which would see Jim's actions and motives in terms of the traditional slave narrative, must remain a partial and conditional one, because of that lack.

To be sure, Jim's words do at times clearly speak his intentions: to get freedom for himself and his family. But W. E. DuBois contends that the black man approaches the dominant white world from behind a 'vast veil', and shares with his fellow African-Americans that double consciousness resulting from his participation in two social systems.[48] If this is so, then we must ask how one who is a slave (Jim) can ever be known from the outside: by Huck or the reader? When Jim says, more than half to himself, 'Dog my cats ef I didn' hear sumf'n' (p. 53) as Huck and Tom disturb him on their midnight escapade, is this his natural mode of speech and part of his deepest being, or is it a highly artificial mode of discourse in a context where he never knows who might be listening: the only kind of (comic and non-threatening) talk available in a society where any note of black self-assertion is taboo? Equally, when Huck paddles off from the raft and Jim calls, 'Dah you goes, de ole true Huck; de on'y white genlman dat ever kep' his promise to ole Jim' (p. 147), is Jim showing his true face (as a trusting and humbly naive black man expressing grateful appreciation for a white superior's kindness) or is he speaking from behind a mask, constructing a 'simulated identity [as] his best defence against white cruelty and infidelity',[49] cleverly playing on Huck's emotions to preserve his own freedom intact?

To read Jim in one way, as a shallow-headed 'minstrel darky', or in another, as a shrewd and self-interested dissimulator, is to impose, I would suggest, a determinate reading on a character who is textually represented in an indeterminate way.[50] Jim's freedom-talk, and the thoughts and actions that give it substance, remain undeveloped in the novel (and especially at its conclusion). It may be that an agenda of cultural pluralism has led some critics to place more stress on the determinate nature of his role than the text justifies. This is not to downplay his importance nor that of the subject of race in the novel. It is, though, to serve as a reminder that the book starts, 'You don't know about me . . . ' (p. 49), with Huck engaging us in direct readerly contact and contract. Huck's voice controls this narrative. It is his story, not Jim's, that is being told.

However it is the authority of Huck's voice and the shape of his narrative that does, *despite* what I have said about the tensions between him and Jim, finally allow the story of race in *Huckleberry Finn* to retain its positive potential. Jim's narrative is taken over, and his thoughts and feelings fade from view. His role in the novel, too, is concluded with a series of anticlimactic and in many ways unsatisfactory turns in the plot. But this ending is balanced, and in many ways countered, by the other, disrupted, narrative that Huck has told: of companionship and equality on the raft. For the raft is not only a place where Huck and Jim engage in a form of dialogic contest. There is a different story told here too, as Huck describes what the raft means to him; and one in which Jim does, provisionally, take on a positive and equal role. It is this other story, when juxtaposed with the change in Jim's status as the novel draws to its end, that has lingered so insistently in the American collective mind.

III

However we reconstruct Jim's character and motives in the novel, it is clear that by its end any measure of autonomy, self-determination and self-respect potentially available to him, once he has made his initial escape from his slave condition, has been pretty well obliterated. The evasion routine reduces Jim to a dehumanised and reified level. He is not even present when Tom reveals he is in fact 'free', but is chained, hands and legs, in a cabin. Jim's brief speaking part in the last chapter focuses on his new financial status, the forty dollars Tom has given him that 'pleased [him] most to death' (p. 368). There is no hint of resentment here at Tom's exploitative behaviour, the way he has been used as a puppet to the latter's (corrupt) imaginative needs.[51] One of the main ironies of the ending, in terms of the discourse of freedom that the text has engaged, is that Jim's own agency counts for nothing in terms of his eventual change in status. The lack of any real final sense of celebration is suggested in William L. Andrews' comment that 'the fugitive slave has got his freedom, but lost his manhood'.[52]

The negative connotations of the ending of the novel are, I would suggest, a product of historical circumstance. For whether we consider the novel in terms of its fictional chronology or in terms of its time of writing, the position of Jim as representative African-American (if this is how we can take him) was bleak. The final sections of the novel implicitly ask questions concerning the nature of 'freedom' for an African-American male in both periods. Jim might be legally free with the forty dollars in his pocket (about two-fifths of per capita income in 1840[53]), but he is left alone, eleven hundred miles from home, and apparently 'all but forgotten by

Huck'.[54] The limits of his freedom are apparent with any knowledge of the status of the free slave in the region at the time. Victor Doyno summarises:

> A manumitted Black would certainly not enjoy genuine freedom in 1845. . . . The likelihood of Jim earning enough money to purchase his wife and children is close to zero. . . . [A]nyone could contest the freed status of a Black such as Jim by claiming that he was not in Missouri when Miss Watson died. In the 1845–1850 era, Jim could very easily be re-enslaved in Arkansas. . . . If a freedman stayed in Arkansas longer than 180 days, he could be imprisoned for a year.[55]

More crucially for the final stages of my argument, freedom was also a highly problematic term as it applied to black lives in the South after the War. The 'web of constraints',[56] in terms of both institutions and attitudes, that bound the free black before the War came, before long, also to characterise race relations in the post-bellum period. The freedom granted by the Thirteenth Amendment signified, for African-Americans, the end of oppressive and dehumanising white authority and a chance for new forms of self-development; was to mean autonomy and equal rights. Such hopes quickly evaporated, together with the first promises of Reconstruction. As W. E. B. DuBois wrote: 'the slave went free; stood a brief moment in the sun; then moved back again toward slavery'.[57] White Southerners (with the implicit and sometimes explicit support of the national political system) gradually re-established authority and control over the African-American population, and enmeshed them, in Eric Foner's words, 'in a seamless web of oppression, whose interwoven economic, political, and social strands all reinforced one another'.[58]

Jim's powerlessness and victimisation as he undergoes renewed imprisonment and a set of imposed discomforts frequently bordering on a form of torture, the meanwhile two members of the dominant white race slowly prepare to liberate his already legally free self, clearly parallels such a historical context. Fishkin sums up what has now become the critical consensus when she says that 'scholars are increasingly coming to understand the evasion as a satire on the way the United States botched the enterprise of freeing its slaves'.[59]

To return to Twain's treatment of Huck and Jim's relationship is not only, however, to justify the artistic logic of the evasion scenes.[60] It is also to suggest that the earlier sequences on the raft work, despite the thrust of my earlier argument, to fuse, as well as to oppose, Jim and Huck's voices and stories. This needs fuller explanation. I have shown that Huck's version of freedom, a relaxed drifting on the margins of the dominant society, differs from Jim's. Huck has, throughout the novel, a divided response to Jim, seeing him as friend, companion and equal, but also (quite otherwise), in socially constructed terms, as 'nigger'. For the catch-22 which limits Huck's 'freedom' at almost every turn is that he gives allegiance to the social charter; mouths the words and shares the values of the dominant culture even as he would (sometimes) resist them. He accepts the language, and thus the institutional and moral assumptions, of the society around him, never questions the validity of slavery as a system, nor its opinions concerning black status (as property). That is why, when Aunt Sally asks 'Anybody hurt?' on the steamboat cylinder head blow out, he can come out with the chilling answer, 'No'm. Killed a nigger' (p. 291). That is why, too, when Huck speculates on the response of his home village community if he were to write Miss Watson a letter telling her of Jim's whereabouts, he says: 'everybody *naturally* despises an ungrateful nigger, and they'd make Jim feel it all the time, and so he'd feel ornery and disgraced' (p. 281, my emphasis). Huck is unable to distinguish culture from nature here; to see Jim's position as enslaved, diminished and rebellious black subject as justifiably different from his 'natural' position – in Southern eyes and mind – as a humble and submissive servant to the requirements of his 'kind' mistress. Huck also accepts those religious values which, hand in glove, accompany the political. His fear 'that people that acts as I'd been acting about that nigger goes to everlasting fire' (p. 282) again marks his acceptance of dominant systems of belief.

Huck's attitude to Jim, though, is split. For at the same time that he accepts such systems, he knows they cannot satisfy his needs on the raft and (often) cannot serve to categorise his relation with Jim. When it comes to immediate action and pragmatic response, he fails, consequently, to share the definitions that he mouths. That is why, for instance, Huck can bring himself both to 'humble myself to a nigger' (p. 143), something his Southern society would consider unthinkable, and later decide to 'steal Jim out of slavery again'

(p. 283) despite the admonitions of his social conscience. This does not mean, though, that Huck rejects the value of conventional belief, but rather that he sees his lack of it as a sign of his own inadequacy as one who is 'ignorant and . . . low-down and ornery' (p. 61).

As Huck comes to know Jim (and vice versa) through their day-to-day comradeship, in a way that escapes the boundaries and norms of the surrounding community, so he becomes a strongly positive presence in Huck's raft narrative. Indeed on the raft, while – however temporarily – their two stories overlap, Huck is at times able to escape his conditioned response to racial difference. This coming together, as the tensions between Huck and Jim disappear, does depend on a certain pause in the action of Jim's narrative: a leaving of his own plans in abeyance as the raft drifts further downstream. For Jim, this is not necessarily a problem. He may want to head north and intend to rebuild his family and re-enter society on a new basis, but, before Cairo, he can share his means (travelling on the raft) with Huck even if their ends (to leave the raft, or stay on it) are different. Huck's version of freedom on the raft is not in the short term, but only ultimately, antithetical to Jim's interests. Even once Cairo is past, and Jim's interests become, in textual terms at least, subordinate (we hear little more of his plans), the raft can still become a place apart where racial tension can disappear. In fact the shelving of Jim's immediate plans contribute to this effect.

When, though, the textual return is made to the matter of Jim's freedom, its thematic centrality is subsumed in the focus on Tom's romantic plots. The evasion sequence, as I have suggested, is a fictional echo of a bleak historical reality: 'an unsatisfying farce that reflected the travesty that "freedom" had become for African Americans in the post-Reconstruction era'.[61] Jim's final manu-mission, too, brings no suggestion of a radical change in his status (if we know anything about ante-bellum Southern history). The effect of this is that, if the reader is looking for a positive version of race relations in the novel, he or she must go back to the sequences on the raft, both before and after Cairo, when Huck and Jim are at ease and at one with each other. It must immediately be recognised that it is Huck who voices this unity. He is the one, after all, who passes such comments as 'we judged that we was free and safe. . . . We said there warn't no home like a raft' (p. 176). But this is consonant with Jim's direct words and actions as they are represented; appropriate to the relationship he has been establishing with Huck, and to a situation where he is back in a kind of limbo (as far as the development of his own slave narrative goes).

Despite the indeterminate representation of Jim's character, then, and despite the fact that his and Huck's needs and narratives tend to run off, when they are most clearly specified, in different directions, there is a powerfully positive (if necessarily undeveloped) social and political charge in the sections of the novel, on the raft, where their two stories do temporarily elide. A positive version of 'freedom' does appear, however hedged in by internal and external circumstance, and whatever the unanswered questions it raises. The form it takes is that of Huck and Jim alone together, naked, talking 'about all kind of things' on the raft, and letting 'her float wherever the current wanted her to' (pp. 178–9). Relaxed and at ease with one another, all tension and competition can and does drop, for the moment, away. Their relationship of two becomes, for one critic at least, a version of 'that redemptive American community which the shore has betrayed'.[62] These moments of social harmony on the raft, and the frustration of what follows, function (I would contend) as a form of narrative incompletion. Such incompletion connects up with an ongoing debate on race in America which had reached a particular crisis point as Twain wrote. The free and equal relation Huck and Jim manage to have – despite all the previously made provisos – acts as a political stimulus, in however loose a sense. It offers, and offered Twain's contemporaries, a model of social possibility which, once depicted, cannot easily be put out of cultural mind.

IV

To present Huck and Jim's relationship on the raft in this way is to modify traditional readings of the novel. These have tended to see the raft as a type of pure space unaffected by the larger social world, and to distinguish between the notion of idyll, which occurs on the raft, and the historical. I would contend that the boundary between the idyllic and the historical is not watertight, and neither (to add a corollary) is that between indirect and explicit forms of social and political comment. Race is a central component in the depiction of

Huck and Jim's relationship in *Huckleberry Finn*. Twain, thus, necessarily engages the wider social and political context of his America. The best version of such racial interaction may be utopian (only possible on the raft) given a set of historical circumstances – in the 1830s–1840s, and in the 1880s – which make a mockery of African-American freedom. It can, though, function to suggest, however tentatively, that rigid current social practice is open to future positive change. On the raft, Twain gives his fellow Americans a different and more progressive version (that is, from a liberal pluralist standpoint where black and white stories can be constructed as potentially running together) of what 'freedom' in the area of racial politics might start to mean than is offered elsewhere in the novel, or in the post-Reconstruction America with which it is in dialogue.

Jonathan Arac argues in a recent influential essay that Twain's novel is 'antihistorical', that 'the form and fable of *Huckleberry Finn* reject the very possibility of public debate'.[63] Richard C. Moreland's analysis of Huck's role, and his tendency to reject the influence of any 'natural, social, or certainly psychological limitations on his own freedom and will', complements that analysis. Referring to the plan 'fixed up' (p. 283) by Huck, following his 'heroic, private moral decision to help Jim escape', Moreland says that:

> The last part of Twain's novel demonstrates in intensely tedious and frustrating detail the inadequacy and ineffectiveness of Huck's unmediated private act of will to set Jim free. . . . Such acts of will prove inadequate and ineffective unless they are also followed up with the positive and specific 'plans' and narrative plots that would articulate and negotiate Huck and Jim's desires in a relationship and a course of action that would resist and counter Tom Sawyer's cultural powers, rather than allow him to write Huck and Jim into his own . . . series of romances into which other stories and plans too often seem to disappear.[64]

Twain's novel, and its frustrating ending, *can* be seen to engage the 'contingencies of history'[65] if we take a different approach. For could Twain imagine (can we imagine) any other ending to *Huckleberry Finn*, given both the status of its narrator and central protagonist and the structures of social and cultural power which bind him?[66] Arac distinguishes between an allegorical interpretation of Twain's text and its direct entry into the field of 'public debate'.[67] In fact, the lines between direct and indirect methods are almost always blurred when fiction, not history, is being written, and an entry into public debate does not necessarily have to be openly announced – especially for a humorist (which Twain was), and especially in difficult political times (which these were).

However intentional the allegorical resonances of *Huckleberry Finn* may be, it is difficult to know, given the historical circumstances in which Twain wrote, and the chosen boundaries of his narrative, how he might otherwise have addressed national political concerns. Oblique and indirect tactics are necessary in a social world which offers no space of freedom for political or collective action,[68] and it is exactly such a world which Twain represents. Moreland speaks of the 'positive and specific "plans"' by which Huck might further his relationship with Jim, and instigate an ongoing 'course of action'. The lack of specificity in these words may mask the historical fact that, for a young, ill-educated and low-class social misfit in the South circa 1840, the likelihood of acting against the socially reinforced authorities, and of helping to right the injustices of slavery (if he were indeed capable of so recognising them), was nil. So read, the temporary merger of Huck and Jim's stories on the raft and the type of freedom found there, come to function, in their very fragility and precariousness, as that form of narrative incompletion previously claimed. Their joint story of (temporary) autonomy, companionship, safety and even equality, reflexively relates to, and interacts with, the larger, more complex and unresolved narrative of American race relations: one that cannot be settled in so relatively easy or exceptional a manner.

The representation of Huck and Jim's relationship on the raft and the frustration that follows can, then, be turned by the cooperative reader into historical engagement: into what Moreland calls 'ongoing cultural work in progress'. That work would explore how black and white stories might begin to be reconciled, put together, reconstituted on a different racial and social basis.[69] Twain's depiction of Huck and Jim points to this historical lack, but also to its possibility. The rhythm of the novel shows Huck moving from various forms of isolation to that 'embryonic model of community'[70] with Jim, on the raft. The undeveloped quality of this model is clear, both in its homosocial nature and the rudimentary form of its two-person base (the minimum for social existence). It is, though, what might grow from this embryo that merits cultural attention.

This may sound like a reworking of Leslie Fiedler, who famously proposed a Whitmanesque and homoerotic harmony between Huck and Jim as 'nearly coeval loving pair' on the river. My reading borders on, but also significantly departs from, his. For Fiedler's main concern is for the personal and not the political, a separation which is enforced by the opposition between nature and culture central to his analysis. The river is thus seen as a 'place out of time and history . . . beyond the bounds of society', while nature itself is described 'as Eden'.[71] I, too, see the idyllic aspects of (some of) the river sequences as central to Huck and Jim's relation. I would, however, keep the link intact between idyll and the social and political; between Huck and Jim's (sometimes) desegregated lives and post-emancipation racial inequities. Indeed, it is the political implication of this relationship I would stress.

Huck's relation to the dominant Southern social order is charac-terised by repression. The terms used to describe this order, if we see Widow Douglas as its early representative, are introduced at the very start of the book: 'dismal regular and decent' (p. 49). It is associated with both temporal and spatial constraint: 'it was rough living in the house all the time. . . . The widow rang a bell for supper, and you had to come to time' (pp. 49–50). Despite the distractions of Tom Sawyer's games, Huck is a passive and often withdrawn figure within this social world, subject to the discourses of mastery of all those – Pap, the Widow, Tom, the Grangerfords, and the King and the Duke – who assume authority over him.

With Jim on the raft, *despite* the fluctuations in their relationship and the battles for power engaged, things can be different. In many ways the raft functions as an estranged or alienated social world where Huck and Jim depart from the accepted norms of interracial behaviour: strip off their clothes; share food; enjoy 'talking, and singing, and laughing' (p. 283) together; rebuke and apologise to each other, as and if the occasion demands. On the raft, not all, but some of the time, the interaction of black and white without fear, prejudice or constraint can be accommodated. In the idyll, for this is what it is, 'all temporal boundaries are blurred and the rhythm of human life is in harmony with the rhythm of nature'.[72]

Mikhail Bakhtin associates the idyll with the restoration of 'folkloric time'. He does not, however, see this as regressive, but rather focuses on its positive and political implications, with the folk figured as the 'untamable, rebellious, and regenerative force that will destroy the status quo', 'newer and finer worlds' rising from the ashes of the old order.[73] The idealising tendencies implicit here, and the revolutionary politics accompanying them, can be modified if we refigure this argument in terms of race not class, and in the American context of Twain's writing. To do so is to look forward to what, with difficulty, might be a future possibility, rather than to trust in a past, and still available, socio-political model (the folkloric) on which one can build.

Approached in this way, Huck and Jim's relationship can be seen in terms of the political and the social, as well as the natural (the idyll). River and riverbank are never, in Twain's novel, neatly containable terms. And if the language and personnel of the riverbank can spill into the river world, then, too, what is established on the raft – the utopian form, however fragile and intermittent, of Huck and Jim's union – can have implications for, potentially spill into, the larger social world. At one remove from the larger social order and its immediate pressures, Huck and Jim's relationship nonetheless reflects back on that order. What is presented as historically rigid, the politics of race relations in the South, is always open to change. The idyllic and utopian (or the indirect, in Arac's terms) are necessarily defined by their opposites, the practical and realisable (the direct), and always call in their direction.

The relaxed discussions Jim and Huck eventually come to have (about, for instance, the origin of the stars – p. 179) and their unpressured togetherness (lying on their backs, legs dangling in the water, talking) democratise the narrative, and realign the boundaries of pleasure and possibility. Though dispute occurs on the raft,[74] the equality of voice also found in their relationship subverts a larger social system which has only one definition of racial interaction. The mutual generosity and potential for harmony realised within the limits of this embryonic interracial community provides a defusing of the accepted power relations and a promise of a new racial dynamic. The celebration of Jim and Huck's bodies on the raft, and their sharing of a language, potentially calls into being a democratic society in which black and white can operate as joint constituents.

The eventual defeat of that community can be read as a sign of incompletion. For its possible rebuilding and re-creation, in the future and in whatever form, necessarily operates to unsettle the resolution of the novel's plot; to resist its final machinations, explanations and closure. The text's balance tilts unavoidably, following the facts of Southern history, back toward authoritarian control, repression and racial inequality, and away from equality, easy companionship and generosity of spirit. As it does, however, so is the remembrance of this latter potential for interracial harmony and community guaranteed; so is the promise of its fuller realisation at some future stage put on the historical agenda.

There are still unresolved issues here. The distance between the model of social possibility the novel offers, operating on a micro-cosmic level and in limited spatial confines, and its realisation as concrete political, economic and social practice, is considerable. The question as to exactly *how* the relationship on the raft might function, when then projected into the wider social world, in terms of any 'positive and specific "plans"', remains unanswered. The historical relevance of Twain's novel lies in its representation of, and challenge to, white supremacist thought and social practice at a time when race relations were rapidly worsening; when, in Christine MacLeod's words:

> what with Northern indifference and the emerging Black Codes in the South – with vagrancy and curfew laws, the sharecropping system, white monopoly of credit, widespread vigilante intim-idation and endemic racism – the average freedman had about as much chance as Jim has at the Phelps Farm of realizing any practical distinction between his current situation and his previous condition of servitude.[75]

The indirect manner in which such a challenge is made, however, necessarily means that the terms I have used to describe Huck and Jim's relationship on the raft and Twain's positive representation of interracial compact – democracy, equality, community, even freedom – must remain abstract signifiers, from a historicist point of view. All language is subject to contested meaning. Harriet Jacobs, in her *Incidents in the Life of a Slave Girl* (1861), would meet ante-bellum celebrations of a polished Southern 'civilisation' head on with her brief words on the punishments meted out to slaves in the region: 'cruelty is contagious in uncivilized communities'.[76] Similarly, words like democracy and equality can carry simple meanings in a two-person relation on a raft, but once a larger and more complex social fabric is re-engaged, any consensus definition of the terms soon disappears. There are only practices of freedom, and those practices are defined differently according to the interests of particular social groups, and in particular historical circumstances. After all, the freedom Jim gets from Miss Watson at the end of the novel is of a different kind than that (outside the normal social boundaries) Huck already has; is a version of that freedom which Huck claims, while in the Widow Douglas's care, to lack. The relative nature of the word in political terms can, moreover, be measured by the fact that Martin Luther King would still yearn, speaking on behalf of his race in the 1963 March on Washington speech, to be 'Free at last!' – to gain the freedom that the emancipation proclamation had supposedly handed over a hundred years before.

To put this in another way, *Huckleberry Finn* does address, though in an indirect manner, the debate about the race question of the 1880s.[77] The evasion sequence functions as 'displaced polemic',[78] serving ironically to critique regional and national political actions and racial ideology in the period following the collapse of Reconstruction. Novels engage with history in a variety of ways, and to approach it 'by de back' (to use Jim's words – p. 134) is as valid a tactic as any. In doing this, questions are left unanswered, not only about the level of authorial intent, but particularly as to just how the forms of freedom found, and built, on the raft might translate to larger, and more complex, social actuality. The problems involved in such a process are indicated in the temporary and provisional nature of the harmony Huck and Jim do find, and the diverging aspects of their stories which continually threaten it. But one might say that the business of the novel is not to suggest concrete and detailed solutions to intractable social problems. Twain's representation of black and white co-operation may not, in terms of text and story time, last long, and might be flying in the face of contemporary historical fact. It does however offer an embryonic model of social (and thus political) possibility – of unity despite difference; of equality and empathy – which has remained in the arena of public debate, however muted that debate may at times have become, from his time to the present.

6

Fantasy and *A Connecticut Yankee in King Arthur's Court*

It is said [that] if you ask a Connecticut Yankee in any part of the world how he is, he will, if not 'sick,' answer 'moving, Sir,' equivalent to saying 'well'; for, if well, he is sure to be on the move.

(Lady Emmeline Stuart Wortley)[1]

Up to this time there had been absolutely no system. Everything was done by guess; nothing was calculated.

(Twain's notebook entry on Webster & Company, the publishing house he had established)[2]

'There,' exclaimed Dr Southwick. 'There is the culmination of ten years' work and study. We live in a higher civilization from this day.'

(On the apparently successful completion of the first legal electrocution in America, 6 August 1890)[3]

I

Hank Morgan, Twain's Connecticut Yankee, is certainly a man on the move. Hit on the head by a crowbar, he 'momentarily tears the fabric of time'[4] as he travels in an instant from the Colt Arms

Factory in nineteenth-century Connecticut to sixth-century Arthurian England. Twain himself is on the artistic move here, too. His turn from the ante-bellum Mississippi setting of *Tom Sawyer* and *Huckleberry Finn* to the England of a much earlier period is accompanied by the shift to fantasy as a literary mode.

Twain constantly experimented with literary genre. In *Tom Sawyer* and *Huckleberry Finn*, his step to an ante-bellum American past allowed him both to engage, but also to evade, his anxieties about the direction of his contemporary American society. As I have suggested, this formal tactic, in the boy book *Tom Sawyer*, provided an effective way of representing ambivalent attitudes both about the past and the present. His use of the retrospective travel narrative in *Roughing It* served parallel ends.

Huckleberry Finn works similarly, though the contentious nature of its central subject makes it an altogether more troubling book. I have used the allegorical fit between the evasion sequence and post-Reconstruction events to suggest that the novel can be read as a criticism of post-bellum American racial practice. The book's peculiar generic mix, though – and quite possibly the unwillingness of its first audience to hear something it preferred not to hear, especially when it came in apparently comic guise – allowed its full implications to pass unnoticed, until (indeed) very recently. This may have entirely suited Twain, or may, indeed, have passed him by. For where I refer to Twain's authorial intentions in my last chapter, this is very much a provisional act: done in the knowledge that the text carries conflicting meanings, *can* be read in quite another way, and that such intentions – allegorical or otherwise – cannot be guaranteed.

Indeed, I would argue that many of the social criticisms I have already identified (and will identify) in Twain's texts, and the doubts about the status and limits of the individual subject that run alongside them, may well not have been deliberately thematised. As I suggest in my first chapter, in the end this is for me beside the point. For it is in the work that Twain's texts do as they engage the cultural dialogues of their times that my main interest lies. Twain was a comic writer dependent on entertaining his audience for his continued financial and literary success. He was also a businessman and a member of respectable society, identified as often with conservative values as with radical ones, at least till the end of his career. Even his attitude to racial issues was not entirely unambiguous.[5]

We repeatedly see in his work both challenges to the assumptions of the dominant culture, and endorsements of them, as his texts move in quite contradictory directions. *A Connecticut Yankee* is no exception to this rule.

Firm definition of literary genres is a difficult matter, and particularly in Twain's case. *Huckleberry Finn* is based, as Harold Beaver points out, on at least four models, 'the picaresque, the epistolary, the autobiographical, and the adventure story'.[6] This, though, is not what causes problems in terms of interpretation and audience response. These come about, I would suggest, as a result of the gap between a number of different perspectives that both control the text and are (potentially) made available as we read it. I have said that the novel works as allegory. To interpret it in terms of American racial issues in the post-Reconstruction era is, though, to see through Huck's voice to a second narrative position: that of the author who writes from the perspective of the 1880s. The possibility of allegory then opens up. But it is very easy to read the novel in another way, as realist literature. To read on this level alone is to remain unaware of the full nature of its racial critique. For the realist techniques Twain uses pull the reader into a direct engagement with his central protagonist and narrator, and the ante-bellum world in which he moves, and work to counter an allegorical alternative.

Realism, of course, is itself a slippery and highly problematic term, and whether the novel fits this category or not is a matter of considerable critical dispute.[7] It is, however, generally associated with an unproblematic rendering of accepted social norms. If there is a gap between an allegorical and realistic reading of *Huckleberry Finn*, I would also argue that, taken at the latter (realistic) level alone, another type of gap – and one this time which has nothing to do with historical periodisation – opens up. This happens as the first-person narrator's account of his own experience is placed beside the different assessment of that experience which his words and actions allow. I point here to the role of the author in manipulating his marginal, naive and alienated protagonist, but I also suggest that Huck's words may tell us (the readers) more than that author intends. For it is in the margin between the recounting of Huck's direct experiences, and the realisation by the reader of their larger implications, that the conventional assumptions associated with realism – assumptions concerning the nature of the self, the values of the social order in which that self moves, and the balance between the individual and his surrounding society – are interrogated. In other words, I see in *Huckleberry Finn* an endorsement of accepted norms and a critique of them running side by side. And though all but the most literal of readers engage at some level with the latter challenge, the extent to which they do so depends on how far they are able to see the fullest implications of Huck's narrative, and to acknowledge the further perspective available (to see meanings in Huck's story that he himself cannot see). This needs further explanation.

The techniques and attitudes in *Huckleberry Finn* in many ways conform to generally accepted definitions of realism. Realism as a term asserts a claim to transparency: what June Howard calls a 'privileged relationship to [the] assumed extra-textual world, invoking an ability to embody "reality" . . . as constitutive of the genre itself'.[8] Twain uses Huck to provide a 'translucent window'[9] on to the immediate world. Huck's vernacular voice leads us into a solidly framed historical context, the small-town ante-bellum Southwest. This is the 'reality' we are asked to take for granted, with all its social practices, its racial distinctions, its cultural codes. Such dominant social assumptions are the given which holds the whole novel in place. Realism firmly embeds individual character in its surrounding environment, focusing on dress, manners, social connections and occupations. This provides a way of exploring the relationship between the individual and his (in Huck's case) environment at a time when prior romantic beliefs in 'the sovereign territory of the individual self'[10] were no longer tenable.

The realistic text, none the less, does generally assume the essential wholeness and coherence of the subject: what Rosemary Jackson calls 'the unity of "character" . . . – that definition of the self as a coherent, indivisible and continuous whole which has dominated Western thought for centuries'.[11] It also binds character and reader within a fixed social framework, the world as it exists. Indeed, the genre is perhaps most often described in terms of the *balance* it depicts between the individual and the social world. Thus Lee Clark Mitchell, loosely bunching Twain, Henry James and William Dean Howells as realists, identifies a shared key concern in the fact that:

they all presented characters as 'subjective selves' who possessed clear capacities for restraint and responsibility. . . . Realist authors enforced a moral perspective on narrative action, a perspective involving the same considerations of intention and responsibility we habitually project on each other (and onto fictional characters as well).[12]

Huckleberry Finn works as a realist text, according to these criteria. Huck can be read as a unified character, a sympathetic and free-speaking (in a sense, he speaks the text) young boy making his way in a difficult Southern world, but responding to it with a clear seeing and pragmatic eye. However, Huck offers no real challenge to the dominant norms of the Southern social order. Though he resists those norms, he sees this as a sign of his own marginality rather than of their inadequacy. An established and unchanging social fabric provides the backdrop against which all Huck's dodgings and weavings occur, and the failings of that order to meet both his and Jim's needs are, to a degree, forgotten, as they are safely (if provisionally) reconciled with Aunt Sally and her world at the finish. We can identify a realist agenda, too, to one of the climactic scenes of the novel where Huck decides to '*go* to hell'[13] (p. 283) rather than letting Jim back into Miss Watson's hands: this can be constructed as an act of individual moral responsibility that counters the 'outer force'[14] of a determining social environment.

There are, however, other ways of reading all of the above. Critics usually argue that the realistic novel upholds 'bourgeois ideology'.[15] But realistic fiction can interrogate social rules and conventions, and the unproblematic nature of subjectivity; does not necessarily take them for granted. And this is what happens in Twain's text. Thus the possibility of escaping social determinants in independent moral action in Huck's decision not to tell on Jim is deeply undermined by Miss Watson's prior actions (for she has already, in fact, set Jim free), by the negative quality of Huck's choice, and by his own consequent position as Tom Sawyer's minion. Equally, the very idea of the intending 'subjective self' is, to a degree, questionned by the extent to which Huck's own language and thoughts are unconscious products of his larger society, and by a textual play on disguise and the slippage of identity (foregrounded, for instance, in Jim's question 'Is I *me*, or who *is* I?[16]) which tends to subvert any notion of fixed selfhood. Finally, though Huck may be a marginal social figure, Twain none the less does use him to launch a penetrating interrogation of the nature of the real. He uses the device of the alienated and uncomprehendingly naive first person narrator and protagonist to mount a serious challenge to the dominant cultural order (though, certainly, the setting of the novel in a prior historical period eases such a task). Bakhtin sees one function of the fool in literature as 'by his very uncomprehending presence . . . mak[ing] strange the world of social conventionality'.[17] Tony Bennett spells out some of the effects of this in Twain's novel when he says that the character of Huck 'functions as a formal device whereby the ideological forms upholding the institution of slavery are turned inside out, made to appear strange and, in the process, called into question'.[18]

In *Huckleberry Finn*, to sum up, both the gap between American present and American past, and that between the naive narrative voice and an informed authorial and readerly presence, establish a number of double effects. The allegorical shift to the racial politics of the 1880s depends on the recognition that the novel need not necessarily be read in terms of realism alone. The critique of dominant values that I identify above, and which does occur within a realistic frame, is both readily available for the reader to see in the text, and yet is possible – at a number of levels – to overlook. Twain's own intentions, as far as this latter critique goes, cannot be entirely determined here. For while the authorial position he constructs is clearly meant to challenge southern social and ideological values, we have no way of going further, and knowing to what degree he was aware of the various questions about subjectivity and moral agency the text also raises. What happens here, where an interrogation of dominant values (which works on a number of different levels) is both conducted and disguised at one and the same time, and where the intentions of the author are unclear, is entirely in line with the patterns of Twain's writing as a whole.

In *Connecticut Yankee*, the type of gaps and distances Twain exploits in his fiction widens. For, if a similar shift occurs between authorial voice, readerly perspective and fictional narrator, Twain now moves the setting of his novel way back in time, and uses fantasy as his fictional mode, to create a whole series of disjunctive effects. As I argue in the rest of this chapter, this latter genre is particularly suitable to Twain's continued critical interrogation of the directions and developments and values of his own America. As I also argue, though, Twain himself remained, at the very most, ambivalent (and even perhaps unconscious) as to the full extent of such a process. Moreover, the very displacements of the novel, its comic effects, and its contradictory thematic elements, mean that it remained (and remains) entirely possible to pass over the criticisms of American culture that the book contains.

In the move to fantasy, however, I see the introduction of a mode that would become increasingly useful to Twain. For fantasy potentially challenges conventional assumptions and norms by moving away from realist forms completely. It turns everyday reality upside down by introducing another *obviously* unreal scenario; an alternative and different world to set against the everyday one. Such generic effects would increasingly meet Twain's artistic needs as his career progressed, and as his unease with American 'realities' (as measured in terms of everyday conceptions of selfhood, value systems and beliefs) became more pressing. And everything in his fiction suggests that this indeed was the case.

II

My placing *A Connecticut Yankee* in the category of the fantastic is not entirely unproblematic. One might choose to describe the novel otherwise, as medieval romance, for example, or as a coming together, and conflict between, romance or sentimentalism and realism, or as a dystopian novel, as burlesque and satire, as displaced western, or science fiction.[19] Rather than giving a detailed analysis of the ways in which *A Connecticut Yankee* conforms to the conventions of fantasy, I follow generally accepted critical opinion here in taking its generic categorisation for granted.[20] Rosemary Jackson's comment on the relation between the mimetic and the marvellous in fantasy is, though, worth recalling, given the particular relation between realism and its opposite in Twain's text:

Fantastic narratives confound elements of both the marvellous and the mimetic. They assert that what they are telling is real – rely on the conventions of realistic fiction to do so – and then they proceed to break that assumption of realism by introducing what – within those terms – is manifestly unreal.[21]

For Jackson, fantasy is 'the inside, or underside, of realism. . . . It is all that is not said, all that is unsayable, through realistic forms.' In Todorov's words, it is 'nothing more than the uneasy conscience of the positivist nineteenth century'. Such definitions ignore realism's own ability to challenge dominant values, and to dislocate what is conventionally taken for granted. But they nevertheless suggest what fantasy can do: violating and upsetting the real, 'opening spaces where unity had been assumed'.[22] In taking his modern American man, Hank Morgan, 'a Yankee of the Yankees',[23] and transporting him to Arthurian England (or at least a fabular version, via Malory, of that England[24]), Twain defamiliarises and questions everyday American assumptions and values. He does so by setting them, through the figure of Hank, in an alien context, alongside a culture which is resistant to them, and which operates on a completely other mental and ideological basis. Nineteenth-century positivist notions are (literally) exploded in the process.

This is, however, only half the story, for again the novel covers up the criticisms of American culture it has to make quite as much as it reveals them. My main interest here is in suggesting the dis-ease with contemporary America which the novel illustrates.[25] But I would not underestimate the extent to which this is masked in *A Connecticut Yankee*; indeed the extent to which it may have been masked to Twain himself. Everett Carter has made a strong case for identifying Hank's values, at least as regards the worth of science, republicanism and technology, with Twain's own while he was writing the book (and before his investments in the Paige typesetter had proved to be the disaster they later turned out to be).[26] And it is certainly clear that most contemporary reviewers focused on the celebration of democratic values, and the defence of 'basic human rights . . . fundamental equalities' represented in the novel.[27] I would argue that the book contains contradictory thematic elements, and that it can be interpreted as a satiric attack on the established church and aristocratic ways of late nineteenth-century British society and a celebration of democracy, just as easily as it can be taken as a critique of Hank's own values and behaviour. It is also easy to forget, in either case, that this is a genuinely funny novel, and that this is the level on which many readers take it. Thus one can, for instance, identify (in a po-faced manner) Hank's lack of humanity in such jokes as the one when he gives Morgan le Fay the go-ahead to 'hang the whole band' (p. 155) after the 'agony' (p. 152) of their performance. But it is equally easy to see the scene as Twain having, and giving his audience, fun, with no regard to thematic consistency. If I am aware my own analysis errs continually in too straight-faced a direction, this does not mean that I am unaware of Twain's comic effects, but that I would concentrate, none the less, on the cultural anxieties I discover here.

Carter marshalls his evidence to say that:

> the meaning of *A Connecticut Yankee* is, as the author repeatedly said it was, that the American nineteenth century, devoted to political and religious liberalism and to technology, was better than the traditional past. The efforts of modern men to continue a progress towards a fulfilment of material goals is shown to be a worthy mission of man.[28]

This may be true. It is clear, however, that there are contrary, and quite possibly unintended, meanings loosed in the novel too. Thus a number of critics, of whom Mark Seltzer, Martha Banta, Ronald Takaki and Cindy Weinstein can be taken as representative, focus on the ways in which *A Connecticut Yankee* fictionally represents the problems facing an American society in the process of rapid and disorienting change as Twain was writing.[29] For these critics, it is modernisation, and the fears, pressures and disruptions that accompanied it, which provide the informing context for analysis of the novel. Thus, Takaki, for instance, reads the text as one in which:

> Twain traveled back in time to assess his own age and its Yankee enterprise and technology . . . offer[ing] a diagnosis of American civilization and its nervousness. . . . His 'Connecticut Yankee' . . . is the modernizer of a feudal society. What he scatters, however, are the seeds of destruction. . . . [Hank is] a scientific manager [who] establishes a centralized bureaucracy to increase efficiency and productivity. Ultimately, however, his aim is not production or profits but control for the sake of control. Here . . . in Twain's novel, we have a condemnation of arrogant Yankee misuse of technology, and a frightening fable which exposed what was actually happening in nineteenth-century American society. . . . As [the 'enterprising' men of white America] built their 'America by design,' they were employing technology as a mode of

production as well as an instrument for the domination and reinforcement of social relations in a capitalist society. Like Hank Morgan, they were creating centralized bureaucracies and placing society under the direction of professionals and scientific managers. They were substituting technology for the body and also channelling men, women, and children into factories and reducing them to machine attendants.[30]

My own reading of the novel runs along similar lines. Carter may be correct in his analysis of authorial intent. Twain's anxieties about the direction of post-Civil War American society (however unconscious or partially formulated they might have been) are, though, as I have shown, consistently evident in both the themes and forms of his work from an early stage of his career. His texts necessarily connect up with the cultural conversations of their times. All Twain's fiction before *A Connecticut Yankee* reveals doubts and ambiguities about both the direction of American history and the shaping of American cultural values. His use of fantasy in this novel significantly extends any prior use of estrangement and dislocation devices. In the manifestly unreal transfer of a type of American everyman into an earlier Arthurian world, and the type of comparisons and disjunctions it allows, Twain releases (despite all the countervailing effects) a more wide-ranging critique of dominant American social assumptions than in any of his work to that point.

III

Recent critical work on late nineteenth-century literature (prompted especially by Walter Benn Michaels's *The Gold Standard and the Logic of Naturalism*[31]) focuses recurrently on the question of individual agency, and how it functions or fails to function within the context of what Martha Banta calls a 'capitalist historiography'.[32] Cindy Weinstein traces such concern over the status of the individual in a modernising economy back to mid-century. She follows Foucault in looking at the way the human body is 'imprinted by history', and illustrates how the literature of that period 'registered a critical cultural moment in which relations between labor, bodies, and agency, were being (re) invented, renegotiated'.[33] Mark Seltzer examines this same cluster of anxieties concerning the boundaries between 'interior states and external systems, and between bodies and persons and machines', with particular reference to the later years of the century, relating such anxieties to what he calls the 'psychotopography of machine culture'.[34] One explanation for the recent revival of critical interest in this latter period is the direct relevance of such concerns to our contemporary awareness (post Foucault) of the relation between the status of the human subject and the politics of the body: that body punished and corrected, supervised and controlled, regulated by the various systems of power and forms of discourse by which a modern bourgeois system, to echo his terms, disciplines its subjects. In this, novels written at the end of the nineteenth century appear increasingly to foreshadow contemporary and even postmodernist concerns.

Twain's interest in the question of agency and identity has been a subject of extended critical enquiry. There is a well-known passage from *A Connecticut Yankee* which serves as an obvious stimulus for discussion of the types of bodily discipline and body–machine interactions described above. Hank's role here is as one who reduces one particular man to a machine, in his drive for both efficiency and profit. The passage comes in Hank Morgan's description of his visit to the Valley of Holiness and his account of one of the 'supremely great' hermits who lives there, one whose 'mighty celebrity' had 'penetrated all Christendom':

His stand was a pillar sixty feet high, with a broad platform on the top of it. He was now doing what he had been doing every day for twenty years up there – bowing his body ceaselessly and rapidly almost to his feet. It was his way of praying. I timed him with a stop-watch, and he made 1,244 revolutions in 24 minutes and 46 seconds. It seemed a pity to have all this power going to waste. It was one of the most useful motions in mechanics, the pedal movement; so I made a note in my memorandum book, purposing some day to apply a system of elastic cords to him and run a sewing-machine with it. I afterwards carried out that scheme, and got five years' good service out of him; in which time he turned out upwards of eighteen thousand first-rate tow-linen shirts, which was ten a day. I worked him Sundays and all; he was going, Sundays, the same as week-days, and it was no use to waste the power. These shirts cost me nothing but just the mere trifle for the materials – I furnished those myself, it would not have been right to make him do that – and they sold like smoke to pilgrims at a dollar and a half apiece, which was the price of fifty cows or a blooded race-horse in Arthurdom. They were regarded as a perfect protection against sin, and advertised as such by my knights everywhere, with the paint-pot and stencil-plate; insomuch that there was not a cliff or a boulder or a dead-wall in England but you could read on it at a mile distance:

'Buy the only genuine St Stylite; patronized by the Nobility. Patent applied for.'

There was more money in the business than one knew what to do with. As it extended, I brought out a line of goods suitable for kings. . . .

But about that time I noticed that the motive power had taken to standing on one leg, and I found that there was something the matter with the other one; so I stocked the business and unloaded, taking Sir Bors de Ganis into camp financially along with certain of his friends: for the works stopped within a year, and the good saint got him to his rest. But he had earned it. I can say that for him. (pp. 205–6)

There are several things to say before I analyse this passage as a critique of Hank's role as an agent of modernisation. The first is that the hermit is very different from the mass of the population, those 'down-trodden people' (p. 176) whom Hank would free from chains of religious and aristocratic servitude and make independent citizens of a new republic. The hermit's status as a Catholic saint, and the futile nature of his activity (in Hank's mind at least), make him a particularly obvious target for manipulation.[35] None the less, I would argue that the religious animus in the episode disguises the fact that Hank's activity is symptomatic of behaviour and attitudes repeated elsewhere, and in circumstances where such qualifications do not apply. They can thus be taken as paradigmatic. My second comment leads in a similar direction. I would want to recognise that Twain is genuinely funny here, as he opposes the rigidity of the hermit's movements (and consciousness) to Hank's quick and pragmatic wit. Certainly it is easier to laugh at the humour of the scene and to see its dehumanising implications more in terms of Twain being carried away by the comedy of the situation, rather than as a serious critique of Hank's values. In line with my former argument, however, I would see this scene as having exactly that double focus previously described. For the comedy in the passage works to veil the alternative response on which I concentrate.

There is an obvious (though implicit) clash of discourse and conceptualisation here between Hank, the 'impatient modernizer', and the medieval Christian world he is engaging. Werner Sollors, in an intriguing article on 'Ethnicity', discusses the prevalence of 'boundary constructing strategies' in Twain's novel. Hank, a 'solitary bourgeois anachronism'[36] in the Arthurian world, imposes his language and set of values on it. The conditions which form Hank's discourse are those of the capitalist economy which initially locates him. Secular and sacred frames of knowledge clash in the dislocations that fantasy brings: the hermit's assumption of religious devotion and freely chosen action are obliterated – or at least overlaid – by Hank's first-person voice and values.

The entry of the moderniser, Hank, into a different medieval world, becomes a way of opening the rationalisations and efficiencies of late nineteenth-century business practice[37] to comparativist criticism and even ridicule. Frederick Winslow Taylor (the time and motion specialist) had not yet achieved national renown when Twain was writing *A Connecticut Yankee*, but was already 'meticulously pursu[ing] "speed" and "feed" studies at Midvale Steel in the mid-1880s'. The principles which he, and other management experts, were introducing in an attempt to 'determine the "one best way" to increase industrial productivity' and bring 'order, rationality, and efficiency out of the disorder, the irrationality, and the wastefulness of the times' had already been grasped by Hank Morgan, and by his creator. For in this novel, Twain represents and assesses what was in 1889 still no more than a 'shadowy [and] yet unnamed idea' – Taylorisation. Efficiency versus waste is the binary structure which Hank uses to conceptualise the hermit and his actions. If Taylor needed to justify and explain his methods of 'tightly fit[ting] factory workers to their assigned tasks',[38] Hank explains, but feels no need to justify, his use of St Stylite to make those ten shirts a day, in Sollors's phrase, 'immigrant, sweat-shop fashion'.[39]

The principles of Taylorisation, the desire for firm management and for business efficiency, that underpin Hank's language and actions are, though, partly modified to his Arthurian circumstances. Martha Banta, from whose *Taylored Lives: Narrative Productions in the Age of Taylor, Veblen, and Ford* (1993) I extract much of my contextual material here, notes the 'elementary ideas' Taylor applied to the management of the workforce. The first two of these were:

First: Holding a plum for them to climb after.
Second: Cracking the whip over them, with an occasional touch of the lash.[40]

Hank's system is even more efficient, since his worker is self-motivated and self-disciplined. The hermit cracks his own whip, with his 'plum' (eternal life) supplied by the framework of his Christian belief. Hank's place in the process is simply to reap the profits, pull his own secular plum from this particular and productive arrangement.

There are other ways too in which Hank acts as a champion of what would later be known as Taylorisation. Hank taylors the hermit's life and actions to the needs both of an efficient production process and of the consumer society whose growth he is stimulating.[41] He brings time, motion and production together and uses the many repetitions his machinery allows to combat what he sees as unacceptable forms of social and industrial waste.

My last sentence suggests, as does much of the quoted passage, how for Hank man and machine are indistinguishable. The incident in Twain's novel here feeds back into, and provides a reflection on, late nineteenth-century social concerns. The 'robotic motions'[42] of the hermit are disassociated, in Hank's mind, from any notion of consciousness or emotion on his part. Hank's monitorings and surveillances of his underlings are a noticeable factor, not just here, but elsewhere in the novel too.[43] His is the hand that governs this business enterprise; his the hand that draws the thread of rational control through the needle of the hermit's religious sensibility.[44] The hermit, the motive power, drives and becomes Hank's well-managed machinery. Hank, to use Seltzer's terms, 'rewrit[es] . . . the [hermit's] natural body in the idiom of machine culture',[45] couples that body with a sewing-machine, and makes capital from the result.

Henry Ford would later convert 'potential waste into gain'[46] by

using workers whom other industrialists discarded, for he calculated that of the 7882 distinct work operations involved in the
production of his Model T, only 12 per cent needed 'strong,
able-bodied, and practically physically perfect men':[47]

> Inspired by the adage 'waste not, want not,' the Ford Motor
> Company employed a legion of disabled workers: in 1914, 680
> legless men, 2,637 one-legged men, two armless men, 715 one-
> armed men, and ten blind men.[48]

So, similarly, Hank uses his hermit. As far as his plans go, the man
might be handless or armless, or even headless for any but the
purposes of basic survival, for it is the legs and trunk doing the work
(the bowing of the body); nothing else matters here. An emptying
out of human agency takes place as the individual subject is
converted into a mechanical object. In Taylorisation, prior notions of
complete manhood are replaced by the worker's function as an
efficient part of a machine. This section of *A Connecticut Yankee* can
be read paradigmatically as a comment on, and critique of, the
workings of the capitalist economy in the late nineteenth century. In
the individual hermit's fate lies the spectre of a mass work force
made to fit, and bound by, a social and industrial system which
reduces its members to mere ciphers. Martha Banta reaches similar
conclusions when she analyses the relation between Hank, Clarence
and the fifty-two cadets who finally carry out his commands, in terms
of the 'transformations over time of relations between the factory
boss and his boys' as represented in Twain's fiction as a whole.[49]

IV

In *A Connecticut Yankee* then, the use of fantasy, with the conflict
between different forms of language and value systems it introduces
as one world intrudes on another, acts to interrogate late nineteenth-
century norms and assumptions. As a businessman, Twain shared
an enthusiasm for the forms of rationalisation and calculability that
marked an emergent modernised culture in America (see the second
prefacing quote to this chapter). His literary works, though, tell
another and more ambivalent story.

Jackson Lears follows Max Weber in stressing the importance of rationalisation in the modernisation process, describing it as:

the systematic organization of economic life for maximum productivity and of individual life for maximum personal achievement; the drive for efficient control of nature under the body of improving human welfare; the reduction of the world to a disenchanted object to be manipulated by rational technique.[50]

Hank Morgan, 'active, restless, and on the make',[51] is directly associated with the idea of disenchantment. His belief in a 'rationally constructed world' (p. 125) runs alongside his pragmatism. For he has the ability to 'invent, contrive, create, reorganise things; set brain and hand to work', once he is stranded, 'just another Robinson Crusoe' (p. 81), in this other society. Hank, who identifies himself with 'the magic of science', takes on Merlin, representative of medieval necromancy and enchantments, of 'the magic of fol-de-rol' (p. 363). An engineer, a technocrat and a scientist, his set of 'superstitions about *unenchanted* and *unmiraculous* locomotives, balloons and telephones' (p. 181, my emphasis) soon transform the world he has entered.

Though the language Hank uses suggests similarity as well as difference between science and magic (I develop this later), his rationalism combats the power of (occult) superstition, and the anti-modern bias it represents. But Hank's rationalism also proves 'disenchanting' in the broader sense, in the loss of charm or delight it implies. For increasing doubts about late nineteenth-century rationalisation, efficiencies and controls can be identified in Twain's novel as it proceeds. Hank organises, as he modernises, the Arthurian world. He develops a 'system and machinery' to ensure the smooth running of the 'civilization' he will put in place. He relies on expertise – newly trained 'experts in every sort of handiwork and scientific calling' (p. 101) – to do his work for him, and to prepare for the flooding of 'the midnight [sixth century] world with light' (p. 103). Anticipating the direct anti-imperialist satires he was to write at the turn of the century,[52] Twain has Hank Morgan bring 'soap and civilization' (p. 146) to a backward country.[53] He also has him introduce advertising, consumerism and modern business methods there. Hank networks the nation with a modern communications system (ground wires carrying telephone and telegraph –

p. 104), and builds up a 'vast system of clandestine factories and workshops', eventually exposed to the view of 'an astonished world' (p. 364). He sits at the centre of a rational and efficient web of control and brings modernisation to a backward world.

The more we learn of Hank's methods and systems, though, the less enchanting they seem. His plan for a 'Man Factory' (p. 130), where promising but common human materials, stifled by unfair and restrictive feudal practices, can be turned from 'groping and grubbing automata into *men*' (p. 159), is apparently based on republican and democratic principles. The implications of reification and rationalisation in its name, however, warn that these men may end up like the hermit – who is no 'man' for Hank, but the tool and agent of a reactionary and corrupt religion. The 'human liberty' (p. 102) Hank espouses operates in highly variable ways. The sound of the Colt factory whistle continues symbolically to resonate here.[54]

If men are made into automata by feudal training, Hank does not necessarily improve their mental condition but simply retrains them to fit his own ideological and social agenda. Thus Ulfius the telephone clerk, 'one of [Hank's] young fellows' (p. 217) met by chance in the Valley of Holiness, has become (like the hermit and his sewing machine) a cog in Hank's system rather than the independent and free-thinking individual his words might promise. Ulfius moves by night and avoids speech with others as he helps in the secret process of getting modern civilisation in place. As he does this, he learns 'naught but that we get by the telephone from Camelot' (p. 218). The plural pronoun used here speaks of Ulfius's status as one of an interchangeable many. In defining himself as Hank's agent, he reveals how narrow are the boundaries of the centralised system of knowledge and information in which he plays his part. For he is uncertain even of his exact location, and is alone, apart from the phone 'back in the gloom' of the cavern, where he has set up his 'office'.

If, in Hank's words, 'the home of the bogus miracle [has] become the home of a real one, the den of a medieval hermit [has been] turned into a telephone office' (p. 217), the underlying ironic turn to this is that little has changed (though in terms of political and religious forms much, of course, has – or will). The hermit's conditioning leads him to a role which only makes sense within the framework of particular religious belief, and where individual identity is measured in terms of the ritual penance undergone. This is not that different from Hank's trainee, whose function and identity exist only as part of the network he is servicing, and who is completely in the dark outside its parameters.[55] Similarly, the boy soldiers who are Hank's 'champions of human liberty and equality' (p. 396) at the narrative's end, are in fact the only fragment of the population not conditioned by prior training (by 'the Church, the nobles, and the gentry' – p. 392) but by Hank's. Thus it is easy to read the Battle of the Sand-Belt in terms of one set of automata fighting another, depending on who has been trained by whom, rather than as standing for any real defence and celebration of democratic principle.

Hank's technological efficiency and scientific knowledge can, by the end of the novel, also be seen from a disenchanted perspective. Hank, speaking undoubtedly for Twain, celebrates modern invention and technical expertise when he looks into the future to criticise England's failures to honour 'the creators of this world – after God – Gutenberg, Watt, Arkwright, Whitney, Morse, Stephenson, Bell' (p. 298).[56] The gap in knowledge and invention between Hank's America and Arthur's England is considerable: 'no gas . . . no candles; a bronze dish half full of boarding-house butter with a blazing rag floating in it was the thing that produced what was regarded as light' (p. 81).[57] Hank has the scientific knowledge to produce (god-like) his own light. By the end of the novel, he is using his 'first great electric plant' (p. 386) to set 'fifty electric suns aflame' (p. 404), and thus to illuminate the slaughter then taking place. Twain's notes for the novel show his interest in the relation between natural and scientific power:

Journal The Sunburst
Electri [sic] Light.[58]

But Hank's drive for an efficient control of nature, and the power and authority it gives him, become identified with mass murder. Indeed the word 'massenmenchemoerder' (p. 212) is part of his incantation in the mending of the holy fountain sequence earlier.

The drive to harness nature's powers was to have disturbing implications in terms of Hank's actions, and in terms, too, of the actions of Twain's late nineteenth-century contemporaries. In both cases, these focused round the 'application of electricity to the human body'.[59] The debate surrounding the introduction of legal electrocution in America took place around the time Twain was writing his novel. Dr Alfred Southwick, a Buffalo dentist and later Professor of Operative Technics at the University Dental School, saw a drunk die instantly after touching an electric wire in 1881. This led him to perform a series of 'lethal electrical experiments on animals'. Following their success, Southwick went on to campaign for a more efficient and less painful form of capital punishment, and, on 1 January 1889, the Electrical Execution Law was passed in New York State. Electrocution thereby replaced hanging, the mode which (as the State-Governor put it) 'has come down to us from the dark ages' as the traditional method for executing criminals. The comparative advance in civilisation that death by electrocution was meant to herald was, however, rather undermined by the fact that the first man to die by this system (William Kemmler, on 6 August 1890) apparently revived after his supposedly lethal shock, and had to be swiftly re-electrocuted.

Kemmler's execution took place at seven in the morning, as 'it was feared that the 1200 convicts at Auburn would be unduly disturbed by a sudden shutdown of the electric power while they were at work in the machine shops'.[60] The connection here between manufacturing needs carried out by an imprisoned and well-supervised labour force, working despite their will, and the use of the same force (electricity) which drove their production to execute one of their fellow criminals seems like a condensed and grotesque version of processes illustrated in Twain's novel. Here Hank gradually moves from his use of the hermit unwittingly to drive his business enterprise to his later use of electricity to slaughter those who oppose his system.

Kemmler's execution took place after *A Connecticut Yankee* was completed. Discussion of electrocution as a mode of criminal execution had been taking place, though, throughout the latter half of the 1880s.[61] Moreover, there were frequent newspaper reports about accidents resulting from electricity, 'deaths resulting from what were called "the deadly wires"'.[62] When Hank sends his electricity through the deadly wires he has set up to trap his enemy, the effect is dramatic:

We would now and then see a blue spark when the knight . . . had touched a charged wire with his sword and been electrocuted . . . ; our current was so tremendous that it killed before the victim could cry out. . . . Our camp was enclosed with a sudden wall of the dead. . . . I shot the current through all the fences and struck the whole host dead in their tracks! *There* was a groan you could *hear*! It voiced the death-pang of eleven thousand men.

(pp. 402–4)

By this point in the novel, Hank's modernisations and rationalisations have come to look very sinister indeed. Twain's nineteenth-century light-bringer becomes a mass-electrocutioner. Scientific and technological knowledge bring destruction and defeat for all the parties involved.

Twain's use of fantasy in *A Connecticut Yankee*, then, interrogates the nature of the 'real' in late nineteenth-century America; confronts and questions generally held norms and assumptions. One such assumption was the 'tendency to equate material and moral progress'.[63] Twain cuts the threads of that particular connection in a novel where material progress, technology and science bring, not human betterment, but moral disaster in an 'annihilating' (p. 396) Civil War, and the Battle of the Sand-Belt that follows.[64] Moreover, the idea of a public order dependent on an individual commitment to, and constraint by, 'an internalized ethic of self-control' (an 'unquestioned norm'[65] at the time) is exploded in a fable of what happens when one self-seeking individual has the edge on his competitors, and how the individual moral gyroscope is upset in such a case. The general belief in a gradual evolution from lower to higher social and historical forms and stages[66] is shattered in a novel whose linear and historical movement ends broken and in tatters.

Again, other readings are possible. Twain has to end his novel in this way, to bring it back in line with the course of real history. The signs of narrative dislocation toward the conclusion and the violence of the Battle of the Sand Belt can be read as Twain's attempts to find a way out of the complicated fictional situation he has set up. It is possible, too, to give equal attention to the defeat of nineteenth-century liberalism by entrenched establishment interests as to Hank's own failings. If, according to my reading, the dominant assumptions of Twain's time are challenged in an explosive text, this is not an interpretation that all critics share. Contradictions and ambivalences have their place in this text too.

V

A further conventional assumption which the use of fantasy in *A Connecticut Yankee* helps to undermine is the belief in 'the most cherished of a human unities: the unity of "character"'. As I have previously shown, anxieties about the sense of self consistently pervade Twain's fictional world. Here, it is possible to read Hank as a consistent and autonomous character, wielding power and sure of his own agency. It is also possible, though, to see an alternative: that the fantastic juxtaposition of the Arthurian and late nineteenth-century worlds acts as a device to illuminate the divided nature of Hank's being. For the use of 'the motif of the double' and of 'otherness' in fantastic texts can provide a way, as Rosemary Jackson suggests, of questioning and destabilising any notion of the coherent subject.[67]

A Connecticut Yankee depends on the contrast between the modern and the medieval. Hank's 'other' is Merlin, the arch-enemy who represents all that is backward about Arthurdom. But the opposition between the two figures is far from stable. I noted earlier that the language Hank uses about himself overlaps with that which describes Merlin. While Merlin, for example, is associated with 'absurd necromancy', the Yankee is seen to represent 'the more splendid necromancy of the nineteenth century'.[68] The use of the same word to describe their two practices starts to blur the apparently firm boundaries between them, and between the science and magic they represent. Such a blurring would be familiar to Twain's contemporaries who, for instance, nicknamed Thomas Edison the Wizard of Menlo Park.

Hank's description of himself as a type of representative nineteenth-century culture hero, his apparent identification with a single and coherent subject position, is challenged by a text which repeatedly illustrates the collapse of the differences between him and those he labels as cultural antagonists. Werner Sollors is just one critic who shows the 'pervasive similarity' between the Yankee and his Arthurian host.[69] Thus, though Hank uses his scientific knowledge, particularly that of high explosives, to out-do and overpower Merlin, he consistently uses the language and techniques of the occult to carry out his purposes. Hank's incantation and use of visible display in his 'Restoration of the Fountain' (pp. 207–14) suggests how the gap between his and Merlin's magic tends to disappear, and especially in terms of the knowledge and reactions of their joint audience. As Michael Davitt Bell puts it, Hank, 'in his conflict with Merlin keeps turning *into* Merlin'.[70]

This collapse of difference between Hank and all that constitutes his medieval opposite is signalled in other ways too. So, in the novel, Arthurians start talking like Yankees, and Hank ends (in the prefacing 'Word of Explanation') speaking like an Arthurian: 'Wit ye well. . . . Give you good den, fair sir' (pp. 34, 38). Hank, too, is consistently shown 'doing the same thing or using the same dehumanising words he criticizes in others'. Not only does he rely on 'fake miracles' to fight superstition, but he models the spreading of his own enterprise on the way the church, his prime enemy, works. And he fights 'the "petrified" system of feudalism . . . [by] transforming knights into "statues"', fixing them rigid as he electrocutes them. Hank ends up inhabiting Merlin's cave, and married to Sandy ('wedded to Arthurianism'[71]). He is, despite his own claims to the contrary, a sentimentalist, who is left mourning his 'Lost Land',[72] 'an abyss of thirteen centuries yawning', as he puts it, between him and Sandy; between him and 'all that could make life worth the living!' (p. 409). The boundaries Hank constructs dividing himself from the Arthurians – who represent all the parts of his subjectivity that he would deny[73] – are in complete disarray at the novel's end. The fantastic use of the sixth century double collapses the firm sense of self that Hank, as the progressive representative of nineteenth-century modernism, would take absolutely for granted.

VI

Hank is, in *A Connecticut Yankee*, finally caught between two historical periods, fully at home in neither. His love for his 'home and his friends', for Sandy and his child (both of whom he addresses in his final 'delirium'), provides his last 'pleasure' and 'gladness' (p. 409). Max Weber wrote in 1918 that 'our greatest art is intimate . . . and not monumental', speaking here of the loss of value in public life at a time 'characterized by rationalization and intellectualization and, above all, by the "disenchantment of the world"'. Hank, too, retreats to the intimate, to that same realm of 'direct and personal human relations' to which Weber refers,[74] at the end of *A Connecticut Yankee* as the world of public history that his rational and 'disenchanted' techniques have brought into being goes smash.

In his analysis of realism, the Marxist critic Georg Lukacs describes the genre as one which allows for the possibility of grasping the 'real causality of events'. He sees the realist writer as one who can chart the direction of 'historical sequence' and show how 'significant human beings' actively participate to effect the lives of their society.[75] Twain never seems to have had quite this kind of confidence either in the ability of humans to shape history,[76] or in the power of the artist to represent it in terms of cause and positive effect. I read *Huckleberry Finn* in terms of the depiction of an interracial relationship operating on the fringes of the existing social system, and pointing in the direction of what might, with great difficulty, become a future public possibility. Such progressive impulses (however minimal) seem, though, completely obliterated at the end of *A Connecticut Yankee*. Hank's final stress on the importance of interpersonal relationships signals a retreat from the public (the monumental); a tacit admission of the disastrous nature of his historical interventions. As so often in this chapter, I have to stop, though, to remind of the alternative reading available. The ending can be read as a mere product of the narrative situation Twain adopts, for Hank *cannot* change history if the basic premises of the novel are to stand. It is as easy, in other words, to read the ending in terms of artistic necessity as of a particular view, on Twain's part, of the historical process and man's relation to it.

But it is the latter interpretation on which I focus. Hank's political values cannot, in terms of the textual development, be separated from his desire for personal power and profit. The corporate civilisation he introduces has dehumanising implications. And the modern financial machinery (the stock-board) he establishes hastens the Civil War that brings both his authority and the regime he has developed to an end. Twain's own fears about the meaning of democracy in America, and about 'social relations in a capitalist society', can be traced far back in his career, certainly to *The Gilded Age*. The shuttling between two worlds he fictionalises in *A Connecticut Yankee*, and the completeness and apocalyptic nature of the historical break that finally occurs between them, can be read in terms of an increasing pessimism about the direction of history, the state of contemporary American culture, and even about basic human nature, on Twain's part. It is perhaps no coincidence that in his later *The Secret History of Eddypus, The World Empire* (1901–2), he would depict history as cyclic, marked by 'a human tendency toward dictatorship on the one hand and subservience and fanaticism on the other'.[77] Twain would not give up on history: his own political involvements and later satiric writing show this. Undoubtedly, though, his attitude toward it became increasingly more pessimistic. The use of fantasy in *A Connecticut Yankee* can be taken as symptomatic of that fact.

Twain's fictional moves between the American past and present, in *Roughing It*, *Tom Sawyer* and *Huckleberry Finn*, end similarly. The attraction of the past is modified by an understanding of its flaws, while the seeds of the present, too, are shown to be contained in that past. In *A Connecticut Yankee*, the nostalgic impulse operates too, but the simpler and agrarian landscape that is mourned is at the same time clearly unsupportable, given the tyrannies, injustices and attitudes of mind with which it is associated (and which Hank can never quite remove). And although the modern political and secular values that Hank introduces are lauded, other sides of his late nineteenth-century value scheme doom them, in this fictional context, to defeat. Twain's ambivalences are clear here. The gaps opening up in his work are becoming wider and wider; more difficult, in any way, to bridge.

7

Severed Connections:
Puddn'head Wilson and Those Extraordinary Twins

You see we were twins – defunct and I – and we got mixed in the bath-tub when we were only two weeks old, and one of us was drowned. But we didn't know which. . . . But I will tell you a secret now, which I have never revealed to any creature before. One of us had a peculiar mark – a large mole on the back of his left hand; that was me. That child was the one that was drowned!

('An Encounter with an Interviewer')[1]

It is hard to see clear in a world of twins.

(Arnold L. Weinstein, *Nobody's Home*)[2]

I

Mark Twain was caught between different stories and literary modes as he wrote *Puddn'head Wilson* (1894). His artistic difficulties with his material are suggested in the late change of title from *Those Extraordinary Twins*.[3] They are clear in his account of the 'literary Caesarean operation' he performed, when he 'dug out' farcical material about Siamese twins to leave the 'tragic aspect' of his tale of Roxy and the two changelings intact.[4] Twain's story of this severance is in the first American edition of the text, published as

134

The Tragedy of Puddn'head Wilson and the Comedy of Those Extra-ordinary Twins. It is told, however, to explain the presence of the farce, which is still retained as supplement to the main narrative.[5] A symbiotic bond, in other words, continues to exist between the two parts of the original body of work. The stories may have been pulled apart, but they remain, none the less, connected.

'Violent separation', as Evan Carton points out, both 'provides a model for the organization of Dawson's Landing' and describes what Twain did in 'severing the double story and disposing of one half'.[6] The twinned publication of the stories, the way they formally interact, and their thematic ties, argue against the success of that disposal. Indeed, as Susan Gillman says:

> *these twin novels must . . . be read together*, despite the fact that the farce makes a mockery of the Siamese twins' grotesque attachment, whereas the tragedy, obsessed with genealogy, race, and miscegenation, offers a critique of an American historical actuality.[7]

One of Twain's most interesting works of fiction is, in other words, made up of two stories still 'tangled together' (p. 229) despite their forced separation. Both *Puddn'head Wilson* and *Those Extraordinary Twins* take as their theme different (but related) types of Siamese connections; share the same textual obsession with violated borderlines, racial and physical. Thus Twain's description in *Those Extraordinary Twins* of Luigi and Angelo as a 'monstrous "freak"' (p. 303)[8] meshes symbolically with Tom's representation in *Puddn'head Wilson* as a mulatto. For, according to one (racist) strand of the racial rhetoric of post-Reconstruction America, the mulatto was defined as 'unnatural hybrid' or '"freak" of natural law'.[9] A cultural scandal replaces a natural one here. Nature, though, is still the court of cultural appeal, as the difference between the two terms is disguised to defend an established and segregated social order. As such overlaps as this occur, additional meanings are released between the two (twinned) narratives which affect our readings of both.

My starting point in this chapter is to lay one twin text against the other to suggest that the tensions and divisions in Twain's work can no longer, here, be contained within a single whole. Cindy Weinstein discusses Twain's 'dis-ease about what does and does not belong in . . . narrative'.[10] She is talking about *Life on the Mississippi*, not about this text, but her comment seems entirely appropriate to it. On one side (*Those Extraordinary Twins*) we have farce, on the other (*Puddn'head Wilson*), tragedy, and Twain cannot reconcile the forms. I suggested in my first chapter that one reading of 'The Stolen White Elephant' implies that extravagant humour (with its anarchic qualities) may not be compatible with a repressive social reality. It is not, however, until this later stage in his career that the gap between the two becomes unbridgeable.[11]

Twain's comedy has already become forced by the end of *A Connecticut Yankee*, as doubts both about dominant American values, and the direction of history itself, are revealed. In *Tom Sawyer* and *Huckleberry Finn*, the use of an ante-bellum setting allows for cultural critique and for nostalgia and escape. The playful and/or idyllic aspects of life on the borders of society carry positive connotations in both novels. Idyll, though, is absent from *Puddn'head Wilson* (set in a similar time and place), and the limits of play are greatly reduced. The view of American history, as seen through a racial perspective, is starkly negative. And wider anxieties about the status of the self, and the determining influence of the environment, are clearly evident. The type of fictional balances found in earlier texts are no longer evident here. And if Twain employs a number of fictional tactics, and particularly the use of the detective genre, which counter the pessimistic tenor of his novel, the use of broadscale humour is no longer one of them.

Cindy Weinstein analyses three of Twain's books (*Life on the Mississippi*, *A Connecticut Yankee* and *No. 44, The Mysterious Stranger*) in terms of a tension in Twain's artistic allegiances between the allegorical representation of personhood and a quite different literary method. On the one hand, character is based – in line with nineteenth-century capitalist values – on 'efficiency and discipline'. Fictional characters come to resemble the 'flattened, mechanical persons . . . in a factory or in a market economy': produced by a determining circumstance and empty of subjectivity. But a different type of *literary* economy competes with that of the market. For literary labour has little to do with the machine-like efficiencies of business. Rather, it 'celebrates an ideal of inefficient . . . narrative that is digressive and, more important, humorous'. This counter-impulse leads in the direction of the type of 'directionless circulations', in which *authorial* efficiency and success consisted. So, in *A Connecticut Yankee*, the comic expansiveness that comes about as a result of Hank's early interactions with Sandy, as their two narrative styles and aesthetic perspectives are contrasted,[12] is subdued at the novel's end as Hank is positioned in the company of 'numbers without stories', the characterless boys he has trained to stand beside him in the cave. Twain's only way of dealing with such 'subversive indistinguishability', in A Connecticut Yankee at least, is by 'the killing of those allegorical characters [he] finds so threatening to his view of the world in which people are people and machines are machines'.[13] The Battle of the Sand-Belt which effectively ends the narrative can be read, consequently, as a type of fictional necessity.

Weinstein's insights here can be carried over to a discussion of the relationship between Pudd'nhead Wilson and Those Extraordinary Twins. Both these texts have allegorical qualities, but it is in Puddn'head Wilson that the stress on flattened character and forming circumstance becomes most bleakly insistent. Indeed, though Twain speaks of the novel in terms of the tragic, it is better described as deterministic. The history of race, though, and not that of labour (Weinstein's focus), imprints the fictional characters here. The text's strongly allegorical impulse comes from the depiction of a society which rigidly categorises and differentiates its members through artificial racial classification; enslaves its members (both 'black' and 'white') within the narrow boundaries of a twinned system built around fixed notions of racial difference. But the term 'slavery' comes to have a wider significance too, for all the characters are enmeshed and constructed, in one way or another, by the social structures which surround them. Any notion of independent agency is strongly qualified, and the nature of identity itself is interrogated.[14]

Those Extraordinary Twins works as allegory too, but not at the expense of humour. The allegorical aspects only start to take their clearest shape at the end of the text, and more particularly, once it is placed alongside Puddn'head Wilson. In the story about Siamese twins, we find the type of extended burlesque missing from its novelistic partner. Twain takes artistic delight in letting his comic situation develop and his narrative ramble every which way, from one humorous incident to the next. The mechanics of farce outweigh those of allegory as his pleasure in the absurdist potential of the twinship device overwhelms (when the text is taken alone) any strong production of additional meaning. The expansive nature of the comedy present here disappears in *Puddn'head Wilson*, no longer compatible with a deepening serious and pessimistic social analysis.

Puddn'head Wilson, taken by itself, is marked internally (like so many Twain novels) by its 'generic swerves'.[15] But it is the formal swerve between the ironic and sardonic minimalism which is the novel's predominant *overall* characteristic, and the farcical and fanciful play of *Those Extraordinary Twins*, which particularly catches my interest. For a tension that has always been evident within Twain's texts now becomes a tension *between* texts. The quest for meaning in *Puddn'head Wilson and Those Extraordinary Twins* becomes a form of collaborative project, as the reader puts the two together to find one broken whole. Such a rupture is a sign that established generic forms (or 'conventions of representation'[16]) can no longer contain Twain's complex and tangled web of materials, nor satisfy his diverging artistic needs. *Puddn'head Wilson* can be read as a self-sufficient novel (though, as many critics have pointed out, a number of obvious traces of the twins' Siamese connection still remain within it). I am suggesting, though, that if it is left to stand independently, an added dimension of its fictional life disappears. Its supplementary text both shadows it, and allows its fullest meanings to emerge. *Those Extraordinary Twins*, however, with its many references to its linked text, cannot be read by itself. It is oddly fitting that the narrative in which the twins are Siamese is the one that cannot stand alone.

I do a number of things, then, in this chapter. I show how *Puddn'head Wilson and Those Extraordinary Twins* interrelate: how, as farce vies with deterministic 'tragedy', Twain's fullest fictional meanings are revealed. The mechanics of extravagant farce in *Those Extraordinary Twins* are used to allegorical ends. But I argue that the allegorical aspects of the text only start to take on their deepest resonance at its rather abrupt and unexpected conclusion. Until that point, the more disturbing meanings of the text are hidden as, for the most part, the broad comedy of the story covers up anxieties about individual identity and difference; about agency, how it can be determined, and its relation to forms of social authority and control. The restored equilibrium brought with the final act of community violence then acts, in a different way, to swiftly suppress such troubling issues. Again, in this chapter, it is the presence of such processes, and the way in which the text's more uncomfortable effects are counteracted, that interests me.

Those Extraordinary Twins is a story of a scandal in nature – Siamese twins, two bodies compellingly and inevitably tied together – and of the legal and social response to it. It describes the battle for power between the two parts of this one whole, and the problems faced by others in telling which twin is master and which slave when they do act. In focusing on these issues, Twain clearly parallels and supplements the story of race relations he tells in *Puddn'head Wilson*. The interrogation of agency and identity in the latter text, too, is replayed at another level in *Those Extraordinary Twins*, to hammer down the point that a belief in autonomy, independence or separate selfhood is nothing more than a bad joke.[17] As the twinned texts are severed, so this supplementary effect is (to significant degree) lost. *Puddn'head Wilson*, too, has its own conflicting elements. The upsetting of the social order that takes place, and the instabilities in identity and assumed categories this reveals, are finally (if not fully) disguised. This happens as the detective genre takes over the novel, and as, consequently, one of the disruptive 'twins' is removed from the scene. In *The Extraordinary Twins*, it is both twins who are finally disposed of.

In *Puddn'head Wilson and Those Extraordinary Twins*, Twain leaves his reader with ragged edges. In the move from one text to its twinned partner, and from one genre to another, he engages two forms, neither of which completely meets his artistic needs. For the world is read both in flatly deterministic and dehumanising terms and as extravagant and comic farce. Shuttled between diverging but related stories, and formally torn between different literary modes, the reader is left finally decentred, the full meaning of this/these twinned text(s) floating somewhere in the gap between them.

II

Siamese twinship, the subject of *Those Extraordinary Twins*, has obvious comic possibility and inevitable allegorical resonance.[18] Two sets of twins seem particularly to have stimulated Twain's literary interest: Chang and Eng (on whom his 1869 sketch 'Personal Habits of the Siamese Twins' was based), and the Italian Tocchi brothers, on whom the physical appearance of Luigi and Angelo is closely modelled.[19] The enforced biological connection of Siamese twins, and the problems of identity and agency, of separateness and togetherness, raised by their status, have a clear carry-over to the story of inescapable racial links in *Puddn'head Wilson*. Further knowledge of Chang and Eng's lives is relevant here. The twins evidently considered themselves a single person, signing their correspondence Chang Eng. The paralysis which came to afflict one side of Chang meant that Eng increasingly bore his weight. Meanwhile, Chang's 'disability turned him into a clinging, surly child'. Eng's death followed inevitably on that of his brother (on 7 January 1874), but apparently Eng awoke on that particular day unaware that Chang had died in the night. All these details have implications for the themes Twain would explore. Most particularly, Chang and Eng, who lived in ante-bellum North Carolina, owned slaves. The allegorical crossover from a permanent bodily connection (with the various types of interdependency involved) to a particular form of social and racial connection, which Twain explores as he moves from text to text, was thus already present in the circumstances of Chang and Eng's lives.[20]

Twain's early description of *Those Extraordinary Twins* as a 'howling farce'[21] suggests the spirit that motivated him as he started writing. Certainly, his subject matter afforded him ready opportunity for extravagant comic effects based on the physical facts of Siamese twinship, their single and joint selfhood, and the problems they posed in terms of the 'familiar boundaries'[22] of small-town American society. Though this material has allegorical implications concerning Twain's view of individual identity and agency, and though the representation of the twins themselves is consequently flat, much of its impact takes the form of what Gillman calls an 'absurd joke'.[23] This, however, is only true *until* we start to relate it to the plots of race and identity in *Puddn'head Wilson*: to tie it down strongly, in other words, *to social and historical circumstance*. For only in the *allegorical correspondence* between Siamese twinship and the depiction both of individual identity and social relationships in the last-named text is further meaning released. Thematically, then, the overt farce of the one text is tightly bound to the savage irony of the other. The severance Twain made between his interconnected stories can be most readily attributed to their lack of *formal* fit.

The jokes in *Those Extraordinary Twins* are often obvious, but they carry the narrative along with an exuberance which always marks Twain's writing when he is at his ease, and when the flow of his comedy follows, apparently effortlessly, from the one basic situational premise. The humorous 'extravaganza' (p. 234) starts with the difficulty of categorisation, as Aunt Patsy conventionally describes each of the two twins as a 'he' or a 'him', but can only respond to the joint and 'uncanny' presence of this 'double-headed human creature' as a monstrous 'it' (pp. 236–9). Problems with the use of singular and plural forms are part of a similar pattern. Thus, for instance, Rowena and her mother discuss 'that young man' with 'both of his faces' (p. 237).

The comedy swiftly develops with the visual play about the twins' four arms, the problem of determining their ownership, and the confused movements and contorted effects displayed. As Aunt Patsy puts it:

Nobody could tell [which twin had taken off which hat]. There was just a wormy squirming of arms in the air – seemed to be a couple of dozen of them, all writhing at once, and it just made me dizzy to see them go. (p. 238)

The narrator follows this up with an inspired, and thoroughly Twainian, image, when he describes the tired and wet twins undressing, and says how 'the abundance of sleeve made the partnership-coat hard to get off, for it was like skinning a tarantula' (p. 239). This comic but dehumanising rhetorical turn implies that the twins' main interest for the author lies in their humorous potential. They are one-dimensional pegs on which he is hanging what is for the most part an equally one-dimensional joke.

The thematic thrust of *Those Extraordinary Twins* concerns matters of agency and control: who is in command of the shared body and when, and how any external observer can possibly tell. These issues surface in farcical form during the duel between Luigi and Judge Driscoll. Here, Angelo is first told by Luigi to 'stop dodging' since 'officially you are not here; officially you do not exist' (p. 283).[24] But Angelo then regains use of the mutual legs, to go 'soaring' over a fence, and 'off like a deer' (p. 285), to his brother's utter dismay. The courthouse scene shares in the same joke. For Luigi cannot be found guilty for assault on Tom, when he kicks him off the platform during a meeting of the town's pro-rum party (which is described only in *Puddn'head Wilson*), since no one can prove who possessed 'the battery' (p. 273) – the joint legs – at the time.

The jury verdict, that the 'identity [of one accused] is so merged in his brother's that we have not been able to tell which was him' (p. 278), and the judge's warning ('Look to your homes – look to your property – look to your lives . . . ' – p. 279) begins, however, to sound a more serious note. For the twins' lack of accountability suggests the 'monolothic fixity'[25] of the law: that it has no way of dealing with that which disrupts conventional and communal systems of categorisation.[26] It suggests, too, a potential for violent disruption that the rigid civic rules and conventions of Dawson's Landing cannot entirely hold in check.

In fact, Twain's Siamese twins story does end, abruptly, in violence. This comes, however, from an entirely unexpected source, that of the citizenry itself. And it acts, paradoxically (for it is outside the law), to restore social authority and order, the limits of which have been exposed by the twins' transgressive presence. The farce turns unexpectedly sour, with the political system of the town stalemated and 'rack and ruin' (p. 302) threatened. This results from Luigi's election to alderman, and a court decision that the (unelected) Angelo cannot legally be allowed to sit on the board with him. 'The people', in Twain's ironic words, then 'come to their senses', deciding to restore civic order by lynching the problem alderman. The narrative then concludes with a bad pun, a grim joke, and an ending which, in its suddenness, mirrors the twins' extraordinary fate. As the citizens refer back to Wilson's advice to hire Luigi to resign, the text continues:

'but it's too late now; some of us haven't got anything left to hire him with.'

'Yes, we have,' said another citizen, 'we've got this' – and he produced a halter.

Many shouted; 'That's the ticket.' But others said: 'No – Count Angelo is innocent; we mustn't hang him.'

'Who said anything about hanging him? We are only going to hang the other one.'

'Then that is all right – there is no objection to that.'

So they hanged Luigi. And so ends the history of 'Those
Extraordinary Twins'. (p. 302)

Though serious issues about personal agency, law, communal
order and violence do come, rather oddly, to take over the story
here, their effect is muted. For the main emphasis of *Those
Extraordinary Twins* is on vivid farce. Once the disruptive effect of
the twins on the community comes to pose any real challenge to its
smooth running, they are rapidly disposed of, and the narrative
abruptly ends. Its ironic and troublesome aspects are thus swiftly
cut short, too. It is only when we read the sketch as a supplement
to *Puddn'head Wilson* that its allegorical aspects resonate and
multiply. Taken alone, it does read as, what Bruce Michelson calls,
a 'dadaist conundrum about the western cult of individuality', with
its play on identity and difference between the two twins, and the
question that raises about what such differences signify.[27] But
further *historical* meaning is released in the connection between this
twinned pair, and Tom Driscoll and Valet De Chambre. The link
between the two sets of Siamese connections is suggested in the
significant (and otherwise pointless) fact that one of the Siamese
twins is 'dark complected' and the other light (p. 245; and see
Puddn'head Wilson, p. 89). Angelo's wish to be '*segregated*' from Luigi,
so as to 'be separate individuals, like other men' (p. 253, my
emphasis), also provides an ironic cross-over to the racial twinnings
of *Puddn'head Wilson*.[28]

Twain's one story of 'conglomerate twins' (p. 234), of two fates
compellingly and inevitably tied together, speaks, as parable, to the
story of race relations he tells in *Puddn'head Wilson*. The difficulty,
in *The Extraordinary Twins*, of telling one twin from the other (p. 238),
and of finally identifying where agency and responsibility lie, spills
over into *Puddn'head Wilson*.[29] So, too, does the struggle for power
between the twins, and the upsets in the relationship of mastery and
subordination that accompany it. The issue of sameness and
difference, crucial in the case of the Siamese Twins, also prefigures
the problems of identity traced in the linked text,[30] not just in the
case of racial exchange, but in the use of the fingerprinting motif
too. For the latter raises questions that reach beyond the limits of
race, about where selfhood lies and how it can be measured,
confirmed and defined. In all these areas, *The Extraordinary Twins*
supplements the subject matter of *Puddn'head Wilson*. What is

considered (in terms of American race relations of the time) an upset in culture is mirrored in an upset of nature.

III

The difficulties readers often have with *Puddn'head Wilson* may, at least in part, stem from its own distinct allegorical nature. Until relatively recently, critics commonly chose to focus on the 'almost geometric' quality of the novel, with its 'iron plot' directed by an author who 'visibly rigs every move',[31] as a sign of its artistic failure. Twain's own admission that he considered Puddn'head Wilson himself not 'as a *character*, but only as a piece of machinery – a button or a crank or a lever, but with no dignity above that',[32] has often been used as further evidence of such a weakness. James M. Cox, who judges the novel flawed, is not atypical. For Cox, 'Puddn'head . . . remains . . . little more than a massive plot device. Neither he nor his "twin," the false Tom Driscoll, is ever freed into character.'[33]

To read the novel as one with a strong allegorical component, however, is to identify exactly the element in it which 'prevents the characters and situations from achieving the dimensions that would give them the illusion of life'.[34] John C. Gerber's suggestion that the text should not 'be measured primarily by the standards of realism' is pertinent here.[35] The chief citizens of Dawson's Landing are described as much as types as in terms of their individual characteristics. They are defined commonly as 'F. F. V.' (First Families of Virginia) and given collective attributes accordingly (p. 139). The highly artificial nature of 'causal relations' in the novel, with its 'improbable visitors . . . coincidental meetings . . . unanticipated conflicts', also works to deny the realist illusion of seamless historical sequence, of 'narrative coherence and continuity', which the specific geographic and historical setting would at first suggest.[36] *Puddn'head Wilson*'s concern with 'allegorical personhood' is evident, too, in its focus on the 'accounting of . . . persons'.[37] For both Roxy's and Tom's identity is decided in terms of fractions of whole numbers: what proportion of their persons is judged 'white' and 'black'. Their loss of civil and legal rights is similarly determined by their categorisation according to the small percentage of 'blackness' their 'blood' contains. In the light of this concern, Puddn'head Wilson's profession as both lawyer and *accountant* takes on further resonance. It is he who conducts the final accounting in the narrative. And in so doing, he reduces Tom once more to owned property, to the non-personhood of slavery.[38]

The allegorical quality of the novel is also clear in the reduction of both the townspeople and main protagonists to elements of geometrical equivalence in a particular narrative formula. Thus the 'group of citizens' who hear Wilson's half-a-dog joke remain indistinguishable, described in the dialogue that follows as numbers (no. 1 to 6, pp. 59–60). Similarly, Wilson's evidence in court at the conclusion of the book depends on a scrutiny of the autographs and pantographs of '*A* and *B*' (p. 219). So Tom and Valet become, literally, interchangeable and equivalent algebraic symbols in a plot over which they have no control:

> *A* was put into *B*'s cradle in the nursery; *B* was transferred to the kitchen and became a negro and a slave. . . . From seven months onward until now, *A* has still been a usurper, and in my finger-records he bears *B*'s name. (p. 222)

The Siamese twins plot of *Those Extraordinary Twins*, and Wilson's early half-a-dog quip in *Puddn'head Wilson*, both reinforce the same sense of interconnection: one half of the dog (or twin) inseparable from the other, their stories symbiotically bound. One figure cannot move without affecting his twin, and, as a Siamese pair, both are finally subject to repressive external force quite beyond their own control. Tom metaphorically ends up losing his bite, for his parricidal aggression and transgressive social role are, at the last, effectively and brutally suppressed with his sale down the river; while Valet (the 'real' Tom Driscoll) has long lost his bark: his use of an African-American vernacular and his lack of social skills bar him from any voice in the community where he is eventually – at least in terms of traditional hierarchies – to become chief citizen. When Tweedledum becomes Tweedledee, both are broken in the exchange.

Puddn'head Wilson not only allegorises the interconnected fates and histories of the two races in America, but also the problematics of identity. Neither the real nor the false Tom Driscoll are 'freed into character', for the very notion of character, of autonomous subjectivity, is interrogated here. 'Conditions', to major extent, '*make character*'.[39] Allegory tends to stark black and white contrasts. The mode is, then, entirely appropriate to a novel where it is the racial status of the protagonists that results in the flattening of their fictional character. Cindy Weinstein shows how allegory, as a rhetorical form, is 'mediated, nuanced, and changed' by its specific historical context.[40] American racial politics, both ante- and post-bellum, form the historical ground for Twain's novel where artificial categories of blackness and whiteness are rigidly determining. The challenge to traditional notions of character that results is, however, not confined to racial politics. For Twain (and this is where the supplementary relevance of the Siamese twins again becomes apparent) destabilises the idea of subjectivity on a more general level too. Indeed, his challenge to 'the fundamental ideology of autonomous individualism in American culture'[41] can be read beside a series of other late nineteenth-century texts where contemporary anxieties about the status of the self are revealed.

First, though, to return to the representation of racial status in *Puddn'head Wilson*. The protagonists of the novel become black and white tokens in the plots of race and identity which structure the text. The novel continually circles round on itself, thus intensifying the thematic sense of entrapment and inevitability. Puddn'head Wilson unwittingly suggests the switch of babies to Roxy at the beginning of the novel (p. 65), only himself to reverse her action (if not all of its consequences) at the end. A stress on the repeated nature of Roxy's thoughts and actions acts to confirm the conditioning effects of race. Roxy threatens suicide three times (pp. 70, 183, 191). Such thoughts, the product of internal and psychological stress, are, however, caused by *external* threats to her physical or emotional well-being; a product of the racially divided society in which she lives. On each occasion, these threats are met with countering acts of aggression or social disruption, and the thoughts of suicide they trigger are accordingly transformed. Roxy's switch of the children first replaces suicide as an option, but both her initial impulse, and the response to it, result from her realisation of the vulnerability of the mother–child bond under slavery. Roxy again acts as racial avenger when she knocks out the Yankee overseer on the Arkansas plantation because he beats a 'little sickly nigger wench 'bout ten year ole dat 'uz good to me, en hadn't no mammy' (p. 183). The suicide decision that follows this act is swiftly replaced, though, by one to flee the plantation. Finally, in St Louis, Roxy carries a knife to kill herself if she should be recaptured by her 'master'. But as she plans an escape from her predicament, she turns the knife onto her son (who has sold her down the river in the first place), threatening to 'jam it into' him if further betrayal occurs (p. 191).

Such repetitions place the reader in a textual world of racial violence and counter-violence. Roxy's illegal and punishable acts here are all responses to the entirely legal cruelties of the slave system in which she is caught. In this repeated cycle, relations of cause and effect spin back on each other. So, for instance, Roxy's first act of switching children originates the novel's sequence of events, but her act is in turn an effect of the social system that harms her. Slavery, its patterns and consequences, come to determine all other relationships and actions. Roxy's disruptive actions are survival tactics in a racial world where self-destruction (suicide), or an acceptance of one's status as will-less property, are the only other options available.

The way race determines events in *Puddn'head Wilson* is also symbolised in the textual motif of the murderous knife. Roxy threatens violence against Tom who, in his role as respectable 'white' master, in turn threatens her freedom. But her action is one element in another three-part repetition. For Luigi too owns a 'murderous blade' with which he has killed a 'native servant' in India, defending his and Angelo's life and property. The native rising 'at the bedside . . . a dirk aimed at [Angelo's] throat' (p. 131) is a nightmare image of that return of the socially and racially repressed on which the larger story expands.[42] Roxy's attitude to 'white' authority is, from early in the novel, a violent one. She reacts to the god-like (p. 68) authority of Percy Driscoll over her life by saying 'I hates him, en I could kill him!' (p. 69). She goes on to talk of her change-ling son as the avenger of the 'crimes against her race' (p. 82).

John Carlos Rowe sees Tom as all but 'a machine' with, so it appears, 'all his actions . . . already determined by cultural or revolutionary forces beyond his control or understanding'.[43] Certainly, Tom acts out a role that seems allotted, as he uses the twins' knife, now in his hands, to commit symbolic parricide. He kills the man who, in a sense, fathered him,[44] and who, in his role as promoter of Dawson's Landing (pp. 96–7) and its chief legal authority ('Judge'), represents law, order and community in his single person. Tom thinks earlier that 'if his father were only alive and in reach of assassination his mother would soon find that he had a very clear notion of the size of his indebtedness to that man' (p. 157). The text makes clear, in all of this, that murderous impulses are produced in the African-American by slavery and by its social system; where a slave-owning father can legally and emotionally disown his slave son to treat him only as a saleable commodity. When Tom, consequently, 'drove the knife home – and was free' (p. 195), these impulses come round to return on that institution's patriarchal representative. The logic of the action and patternings of the novel is driven by racial and historical determinants beyond the ability of any single individual to contain and control.

IV

Race strongly determines both plot and character in *Puddn'head Wilson*. Though Roxy seems to act as free agent in her chaotic reversal of the social order of Dawson's Landing, in fact her action is prompted from without (Puddn'head). It is also psychologically and historically determined, not just by the general injustices of slavery as an institution, but also by the gap between a strong sentimental valuation of the family unit (a dominant cultural trait which she has imbued)[45] and her own position as a slave mother. Twain does not offer a single determinate explanation of Roxy's actions. Rather, he leaves his reader uncertainly hanging between nature – the strength and power of Roxy's individual personality – and nurture – the environmental and institutional circumstances that condition how she speaks and what she does. In a repeated tactic in this novel, any attempt firmly to distinguish nature from nurture as the direct cause of plot or action quickly founders in a spiralling uncertainty of origin. While conditions make character, then, they are not quite *all* that make it.

None the less, the recognition of individual difference takes second place to the power of cultural determinants in this novel. And the efficacy of individual action is strongly questioned here. Thus a certain irony lies in the fact that Roxy's switch of children confirms (at the same time that it *secretly* collapses) the inequitable social structure which dehumanises her. For the master–slave

relationship between changeling son and 'black' servant over-
takes and destroys the bond between mother and child which
caused Roxy initially to act. This stress on the power of racial
circumstance is furthered by the overall structure of the novel, for
'from the opening moment when she decides to drown her child,
to the closing one in which he is sold down the river, death [either
literal or social] is the slave mother's predetermined legacy that
Roxana tries to, but finally cannot, abort'.[46] Her final position,
textually silenced, laughter quashed and 'martial bearing
departed' (p. 225) is a measure of her defeat. Roxy now is reduced
to little more than a shadow, the havoc she has loosed once more
(as it seems to have been determined) safely contained.[47] Any
sense of independent agency on her part vanishes from the novel's
range of possibilities.

Roxy's initial switch of the children completely upsets, and
reveals as a lie, the distinction between supposed racial superiority
and inferiority on which the social system of Dawson's Landing
depends. The switch is made possible because Roxy and her son
are, in terms of physical appearance, both white. They are 'negro . . .
by fiction of law and custom' alone (p. 64, my emphasis), since Roxy
is one-sixteenth, and Tom is one-thirty-second, 'black'. Twain here
shows up the entirely illusory base on which American racial
difference was constructed, and enforced. Shelley Fisher Fishkin ties
Puddn'head Wilson to *Huckleberry Finn* in saying that their 'subliminal
subject is American race relations, not in the time in which the books
were set, but during the period in which they were written'. She
continues:

In the 1890s . . . laws designed to separate white from black . . .
proliferated. And what could not be done within the law was
accomplished extralegally by lynch mobs. The price one paid for
the color of one's skin was higher than ever before. . . . The fiction
of 'racial purity' – the notion that it was, in fact, possible to divide
society into 'white' and 'black' – remained the precious tenet
which underlay the enormously cumbersome workings of the
segregation laws. While white society tried to secure the dividing
line between black and white through the courts and the law on
the one hand, and through mob terror on the other, the
population of Americans of mixed blood was increasing
geometrically.

Fishkin points out that racial categorisation according to a rigid rule of descent – the 'one-drop rule' that meant that 'all descendants of mixed unions' were classed 'with their black progenitors' – stayed, for the most part, 'intact throughout the nineteenth and much of the twentieth century' in America.[48] Susan Gillman, in turn, reveals that 'as late as 1970 . . . in Louisiana the legal fraction defining blackness was still one-thirty-second "Negro blood"'.[49]

In *Puddn'head Wilson*, Twain reduces such discriminatory legal and social classifications to absurdity. Again the Tweedledum and Tweedledee analogy comes to mind. Once Roxy has swopped the officially 'black' and 'white' babies, absolutely no one (until Puddn'head Wilson's late intervention) can tell the difference. If 'black' can be 'white', and vice versa, so easily, then any categorisation of difference in terms of race collapses in on itself. Roxy's initial smearing of jam round Tom and Valet's baby mouths (p. 73) is quite unnecessary as even the 'white' child's father is oblivious of the switch.[50]

Twain is doing several things here. He uses the Tom–Valet twinning motif both to illustrate the starkness of the socially constructed contrast between 'black' and 'white', and to reveal its fraudulence. But he also uses that exchange to question the idea of autonomous subjectivity. For as Twain undermines a social system built on racial difference, he shows the extent to which that system structures the subjectivity of its members. It is the respective environments in which Tom and Valet are brought up that, to major degree, explain their individual differences.

Valet can be quickly dealt with. Entirely the product of his circumstances as a slave, he is 'made' as a man accordingly. When he is restored to his rightful position (a right which rests, of course, on a fundamental moral wrong) he is, in consequence, like a fish out of water, unable to adjust to his new environment. Conditioning is all in his case:

> he could neither read nor write, and his speech was the basest dialect of the negro quarter. His gait, his attitudes, his gestures, his bearing, his laugh – all were vulgar and uncouth; his manners were the manners of a slave. Money and fine clothes could not mend these defects or cover them up. . . . The family pew was a misery to [the poor fellow], yet he could nevermore

enter into the solacing refuge of the 'nigger gallery' – that was closed to him for good and all. (p. 225)

Tom, as most critics have recognised, is a more complicated case, for it is difficult to separate out his 'native viciousness' (p. 79) from his nurtured being. The 'evil light in his eye' (p. 190) and his violent actions may reveal a flawed individual nature. They may, though, reveal a hereditary racial characteristic, the 'one part nigger' (p. 157)[51] in him which makes him first a coward, and then a murderer. But there are further possibilities too. For, if Tom is morally depraved, such depravity may be bred by the social environment in which he has been raised *since* Roxy's switch. And his capacity for violence may relate to yet a further source, determined by race, but not through any equation of racial and moral 'blackness'. For it may arise from an unconscious, or part-conscious, historical conditioning that makes the death of the Judge a 'justifiable homicide', as Tom, now in blackface, acts to avenge past crimes against his race.[52]

Tom's viciousness does seem to distinguish him from the other F.F.V.'s of the class into which he has been raised. On the other hand, Twain writes that he 'was a bad baby from the *very beginning of his usurpation'* (p. 75, my emphasis). In both *A Connecticut Yankee* and *The American Claimant,* Twain appears to show the impossibilty of separating out nature from nurture (or first from second nature, as he puts it in the latter text).[53] So here, one can equally argue that Tom is innately evil (which may or may not be related to his 'blackness') or that, in Rowe's words, his 'dissolute habits are less attributable to his black origins than to the historical deterioration of aristocratic authority'.[54] Whatever the case, as we chase round the nature/nurture argument, it would still seem that much of Tom's 'identity' stems from Roxy's first act in putting him in that other set of clothes and cradle. And if it is at least possible to claim that Tom's worst traits are 'a sign . . . of aristocratic degeneration',[55] then what follows is the implication that if Tom had been Valet and Valet, Tom, the story *could* have remained the same. And if this is so, then the notion of autonomous selfhood collapses. This latter possibility haunts Twain's novel and leads it beyond the boundaries of race to a more general exploration of selfhood itself. As this occurs the links between *Puddn'head Wilson* and *Those Extraordinary Twins* once more clearly emerge.

In making Valet into Tom and Tom into Valet, Twain introduces a theme of identity and imitation which dizzyingly spins his reader in circles. It is difficult even to know how to refer to the novel's characters, but I have followed convention in calling the false Tom, Tom (for this is how he is textually known once the switch has occurred) and the real Tom, Valet. Just the matter of names, then, introduces considerable confusion as far as identity goes. When Tom comes home from Yale, dressed in the height of fashion, his 'fancy Eastern graces' are mocked by the imitations of 'the old deformed negro bell-ringer straddling along in his wake tricked out in a flamboyant curtain-calico exaggeration of his finery' (p. 85). An old black man, in other words, imitates a young white man. That young white man is, though, being imitated by a young 'black' man who is in fact not black at all. In turn, the young white man is imitating this 'black' twin. As Arnold Weinstein puts it: 'One has a "wake" in Twain's book, as if we did not stop where we thought our contours ended'.[56]

When Roxy calls Valet 'you mis'able imitation nigger', and he replies 'If I's imitation, what is you? . . . Bofe of us is imitation *white* . . . – en pow'ful good imitation too' (p. 103), similar doublings and redoublings occur. Roxy's imitation of whiteness is based on the fact that she *is* white, even if social classification denies her that label. When, in her rage, she calls Valet, who is white both by social definition and appearance, an imitation 'nigger', she exactly describes what he is, and what she herself has made him – though this has apparently slipped her mind here. In denying her charge he claims, in self-mockery, imitation whiteness; unconscious that the original he claims to copy is in fact his own self.

This concern with imitation and originality does not merely relate to matters of race. Susan Gillman points to the number of gender as well as racial imitations occuring in the text to assert that 'this is a society radically confused about what people are, who is black and who is white, what is imitation and what is real, a society whose laws create and enforce strict boundaries to mask those confusions'.[57] Tom, who is already disguised as a 'white' man, puts on a further series of disguises when he kills the Judge. First, he makes himself up in blackface (p. 194), so becoming an imitation version of the African-American he is already socially categorised as being. He then puts on a 'suit of girl's clothes' (p. 196) on top of his male attire, veiling his face as he escapes the house. Finally, in the haunted house, he burns both these sets of clothes and disguises himself as a tramp. The question of what identity *is*, how it can be propped up (by social circumstance, and by clothes, title and outward appearance), and how a false role can be distinguished from a real one, resonates through the whole novel.

This question takes us back in turn to the Siamese connection of *Those Extraordinary Twins*, and how twin can be told from twin. For, as Puddn'head Wilson says in the final court scene of *Puddn'head Wilson*: 'You have often heard of twins who were so exactly alike their own parents could not tell them apart' (p. 217). Selfhood becomes even more indefinable in the case of Siamese twins, where singularity and plurality overlap in one confused whole. The question of original and copy collapses with their (transgressive) bodily connection. In the case of this 'twin-monster' (p. 303), it is finally impossible to separate self from self. In *Puddn'head Wilson*, Wilson himself finally sorts out the identity confusion in the novel. In doing so, he ironically (for one who is represented as possessing the 'objective detachment [of] the behavioural scientist'[58]) trium-phantly re-establishes the stability of a social order which the whole text has proved to be morally corrupt, and which is founded on the absolute lie of racial inferiority and difference. Twain here uses the detective genre as (through Wilson) he 'clears the world of doubles . . . [and] disposes of . . . the spectre of an open-ended world where lines do not hold between the sexes and the races'.[59] If the cover-up that occurs as Wilson puts the community order back to rights is full of holes, it nonetheless acts (partially) to suppress the more disturbing aspects of the text. For Wilson puts a lid on the deep anxieties about the relation between the individual and her or his social circumstance, and about American racial politics, that would otherwise remain openly apparent. This movement, where uncomfortable issues are raised only then to be disguised or overlooked, as we have come to recognise by now, is a standard feature of Twain's art.

V

As Twain's career progressed, so the anxieties and social criticism apparent in his work became more and more difficult to hide.

Accordingly, the gaps and cracks in his fictional constructs show more and more clearly. Thus the jagged forms of the ending of *A Connecticut Yankee*, and its climactic violence, are signals that the criticism of commonly held assumptions about American culture and the pessimistic view of history that are parts of the novel can no longer be reconciled with their thematic opposites. In *Puddn'head Wilson*, too, a whole series of fissures disturb the apparent logic and aptness of the novel's formal resolution.

This partly relates to the view of American racial history the text implies. It is now generally accepted that here (as in *Huckleberry Finn*) Twain's novel is not just about slavery but also about 'the second slavery'[60] of post-Reconstruction racial practice. Puddn'head Wilson's restoration, by means of the law, of rigid segregation, following the crisis over racial and social boundaries which has occurred, can thus be read as a bleak allegory of the events of this later period. The note of community celebration which accompanies the final cover-up of the novel (Wilson's, and Twain's, restoration of the racial status quo) is, though, questioned by the final position of both 'black' and 'white' twins. For Tom 'goes from black to white to murderer to thing that will be sold down the river';[61] while Valet is left dangling on the fringes of the community, the living symbol of the breakdown of its codes, boundaries and beliefs. The damage done to both parties in a system that depends on binary racial distinctions cannot be hidden here. That *Those Extraordinary Twins* ends with a lynching, a different but more immediate and convenient way to solve a complicated social and legal problem, is no coincidence in a period when this means of *racial* punishment and repression was dramatically on the rise.[62] Again, the fluidity of the boundaries between twinned texts becomes apparent. Twain's story points to the problems of the racial present as everything is put back into its apparently comfortable place in the fictional past.

The cover-up and closure that occurs in the last pages of *Puddn'head Wilson* raises, for the alert reader, as many questions as it solves. The novel ends as a detective story, with Wilson as the possessor of knowledge that allows him to solve the crime and Twain to close his book. The scientific techniques associated with Wilson's hobby of finger-printing allow him to unravel the tangle of identity caused by Roxy's initial act, and, at the same time, to discover the perpetrator of the Judge's murder. Twain's use of the detective genre here partly distracts from the force of his historical materials about race and slavery. For Wilson's investigations, in fact, reveal two 'crimes' at once: the *original* act by which Roxy has upset the town's *racial* order, *and* Tom's later act of murdering his 'uncle', the prompt for the immediate criminial proceedings. These two stories cannot be separated out from one another. The novel brings us back to the broad-scale nature of its racial theme even as its grounds are shifted to the punishment of one black individual for the one black crime. As in 'The Stolen White Elephant' an ironic humour operates as the detective ends up being celebrated by a community that fails to see his, or its, blindness. A similar sense of incongruity exists here, as the disruptive presence which cannot be hidden from sight (race) is entirely overlooked in the shift of focus to the puzzling out of clues that solves a particular murder mystery.

If Wilson's activity distracts from, but also (unwitttingly on his part) draws attention to the racial issue, as far as the larger question of character and self-definition goes, all his intervention does – as he sorts out who is who – is to confirm the instability of subjectivity. The *only* way Tom can be told from Valet, and Valet from Tom (and thus, implicitly, one individual from another) is by their fingerprints. In terms of the exchange that has occurred here, there is absolutely no other way of telling the two individuals apart. Identity is reduced to its basic essence, the lines on one's skin. There is no more to it than that. The idea of the self as fixed, centred and stable in an environment which it can effectively control is revealed here as patent nonsense as Twain questions the fundamentals of nineteenth-century value and belief.

I have suggested how *Puddn'head Wilson and Those Extraordinary Twins* are bound in a Siamese connection. Once this is recognised, the allegorical aspects of the text(s) gain additional resonance. Twain's move from one genre to another, from ironic 'tragedy' to farce, can be seen in terms both of an acceptance of the artistic appropriateness of the rigidities of allegory to the material of *Puddn'head Wilson,* and a counter-impulse toward the extravagant burlesque of the Siamese twins story. This is not to deny the allegorical aspects of the latter, nor the humour of *Puddn'head Wilson,* but to identify a significant tension in the writing – a difference in narrative style and attitude which, despite the symbiotic nature of the two texts, could not be bridged. The peculiar quality of the narratives lies in the lack of formal unity, the sense of incompletion and deferral, that results from their twinning. To suggest this is to see Twain on the verge of the type of artistic understanding which would only become commonplace in later, post-structuralist, times: that our representation of reality can only end in deferral and incompletion.[63]

8

The Late Works:
Incompletion, Instability,
Contradiction

Damnation! I said to myself, are we real creatures in a real world, all of a sudden, and have we been feeding on dreams in an imaginary one since nobody knows when – or how is it? My head was swimming.

(*The Great Dark*)[1]

I

The general critical consensus is that, with the completion of *Puddn'head Wilson and Those Extraordinary Twins*, Twain's best work was done. But that is not to say that the vast amount he wrote after 1894 (and particularly in the next twelve years[2]) is without interest. Indeed, the range and variety of his writing in this period is extraordinary. Twain published a good part of this material in his lifetime. However, much remained unfinished, or self-censored, and unpublished (or published only in bowdlerised or 'laundered' form[3]) until comparatively recently. *Which Was the Dream? and Other Symbolic Writings* and *Mark Twain's Mysterious Stranger Manuscripts* came out in 1967 and 1969 respectively.[4]

This surge of new material has prompted a re-evaluation of the final stages of Twain's career. Earlier commentary tended to concentrate on his 'slide into despair and artistic impotence'.[5] More

157

recently, Bruce Michelson has warned against 'dividing Mark Twain's career into theater acts', and has emphasised a turbulent, resilient and liberating quality to the late texts matching that found in his earlier writing.[6] Other critics, such as Susan Gillman, Maria Ornella Marotti and David Sewell, focus particularly on Twain's unfinished narratives, especially the dream tales and the different versions of *The Mysterious Stranger*. Though taking different critical perspectives, they agree on the importance of this late work.[7] Each variously recognises that the formal incompletion of these narratives, and their strong sense of deferral, arises out of the duplications, contradictions and relativistic uncertainties, which they obsessively represent. The fragmented nature of these texts point, in Marotti's words, toward 'modern fiction, the open form, and the endless chain of signs'.[8]

I argue in my previous chapter that to read *Puddn'head Wilson and Those Extraordinary Twins* as twinned texts is already to identify a sense of deferral and incompletion in Twain's work. However, *Pudd'nhead Wilson* can still stand alone as a single text, and is brought to an end, albeit with that type of uneasy closure that is a repeated feature of Twain's narratives. The late texts I discuss in this chapter are all unfinished. Formal completion, and the masking of thematic and generic tensions this involved, just could no longer be managed by Twain. Fixed endings could not serve to seal down either the instabilities of the world he was to represent or his conflicting responses to it.

Michelson suggests that earlier critical responses to Twain's late texts were predicated on the basis that he was struggling to create 'shapely, polished' stories. His counter-reading rests instead on their creative instability, which he directly relates to the intellectual and cultural climate of a period when 'structural and thematic unities were . . . coming under unprecedented challenge as aesthetic virtues'. Marotti pursues a similar argument but goes a step further. For while Michelson sets this late work in a modernist context, she stresses, too, its links with postmodernist art. Marotti points to the 'probing of form' which intensifies in the Mark Twain Papers, the generic heterogeneity of these texts, and their thematic content, to conclude that Twain here 'anticipates both our contemporary awareness of the fragmentation of experience and some modern and postmodern literary procedures'.[9]

In my last chapter, I show how the fragmentary and open-ended forms of such narratives as *The Great Dark* (1898), *Three Thousand Years Among the Microbes* (1905) and *No. 44, The Mysterious Stranger* (1902–8), inevitably result from their thematic contradictions, generic instabilities and epistemological uncertainties. While agreeing that Twain anticipates postmodernism here, I would resist identifying him closely with that later movement. For I would argue that, though the fragmentary, repetitious and unfinished nature of these stories reflects Twain's understanding of the relation between text and world, it remains, too, a sign – and here I depart both from Michelson and Marotti – of his artistic frustrations.[10] Twain *could* not finish these texts. That is a very different matter than mounting a fully realised challenge to accepted artistic convention; and from the *deliberate* incompletions and formal ruptures of postmodernism.

II

Twain published a considerable number of finished texts after *Puddn'head Wilson and Those Extraordinary Twins*. My approach in this chapter is once more, and necessarily, highly selective. After brief comment on Twain's last travel book, *Following the Equator* (1897), I focus on two of the dream tales and just one of the *Mysterious Stranger Manuscripts*. I see here a culmination to the thematic and formal anxieties I have traced throughout Twain's career, and which are particularly apparent from *A Connecticut Yankee* onward. The return to fantasy in the late fiction provides, indeed, an important connection with this latter text.

The thematic and generic tensions in Twain's narratives increasingly threatened their artistic shape, so his turn once more to travel narrative can be seen as a temporary reprieve from such concerns. *Following the Equator: A Journey Around the World* (published in England as *More Tramps Abroad*[11]) is the record of Twain's global lecture tour, made to help pay off his debts following the voluntary bankruptcy of 1895. The travel book, as Twain practised it, was a catch-all form. He was never bound by the limits of the conventional non-fiction travelogue, but rather wandered from fact to fiction, from autobiography to history to cultural anthropology, and from burlesque and satire to philosophy and political denunciation, as he wrote. The genre suited Twain's varying artistic needs, perhaps

better than any other. He travelled through countries, rather than
engaging – in *Following the Equator* at least – in much dialogue with
their people. As he went, he commented as he pleased on various
individuals, places, aspects of culture and associations,[12] before
moving his narrative, at whatever pace suited him, to the next place
and topic.

The return to travel writing gave Twain the type of formal
looseness that entirely suited him. However, *Following the Equator*
lacks the vivacity of his earlier works in the genre. Bruce Michelson
notes the fascination with death that pervades the book, and rightly
suggests that it is 'not a narrative that waves its hat very much in
moments of glee and broad comedy'.[13] The passivity of the narrator,
his (often) marginal position in terms of the described environment,
histories and events that he recounts, and the noticeable lack of
detail concerning his professional activities and personal relationships, are in marked contrast to his construction as an active and
fully engaged central persona in *Innocents Abroad* or *Roughing It*.

Susan Gillman links *Following the Equator* to Twain's other late
texts in its use of the device of 'occult travel', and in its repeated
returns to the matter of race and imperialism. She sharply illustrates
how 'the logic of US racial division, based on the "one-drop"
rule . . . is exploded within the context of colonial race relations',
and looks at examples of Twain's 'close readings of native dress,
skin, and bodies' to suggest his 'identification with otherness' here.
Tracing such connections, she calls *Following the Equator* the
'companion travel narrative' of the dream tales: where the race
problem, she suggests, also strongly figures.[14] I would make a
different type of connection. For a sequence of incidents and
anecdotes narrated in *Following the Equator*[15] foreshadows other
dominating concerns and obsessive repetitions of the late fiction.

In *Following the Equator*, Twain tells a series of (often very short)
stories, and uses descriptive terms, which point to his imaginative
engagement with a particular set of themes that recur over and over
in his writing from this time on. My examples here must necessarily
be brief, but are indicative of a more general pattern. Thus Twain's
description of a dream he has in Sydney, with the relativistic shifts
of scale involved, reads like a close working note for *Three Thousand
Years Among the Microbes*:

I dreamed that the visible universe is the physical person of God;

that the vast worlds that we see twinkling millions of miles apart
in the fields of space are the blood corpuscles in His veins; and
that we and the other creatures are the microbes that charge with
multitudinous life the corpuscles. (p. 132)

The possibility of losing one's bearings, a constant threat in the late
Twain, connects up with the startling change in perspective
described here. The use of charts and maps, and their failure to
match known geophysical facts, is a recurrent motif both in
Following the Equator and the dream tales. When maps, in the former
text, are set against direct perception, curious disjunctions occur. So
the narrator refers to islands 'so thick on the map that one would
hardly expect to find room between them for a canoe: yet we seldom
glimpse one' (pp. 80–1). And in this travel book, the type of strange
and unsettling events which recur throughout the late fiction take
place on Twain's own reported sea journey. As his ship enters the
doldrums, so a 'wobbly and drunken motion' overcomes it, and a
'total eclipse of the moon' (p. 65) follows. Exceptional and disturbing changes in the natural environment prefigure the unsettling
links between geophysical and psychic disturbance in the dream
tales. Descriptions of the 'eternal monotonies' (p. 66) of the voyage
at sea, and, later, of a porpoise which takes (as it first appears) the
'corkscrew shape and imposing length of the fabled sea-serpent'
(p. 109), are suggestive of the doomed encirclings of *The Enchanted
Sea-Wilderness* and the monstrous forms of *The Great Dark* respectively.[16] Such disturbing notes are crucial to Twain's late fiction, and
connect with the motif of shipwreck, or disaster at sea which
became such a dominant trope there.

If the reuse of the travel genre in *Following the Equator* meant, then,
a temporary release from Twain's formal problems as a writer,
material in the book anticipates that in the late and unfinished
fictional texts. Any attempt to divorce Twain's fictional and
non-fictional writing too firmly, or to insist on too rigid a definition
of the latter term, cannot be sustained. Biographical detail (Twain's
journey round the world in financial disarray; the emotional
bombshell of Susy's death from meningitis before his return to
America), late nineteenth-century cultural anxieties (about race,
technology, knowledge and the status of the self), the travel book
he wrote, and the unfinished fictions he would produce, are all
bound together in one interrelated whole.

III

In the dream tales and the *Mysterious Stranger Manuscripts*, Twain, as was his normal practice, mixes genres within the same text. Thus *The Great Dark* includes elements of farce, as the invisible Superintendent of Dreams playfully empties and refills the mate's cup of coffee to the latter's consternation: 'I'm dumm'd if *I* recollect drinking that' (p. 115). The story later, however – at least, in the notes Twain made toward a conclusion – turns to tragedy:

> The sea begins to dry up. . . . Capt. & Edwards & others take several days' provisions & walk overland. Arrive too late. All hands dead. They carried the mummied bodies (aged 16 and 25) back to their ship. Too late again. All dead – & he was going to ask forgiveness of her and Jessie. Looks up – is at home – his wife & the children coming to say goodnight. His hair is white.[17]

The narrative shifts between science fiction and fantasy, as Edwards's account of the scientific experiment that reveals a whole ocean in a drop of water is replaced by his shipboard life on that same strange sea.[18] It moves, too, between sentimentalism, with its focus on home and family, and horror story, with the threat of the colossal squid and other 'uncanny brutes' (p. 111). Michelson talks of a 'delight in subverting the ground rules for literary art'[19] running through Twain's whole artistic career, but that does not quite explain what is happening here. The formal choices and instabilities of the late work are inseparable from their *incomplete* status. Twain ends up caught between genres and ideas, unable to finish his texts. His formal frames can no longer accommodate an artistic vision which is marked by a dizzying relativism, and which moves in unreconcilable and contradictory directions. The fragmentation of this work is a measure of Twain's thinking about the nature of identity, the direction of history and the foundations of knowledge. Formal incompletion and thematic instability are the necessary correlatives of his doubts, ambivalences and hesitations on these subjects.

The dream tales and the *Mysterious Stranger Manuscripts* tell, in part, an unfinished story of anxieties about subjectivity and of epistemological uncertainty. Twain's return to fantasy as a genre –

for all the texts I now discuss are fantastic, or contain elements of fantasy[20] – is, accordingly, highly significant. Fantasy's function as a reminder of 'all that has been silenced in the name of establishing a normative bourgeois realism'[21] is particularly relevant. For one of the things Twain does, in these late tales, is to explode with renewed force conventional realist assumptions of the stable, centred and autonomous self.

Rosemary Jackson links the idea of the stable self to the seeing eye. Implicit in the ability to see clearly, and the sense of control that accompanies the eye's dominance over a perceptual field, is that sense of authority and comprehension associated with the sovereign subject. From such a perspective '"I see" [is] synonymous with "I understand". Knowledge, comprehension, reason, are established through the power of the *look*, through the "*eye*" and the "*I*" of the human subject.' Accordingly, so Jackson suggests, the loss of the sense of visual control is a sign of deep uncertainty about identity, the authority of the self, and the relation between self and world. 'Many Victorian fantasies', she writes, 'employ the device of a lens or mirror to introduce an indeterminate area where distortions and deformations of "normal" perception become the norm.'[22]

The use of the microscope in *The Great Dark* has just such a function. Henry Edwards changes from a spectating subject, using the increasingly powerful lenses of his scientific tool to open up the mysteries of nature, to 'observed object'.[23] In the transformation that occurs, he finds himself, and the ship in which he travels, a specimen on the microscope slide. He is still in charge of the narrative he writes but of little else, and, in his change of role and status, he is thrown increasingly off balance. In this other world, 'there ain't any *sun* [and] there *ain't* any . . . moon' (p. 120), and the sky is 'solid black' (p. 119). Vision, beyond the lamps on board ship and the phosphorescence of the sea spray, is 'dimmed to obliteration' (p. 106). The loss of sight is matched by a loss of geographical bearings on the part of the narrating subject and his companions. Compass readings fail completely to match the boat's expected location, thus the mate, for instance, reports that 'the Gulf Stream's gone to the devil!' (p. 118).

The collapse of knowledge and the loss of bearings signify, in line with Jackson's analysis, a slipping sense of authority and identity. Bruce Michelson expresses this very nicely, and suggests the larger implications of the tale, in describing Edwards and his wife as:

middle-class American everybodies and nobodies, distinguished only for their bad luck in losing track of who and where they are. . . . In other words this is a story in which nonpeople from nowhere [typecast fictional characters who come from Springport, a non-existent American town] get lost between realities . . . in an endless nowhere, a nonworld where Pirandello and Stoppard might feel right at home.[24]

Interestingly, though, and in line with other Twain texts at the time, this sense of slipping identity has a double focus to it. For Twain's representations of uncertain subjectivity look in two directions, both outward to the surrounding world, and inward to the psyche. Edwards loses track of things. He finds himself, as middle-class American type, at the absolute mercy of circumstances of which he has no knowledge and which he cannot control. His role, then, is paradigmatic, suggesting Twain's anxieties concerning the status of the subject in a disorienting and unknowable world. But Edwards is also a divided self. In line with his understanding of 'the new psychology of the unconscious', Twain introduces the figure of the Superintendent of Dreams into his story to indicate that the subject is split internally between a dream self and waking self. He then suggests that to insist on the primacy of the waking self is not necessarily an accurate reflection of the way things are.[25] So, according to a holograph note, the Superintendent of Dreams would claim the 'S[uperintendent] of R[ealities]' (p. 131) as his real name, while the life Edwards apparently dreams on shipboard becomes more convincing than his supposedly real prior life (p. 139).

A similar concern with identity loss and self-division also haunts *Three Thousand Years Among the Microbes* and *No. 44, The Mysterious Stranger*. The narrator of the former text, Huck (a diminutive of Huxley[26]), has been transformed by a magician into a cholera germ. He now lives in the bloodstream of Blitzowski, an 'incredibly dirty [and] unspeakably profane' Hungarian-American tramp, whose 'body is a sewer' (p. 436). The value of the individual subject is implicitly mocked in several ways as this (fantastic) change of scale occurs. Blitzowski's name and status contain a veiled reference to contemporary American fears about immigration. A further reminder of this historical context is also present in the description of Huck's own instant naturalisation in his new home: 'I was become intensely, passionately, cholera-germanic; indeed, I outnatived the natives themselves' (p. 435). The allusion to the 'swarming nations of all the different kinds of germ-vermin' (p. 436) that inhabit Blitzowski's body has a double effect. It acts as a reminder that, for many native-born Americans, the new immigrant 'other' (from Eastern Europe) was seen as an alien and proliferating foreign 'germ', lacking any individual identity in its mass infection of the American social body.[27] It also, though, relativises such a perspective in the detached view given of the *universal* body. For, from outside that Blitzowskian cosmos (the narrator's original position), the inhabitants of the host country he will enter lack just as much individualisation as those who would 'invade' them. They are *all*, indeed, 'germ-vermin'.

The destabilising relativism of the narrative, introduced through the use of fantasy, thus provides a way of critiquing both nationalist xenophobia and conventional views of the self as 'unique, distinguishable, irreplaceable'.[28] The microbic world is represented throughout as a microcosmic version of the human one. This opens the way for satire as, for example, the conventional Christian belief that '*all* of God's creatures are included in his Merciful scheme of salvation' (p. 497) is translated to a microbe context. Its effect is both to question the assumed self-importance of the individual human being in the divine scheme of things, and the related sense of the preciousness of distinct identity. Such satiric play continues as Huck claims that American scientists, in their 'torturing' of microbes on microscope slides, commit 'germicide', going on to say that 'there is no moral difference between a germicide and a homicide . . . not even a germ falls to the ground unnoticed' (p. 504).

The interrogation of the idea of stable and autonomous individualism takes a further turn when Huck reveals that, seen from a microbe perspective, all things are alive. Even an atom, he reveals, has 'a certain degree of consciousness [and] a *character*, a character of its own' (p. 448). Death itself does not exist. Rather the molecules which compose living bodies scatter to 'take up new quarters' elsewhere, in 'hundreds of plants and animals'. A complete decentring and radical collapse of the sense of consistent and coherent identity and consciousness occurs here. For as Huck says:

What would become of me if [Blitzowski] should disintegrate? My molecules would scatter all around . . . but where should *I* be?. . . . There would be no more me. . . . I should still be alive, intensely alive, but so scattered that I would not know it. (p. 458)

At this point, Twain's ongoing anxieties about identity reach a climax in the epiphanic vision of subjectivity dissolved into a fluid and boundary-less amorphousness.

No. 44, The Mysterious Stranger, like *The Great Dark*, throws a double focus on the problem of identity. For August Feldner, the sixteen-year-old apprentice printer and narrator, is divided without and within. The description of his two selves acts to suggest both the subjection of the body to the imprint of historical circumstance (in the allegory of modernisation that is implied), and the split nature of the psyche. For August, and all his fellow printers, have duplicates of themselves brought into being by the young stranger who bears the strange name, No. 44, New Series 864,962.[29] These 'exact reproduction[s]' (p. 305) are a 'flesh and bone' (p. 315) version of 'invisibles'[30] conjured up previously by No. 44 to provide labour when a strike brings the printing works to a standstill. The invisibles then function as more efficient and automatic versions of the original human workforce:

there before our eyes the press was whirling out printed sheets faster than a person could count them – just *snowing* them onto the pile, as you may say – yet *there wasn't a human creature in sight anywhere*!. . . . When *they* did a thing, they did it right . . . and it hadn't any occasion to be corrected. (pp. 281–2)

This reads like a description of a successful version of the Paige typesetter in which Twain had sunk so much wasted money.

Human forms (the duplicates) of abnormal strength (p. 291), however, replace these invisibles. As this happens, and as the 'original' strikers plan to murder their doubles (p. 387), so an interpretation of such duplication in terms of contemporary anxieties about the status of the subject in a Taylorised work force is prompted. This, in turn, takes us back to Twain's earlier representations of this theme in *A Connecticut Yankee* and *The American Claimant*.[31] To read this part of *No. 44, The Mysterious Stranger* in this way is to see the original workers – with all their inefficiencies, human weaknesses and disruptive economic potential[32] – faced with the threat of conversion into components of a smooth and efficient industrial system, where personal visibility or invisibility is scarcely to the point.

But if one can see the duplicates in terms of Twain's concern with the processes of American social and industrial history, there is an alternative and opposite reading contained in the text. For the division in the subject represented here is internal as well as external. August's other duplicate self is, in fact, part of his single first self. When August speaks of the shock he receives 'every time I met myself unexpectedly' (p. 311), that shock comes to signal recognition of internal self-division.[33] For August discovers that his duplicate, Emil Schwartz, is in fact the dream self that has always lived 'Box and Cox lodgers in the one chamber' (p. 343) with his waking self. Only with No. 44's fleshing forth of this duplicate into the waking world has contact between the two selves become any more than hazy.[34] The dream self is, it turns out, far imaginatively superior to the waking self: 'he had all the intensities one suffers or enjoys in a dream!' (p. 344). Twain works his way out of the problems such self-divisions represent for the completion of his narrative by exploding them, together with all that remains of the conventional notion of selfhood, at the end of the manuscript as it stands. Here, No. 44 declares both himself and the universe a dream: a creation of the imagination, of the pure 'thought' of which Feldner is comprised (pp. 404–5). Though the logic of these various interrelationships is problematic, it is clear that Twain's concern with the psychology and composition of the individual subject has taken a sharp turn away here from the social and historical resonance with which the notion of the double is also (previously) invested. The fact that the narrative is unfinished, or part finished, suggests that the different components of the fiction cannot satisfactorily be brought together; that the contradictions in Twain's art can no longer be formally contained.

IV

The fantastic elements of the dream tales and *No. 44, The Mysterious Stranger* disrupt any normative version of centred and coherent subjectivity. They act too, however, to rupture the 'ground rules'[35] by which we conventionally frame and order our world. The displacements and 'disturbing transformation[s]' of Twain's late fantasies undermine what is homely, familiar and 'comfortably "known"', replacing them with a spiralling relativism, where uncertainty and disorder ('areas normally kept out of sight') predominate.[36] The challenge posed to any firm knowledge of 'reality' in these late texts runs hand in hand with a narrative technique which is similarly disconcerting, and to the same ends.

A disorienting epistemological uncertainty permeates the late work. This is suggested in the number of times a statement like 'It makes me dizzy; I don't know quite where I am' is echoed by words and phrases connoting acute confusion and estrangement: 'uncanny', 'uncharted', 'dizzy', 'my head was swimming', 'dazed' and 'a good deal jumbled up'.[37] The sense of the ground being removed from under both Twain's characters' and his readers' feet commences in *The Great Dark* with the transformation of the narrator from the scientific controller of a miniature world to a disoriented participant in the uncanny and nightmare sea-scape the lens of his microscope reveals. Then, in the 'Mad Passenger' extract, written as part of the same story, Edwards' children find a microscope in this fellow voyager's shipboard locker. Edwards undergoes a dream-like sense of recall as he watches the Mad Passenger 'put a drop of water on a glass slide', and the children 'exclaiming over the hideous animals they saw darting about and fighting in the bit of moisture'.[38]

A sense of boundless repetition, and an undercutting of any sense of firm narrative and epistemological ground and level occurs here. This latter becomes even more overt in the dialogues concerning the comparative status of shipboard life and the domestic life which (for Edwards, and in the narrative) preceded it. For Edwards starts to loses his hold on which life is dream and which reality. First, the Superintendent of Dreams, on board ship, questions and reverses his assumptions on this matter: 'And this is *real* life. Your other life was the dream!' (p. 124). Then his own wife says that the shared (other) family life they both recall took place in 'dream-homes, not real ones' (p. 130). Finally, Edwards himself starts to recover memories of an earlier shipboard existence. The extreme nature of the uncertainty introduced into this story is evident in the way that the wife's assertion that life on board ship is their joint reality is positioned. For it is given as part of an inner narrative (the sea journey) placed *within* two outer frames. And the first of these two framing statements, which describe and apparently validate –

in their earlier turn – the reality of those events which have occurred in the family *prior* to their fantastic transformation, is also made by her. Edwards' wife, then, validates *both* (unreconcilable) realities.

The text is full too of other destabilising effects. The Superintendent of Dreams has a curious indeterminate status in terms of the two worlds described. The narrator's own acts of writing appear to transgress any clear boundary between the different levels of narrative. And the story itself is incomplete. All these together make Edwards' comment, 'we seldom really know the things we think we know' (p. 125), resonate uncontrollably. The sense of any absolute authority over, or firm knowledge of, experience, and of the ability to represent it in any transparent or straightforward narrative form, disintegrates in the course of the inconclusive and fragmented story.

A similar sense of epistemological uncertainty and narrative incompletion pervades *Three Thousand Years Among the Microbes*. A spiralling sense of cosmic relativism is first prepared for, with the Darwinism of the microbe world – the satire at this point clearly pertains to late nineteenth-century social realities – where the Nobles munch on the SBEs (Soiled-Bread Eaters) and, when the chance is given, the reverse occurs too (p. 512). The chain of eaters and eaten, victimisers and victims, in the natural and social economy that this introduces, is then widened as the narrator, speaking to Franklin, a Yellow Fever germ, undercuts Franklin's providential sense of self-importance with his own knowledge that '[Franklin] and all the swarming billions of his race' were, in complete ignorance, 'gnawing, torturing, defiling, rotting, and murdering a fellow-creature', the tramp, Blitowski. He then continues, to suggest the further implications of this:

> It hints at the possibility that the procession of known and listed devourers and persecutors is not complete. It suggests the possibility, and substantially the certainty, that man is himself a microbe, and his globe a blood-corpuscle drifting with its shining brethren of the Milky Way down a vein of the Master and maker of all things . . . (p. 454)

A mind-stretching relativism develops here, as the initial shift in scale, from human to microbe, prompts the vision of a groundless sequence stretching from the Universal body of God down through layers of infestation to, and implicitly beyond, the 'infinitely microscopic microbes that infest *microbes*' (p. 513).

The loss of centre that such relativism signifies is reinforced by the multi-levelled and inconclusive quality of *Three Thousand Years Among the Microbes*'s narrative form. A kind of double translation appears to take place, as the narrator first writes in 'microbe tongue', then 'laboriously translate[s] it into English' (p. 461). The two framing prefaces further complicate things. For in the first, 'Mark Twain' says that he himself 'translated [the story] from the Original Microbic' (p. 433). In the second, and more consistently,[39] he claims only to have further 'translated the author's style and construction'. He also, however, comments to disorienting effect that the original 'title-page is incorrect' (p. 434). The inside main story is then told from a number of perspectives. So Huck, at one stage, recounts his experience, only to interrupt himself with a later comment on his text. He then interrupts his first interruption to note, from a later perspective still, the inaccuracy of the information he has just added (pp. 439–41). Asterisks, added notes and apparently independent textual fragments ('xxxxx. But really no one was to blame, it was an accident' – p. 43) heighten the sense of dislocation and textual instability. The narrative concludes suddenly with Huck, apparently absorbed in the Blitzowski present, dazzled by the 'incredible wealth' he hopes to mine there (from a gold tooth). The problem of how to reconcile the various levels and voices of the text, and how satisfactorily to end it, is left – one suspects necessarily – unresolved.

The conventional ground rules by which we 'know reality' are also turned topsy-turvy in *No. 44, The Mysterious Stranger*. No. 44 represents the spirit of exuberant play and imagination. He can be seen to stand in self-reflexive relation to Twain himself: a liberating figure who by the means of his artistic imaginings can escape and subvert conventional belief systems and restrictions.[40] If playfulness undermines all normal constraints here, however, it can never be brought into any kind of balanced relationship with the social and historical world it disrupts. To focus just on No. 44's actions, however – for it is these that provide the mainspring of the text – is to see the usual ways of ordering the world completely undermined. Thus No. 44 transcends space and time, for his race is not limited by their rules (p. 331). Accordingly, he brings August canvas-back duck to eat from America, a country not yet discovered

(p. 313), and can transport him, in the instant, to China (p. 399). The human race, to No. 44, is indistinguishable from the 'other bugs' (pp. 319–20), and he reveals to August that the various ways it conducts itself, and socially and morally orders its world, are completely ridiculous.[41]

No. 44 is a boisterous jokester who upsets the frameworks and systems by which those around him pattern their lives, and mocks their rules and customs. He takes human time and history and reverses and rearranges them. He even replays conversations backwards, radically disorienting both August and the reader as he does so (pp. 397–8). August assumes a pious demeanour, in line with his religious beliefs, to pray for the soul of No. 44 when the latter professes his indifference to religion. He is, though, ignored completely, as No. 44 entertains himself, spinning about in the air, making gay and vibrant music with a jew's harp, and whooping with joy as he does so (pp. 298–9).[42] Equally, when Father Adolf invokes divine power against him, No. 44's only response is to indulge in what August calls 'coarse and vulgar horse-play' (pp. 328–9). As Bruce Michelson says, a 'kind of vertigo' affects the reader as the narrative proceeds. For not only does No. 44 playfully upset time, space, history and religion, he undermines confidence in language itself, and its expressive abilities (pp. 318–19); throws the difference between dream and reality, self and world, in doubt. And if everything No. 44 does disorients in one way or another, so does the entire narrative when read as Twain left it. For the story as it stands is marked both by contradiction – between solipsism and historical engagement – and by disjunctive shifts in tone, as satire, deterministic pessimism and (No. 44's) celebratory comic performance each are (separately) introduced. The reader is left 'with every structural and thematic rug pulled out from under'[43] her or his feet. The incomplete quality of the text is a logical result of its internal tensions and vertiginous effects.

V

Fantasy works to produce a form of readerly hesitation as the borders between reality and the unfamiliar or uncanny are blurred. The dislocation that occurs acts to deny the solidity of what is normally taken to be real.[44] But fantasy is not normally associated with textual incompletion and fragmentation. The spiralling relativisms and disturbing vacuums (the self 'alone in shoreless space'[45]) of Twain's late work in this mode problematise any sense of narrative completion. The conventional device of fantasy is to move the central protagonist between two adjacent worlds: as happens, for instance, in *A Connecticut Yankee*. In his late manuscripts, Twain complicates and extends his use of the mode. He denies the centred subjectivity of his characters in exposing the internal divisions that compose the self. Further destabilisation occurs in the final loss of any kind of firm ground. For his protagonists are unmoored, either left with no sense of solid reality at all, or caught between worlds and unable to tell which is real; which has authority over which. All frameworks of knowledge and belief are shown to be arbitrary and untrustworthy. Any sense of narrative resolution or final closure consequently becomes impossible.

This, though, is not quite all. For the sense of internal contradiction and paradox present in all Twain's work to one degree or another becomes, in these late works, overt. Opposed thematic impulses drive these fictions, and no straightforward narrative closure can overcome such inbuilt divisions. So Twain's exploration of individual psychology cuts against his social and historical interests. The focus on the split subject, the dream and waking self, in *The Great Dark* cannot ultimately be thematically reconciled with the allegorical concern with late nineteenth-century science and technology in the same text: the exploration of the 'demonic nature of crossing limits' which the initial use of the microscope introduces.[46] Similarly in *No. 44, The Mysterious Stranger*, the manuscript ends in solipsism; an escape from reality by using the imagination to extinguish it, 'transforming it into a fiction'.[47] But this is desperately at odds with the socio-historical interest in technology and duplication, and the continued anxiety about current events, racial issues and (other) social injustices, that – at times, subliminally, at others, overtly – informs the text.[48] The gap between these two aspects of the narrative is clear as specific references to contemporary occurrence (the Russo-Japanese war, for example, p. 393), and the historical procession described in the penultimate chapter, give way, in a sudden wave of the hand, to the vision of 'an empty and silent world' (p. 403). The structure of dream and the engagement with history are incompatible with one another here, in terms of a coherent narrative.[49]

Thus Twain's continued artistic involvement with, and satiric comment on, late nineteenth-century social and political history stands in contradictory relationship with his impulse to celebrate the creative self-sufficiency of the individual imagination: 'Dream other dreams, and better!' (p. 404). Likewise, the cool detachment and deterministic philosophy that is such a strong element in these late works cannot be reconciled with the 'moral indignation' that continued to motivate their author, and to influence him as he wrote.[50] Something of this contradiction comes across in the moves between satire and comic relativism in *Three Thousand Years Among the Microbes*. In modern forms of black humour, any faith in satire as an instrument of reform is suspended in favour of a comic acceptance of the absurd: that all values are relative, and that humour lies in seeing the joke in the human situation rather than attempting to remedy it.[51] Much of Twain's late work can be placed in this category. The switch in perspective that sees man's 'mission' and 'reason for existing' in providing 'a home and nourishment' for the microbe and bacillus (pp. 447–8) engages just such comic play. The subjective nature of knowledge and belief – 'truth [as] the concoction of the subjective mind'[52] – is also the target of such humour. Thus the narrator's certainties about his previous life and universe are 'dubbed an illusion,' and met with expansive laughter, by the 'able minds' of his microbe friends (p. 492). The conclusion Huck draws from this difference in perception, with each party convinced of its own rationality, is that 'there isn't anybody that isn't right, I don't care what the subject is. It comes of our having reasoning powers' (p. 495). Black humour depends on such relativistic uncertainty as this. It envelops *Three Thousand Years Among the Microbes*, with the relationships and analogies between the worlds of microbes and men on which it plays.

But humour is also used as a satiric weapon in the text. America is satirised in the name given its Blitzowskian equivalent, 'Getrichquick'. Its imperialist policies in the Phillipines are comically savaged in the account given of 'Benevolent Assimilation': the ingenious territorial gain of the 'collection of mud islets inhabited by those harmless bacilli which are the food of the fierce *hispaniola sataniensis*' (pp. 442–3).[53] The textual juxtaposition of remarks about the English monarchy with the account of the long-ruling Pus family of Henryland works to similar satiric effect. Thus Henryland's colonial practices are described, with obvious but none the less apt wit, as the spreading of 'pus and civilisation' (pp. 438–9). Indeed, in *Three Thousand Years Among the Microbes*, Twain aims his comic barbs at a whole range of nineteenth-century practices and institutions. Such satire, based, as it finally is, on the desire for reform, sits uneasily with the comic and cosmic relativism beside it.

Twain, then, was caught between themes and philosophies as he wrote these late texts. Given this, their fragmentary and incomplete nature is no great surprise. In *No. 44, The Mysterious Stranger*, Schwartz, August's dream self, pleads for freedom from 'these bonds of flesh – this decaying vile matter' (p. 369), the human body to which he has become tied. He describes the shape-shiftings and transcendences of 'spirit[s] of air' like him:

> *We* have no morals; the angels have none; morals are for the impure; we have no principles, those chains are for men. . . . We have no character, no *one* character, we have *all* characters. . . . We wear no chains . . . we have no home, no prison, the universe is our province; we do not know time, we do not know space . . . our playgrounds are the constellations and the Milky Way.
>
> (p. 370)

In this dream version of the human self, Twain's imagination works itself free of all the conditioning influences that chain August and his other human protagonists. But the gap between this dream ideal (brought to life in the figure of No. 44) and everyday human realities cannot be closed. In this, it refigures the impossibility of reconciling in one text the 'self-enclosed mental world'[54] of the novel's provisional ending with the external realities of history, time and social being which are there cast aside.

The dream sprite, Schwartz, can scarcely communicate his experiences to August, his 'flesh-brother' and 'Waking-Self'. For to try to do so 'was like "emptying rainbows down a rat-hole"' (p. 378). Twain's late work leaves his reader between incompatible realities, surreally stranded (as the above quote indicates) between transcendent vision and the mundane. To read *No. 44, The Mysterious Stranger* alongside the dream tales is to find Twain still writing extraordinary and interesting narratives, but narratives that cannot be closed or completed. He is artistically trapped here between relativistic black humour and satiric critique; between spinning personal and epistemological disorientation and the desire for community, home and known; between cacophony and incomprehensibility, and a belief in the power of language and communication;[55] between psychology and history; and between a belief in the agency of the subject[56] and a mechanical determinism that undermines the concept of the self as a meaningful category. A separate stress on the divisions within the self also calls coherent subjectivity into question.

There is, of course, much more to the late Twain than the particular works I study here.[57] The divisions, fragments and incompletions of these texts, however, seem an apt conclusion to his writing career. Their inconclusive and anxiously repetitive explorations of individual and social identity, of history and of the status of knowledge, are the end of a long artistic process, with Twain's forms proving increasingly unable to satisfactorily contain his divergent and complex themes. If the fragmentation of these works, moreover, anticipates some aspects of modernist and postmodernist literary practice, it also diverges crucially from them. Twain's formal experiments and incompletions do provide a way artistically to represent his developing understanding of self and world, but he does not produce *finished* texts. Their ragged edges are not formally shaped, there by deliberate choice, but act to signal paradox, contradiction and the artist's *inability* to complete. They are, though, no less valuable for that. To do much more was, one might indeed argue, near to impossible[58] for one writing at the time.

There is a statement attributed to Twain at a school prize-giving, when – so the story goes – he presented a boy with a large Webster's dictionary: 'This is a very interesting and useful book, my son. . . . I have studied it often, but I never could discover the plot.'[59] Whether apocryphal or not, the anecdote provides a suitable note on which to conclude. Twain's study of human behaviour, of philosophy and of socio-historical conditions was finally to leave him, not exactly plotless, but caught between plots; unable formally to contain the spiralling complexities of his vision. The manuscript of *The Great Dark* ends with the ship's captain saying, 'We haven't had an observation for four months, but we are going ahead, and do our best to fetch up somewhere' (p. 150). The words might stand for Twain at his career end, still writing, not quite sure of his direction, left with unfinished manuscripts, but fetching up, despite, as one of the most productive, important and interesting writers of his time.

Notes

Chapter 1 Keeping Both Eyes Open: 'The Stolen White Elephant'

1. Mark Twain, 'The Stolen White Elephant' in *The Stolen White Elephant Etc.* (London: Chatto and Windus, 1897 [1882]) p. 24. Page references to follow quotes hereafter. Twain originally wrote 'The Stolen White Elephant' in November or December 1878, intending it to be part of *A Tramp Abroad*. See James D. Wilson, *A Reader's Guide to the Short Stories of Mark Twain* (Boston, Mass.: G. K. Hall, 1987) p. 247. A version of this, my present, chapter appears in *Studies in American Humor*, new series 3, no. 2 (1995). I am grateful to the American Humor Association for permission to reprint.
2. There is extended critical commentary on Samuel Clemens's use of his pen name, Mark Twain (which he adopted in 1862). For a summary, see R. Kent Rasmussen's *Mark Twain A to Z: The Essential Reference to His Life and Writings* (New York: Facts on File, 1995) pp. 188–9, 303. Recent critics tend to use Twain when speaking of the writer's persona and Clemens as the historical person. For reasons suggested in chapters 2 and 3, I use the former name throughout.
3. Limits of space prevent me analysing this other important story too. But see my 'Caught on the Hop: Interpretive Dislocation in "The Notorious Jumping Frog of Calaveras County"', *Thalia: Studies in Literary Humor*, vol. 15, nos. 1 and 2 (1995) pp. 33–49.
4. The term is borrowed from Gerald Mast's comment on the films of Buster Keaton, and is quoted in Marcel Gutwirth, *Laughing Matter: An Essay on the Comic* (Ithaca, NY: Cornell University Press, 1993) p. 157. I use Gutwirth's book extensively as my theoretical model here, and acknowledge my debt to him.
5. Gutwirth uses this term 'frustrated expectation' in his description of the comic. He links it with another phrase which is particularly provocative once applied to Twain's comic work: a '[rupture] in determinism'. See *Laughing Matter*, pp. 91–3.
6. My move from first-person singular to plural, and the related identification between first- and third-person 'reader', indicates that, in reconstructing the reader's role, I let my own response stand as

representative. For my recognition of the problems involved in such a tactic see the chapter on 'The Dynamics of Reading: *A Lost Lady*' in my *New Readings of the American Novel: Narrative Theory and its Application* (Basingstoke: Macmillan, 1990) pp. 130–61.

7. I reapply the phrase Gutwirth uses to discuss Samuel Beckett's *Waiting for Godot*. See *Laughing Matter*, p. 184. The appropriateness of the implied analogy will emerge later in the chapter.

8. James D. Wilson, *A Reader's Guide to the Short Stories of Mark Twain*, p. 248

9. Twain's own acquaintance with Barnum is noted in Robert Pack Browning, Michael B. Frank and Lin Salamo (eds), *Mark Twain's Notebooks & Journals: Volume III (1883–1891)* (Berkeley: University of California Press, 1979) p. 547. Twain's fictional elephant has, as it happens, the same name as had 'Barnum's celebrated British acquisition, "Jumbo" . . . [which] arrived from London on 9 April 1882'. See Frederick Anderson, Lin Salamo and Bernard L. Stein (eds), *Mark Twain's Notebooks & Journals: Volume II (1877–1883)* (Berkeley: University of California Press, 1975) p. 509. Twain, however, originally wrote his story three and a half years earlier.

10. Susan Gillman, *Dark Twins: Imposture and Identity in Mark Twain's America* (Chicago: University of Chicago Press, 1989) pp. 14–15.

11. Forrest G. Robinson, '"Seeing the Elephant": Some Perspectives on Mark Twain's *Roughing It*', *American Studies*, vol. 21, no. 2 (Fall 1980) pp. 55–6.

12. Marcel Gutwirth, *Laughing Matter*, p. 91.

13. Susan Gillman, *Dark Twins*, p. 22. See too my 'Caught on the Hop'.

14. The fact that the several story frames given are *all* part of the same fictional representation to a degree problematises the making of such distinctions. My repeated use of the words 'seem' and 'appear' suggests, too, the difficulty of any definitive reading of a text which operates as hoax; where the line between deception and the hiding of deception is always marked as problematic. So often in Twain, we cannot be sure who is hoodwinking whom, nor on quite what level we are meant to be reading and responding.

15. Quoted in Marcel Gutwirth, *Laughing Matter*, p. 105.

16. Marcel Gutwirth, *Laughing Matter*, p. 99.

17. Alternatively, or additionally, once we realise that the story does not work satisfactorily as a conventional hoax, we may look for another narrative or allegory which will allow us to make more sense of it. My following sections illustrate what happens when we do this.

18. Marcel Gutwirth, *Laughing Matter*, p. 80.

19. In his valuable study of the sources of Twain's story, 'Of Detectives and Their Derring-Do: The Genesis of Mark Twain's "The Stolen White Elephant"' (*Studies in American Humor*, vol. 2, January 1976, pp. 183–95), Howard G. Baetzhold describes how it had its specific base in the Alexander T. Stewart grave-robbery case of 1878. Twain's contemporary audience would have been aware of the theft of the corpse of the wealthy dry-goods merchant (from St Mark's churchyard

in New York City) on 7 November 1878, and the absurdities of the investigation that followed. Despite reports of a ransom paid and of the recovery of the corpse (in 1880), there still remains some question as to whether the body was in fact ever returned: see Baetzhold, pp. 188–9. Twain's story thus operates first and foremost as burlesque: 'When the detectives were nosing around after Stewart's loud remains, I threw a chapter into [*A Tramp Abroad*] in which I have very extravagantly burlesqued the detective business – if it *is* possible to burlesque that business extravagantly' (*Mark Twain–Howells Letters*, quoted in Baetzhold, p. 184). The 'loudness' of these remains and the 'nosing around' of detectives after a body in a state of two and a half years' decomposition – which rendered it, in the words of the police inspector, Dilks, in charge of the case, 'so offensive that [it] cannot be concealed' (Baetzhold, pp. 186–7) – clearly parallel Twain's depiction of the comic nature of the elephant–detective relationship in his story.

20. Twain's use of foreign names for comic ends indicates his attraction to common forms of ethnocentric humour. See my 'Racial and Colonial Discourse in Mark Twain's *Following the Equator*', in *Essays in Arts and Sciences*, vol. 22 (October 1993) pp. 67–83. The nub of Twain's joke here, however, lies in the reductive move from the formal complexity of the long, ornate and polysyllabic Indian name to the most common and mundane of elephant nicknames. This is a common technique in Twain's comic armoury – that sudden overturning of expectation; the deflationary shift from one level of discourse to another (so-called 'lower' and vernacular) level.

21. Marcel Gutwirth, *Laughing Matter*, p. 85.

22. Marcel Gutwirth, *Laughing Matter*, pp. 97–8.

23. Meanwhile, Blunt may well be playing a double game as he apparently 'cons' the narrator out of $142,000 (the lack of certainty here is a product of Twain's use of the first-person voice).

24. Marcel Gutwirth, *Laughing Matter*, pp. 55, 107.

25. The notion of an allegorical reading of the white elephant tempts further speculation on a possible relationship between this story and Herman Melville's *Moby Dick*. The relation between white whale and white elephant and what each signifies (or *fails* to signify), between the detective (the representative of a secular society, on the trail of the animal for the monetary reward it will bring) and Ahab (whose quest is more of a 'sacred', spiritual and metaphysical, kind), and between the use of tragedy and comedy in the two texts, deserves more extended treatment than I can give it here. The thought of Melville as a literary father figure to this narrative is an intriguing one. The connection with Edgar Allan Poe, and his use of the hidden and the obvious in 'The Purloined Letter', is also worth pursuing.

26. See Marcel Gutwirth, *Laughing Matter*, pp. 50–1, 58, 57.

27. Marcel Gutwirth, *Laughing Matter*, p. 29. This is just one of the series of approaches to the analysis of humour that Gutwirth discusses.

28. Mark Twain, *The Mysterious Stranger*, ed. William M. Gibson (Berkeley: University of California Press, 1969) p. 166.

29. Marcel Gutwirth, *Laughing Matter*, pp. 57, 66
30. See Michael Denning, *Mechanic Accents: Dime Novels and Working-Class Culture in America* (London and New York: Verso, 1987) pp. 118–48. Denning describes both how dime novelists quickly capitalised on the Molly Maguires case and, in relation to this, how the figure of the detective became a common one in American popular fiction of the 1870s and 1880s. There are clear allusions both to the Pinkertons and to detective fiction as a popular genre in Twain's story (and to the two combined, for Allan Pinkerton's fictionalised versions of the cases involving his 'National Detective Agency' were to appear from 1874 onward). The 'wide-staring eye' and the 'WE NEVER SLEEP' legend of the detective badge 'printed in gold on the back of popular novels' ('The Stolen White Elephant' – p. 23) is, as Howard G. Baetzhold points out, that which 'grace[d] the spines – and covers – of Pinkerton's books'. 'What seems to have irked [Twain] most', he continues, 'was the assumption of infallibility implied in the badge and motto, and in Pinkerton's books themselves.' See 'Of Detectives and their Derring-Do', p. 192.
31. See Paul Smith, *A Reader's Guide to the Short Stories of Ernest Hemingway* (Boston, Mass.: G. K. Hall, 1989) p. 208, and Richard Godden, *Fictions of Capital: The American Novel from James to Mailer* (Cambridge: Cambridge University Press, 1990) p. 67. Both refer to Ernest Hemingway's story 'Hills Like White Elephants', a later American narrative which operates round the divergent meanings of the latter term.
32. Though, at the same time, we are aware that part of Twain's joke lies at a simpler level; precisely in the making literal of a figure of speech (something which dreams often do) and the comic move between conceptual boundaries (the real and the surreal) which then follows.
33. Marcel Gutwirth, *Laughing Matter*, pp. 98–9.
34. Marcel Gutwirth, *Laughing Matter*, pp. 108, 99.
35. Marcel Gutwirth, *Laughing Matter*, p. 108 (my emphasis).
36. As my reading of 'Jim Smiley and His Jumping Frog' would confirm (see note 3 above).
37. See Justin Kaplan, *Mr. Clemens and Mark Twain* (Harmondsworth, Middx.: Penguin, 1967 [1966]) pp. 320–3, and Gregg Camfield, *Sentimental Twain: Samuel Clemens in the Maze of Moral Philosophy* (Philadelphia: University of Pennslyvania Press, 1994) pp. 223–4.
38. Though my analytic procedures do not match Mailloux's rigorous interest in 'rhetorical hermeneutics', I am influenced here by his concentration on the way the rhetoric of a text 'participat[es] in the cultural debates of a specific historical period and place', and the way critical analysis then functions to locate 'the intersecting dialogues of the cultural conversation within the social practices, institutional disciplines, and material circumstances that made up American society at the moment the text was produced'. See Steven Mailloux, *Rhetorical Power* (Ithaca, NY: Cornell University Press, 1989) p. 104.
39. See Jane Tompkins, *Sensational Designs: The Cultural Work of American*

Fiction, 1790–1860 (New York: Oxford University Press, 1985) pp. xv–xvii.

Chapter 2 Old World Travel: *The Innocents Abroad*

1. Frederick Anderson, Michael B. Frank and Kenneth M. Sanderson (eds), *Mark Twain's Notebooks & Journals, Volume I (1853–1873)* (Berkeley: University of California Press, 1975) pp. 352, 426, 433.
2. Mark Twain, *The Innocents Abroad or The New Pilgrim's Progress* (1869). I use the version of the text published in *The Innocents Abroad and Roughing It* (New York: Library of America, 1984), here p. 17. Page numbers to follow quotes hereafter. Twain also used letters sent to the New York *Tribune* and *Herald* in the writing of his book.
3. The narrator's role in the book varies. At times he apparently speaks for the author; at others, his naive persona is constructed in comic relation to the superior knowledge and sophistication of that author. I use Mark Twain from now on (necessarily uncomfortably) to refer both to author and protagonist.
4. Jeffrey Steinbrink, *Getting to be Mark Twain* (Berkeley: University of California Press, 1991) p. xiii.
5. James Buzard, *The Beaten Track: European Tourism, Literature, and the Ways to Culture, 1800–1918* (Oxford: Clarendon Press, 1993) p. 219. '[S]teamship lines and travel agencies', he continues, 'competed for and stimulated a broadening demand'.
6. See Jeffrey Steinbrink, 'Why the Innocents Went Abroad: Mark Twain and American Tourism in the Late Nineteenth Century', *American Literary Realism*, vol. 16 (1983) p. 279.
7. Michael Kammen also refers to the urge to promote a 'nationally desired note of reconciliation' following the Civil War, which ended just two years before Twain's journey. See *Mystic Chords of Memory: The Transformation of Tradition in American Culture* (New York: Alfred A. Knopf, 1991) p. 103.
8. William W. Stowe, *Going Abroad: European Travel in Nineteenth-Century American Culture* (Princeton University Press, 1994) pp. 36, 17, 34. Stowe provides the best study I have read of *The Innocents Abroad* and the development of American travel writing.
9. I follow Twain in the gender specificity of this phrase. William W. Stowe, in *Going Abroad*, has interesting material on the gendered aspects of *The Innocents Abroad*, and its 'bad-boy bluster', and how they mutually relate to the sense of 'embattled manhood' (p. 128) in the period. J. D. Stahl also discusses the sexual politics of the book in *Mark Twain, Culture and Gender: Envisioning America through Europe* (Athens: University of Georgia Press, 1994).
10. Directly associated by J. D. Stahl with 'the newfound economic and cultural self-confidence of post-Civil War America', in *Mark Twain, Culture and Gender*, p. 31.
11. William W. Stowe, *Going Abroad*, p. 125.

12. Bruce Michelson, 'Mark Twain the Tourist: The Form of *The Innocents Abroad'*, *American Literature*, vol. 49 (1977–8) p. 392.
13. In *Going Abroad*, William W. Stowe shows how Twain's tactics and concerns in *The Innocents Abroad* were anticipated by other writers (pp. 129–46). I follow his analysis of what it is that makes Twain's text distinctive (pp. 146–7).
14. Jeffrey Steinbrink describes it as 'the most successful travel book in the country's literary history', with sales of 100,000 within two years of its publication. See *Getting to be Mark Twain*, p. 62, and 'Why the Innocents Went Abroad', p. 278.
15. Alfred Kazin, 'Introduction' to *The Innocents Abroad* (New York: Bantam, 1964) pp. vi, vii.
16. Bruce Michelson's analysis of the text is based on this conflict. See *Mark Twain on the Loose: A Comic Writer and the American Self* (Amherst: University of Massachusetts Press, 1995) pp. 55–63. I acknowledge my critical debt to Michelson, though my commentary runs in different directions.
17. William W. Stowe, *Going Abroad*, p. 126.
18. William W. Stowe, *Going Abroad*, p. 48. Stowe uses the work of Dean MacCannell to suggest the relation between the tourist and the ethnographer here.
19. See Bruce Michelson, *Mark Twain on the Loose*, p. 53.
20. Henry B. Wonham says that as Twain added new episodes to the original travel letters, as he prepared his book for publication, so he prioritised 'dramatization over description'. See *Mark Twain and the Art of the Tall Tale* (New York: Oxford University Press, 1993) p. 81.
21. Richard Bridgman, *Traveling in Mark Twain*, pp. 9, 1. As part of his discussion of the influence of Sentimentalism on Twain, Gregg Camfield discusses the links between Twain's writing and the 'associationist model of human psychology' (p. 45) adopted by some members of the Common Sense school of philosophy. See *Sentimental Twain: Samuel Clemens in the Maze of Moral Philosophy* (Philadelphia: University of Pennsylvania Press, 1994). The importance of this model in terms of Twain's general literary practice cannot be overestimated. See, also, Forrest G. Robinson, 'The Innocent at Large: Mark Twain's Travel Writing', in Robinson (ed.), *The Cambridge Companion to Mark Twain* (Cambridge: Cambridge University Press, 1995) pp. 27–51.
22. Richard Bridgman, *Traveling in Mark Twain*, p. 2.
23. Contemporary reviews were more likely to comment on the distinctive quality of the American brand of humour than anything else, if Frederick Anderson's selection is representative. The review in the Buffalo *Express* spoke of the 'panorama of Europe and the Holy Land as they were seen by one who went abroad with no illusions; who carried about him a shrewd pair of American eyes', but this sounding of a nationalistic note in the context of the Old–New World contrast was the exception, not the rule. British reviewers seem to have been more open to such a reading. See Frederick Anderson (ed.), *Mark Twain:*

The Critical Heritage (London: Routledge & Kegan Paul, 1971) pp. 25–6 and *passim*.

24. William Woodruff, *America's Impact on the World: A Study of the Role of the United States in the World Economy, 1750–1970* (London: Macmillan, 1975) p. 64. William W. Stowe says, of American travel abroad in the period, that 'the tide of the early nineteenth century became a torrent, and the American tourist in Europe became a commonplace'. See *Going Abroad*, p. 8.

25. This episode, where the representative American democrat becomes 'bloated aristocrat' already points to that destabilising of expected polarities which occurs throughout the text. It also raises the question of the nature and consistency of the ironic gap between the author and his narrator. Steinbrink comments on the costs of foreign travel, noting that 'some [Americans] were actually able to economize by going abroad', in 'Why the Innocents Went Abroad', p. 280. See, too, *The Innocents Abroad*, p. 65.

26. J. D. Stahl's analyses the doctor's buying of a kiss from the attractive girl who acts as guide at the Palazzo Simonetti (see *The Innocents Abroad*, p. 156) to show how a relationship based on the 'cash nexus' of tourism is complicated by the sexual politics involved. See *Mark Twain, Culture and Gender*, pp. 41–2. Stahl, William W. Stowe in *Going Abroad*, and Robert Regan, in 'In the Wake of the *Quaker City*', in Robert Sattelmeyer and J. Donald Crowley (eds), *One Hundred Years of Huckleberry Finn: the Boy, His Book, and American Culture* (Columbia: University of Missouri Press, 1985) pp. 231–41, all discuss the gender politics of the text.

27. See 'Why the Innocents Went Abroad', p. 283, for Jeffrey Steinbrink's comments on the 'materialist mindset' of the tourists, and also their buying into both European art and European aristocracies. William W. Stowe's discussion of the guidebook is also relevant here: 'one of [its] most important functions was to endow the traveler with all the freedom and power of the bourgeois consumer by serving as a catalog of tempting products among which he or she was free to choose'. See *Going Abroad*, p. 45.

28. Robert Regan, 'Huck Finn in the Wake of the Quaker City', pp. 233, 234, 236. Regan also suggests that *The Innocents Abroad* invokes a posterior discourse (his term, p. 240); establishes a context for the books he would later write. So, for example, the reference to the monk in the Capuchin Convent in Rome some day being 'taken apart like an engine or a clock' (p. 238) anticipates Twain's later interest in the links between the human body, the machine and the question of identity. Similarly, the puzzle of the veins of oyster shells in the hill of the citadel in Smyrna (pp. 328–9) points forward to the uneasy parody of evolutionary discourse, and a similar lack of firm historical knowledge or ground, in 'Was the World Made for Man?', in Bernard DeVoto (ed.), *Mark Twain: Letters from the Earth* (New York: Harper & Row, 1962) pp. 211–6.

29. Alfred Kazin, 'Introduction' to *The Innocents Abroad*, p. ix.

30. Edward Said, *Culture and Imperialism* (London: Vintage, 1994 [1993]) p. 42.

31. Twain gives an example of this ruinous English in his notebook: 'Muleteers sang "We hang Jaf Deevez on sowly abbla tree/Glory halleluiah – and his soul go"'. In the *Alta* letters, Twain changed this to: 'We 'ang Jeffah Davis on sowlah applah tree,/So we go *molloching* on!' See Frederick Anderson, Michael B. Frank and Kenneth M. Sanderson (eds), *Mark Twain's Notebooks & Journals, Volume I (1853– 1873)*, p. 346. My emphasis anticipates the argument in the final section of this chapter

32. A late comment, where Twain refers to foreign attitudes to America, both obliquely acknowledges, and diverts from, the war: 'When we found that a good many foreigners . . . knew [America] only as a barbarous province away off somewhere, that had lately been at war with somebody, we pitied [their] ignorance' (pp. 515–16).

33. This sense remains intact despite the sailors' burlesque of the passengers, their false humility, and the formal circumlocutions of their rhetoric in the presence of royalty, that follows (pp. 320–2).

34. David E. E. Sloane, 'Toward the Novel', in Sloane (ed.) *Mark Twain's Humor: Critical Essays* (New York: Garland, 1993) pp. 125–6. The essay is reprinted from *Mark Twain as a Literary Comedian* (Baton Rouge: Louisiana State University Press, 1979).

35. Mark Twain, *The Adventures of Huckleberry Finn* (Harmondsworth, Middx.: Penguin, 1987 [1885]) p. 50.

36. See Bruce Michelson on the larger resonances of the 'Is he dead?' gag, *Mark Twain on the Loose*, pp. 49–50, 52–4. The impossibility of such a permanent erasure counterbalances such an episode.

37. So Christopher Mulvey describes transatlantic tourism in the nineteenth century in *Anglo-American Landscapes: A Study of Nineteenth-Century Anglo-American Travel Literature* (Cambridge: Cambridge University Press, 1983), where he speaks of the reduction of 'everything to the condition of things "which tourists travel to see"'. His comment that the word *did* 'was eventually to become the verb to describe the typical activity of the tourist' (all quotes, p. 249) recalls Twain describing his and his fellow tourists' activity as 'we galloped through the Louvre, the Pitti, the Ufizzi, the Vatican – all the galleries' (p. 517), and his first explorings of Marseilles when 'we only wanted to glance and go – to move, keep moving!' (p. 78). James Buzard bases *The Beaten Track* on the 'binary opposition' between travel and tourism that he sees as 'fundamental to and characteristic of modern culture', p. 18.

38. William W. Stowe notes that European art is associated with a repugnant social system. He shows how Twain's 'common-sense solution to the problem of art appreciation' (to look at the painting 'with unprejudiced American eyes and trust one's "natural" judgement') is to deny both that 'beauty is . . . a cultural product' and that the supposedly 'natural eye has already received . . . [an] education' in how to judge it. See *Going Abroad*, pp. 157–9. An implicit

contradiction exists here with comments on art elsewhere in Twain's book.

39. As so often in the book, Twain's position lacks consistency. On other occasions Twain is genuinely moved and impressed by European culture and the aura that surrounds its originals, though such enthusiasm generally refer to places rather than paintings. Even in the case of paintings and sculpture, Twain counter-balances the dismissive quality of his comments by admitting that 'one has no opportunity in America to acquire a critical judgement in art' (p. 187). To read the original/copy relationship in terms of international cultural difference is to problematise any American claim to originality. Such a problematisation is well recognised in any discussion of American cultural identity.

40. The French and the English are represented more positively than other nationalities. That 'otherness' becomes more noticeable in the Holy Land and Africa is unsurprising, for the civilisation/savagery binary had prior existence along European/non-European lines. The Holy Land is also, as I show, associated with the sacred, so representations of the area are not for Twain (or for prior European writers) homogeneous.

41. William W. Stowe uses this term in *Going Abroad*. He usefully describes the complexities and contradictions of the variety of identities Twain assumes in terms of 'a rhetoric of noncommittal enthusiasm' – 'playing every role with brief, sincere commitment and then undercutting the commitment, the sincerity, and the role itself' (p. 156). Bruce Michelson similarly speaks of the quality of 'perilous renewal' in Twain's persona, the trying on of 'new masks, new mentalities, costumes, ways of being', *Mark Twain on the Loose*, p. 44. I would argue (as Michelson also suggests) that the moves between such identities are not always so easily put on and off as Stowe suggests; that the adopting of incompatible roles leads to a sense of some anxiety and dis-ease.

42. Another strain running through the book is its one-dimensional representation of women. Women are consistently described in terms of physical attractiveness alone, or more often the lack of it. An overt misogynistic note appears in the *Alta* letters where the description of the 'atrocious ugliness' of the Moorish women of Tangier that appears in *The Innocents Abroad* (p. 69) is followed by the statement that 'If I had a wife as ugly as some of those I have seen, I would go over her face with a nail-grab and see if I couldn't improve it' (see *Mark Twain's Notebooks & Journals: Volume 1*, p. 365).

43. In the late work, *Three Thousand Years Among the Microbes* (1905), turn-of-the-century colonial practice is satirised as the spreading of 'pus and civilization'. See Chapter 9.

44. David R. Sewell, *Mark Twain's Languages: Discourse, Dialogue and Linguistic Variety* (Berkeley: University of California Press, 1987) p. 60. Sewell has interesting material on Twain's illusion 'that he can pass as a cosmopolitan polyglot', relating it to Emerson's romantic conception of language(s), pp. 64–5.

45. David Sewell refers to the way that 'American gold pieces spea[k] the universal language of economic power' in a prior episode (pp. 42–3) in *Mark Twain's Languages*, p. 61. So, too, the American dollar becomes *like* gold, a *lingua franca*.
46. See David Sewell's astute analysis of the fact that often, in *The Innocents Abroad*, '*less* language equals more power', *Mark Twain's Languages*, pp. 58–9.
47. Forrest G. Robinson, 'The Innocent at Large', p. 31.
48. Alfred Kazin, 'Introduction' to *The Innocents Abroad*, p. x.
49. In both these cases, there are also negative aspects to Twain's descriptions. In the latter, one can also see that 'recoil from the consciousness of the present, proximate, familiar and human' which Forrest G. Robinson identifies as a repeated pattern in the book. See 'Patterns of Consciousness in *The Innocents Abroad*', *American Literature*, vol. 58 (1986) pp. 58, 62.
50. Neither, despite what Robert Regan says in ' Huck Finn in the Wake of the *Quaker City*', can Huck.
51. James Buzard, *The Beaten Track*, p. 158. Buzard has detailed discussion on the problems of asserting 'originality in spite of . . . belatedness'. He describes how: 'nineteenth century visitors to the Continent had to reconcile the essentially repetitive nature of *acculturating* tours – to places known and valued in one's own culture – with that countervailing 'adversary' pressure to demonstrate some measure of originality and independence. . . . Writers . . . saw themselves moving through a domain of texts, seeking the complex satisfaction of participating in a process of cultural accreditation while also standing aloof from such participation as a form of imitation' (p. 161). Though Buzard is speaking of English travellers at this point, his words can be directly applied to Twain's case.
52. I am adapting what Edward Said says here about the 'huge library of Africanism', *Culture and Imperialism*, p. 79. Said's comment on the same page that 'there is no such thing as a *direct* experience, or reflection, of the world in the language of a text' is immediately relevant here.
53. Shades of difference between reverence and a deadpan comic version of it, and the exact nature of the tone being used, are not always easy to distinguish in the text. So, for an alternative interpretation, see J. D. Stahl, *Mark Twain, Culture and Gender*, p. 29.
54. Edward W. Said, *Orientalism* (London: Routledge & Kegan Paul, 1980 [1978]) p. 42. See Said's general argument, and especially pp. 65, 71–3, 102.
55. The phrase is Mary Louise Pratt's, though in a different context, in *Imperial Eyes: Travel Writing and Transculturation* (London: Routledge, 1992) p. 125.
56. See William W. Stowe, *Going Abroad*, p. 148.
57. See Bruce Michelson for a penetrating reading of this opposition, in *Mark Twain on the Loose*, pp. 55–63. I follow Michelson's lead here in linking the Holy Sepulchre and Adam's tomb sequences.

58. Dennis Welland, *The Life and Times of Mark Twain* (London: Studio Editions, 1991) p. 42.
59. Twain's worsening relationship with the *Quaker City* party and their complaints about him (and the other 'fast young men') can be traced in Harriet Elinor Smith and Richard Bucci (eds), *Mark Twain's Letters, Volume 2, 1867–1868* (Berkeley: University of California Press, 1990) pp. 102–3, 106, 108, 400–406.
60. See Robert Regan, 'The Reprobate Elect in *The Innocents Abroad', American Literature*, vol. 54, no. 2 (May 1982) pp. 240–57.
61. Tony Tanner, 'Writers of the Bible of America', *Times Higher Educational Supplement*, 22 November 1985, p. 17.
62. See Frederick Anderson, Michael B. Frank and Kenneth M. Sanderson (eds), *Mark Twain's Notebooks & Journals, Volume 1*, p. 390.

Chapter 3 *Roughing It* and the American West

1. Edgar Marquess Branch, Michael B. Frank and Kenneth M. Sanderson (eds), *Mark Twain's Letters, Volume 1: 1853–1866* (Berkeley: University of California Press, 1988) p. 150. A close version of this present chapter is scheduled to appear in the *Canadian Review of American Studies*, vol. 26, no. 1 (Winter 1996). My thanks to the journal editors for permission to reprint.
2. From Frederick Jackson Turner, 'The Significance of the Frontier in American History' (1893). See George Rogers Tyler (ed.), *The Turner Thesis Concerning the Role of the Frontier in American History* (Lexington, Mass.: D. C. Heath, 1956) p. 2. Hereafter, 'The Significance of the Frontier'.
3. *Mark Twain's Letters, Volume 1*, p. 132.
4. Stephen Fender, '"The Prodigal in a Far Country Chawing of Husks": Mark Twain's Search for a Style in the West', *Modern Language Review*, vol. 71, no. 4 (October 1976) pp. 740–1. Fender's comments on the rhetorical shaping of the letter for possible publication (p. 741) is confirmed in *Mark Twain's Letters, Volume 1*, p. 139. Twain wrote two versions of this piece, one of which was published in the Keokuk *Gate City*, 20 November 1861.
5. Turner, 'The Significance of the Frontier', pp. 18, 2, 3. Turner first delivered his frontier thesis to the American Historical Association in Chicago. In it, he does distinguish between different types of frontier (farmer's and miner's, for example) and their different rates of development, and allows, too, for geographical discontinuities (the irregularities of such western movement).
6. One that Twain himself would consistently employ (and, as protagonist of *Roughing It*, be the victim of). Stephen Fender discusses the western newspaper hoax, and Twain's breaking of its conventions in his 'A Bloody Massacre' (1863), in '"The Prodigal in a Far Country Chawing of Husks"', pp. 748–50.
7. Turner, 'The Significance of the Frontier', pp. 4–5. Both Lee Clark

Mitchell and Bruce Michelson interpret the Buncombe incident in related ways. Mitchell sees it in terms of the unpredictability of the West, compared to the 'fully predictable' East, in 'Verbally *Roughing It*: The West of Words', *Nineteenth Century Literature*, vol. 44 (1989–90) p. 71. Michelson places Buncombe's 'overthrow' in the context of a West which 'flourishes upon [the] . . . absence' of 'rules, precedents, . . . cultural institutions and common sense . . . '. He sees the 'resistance to "serious" interpretation' here in terms of Twain's general narrative tactics in the book. See *Mark Twain on the Loose: A Comic Writer and the American Self* (Amherst: University of Massachusetts Press, 1995) p. 70.

8. See Bruce Michelson, *Mark Twain on the Loose*, pp. 63–4, 74.
9. Martha Banta, 'The Boys and the Bosses: Twain's Double Take on Work, Play, and the Democratic Ideal', *American Literary History*, vol. 3, no. 3 (Fall 1991) p. 489.
10. Turner, 'The Significance of the Frontier', p. 4.
11. Similar to his method on stage. Within two pages of the start of the transcribed version of the 'Sandwich Islands Lecture' (given by Twain on his return to San Francisco) he says: 'But I am losing time; what I have been saying don't bear strictly on the Sandwich Islands, but one reminiscence leads to another, and I am obliged to bring myself down in this way. . . . It is not safe to come to any important matter in an entirely direct way.' See Paul Fatout (ed.), *Mark Twain Speaking* (Iowa: University of Iowa Press, 1976) p. 5. At this very early stage of his career, Twain is already describing some of the vital techniques of his lecturing (and literary) art.
12. Mark Twain, *Roughing It* (Harmondsworth, Middx.: Penguin, 1985 [1872]), p. 54. Page references to follow quotations henceforth.
13. Turner, 'The Significance of the Frontier', p. 17.
14. Jeffrey Steinbrink, *Getting to be Mark Twain* (Berkeley: University of California Press, 1991) p. 139.
15. Turner, 'The Significance of the Frontier', p. 2. But, pointedly, social pressures too have a major part to play in the clothes and habits the narrator adopts.
16. The book is based on Twain's experiences in the West from the summer of 1861 to December, 1866. The difference between the naive narrator depicted at the start of *Roughing It* and the experienced twenty-five year old who actually made the journey is the subject of extended critical comment. See, for instance, Jeffrey Steinbrink, *Getting to be Mark Twain*, p. 138. Hamlin Hill refers to Twain's 'enormous violation of the facts of his biography' in the construction of his narrative persona in his 'Introduction' to *Roughing It*, p. 16.
17. Henry Nash Smith identified a structural move from innocence to experience in the contrast between these two narrative positions. See 'Mark Twain as an Interpreter of the Far West: The Structure of *Roughing It*', in Walker D. Wyman and Clifton B. Kroeber (eds), *The Frontier in Perspective* (Madison: University of Wisconsin Press, 1957) p. 212. Though, undoubtedly, one of the ways the book works is as a Bildungsroman, the extent and type of maturation associated with the

narrator, and the way it relates to a gradual closing of the gap between the two textual voices, is considerably more problematic than Smith (and the critics who follow his lead) suggests. For the move from tenderfoot to old-timer he describes can, alternatively, be viewed as yet another of the book's 'blind leads'. If the recollecting voice is positioned further back (i.e. identified with the Mark Twain writing in Buffalo and Elmira in 1870–1) some of these problems disappear, though a new one is raised as the tension between naivety and experience has to be reformulated. As in *The Innocents Abroad*, consistent distinction between author and protagonist is problematic. Despite the retrospective gap, at times (and especially when in serious descriptive mode) the narrator's voice becomes one with the author's. 'Mark Twain' accordingly signifies variously.

18. See Turner, 'The Significance of the Frontier', pp. 5, 8. Turner identifies East and West with different orders of the 'civilised'. See note 20 below.

19. Helen L. Harris argues that Twain is 'unfailingly hostile' to American Indians: 'Mark Twain's Response to the Native Americans', *American Literature* vol. 46 (1975) p. 495. Walter Benn Michaels, though, in the context of *A Connecticut Yankee*, sees the Indian as a positive figure of individual resistance to social pressures: 'An American Tragedy, or the Promise of American Life', *Representations* vol. 25 (Winter 1989) pp. 71–98. In my 'Racial and Colonial Discourse in Mark Twain's *Following the Equator*', *Essays in Arts and Sciences*, vol. 22 (October 1993), I argue that there is a sub-text in Twain's late travel book which criticises the dispossessions and depredations to which American Indians were historically subject (see pp. 70–1).

20. As Twain unexpectedly switches his verbal attack to the Baltimore and Washington Railroad Company and its employees (in their resemblance to the Gosiutes), Twain introduces a note of relativistic uncertainty which unsettles his savage–civilised binary. Twain operates here from a similar position that Turner will later adopt, in establishing a three-way set of oppositions between 'savage', frontier and eastern. The advance of capitalism and incorporation associated by Twain with the East, and the corruption that goes with it, are contrasted accordingly with western individualism. I suggest the problematic nature of this contrast later. Any straightforward notion of historical evolution and racial difference is, though, disrupted in the new hierarchy established here. See John E. Bassett, '*Roughing It*: Authority through Comic Performance', *Nineteenth Century Literature*, vol. 43 (1988–9) pp. 227–8.

21. Henry Nash Smith, 'Mark Twain as an Interpreter of the Far West', pp. 214, 212. Forrest G. Robinson argues for a much bleaker reading of the incident and the text, seeing the dog as 'not educated or initiated' by the coyote, but 'utterly crushed', in line with the general movement of a book which recurrently speaks of 'gross self-deception and inevitable failure': '"Seeing the Elephant": Some Perspectives on Mark Twain's *Roughing It*', *American Studies*, vol. 21, no. 2 (Fall 1980) pp. 50, 55.

22. William Bright, quoted in Arnold E. Davidson, *Coyote Country: Fictions of the Canadian West* (Durham, NC: Duke University Press, 1994) p. 2. Warwick Wadlington makes the same connection, writing that 'the coyote is a pivotal metaphor that allows Twain to . . . both . . . establis[h] a pyramid [of superiority] and then pivo[t] it onto its head, giving priority to neither pyramid nor inversion'. See *The Confidence Game in American Literature* (Princeton, NJ: Princeton University Press, 1975) p. 216.
23. Turner, 'The Significance of the Frontier', p. 5.
24. Drewey Wayne Gunn attributes positive value to the dictionary. He says that Twain's 'triump[h] in American letters was in his realization that he must graft the natural speech of the West . . . onto the literary diction of the Eastern establishment': 'The Monomythic Structure of *Roughing It*', *American Literature*, vol. 61 (1989) p. 570. I would resist the assumptions of organic growth and unity behind Gunn's metaphor. The notion of a single pure American form of language (a linguistic gold or silver standard) which could contain the nation's disparate ways of speaking and thinking is shown by Twain also to be illusory. Bruce Michelson suggests a different reading of the sequence, when he discusses 'Life After the Unabridged Dictionary' in terms of a *tension* between constrictive and inherited 'rules of discourse' and a 'tormenting [linguistic] anarchy, a pestilential, "decomposed" composition [the Sphynx]'. See *Mark Twain on the Loose*, pp. 46–7. See also Lee Clark Mitchell, 'Verbally *Roughing It*: The West of Words', p. 82.
25. Kenneth Lynn, *Mark Twain and Southwestern Humor*, quoted in David Sewell, *Mark Twain's Languages: Discourse, Dialogue and Linguistic Variety* (Berkeley: University of California Press, 1987) p. 132.
26. David Sewell, *Mark Twain's Languages*, p. 132.
27. Philip D. Beidler, 'Realistic Style and the Problem of Context in *The Innocents Abroad* and *Roughing It*', *American Literature*, vol. 52 (1980–1) p. 46. These ways of knowing the world are not *quite* separate, thus Briggs leads in with a phrase 'doxology works' which makes use of specialised and sophisticated religious terminology but converts it to his own stylistic needs; reduces its cultivated effect, by combining it with his use of the (formally) inappropriate and (linguistically) casual and imprecise 'works'.
28. M. M. Bakhtin, *The Dialogic Imagination: Four Essays*, trans. Caryl Emerson and Michael Holquist (Austin: University of Texas Press, 1981) p. 297.
29. Philip D. Beidler, 'Realistic Style and the Problem of Context in *The Innocents Abroad* and *Roughing It*', p. 47. Twain's own narrative incorporation of such conflict and difference suggests an understanding of his role as an artist in a heterogeneous society, and a commitment to linguistic (and social) variety. However, such a commitment has its limits, and to speak of the narrator's 'neutrality' is problematic, given the omnipresence of ideological interestedness. The representation of race is ambiguous in *Roughing It*. If, here, Twain interrogates the racist assumptions of Briggs, elsewhere he privileges

the dominant racial and ethnic groups; as when, for instance, he contrasts 'native American' (white) men with Mexican 'Greasers' (p. 435).

30. See Stephen Fender for discussion of the problems involved in Twain's attempt to find a literary style to register a western community which was in itself socially complex (but also deracinated): '"The Prodigal in a Far Country"', pp. 746, 748, 753–5 and *passim*.

31. Lee Clark Mitchell, 'Verbally *Roughing It*: The West of Words', pp. 71–2.

32. John E. Bassett, '*Roughing It*: Authority through Comic Performance', p. 225. Bruce Michelson focuses on the 'refusal of rules, reason, stabilized identities, and recognition of things as they are' the 'blind lead' episode suggests. He associates it with other 'leads' followed and lost, as the narrator attempts to 'inven[t] or discove[r] an identity', and as the narrative itself 'flips and spins' in one direction then another. See *Mark Twain on the Loose*, p. 68. His discussion of unstable identity here usefully connects with my comments on *The Innocents Abroad*. I focus here on other, but related, issues.

33. See Henry Nash Smith (ed.), *Mark Twain of the Enterprise* (Berkeley: University of California Press, 1957) pp. 25–9, for information on the Sanitary Fund controversy, explaining reasons for the move to San Francisco.

34. See Neil Schmitz's stimulating reading of this episode in terms of Twain's use of 'Jacksonian dreaming' as a subject: 'Mark Twain, Henry James, and Jacksonian Dreaming', *Criticism*, vol. 27 (Spring 1985) p. 168.

35. Richard Bridgman, *Traveling in Mark Twain*, p. 56. Twain's attitude in the first Appendix is, I would suggest, itself more ambiguous than Bridgman suggests. His reading of Twain's puzzling third Appendix is, though, illuminating. The analysis Bridgman gives (pp. 39–48) of the Horace Greeley letter about turnips (in the Hawaiian section of *Roughing It*, pp. 501–9) as an embodiment of 'precisely the enigma that Twain himself had to deal with: a scrawled world that yielded a variety of uncertain and by and large unwelcome interpretations' (p. 41) is brilliant (though I disagree with the pessimistic thrust of his general conclusions). In this incident, though the correct version of the letter is finally known, such knowledge comes too late to save the sanity of the preacher.

36. Though I agree with Forrest G. Robinson that any quest for 'knowledge and wisdom' in *Roughing It* is frustrated, I would resist the single stress on self-contempt and cynicism which he reads not only in Twain's own letters from the West but also in his book about it. See his '"Seeing the Elephant"', pp. 44, 53. Twain does, however (as Robinson also notes), seem to have had thoughts of suicide sometime in the last months of 1865 or the very early period of 1866 when he was 'in trouble, & in debt . . . utterly miserable' in San Franciso. See Edgar Marquess Branch, Michael B. Frank and Kenneth M. Sanderson (eds), *Mark Twain's Letters, Volume 1*, pp. 320, 324 (the source of my quote) and 325.

37. Warwick Wadlington, *The Confidence Game in American Literature*, p. 203.

38. As Twain visits the Sandwich Islands, so his narrative continues to bristle with contradictions. Hawaii is both a place of commercial opportunity, and the 'sunniest, balmiest, dreamiest haven of refuge for a worn and weary spirit the surface of the earth can offer'. The latter quote comes from the manuscript fragments of Twain's novel set in Hawaii: see Stephen H. Sumida, 'Reevaluating Mark Twain's Novel of Hawaii', *American Literature*, vol. 61 (1989) p. 593. The attraction of the 'primitive' is obvious in much he says about the country. The missionaries are correspondingly ironically pilloried for the 'improvements' they have brought to these 'simple children of the sun' (p. 481, and see p. 461). But the missionaries are also praised for their improvements, as the idea of savagery as noble is ruthlessly demolished in a description of the violence and 'brutal and unbridled licentiousness' (p. 494) of earlier times.

39. California is described as 'the Garden of Eden reproduced' in one of Twain's 1862 letters from Carson City. See *Mark Twain's Letters, Volume 1*, p. 155.

40. Jeffrey Steinbrink, *Getting to be Mark Twain*, p. 139.

41. Alan Trachtenberg, *The Incorporation of America: Culture and Society in the Gilded Age* (New York: Hill and Wang, 1982) pp. 23, 20.

42. See, too, the reference to the ignorance, of all the Virginia City population but its telegraph operator, of the Civil War victory by Union troops at Gettysburg. This resulted from the 'journalistic monopoly that forbade the slightest revealment of eastern news till a day after its publication in the California papers' (p. 406).

43. See Martha Banta, 'The Boys and the Bosses', pp. 493–4.

44. Howard Horwitz, *By the Law of Nature: Form and Value in Nineteenth-Century America* (New York: Oxford University Press, 1991) p. 112.

45. Edgar Marquess Branch, Michael B. Frank and Kenneth M. Sanderson (eds), *Mark Twain's Letters, Volume 1*, p. 245; and 'Bigler vs. Tahoe', in Edgar Marquess Branch and Robert H. Hirst (eds), *The Works of Mark Twain: Early Tales and Sketches, Volume 1: 1851–1864* (Berkeley: University of California Press, 1979) p. 290.

46. See Leo Marx on Twain's problems of describing nature in any but formulaic and received terms: *The Machine in the Garden: Technology and the Pastoral Ideal in America* (New York: Oxford University Press, 1967 [1964]) pp. 319–25.

47. Peter Stoneley examines this incident in terms of the homoerotic impulse in western literature and life. For him, 'idealized moments of same-sex relationship in *Roughing It* are always curtailed by a retributive violence'. See 'Rewriting the Gold Rush: Twain, Harte and Homosociality', *Journal of American Studies*, forthcoming. Twain implicitly asserts his own manliness (in contrast to a scorned effeminacy) where, for example, he contrasts western horsemanship to 'the silly Miss Nancy fashion of the riding-schools' (p. 197): better to be bucked and jolted by a Genuine Mexican Plug than ride in such a manner.

48. The major thrust of the book, whether through silver mining, speculating, lecturing etc. This episode recalls Locke, for whom 'property results from "workmanship" that "puts[s] the difference of value on everything," which untreated has none'. The West promises such value with only token amounts of work. See Howard Horwitz, *By the Law of Nature*, p. 90.

49. Dan De Quille (William Wright), *The Big Bonanza: An Authentic Account of the Discovery, History, and Working of the World-Renowned Comstock Load of Nevada* (London: Eyre & Spottiswoode, 1969 [1876]) pp. 174–7. See Oscar Lewis's introduction to this edition for an account of Twain's active involvement in, and encouragement of, De Quille's project.

50. See Martha Banta on *Roughing It*'s opposition between playful 'boys' and efficient 'bosses', and the way this affects the book's structure, 'The Boys and the Bosses', pp. 493–7.

51. Martha Banta, 'The Boys and the Bosses', p. 495.

52. See Martha Banta, 'The Boys and the Bosses', p. 496.

53. Walter Benn Michaels, *The Gold Standard and the Logic of Naturalism: American Literature at the Turn of the Century* (Berkeley: University of California Press, 1987) pp. 65–6. He takes the phrase 'fictitious dealings' from a 1921 House Committee enquiry on *Future Trading*.

54. Elisha P. Douglass, *The Coming of Age of American Business: Three Centuries of Enterprise, 1600–1900* (Chapel Hill: University of North Carolina Press, 1971) p. 389. In *The Confidence Game in American Literature*, Warwick Wadlington agrees that 'the importance of financial enterprise in the official national culture finds a dramatic parallel in the flush times of silver and gold mining' but claims that 'the arbitrary luck that usually separates great wealth from hopeful scrounging, as well as the Western habit of spending sprees, completely flaunts the official morality of acquisition through orderly stages of work and capitalization through sober saving' (pp. 203–4). As my argument suggests, I would focus on the similarities of the workings of the capitalist system in the East and the West rather than on their differences, and would ask just how far the type of 'official morality' to which Wadlington refers operated even in the East in Gilded Age America.

55. Earl Pomeroy, *The Pacific Slope: A History of California, Oregon, Washington, Idaho, Utah, and Nevada* (Lincoln: University of Nebraska Press, 1991 [1965]) p. 51.

56. Earl Pomeroy, *The Pacific Slope*, p. 53.

57. See Edgar M. Branch, 'Fact and Fiction in the Blind Lead Episode of *Roughing It*', *Nevada Historical Society Quarterly* 28 (Winter 1985) pp. 234–47. What is suggested in the factual base of this incident is, however, that Twain's ambiguities about individual agency and the market economy may be, in part, a reflection of the rapidity of the changes in American social and economic life. The general relation between fact and fiction in Twain's text is more complicated that Branch's title would imply.

58. Elisha P. Douglass, *The Coming of Age of American Business*, pp. 390–1.

Douglass also gives figures concerning the number and profitability of the Nevada mines: 'Perhaps as many as 5000 claims were located and traded within thirty miles of Virginia City. Only 300 were ever opened, only 20 became mines, and of these only 8 or 9 paid dividends.' Looking at the slim chances of profit from western mining, he comments that 'it is hard to explain the tremendous investment on purely economic grounds' (p. 392).

59. I am extracting here from Walter Benn Michaels's account of late nineteenth-century disputes over the value of money in *The Gold Standard*, pp. 144–9. The quotations given are generally taken from the theorists of the time.

60. Bruce Michelson, accordingly, takes the comic performance which is Jim Blaine's story about his grandfather's old ram as paradigmatic of the conversion to artistic ends of the lack of 'linearity, form, or common sense . . . in the insane world of the American West', *Mark Twain on the Loose*, p. 63.

61. Twain's awareness of such an audience can be implied from the repeated use he makes of the tall tale to reveal its function as a distinctive western type of humour, but also to show its limitations. For the tall tale fails to provide any firm base from which to construct an authoritative version of reality. Instead, deflation (the exaggerations of the tall tale are fabulations, and rest on no solid basis) follows deflation (of the greenhorn victim's naive expectations) in what Neil Schmitz suggests is a kind of 'nihilist joke'. See 'Mark Twain, Henry James, and Jacksonian Dreaming', p. 169. Twain's achievement here is to take that particular western form and represent it as part of a larger literary whole for a *national* audience; allowing that audience both to see the joke, how that joke works and at whose expense, and its final insufficiencies as an alternative and hyperbolic way of representing reality. As a form of humour it does not, like Twain's westward journey itself, finally lead anywhere in terms of constructing a satisfactory stance from which to interpret experience. For an alternative view of Twain's use of this form in *Roughing It*, see Henry B. Wonham, *Mark Twain and the Art of the Tall Tale* (New York: Oxford University Press, 1993) pp. 89–111.

62. See Bruce Michelson, *Mark Twain on the Loose*, pp. 72–4.

63. Lee Clark Mitchell, 'Verbally *Roughing It*', p. 74.

Chapter 4 *Tom Sawyer* and American Cultural Life: Anxieties and Accommodations

1. From *Time* magazine's review of Melvin and Mario Van Peebles's film on the Black Panthers, *Panther*. Quoted in David Gritten, 'The Panthers: Heroes or Villains?', *Independent on Sunday*, 4 June 1995, p. 27.

2. Lee Clark Mitchell, 'Introduction' to *The Adventures of Tom Sawyer* (Oxford: Oxford University Press, World's Classics, 1993) p. x. This is one of the best recent essays on the novel.

3. Described by Gregg Camfield as 'Like the entire park, . . . [offering] a self-contained haven of adventure, where fantasies of piracy and treasure hunting, of endless summertime and endless youth, are colored with enough that is frightful to make them interesting, but are perfectly safe, endlessly repeatable, always charming, and quite saccharine.' See *Sentimental Twain: Samuel Clemens in the Maze of Moral Philosophy* (Philadelphia: University of Pennsylvania Press, 1994) p. 1.

4. Fred G. See, 'Tom Sawyer and Children's Literature', in Gary Scharnhorst (ed.), *Critical Essays on The Adventures of Tom Sawyer* (New York: G. K. Hall, 1993) p. 179.

5. Lee Clark Mitchell, 'Introduction' to *The Adventures of Tom Sawyer*, p. x.

6. Louis J. Budd, 'Mark Twain as an American Icon', in Forrest G. Robinson (ed.), *The Cambridge Companion to Mark Twain* (Cambridge: Cambridge University Press, 1995) p. 6.

7. Cynthia Griffin Wolff, '*The Adventures of Tom Sawyer*: A Nightmare Vision of American Boyhood', *Massachusetts Review*, vol. 21, no. 4 (Winter 1980) pp. 99, 94.

8. 'Preface', *The Adventures of Tom Sawyer* (London: Penguin, 1986 [1876]). Page numbers follow quotes from henceforth.

9. Marcia Jacobson, *Being a Boy Again: Autobiography and the American Boy Book* (Tuscaloosa: University of Alabama Press, 1994) pp. 4, 7, 13.

10. Thus Marcia Jacobson's central argument is that the boy book 'could simultaneously be accepted as offering a vicarious escape from and implicit critique of the culture that produced it and as an instrument for furthering the ends of that culture' (*Being a Boy Again*, p. 13). This leads in fruitful directions, as far as *Tom Sawyer* goes, but does not for me quite explain all the complex effects of the book.

11. Lee Clark Mitchell, indeed, discusses the 'mix of contrasts' in *Tom Sawyer* as matching 'the contradictions many have felt about coming of age in American culture', 'Introduction' to *The Adventures of Tom Sawyer*, p. xv.

12. Hannibal was incorporated in 1845. Its citizens (and particularly Twain's father) shared in 'the speculative ferment . . . sparked by the promise of the vast frontier' in the 1830s. The Panic of 1837 and the decade long depression that followed were the most likely cause of Judge Clemens' financial ruin. See John Carlos Rowe, 'Fatal Speculations: Murder, Money, and Manners in *Puddn'head Wilson*', in Susan Gillman and Forrest G. Robinson (eds), *Mark Twain's Puddn'head Wilson: Race, Conflict, and Culture* (Durham, NC: Duke University Press, 1990) pp. 141, 144–5.

13. For a biographical explanation which connects Twain's writing of the book to his marriage to Livy, see, for instance, Charles A. Norton, *Writing Tom Sawyer: The Adventures of a Classic* (Jefferson, NC: McFarland, 1983) pp. 48–51. Although *The Gilded Age* (1873), the novel Twain wrote with his Hartford neighbour, Charles Dudley Warner, was published three years earlier than *Tom Sawyer*, it is generally agreed that Twain had in fact started working on the latter text first. It may be that his work with Warner gave him the confidence for the clear

move away from the autobiographical which takes place as *Tom Sawyer* proceeds.

14. See Alan Gribben, '"I Did Wish Tom Sawyer Was There": Boy-Book Elements in *Tom Sawyer* and *Huckleberry Finn*', in Robert Sattelmeyer and J. Donald Crowley (eds), *One Hundred Years of Huckleberry Finn: The Boy, His Book, and American Culture* (Columbia: University of Missouri Press, 1985) pp. 154, 156.

15. Bruce Michelson argues that Tom's 'psychological immunity, or perhaps superficiality' is seen as he goes from 'mood to mood, sentiment to sentiment, in a flash'. Tom's ability to forget the graveyard murder and the trial for long textual periods has its formal match in the ability of Twain's omniscient narrator to 'contentedly . . . forge[t] with him', *Mark Twain on the Loose: A Comic Writer and the American Self* (Amherst: University of Massachusetts Press, 1995) p. 105.

16. Marcia Jacobson suggests that some of these disjunctions may be explained by the 'constant shifting of attitudes' between 'the narrator and his younger self' that characterises the boy book: 'as the narrator relives his past in recalling it, and brings his present condition to bear on it in interpreting it'. Thus, for example, in *Tom Sawyer*, the narrator takes a clearly ironic position as he mocks, and then literally dashes (possibly cold and certainly dirty) water on, Tom's sentimental maunderings as he lies under what he thinks is Becky Thatcher's window (pp. 25–6). This, however, later gives way to an apparently straightforward romantic perspective in the description of Tom's waking to the new day on Jackson's Island, and in the use of conventional sentimental discourse ('not a sound obtruded upon great Nature's meditation', p. 96) that accompanies it. This latter is 'Childhood . . . seen from the remembered perspective of youth [and] . . . consequently presented in a lyrical or elegiac mode'. See *Being a Boy Again*, pp. 20–3. We are still left here with the rather unexpected fact that Twain uses that type of 'naively romantic perspective' which in his earlier humorous works was generally subject to 'corrective explosion'. See Henry B. Wonham, *Mark Twain and the Art of the Tall Tale* (New York: Oxford University Press, 1993) p. 128. See Wonham, too, for an alternative explanation of such effects as a sign of Twain's 'increasing dexterity as a writer' (pp. 132, 139).

17. Wayne Fields, 'When the Fences are Down; Language and Order in *The Adventures of Tom Sawyer* and *Huckleberry Finn*', *Journal of American Studies*, vol. 24, no. 3 (December 1990) p. 370. Jerry Griswold compares British and American children's books of the period to argue that whereas 'British books . . . move outward to create imaginary paradises', American ones are concerned with 'an internal world we might call the Theater of Feelings'. Though Griswold's description of Tom and his attempts 'to re-create the Protestant Pieta' (as Twain burlesques 'the figure of the literary child as pallid sufferer') is accurate, his attempt to impose outer/inner binaries on the book is (as my use of the fence metaphor suggests) faulty: *Audacious Kids: Coming of Age*

in America's Classic Children's Books (New York: Oxford University Press, 1992) pp. 143, 144, 150, 151.

18. Neil Schmitz, *Of Huck and Alice; Humorous Writing in American Literature* (Minneapolis: University of Minnesota Press, 1983) p. 66.

19. Neil Schmitz, *Of Huck and Alice*, p. 66.

20. Sanford Pinsker writes that 'Tom's . . . abiding sense of play, transmogrifies a dull St Petersburg into a world more attractive'. See 'The Adventures of Tom Sawyer, Play Theory, and the Critic's Job of Work', *Midwest Quarterly*, vol. 29 (Spring, 1988) p. 360.

21. The Penguin text ('having a holiday') is inaccurate here. I amend accordingly.

22. For *Tom Sawyer* is much concerned with disciplinary practice and its resistance. The world of power that the book sketches (with its judges, teachers, guardians) may be that of the small town rather than of the industrial workplace, but the concern with the socialisation of identity *prefigures* later forms of childhood discipline, by which boys would be trained into efficient workers for an industrial 'economy that has no time for kidding around'. See Martha Banta, 'The Boys and the Bosses: Twain's Double Take on Work, Play, and the Democratic Ideal', *American Literary History*, vol. 3, no. 3 (Fall 1991) p. 511 (see, too, pp. 507–11).

In 'Sparing the Rod: Discipline and Fiction in America in Antebellum America', Richard H. Brodhead traces the move from corporal correction to a new form of domestic discipline ('correction-by-interiority') in 1830s and 1840s America. The relation between Tom and Aunt Polly might be re-examined in the light of Brodhead's arguments to suggest (though evidence for this is incomplete) that it is through the influence of 'inward colonization, not outward coercion' that Tom's acceptance of the dominant social norms is guaranteed. See *Representations*, no. 21 (Winter 1988) pp. 67–96. I quote from pp. 78, 73.

23. *Michael Oriard, Sporting with the Gods: The Rhetoric of Play and Game in American Culture* (Cambridge: Cambridge University Press, 1991) pp. xi, 11, 369, 394. *Tom Sawyer* is a book written about a boy and one primarily directed toward male readers (see for instance the remark on whistling, p. 11). Oriard is particularly interesting on the difference between boy and girl books at this time, and makes the revealing comment that, if play can be linked to such a 'countercultural desire for work-oriented men', then 'work embodied the reformist desire of play-burdened women' (p. 394; and see pp. 394–9). See also Steven Mailloux's valuable essay, 'The Rhetorical Use and Abuse of Fiction: Eating Books in Late Nineteenth-Century America', in Donald E. Pease, *Revisionary Interventions in the American Canon* (Durham, NC: Duke University Press, 1994) especially pp. 140–50.

24. *Sporting with the Gods* pp. 399, 398.

25. John Seelye, 'Introduction' to *The Adventures of Tom Sawyer* (Penguin) p. xi.

26. My approach, and the terms I use here, are influenced by Scott Michaelsen's unpublished article, 'Tom Sawyer's Capitalisms and the

Destructuring of Huck Finn'. My thanks to him for allowing me to make use of it. Other critics, too, refer to this aspect of the novel. See, for example, Lee Clark Mitchell, who says that Tom anticipates many techniques 'we accept today as commonplace business ploys', 'Introduction' to *The Adventures of Tom Sawyer* (World's Classics) p. xiv.

27. Though Oriard's analysis of the novel and especially his insistence on the 'safe' quality of Tom's play is still to the point: *Sporting with the Gods*, p. 401.

28. Quoted in Alan Gribben, '"I Did Wish Tom Sawyer Was There"', p. 149. Forrest Robinson refers to Tom's 'consummate mastery of face' and calls him 'the leading gamesman in St Petersburg'. He also says that 'in winning his way to the top, Tom outwits and exploits every age group and class in the community', *In Bad Faith*, pp. 31, 28–9, 25.

29. See Karen Halttunen, *Confidence Men and Painted Women: A Study of Middle-class Culture in America, 1830–1870* (New Haven, Conn.: Yale University Press, 1982) pp. 3, 1, 7, 23, 25, 33–4.

30. John Carlos Rowe speaks of the intense economic activity on the ante-bellum southwestern frontier as helping 'Jacksonian America enter the modern industrial age', 'Fatal Speculations', p. 141.

31. See too the links Neil Schmitz makes between Jacksonian values and Twain's representations of the Gilded Age in 'Mark Twain, Henry James, and Jacksonian Dreaming', *Criticism*, vol. 27 (Spring 1985) pp. 155–73.

32. *Confidence Men and Painted Women*, pp. 31, 34, 187, and Michael Oriard, *Sporting with the Gods*, p. 51. Oriard is talking about Southwestern humour here, but his statement bears equal relevance to the city world that Halttunen describes.

33. *Tom Sawyer: A Play*, in Walter Blair (ed.), *Hannibal, Huck & Tom* (Berkeley: University of California Press, 1969) p. 281.

34. Karen Halttunen suggests that by the second half of the nineteenth century, 'aggressiveness, charm, and the arts of the confidence man' had become new components of accepted American success ideology, and were no longer treated with suspicion; rather 'the manipulation of others through artifice was coming to be accepted as a necessary executive skill', *Confidence Men and Painted Women*, pp. 202, 204.

35. See too Cynthia Griffin Wolff, '*the Adventures of Tom Sawyer*: A Nightmare Vision of American Boyhood', pp. 93–105. The fact that both the town doctor and Joe are involved in the grave-robbing also suggests that the relation between community and its 'other' is not as clear cut as one might first imagine.

36. See Scott Michaelsen, 'Tom Sawyer's Capitalisms', unpublished ms, note 26. See, too, Paul Taylor, '*Huckleberry Finn*: The Education of a Young Capitalist', in Robert Sattelmeyer and J. Donald Crowley (eds), *One Hundred Years of Huckleberry Finn*, p. 343. Tom is both like and unlike Joe here. If Tom's intent is robbery, while Joe is innocent of this, Joe's antisocial criminality and displacement of Tom in the cave suggests their likeness.

37. Enterprise and theft continue to stand for one another here. An

alternative interpretation would focus on the *difference* between Tom's earlier exploits and the 'finding of gold in the ground' motif. There are parallels here with *Roughing It*: nostalgia for an imaginary time when individual luck, pluck and financial success went hand in hand, prior to the coming of systematised forms of corporate activity and the creation of a wage-earning middle class. The possibility of such variants suggests the ambiguities of the novel.

38. See Marcia Jacobson, *Being a Boy Again*, p. 16.
39. *Saturday Review*, 8 July 1876. Reprinted in Gary Scharnhorst (ed.), *Critical Essays on the Adventures of Tom Sawyer*, p. 36.
40. T. J. Jackson Lears, *No Place of Grace: Antimodernism and the Trans-formation of American Culture, 1880–1920* (New York: Pantheon, 1981) p. 146.
41. Eric Sundquist, 'Introduction: The Country of the Blue', in Sundquist (ed.), *American Realism: New Essays* (Baltimore, Md.: The Johns Hopkins University Press, 1982) p. 8.
42. Fred G. See, 'Tom Sawyer and Children's Literature', p. 180.
43. An ironic name, in the light of Twain's own later book, *Following the Equator*; the record of the world lecture tour determined by financial necessity.
44. Cynthia Griffin Wolff, '*The Adventures of Tom Sawyer*: A Nightmare Vision of American Boyhood', p. 99. See, too, my earlier note 23 on disciplinary practice.
45. Fred G. See, ' Tom Sawyer and Children's Literature', p. 180.
46. Elizabeth G. Peck, 'Tom Sawyer: Character in Search of an Audience', *American Transcendental Quarterly*, vol. 2 (September 1988) p. 224.
47. See Judith Fetterley, 'The Sanctioned Rebel', *Studies in the Novel*, vol. 3 (Fall 1971) pp. 293–304.
48. My interpretation of *Tom Sawyer* differs considerably from that of Bruce Michelson, who argues that 'the main thematic taproots of *Huckleberry Finn*' are in this earlier novel, present in Tom's 'quest for . . . uncompromised freedom' and his lack of a 'stable self'. See *Mark Twain on the Loose*, p. 102, and, more generally, pp. 101–8.
49. It is a critical commonplace that a central reason for *Huckleberry Finn*'s importance is due to its adoption of the vernacular narrative voice. More acknowledgement, though, should be given to the extent to which *Tom Sawyer* foreshadows this literary revolution. It is noticeable that contemporary English reviews focused repeatedly on the book's distinctive use of language. Thus one reviewer (the London *Standard*) says that 'the language is certainly extraordinary. It is that strange tongue which has grown up on the other side of the Atlantic which, although founded upon English, is yet not English, whose grammar, whose idioms, and whose slang differ wholly from our own'. See Gary Scharnhorst (ed.), *Critical Essays on The Adventures of Tom Sawyer*, p. 35. See too pp. 41, 43. Significantly, the last voice in the main body of the text (to which the distanced narrator then adds his formal closure) is not that of Tom but of Huck. His vigorous vernacular ends with an expression of loyalty to the Widow, suckered into it by Tom's threat

that 'we can't let you into the gang if you ain't respectable' (p. 219): 'I'll stick to the widder till I rot, Tom; and if I git to be a reg'lar ripper of a robber, and everybody talking 'bout it, I reckon she'll be proud she snaked me in out of the wet' (p. 221). The voice that sounds here, and the values that it would speak, cannot, though, be satisfactorily contained either within a conventional narrative frame or by the respectabilities of the small-town world. In *Huckleberry Finn*, Twain would give this voice its fuller freedom.

50. My prior argument about the free expression of self starts here to take on more sinister connotations. Freedom from social convention, being outlaw, has both positive and negative implications in Twain. See, for instance, the difference between Huck and Pap Finn.

51. Cynthia Griffin Wolff, 'The Adventures of Tom Sawyer: A Nightmare Vision of American Boyhood', pp. 102, 100, 99–100, 101, 104. See too Tom H. Towers, '"I Never Thought We Might Want to Come Back": Strategies of Transcendence in *Tom Sawyer*', *Modern Fiction Studies*, vol. 21 (1975–6) pp. 513–14.

52. 'Introduction' to *The Adventures of Tom Sawyer* (Penguin) pp. xix–xx.

53. Tom H. Towers, '"I Never Thought We Might Want to Come Back"', p. 518.

54. *The Adventures of Tom Sawyer* (London: Chatto & Windus, 1885 edition) p. 182. The words 'stark naked' are edited out of the Penguin text!

55. *In Bad Faith*, pp. 97-8.

56. A self-justifying mythologising and mystification of master–slave relations. The master, the head of the plantation 'family', saw himself in the role of fatherly authority and carer to his 'children', the (supposedly) child-like slaves.

57. Robert Tracy, 'Myth and Reality in *The Adventures of Tom Sawyer*', in Gary Scharnhorst (ed.), *Critical Essays on The Adventures of Tom Sawyer*, p. 110.

58. See the London *Times*, 28 August 1876, and also Moncure Conway's two reviews of the book, reprinted in *Critical Essays on The Adventures of Tom Sawyer*, pp. 40, 24, 27.

59. Ronald T. Takaki, *Iron Cages: Race and Culture in Nineteenth-Century America* (London: Athlone Press, 1980 [1979]) p. 84.

60. Dee Brown, *Bury My Heart at Wounded Knee* (London: Pan, 1974 [1970]) p. 11.

61. Robert Tracy, 'Myth and Reality in *The Adventures of Tom Sawyer*', p. 110.

62. Forrest Robinson, *In Bad Faith*, p. 52. See too Robert Tracy, 'Myth and Reality in *The Adventures of Tom Sawyer*', pp. 110–11.

63. Where, none the less, the signs of industry are present in the 'boiler iron' which sheathes the (triple-locked) big doors to McDougal's cave (p. 202) and behind which Indian Joe dies. This is not a pre-industrial society. The actions of the small boy in the school Examination Day ritual who accompanies his recitation 'with the painfully exact and spasmodic gestures which a machine might have used – supposing the machine to be a trifle out of order' and who makes his 'manufactured bow' as he finishes (p. 137) is symptomatic though, I would suggest,

of a post-bellum concern (about man–machine coordinates) that would gradually cause much more anxiety on Twain's part as the century progressed. The description seems irrelevant, though, to the St Petersburg of the 1830s–1840s represented in the text.

64. Only in the superstitions which are so much a part of the imaginative life of both children, and adults, in the village (see pp. 77, 121) do we see signs of interculturalism, of the African-American influence on the dominant culture.

65. Wayne Fields, 'When the Fences are Down', p. 372.

66. Steven Mailloux connects this with the 'more tolerant attitude toward temporary youthful deviance' (p. 147) in the period. He distinguishes strongly, though, between the disciplinary use of juvenile fictions for boys and for girls. See 'The Rhetorical Use and Abuse of Fiction', pp. 140–50. My earlier use of Brodhead suggests a possible bridging of this divide.

Chapter 5 Racial Politics in *Huckleberry Finn*

1. Mark Twain, *The Adventures of Huckleberry Finn* (Harmondsworth, Middx.: Penguin, 1987) p. 348. Page numbers to follow quotes from henceforth. The correct, original title of the novel is *Adventures of Huckleberry Finn*. It was published in the United States in 1885, after prior publication in England and Canada in 1884.

2. John C. Gerber, 'Introduction: The Continuing Adventures of *Huckleberry Finn*', in Robert Sattelmeyer and J. Donald Crowley (eds), *One Hundred Years of Huckleberry Finn: The Boy, His Book, and American Culture* (Columbia: University of Missouri Press, 1985) p. 3.

3. See Laurie Champion (ed.), *The Critical Response to Mark Twain's Huckleberry Finn* (Westport, Conn.: Greenwood Press, 1991) pp. 3, 44.

4. The *New Yorker*, 26 June–3 July 1995, pp. 128–33 (Styron's quote is on this last page). The brief extract, where Jim is ordered, by the medical student who is his master, to warm up the body of a dead man to render him pliable for dissection, rehearses – in comic/grotesque manner – the themes of resurrection (and false resurrection) and of symbolic exchange that run through the whole novel. The sexual undercurrents of the episode readily explain its eventual omission from the novel.

5. Eric Solomon, 'My *Huckleberry Finn*: Thirty Years in the Classroom with Huck and Jim', in Robert Sattelmeyer and J. Donald Crowley (eds), *One Hundred Years of Huckleberry Finn*, p. 246. Solomon's essay provides a good critical account as to why the novel has this canonic status, though he underemphasises the reception of the text in its developing historical context; the way in which each generation of critics has been able (to date) to renegotiate the multiple meanings available in the novel to fit its own academic, cultural and ideological needs.

6. David R. Sewell, *Mark Twain's Languages: Discourse, Dialogue and Linguistic Variety* (Berkeley: University of California Press, 1987) p. 86.

7. See Lee Clark Mitchell, '"Nobody but Our Gang warn't Around": The Authority of Language in *Huckleberry Finn*', in Louis J. Budd (ed.), *New Essays on Huckleberry Finn* (Cambridge: Cambridge University Press, 1985) especially pp. 88, 102, 104. See too Gregg Camfield, *Sentimental Twain: Samuel Clemens in the Maze of Moral Philosophy* (Philadelphia: University of Pennsylvania Press, 1994) especially pp. 6–13.

8. For a good selection of the more recent critical work on the novel, I would recommend Louis J. Budd (ed.), *New Essays on Huckleberry Finn*; Robert Sattelmeyer and J. Donald Crowley (eds), *One Hundred Years of Huckleberry Finn*; Laurie Champion (ed.), *The Critical Response to Mark Twain's Huckleberry Finn*; and the relevant essays in Forrest G. Robinson (ed.), *The Cambridge Companion to Mark Twain*.

9. See Marcia Jacobson on the use of the narrating adult and of autobiographical and fictional materials in the boy book: *Being a Boy Again: Autobiography and the American Boy Book* (Tuscaloosa: University of Alabama Press, 1994) pp. 20–3. *Huckleberry Finn* is not, according to this definition, in the genre.

10. Steven Mailloux, *Rhetorical Power* (Ithaca, NY: Cornell University Press, 1989) pp. 102, 117. Mailloux sites the book's reception in terms of the 'cultural debates and social practices concerned with juvenile delinquency'.

11. See Laurie Champion (ed.), *The Critical Response to Mark Twain's Huckleberry Finn*, p. 46

12. Jonathan Arac sees such readings as a type of self-reflexive critical activity on the part of a scholarly community, which thus takes its own 'countercultural' stance against 'actually existing America'. See 'Nationalism, Hypercanonization, and *Huckleberry Finn*', *boundary 2*, vol. 19, no. 1 (1992) pp. 20–4. Arac starts with Henry Nash Smith (1962) and moves forward from there. I would tend rather to contextualise such activity in terms of New Criticism and its legacy, and the focus on myth and symbol it fostered, and would see its influence on criticism post 1970 (though any choice of date will be somewhat arbitrary) as much more limited than Arac suggests.

13. Laurence B. Holland suggests the unstable nature of the difference between liberation and enslavement throughout much of the novel in 'A "Raft of Trouble": Word and Deed in *Huckleberry Finn*', in Eric Sundquist (ed.), *American Realism: New Essays* (Baltimore, Md.: Johns Hopkins University Press, 1982), p. 71.

14. Shelley Fisher Fishkin, *Was Huck Black? Mark Twain and African-American Voices* (New York: Oxford University Press, 1993) pp. 70–1.

15. R. J. Ellis, '"I Knowed He Was White Inside": Huck Finn's Dangerous Language', *Overhere: Reviews in American Studies*, vol. 14, no. 2 (Winter 1994) p. 10.

16. Jonathan Arac, 'Nationalism, Hypercanonization, and *Huckleberry Finn*', p. 26. Christine MacLeod argues for exactly such a sense in 'Telling the Truth in a Tight Place: *Huckleberry Finn* and the Reconstruction Era', *The Southern Quarterly*, vol. 34, no. 1 (Fall 1995) pp. 5–15. She contends that the 'social and political implications' of the

novel's subtext are for the reader to reinstate; that 'Twain in *Huckleberry Finn* offered a cogent critique of America's failure to live out the true meaning of the emancipation it had proclaimed. . . . But . . . [Twain] knew that in a society still wedded to the doctrines and practices of white supremacy, direct truth-telling was a high risk strategy. Hence the masks, the narrative displacements, and the signifying silences' (p. 14). The problem of audience response in Twain's own time must remain unresolved. Mailloux's argument in *Rhetorical Power* does not fully explain why a concern with the question of juvenile delinquency should necessarily have meant a complete denial of the race issue. The questions which still need addressing may, as MacLeod starts to suggest, have to do with the relation between humour and hegemonic codes; between realist techniques and countervailing (allegorical) strategies of indirection.

17. Steven Mailloux, *Rhetorical Power*, pp. 103, 64–5, 69.
18. Toni Morrison, *Playing in the Dark: Whiteness and the Literary Imagination* (Cambridge, Mass.: Harvard University Press, 1992) pp. 5, 33.
19. *Was Huck Black?*, pp. 140, 14, 15.
20. Quoting Werner Sollors and Charles Johnson respectively. See *Was Huck Black?*, p. 141.
21. I take my terms from J. L. Dillard, *Black English: Its History and Usage in the United States* (New York: Random House, 1972).
22. For a critical challenge to Fishkin's thesis, see Myra Jehlen, 'Banned in Concord: *Adventures of Huckleberry Finn* and Classic American Literature', in Forrest Robinson (ed.), *The Cambridge Companion to Mark Twain*, p. 113. Jehlen's description of Jimmy's voice as 'impersonated' by Huck does not, though, do entire justice to Fishkin's argument, and her assertions about 'Huck's cultural power' need some modification, at least.
23. *Was Huck Black?*, p. 107.
24. Michael Holquist, 'Introduction' to M. M. Bakhtin, *The Dialogic Imagination: Four Essays*, trans. Caryl Emerson and Michael Holquist (Austin: University of Texas Press, 1981) p. xviii.
25. In *Civil Rights and the Idea of Freedom* (New York: Oxford University Press, 1992), Richard King defines the different meanings of the concept 'freedom' as it has been used in the American (and Western) political context.
26. Neil Schmitz, *Of Huck and Alice: Humorous Writing in American Literature* (Minneapolis: University of Minnesota Press, 1983) p. 103.
27. Both Huck and Jim experience institutional oppression. It is, however, in Huck's case, the internal and psychological results of such oppression that have the most effect. Though Huck's legal status is at issue (as far as his father's rights over his money is concerned), it is not the dominant and determining factor it is for Jim.
28. The terms I use here are all taken from Harriet Jacobs, *Incidents in the Life of a Slave Girl*, in Henry Louis Gates (ed.), *The Classic Slave Narratives* (New York: Mentor, 1987 [1861]) pp. 408, 380, 342. The relation between

Twain's novel and the (ante-bellum) slave narrative becomes more obvious as I proceed.

29. As Howard Horwitz points out there is a Lockean self-legislative charge to this. Our first property is precisely ourselves. See *By the Law of Nature: Form and Value in Nineteenth- Century America* (New York: Oxford University Press, 1991) p. 102.

30. The Exodus motif is a repeated one in the novel. Richard King notes that its particular definition of 'freedom as collective deliverance is ambiguous as to whether it is a story of being freed or of self-liberation, of chosenness or self-initiated rebellion'. Such an ambiguity is relevant to the way Twain's narrative works. See *Civil Rights and the Idea of Freedom*, p. 28.

31. After the threat to Jim posed by the two men in the skiff, he immediately starts to use the first-person plural again (p. 150). The generally fluid nature of pronouns in the text repeatedly raises questions of identity and interest.

32. My use of this term is drawn from Richard King, *Civil Rights and the Idea of Freedom*, p. 13.

33. Laurence B. Holland, '"A Raft of Trouble"', p. 70.

34. Frederick Douglass, *Narrative of the Life of Frederick Douglass, An American Slave* (Harmondsworth, Middx.: Penguin, 1982 [1845]) p. 138.

35. My analysis overlaps and runs parallel to that of Neil Schmitz, in *Of Huck and Alice*, here. I acknowledge my critical debt to this landmark study in my own tracing of Huck and Jim's diverging stories.

36. Huck's double-voicedness, and the way this relates to his sense of self, explains his failure to proceed, to actually betray Jim here. A second discourse has already developed in the context not of the surrounding world, but of the community of two on the river; one which arises out of the shared aspects of their narratives to this point. Huck wavers between these forms of discourse throughout. See my *New Readings of the American Novel* (Basingstoke: Macmillan, 1990) for fuller development of this argument.

37. Neil Schmitz, *Of Huck and Alice*, p. 103.

38. As many critics have pointed out, the more attractive aspects of Tom's character are marginalised in this novel.

39. See Eric Lott, who sees Jim's appearance here as 'recall[ing] the art of blackface at the same time that it explodes the very idea of racial performance'. 'Mr, Clemens and Jim Crow: Twain, Race, and Blackface', in Forrest Robinson, *The Cambridge Companion to Mark Twain*, p. 140. In his fascinating essay, Lott argues that 'blackface minstrelsy underwrote one of the nineteenth century's most powerful antiracist novels – a tribute to the political fractures of minstrelsy and *Huckleberry Finn* both', p. 133.

40. See Myra Jehlen, 'Banned in Concord', p. 100.

41. David L. Smith, 'Huck, Jim, and American Racial Discourse', in James S. Leonard, Thomas A. Tenney, Thadious M. Davis (eds), *Satire or Evasion? Black Perspectives on Huckleberry Finn* (Durham, NC: Duke University Press, 1992) p. 104.

42. I am using terms taken from Eric Lott, 'Love and Theft: The Racial Unconscious of Blackface Minstrelsy', *Representations*, vol. 39 (1992) p. 28.

43. For part of the novel's achievement is in the tension it creates between the *social* powerlessness of Huck's voice and his *narrative* control over the more authoritative social voices represented through it (Jim, with his low social status, is the exception to this rule). Huck is consistently seen in passive relationship to the larger riverbank society, finally bound by its words and value schemes. As narrator, however, he lays out the different voices of southwestern culture for us to hear (in their power, their typicality and their interweavings) and, through that very narrative authority, unwittingly but effectively critiques them. Huck's voice, then, challenges and tears the mask from these languages, even while it cannot escape their influence.

44. Thomas R. R. Cobb, a major legal scholar in the ante-bellum South, wrote that: 'Of the three great absolute rights guaranteed to every citizen by the common law [personal security, personal liberty and private property], the slave, in a state of pure or absolute slavery, is totally deprived.' See James Oakes, *Slavery and Freedom: An Interpretation of the Old South* (New York: Alfred A. Knopf, 1990) pp. 69–70.

45. Huck's voice is not a unified one, and the degree to which Jim's story is, and remains, separate from and subordinate to his, varies. One can argue that Huck's intention to free Jim, articulated in Chapter 31 of the book, remains constant, even when he (disturbingly) acts as Tom's double in the evasion sequence.

46. John H. Wallace, 'The Case Against *Huck Finn*', and David L. Smith, 'Huck, Jim, and American Racial Discourse', both in James S. Leonard, Thomas A. Tenney and Thadious M. Davis (eds), *Satire or Evasion?*, pp. 16, 107. In 'Black Critics and Mark Twain', in Forrest Robinson (ed.), *The Cambridge Companion to Mark Twain*, pp. 116–28, Smith argues that the fact that critics (both black and white) interpret the racial implications of the text so differently is not a sign of 'authorial failings' (p. 122). Rather it indicates their different political position on the question of race. For discussion of the critical debate concerning Jim's role, see too Shelley Fisher Fishkin, *Was Huck Black?*, pp. 79–92. The use of the word 'nigger' does mean that, whatever one thinks of the representation of Jim, and regarding the level of irony in the book, a problem remains in the teaching of it to an American (and British) audience where racism remains a part of everyday life. For one positive response to this, see Jocelyn Chadwick-Jones, 'Mark Twain and the Fires of Controversy: Teaching Racially-Sensitive Literature: Or, "Say That 'N' Word and Out You Go!"', in Laurie Champion (ed.), *The Critical Response to Mark Twain's Huckleberry Finn*, pp. 228–37.

47. Fredrick Woodard and Donnarae MacCann, 'Minstrel Shackles and Nineteenth-Century "Liberality"'; David L. Smith, 'Huck, Jim, and American Racial Discourse'. Both in *Satire or Evasion?*, pp. 142, 112.

48. W. E. Du Bois, *Souls of Black Folk* (Chicago, Ill.: A. C. McClurg, 1903) pp. 2–3.
49. Forrest G. Robinson, 'The Characterization of Jim in *Huckleberry Finn*', in Laurie Champion (ed.), *The Critical Response to Mark Twain's Huckleberry Finn*, p. 220.
50. This is not at all to argue against Jim's intelligence. It is though to posit an unbridgeable gap between what he says and does, and how they can be interpreted.
51. Bruce Michelson examines the whole cycle of texts about Tom and Huck to warn against necessarily seeing them as dissimilar figures. See *Mark Twain on the Loose: A Comic Writer and the American Self* (Amherst: University of Massachusetts Press, 1995) pp. 95–141.
52. From an unpublished paper by William L. Andrews, '*Huckleberry Finn* and the Slave Narrative Tradition', pp. 18–19. My thanks to the author for his permission to quote. I would be more tentative than Andrews in making the connection between Jim's loss of agency and of manhood, again in line with the fact that we are given Jim from the outside only.
53. Robert William Fogel, *Without Consent or Contract: The Rise and Fall of American Slavery* (New York: W. W. Norton, 1989) p. 191. Fogel estimates this at six thousand dollars at 1989 rates.
54. Laurence B. Holland, '"A Raft of Trouble"', p. 71.
55. Victor A. Doyno, *Writing Huck Finn: Mark Twain's Creative Process* (Pennsylvania: University of Philadelphia Press, 1991) p. 230.
56. Ira Berlin, *Slaves Without Masters: The Free Negro in the Antebellum South* (New York: Pantheon, 1974) p. xiv.
57. Quoted in Eric Foner, *Reconstruction: America's Unfinished Revolution, 1863–1877* (New York: Harper and Row, 1989 [1988]) p. 602.
58. Eric Foner, *Reconstruction*, p. 598.
59. Shelley Fisher Fishkin, *Was Huck Black?*, p. 75. Fishkin gives further bibliographical detail.
60. See Christine MacLeod, 'Telling the Truth in a Tight Place', for a full and strong refutation, based on a post-bellum historical contextualisation, of charges that the evasion sequence is artistically inept.
61. Shelley Fisher Fishkin, *Was Huck Black?*, p. 74.
62. Joyce Rowe, *Equivocal Endings in Classic American Novels* (Cambridge: Cambridge University Press, 1988) p. 48.
63. Jonathan Arac, 'Nationalism, Hypercanonization, and *Huckleberry Finn*', pp. 26, 33. I take strong issue here with Arac and his argument that Twain's novel is 'antihistorical' (p. 26). For to use indirect or allegorical methods is not, as he suggests, to '[cut] off the address to . . . acknowledged national concerns' (p. 18). Arac's argument starts by using a four-part scheme (national, local, personal and literary). As it proceeds, though, it comes to turn on the literary/national binary; one which, like all other binaries, is suspect. This may be a useful ploy for suggesting a variable relationship, even an increasing gap, between literary culture and national history as the nineteenth century progressed, but to conclude that Twain's novel rejects the possibility of

public debate – operates in some way outside the province of history – seems to me a bizarre interpretive move. Arac's article is reprinted in Donald E. Pease (ed.), *National Identities and Post-Americanist Narratives* (Durham, NC: Duke University Press, 1994) pp. 14–33.

64. Richard C. Moreland, '"He Wants to Put His Story Next to Hers": Putting Twain's Story Next to Hers in Morrison's *Beloved*', *Modern Fiction Studies*, vol. 39, nos. 3 and 4 (Fall/Winter 1993) p. 505. See Arac, 'Nationalism, Hypercanonization, and *Huckleberry Finn*', pp. 18, 30, 31, for similar arguments.

65. Moreland uses this term just before the above quotation, '"He wants to Put His Story Next to Hers"', p. 505.

66. Other endings have been suggested. For example, John Seelye, in his *The True Adventures of Huckleberry Finn* (New York: Simon and Schuster, 1970) has Jim, weighed down by his chains, drowning in the Mississippi as he attempts escape from the Phelps' and before Huck can get to help him. Though this foregrounds the pessimistic implications kept below the surface in Twain's narrative, I am not sure it engages 'the contingencies of history' any more effectively.

67. See 'Nationalism, Hypercanonization, and *Huckleberry Finn*', pp. 18, 33.

68. I borrow the words used by Richard King in his analysis of Faulkner's *Go Down, Moses* here, and in the passages that directly follow. See *The Southern Renaissance: The Cultural Awakening of the American South, 1930–1955* (New York: Oxford University Press, 1980) p. 138.

69. Richard C. Moreland, '"He Wants to Put His Story Next to Hers"', p. 506. I take the idea of stories being put together from Moreland too as he (mainly) focuses on Paul D. and Sethe in *Beloved*. To stress, this is not to deny the important differences in Huck and Jim's narratives but to argue for sameness too: on the raft, if provisionally, they share at times both interests and story. Sameness and difference are not incompatible, as any theory of multiculturalism would recognise.

70. Roderick Waterman, *Reclaiming the Perverse: Some Readings of Sherwood Anderson and Carson McCullers* (unpublished MA dissertation, University of Nottingham, 1992) p. 24. Waterman uses Bakhtin to argue for a new reading of the grotesque. I redirect here some of his argument to my different context, and thank him for his permission to do so.

71. Leslie A. Fiedler, *Love and Death in the American Novel* (New York: Stein and Day, 1966 [1960]) pp. 352, 355.

72. Mikhail Bakhtin, *The Dialogic Imagination: Four Essays*, trans. Caryl Emerson and Michael Holquist (Austin: University of Texas Press, 1981) p. 229. In writing this, Bakhtin might have been using *Huckleberry Finn* as his model. For more detail on way the rhythms of nature and of human life interrelate in the idyll and in Twain's novel, see my *New Readings of the American Novel*, p. 227.

73. *The Dialogic Imagination*, p. 224, and Katerina Clark and Michael Holquist, *Mikhail Bakhtin* (Cambridge, Mass.: Harvard University Press, 1984) pp. 310–11.

74. See Steven Mailloux, *Rhetorical Power*, pp. 72–6, 83–6.

75. Christine MacLeod, 'Telling the Truth in a Tight Place', p. 7.

76. Harriet Jacobs, *Incidents in the Life of a Slave Girl*, p. 378.
77. For more detail and further analysis, see Steven Mailloux, 'Reading *Huckleberry Finn*: The Rhetoric of Performed Ideology', in Louis J. Budd (ed.), *New Essays On Huckleberry Finn*, pp. 107–33.
78. Christine MacLeod, 'Telling the Truth in a Tight Place', p. 8.

Chapter 6   Fantasy and *A Connecticut Yankee in King Arthur's Court*

1. Lady Emmeline Stuart Wortley, a British traveller in America in the 1840s, quoted by Karen Halttunen in *Confidence Men and Painted Women: A Study of Middle-class Culture in America, 1830–1870* (New Haven, Conn.: Yale University Press, 1982) p. 31.
2. Robert Pack Browning, Michael B. Frank and Lin Salamo (eds), *Mark Twain's Notebooks & Journals, Volume 3 (1883–1891)*, p. 311.
3. Quoted in Arnold Beichman, 'The First Electrocution', *Commentary*, vol. 35 (1963) p. 417.
4. William J. Collins, 'Hank Morgan in the Garden of Forking Paths: *A Connecticut Yankee in King Arthur's Court* as Alternative History', *Modern Fiction Studies*, vol. 32 (1986) p. 111.
5. Shelley Fisher Fishkin says his writings on race are 'complex and ambiguous', *Was Huck Black? Mark Twain and African American Voices* (New York: Oxford University Press, 1993) p. 125.
6. Harold Beaver, *Huckleberry Finn* (London: Allen and Unwin, 1987) pp. 48–9. See my *New Readings of the American Novel* (Basingstoke: Macmillan, 1990) p. 239, for further discussion of the polygeneric aspects of the book.
7. Roger George calls Twain 'one of the pioneers of nineteenth-century realism', in '"The Road Lieth Not Straight": Maps and Mental Models in *A Connecticut Yankee in King Arthur's Court*', *American Transcendental Quarterly*, vol. 5 n.s. (March, 1991) p. 64. See too, with specific reference to *Huckleberry Finn*, Alan Trachtenberg, *The Incorporation of America: Culture and Society in the Gilded Age* (New York: Hill and Wang, 1982) p. 190. Bruce Michelson points to the problems in categorising Twain as a realist, describing 'things as they are', when he writes: 'But what if [the] "real world" . . . is seen to be saturated with delusion, pretence, fantasy? The task of the realist in such straits may call not for box-cameras, but rather for dynamite: disorienting and even violent breakthroughs into the concealed truth about human experience. And if such breakthroughs require strange pyrotechnics – dream-selves, fantasies of time-travel, or 'whoppers' embedded in supposedly factual travel narratives and personal histories – so be it.' See *Twain on the Loose: A Comic Writer and the American Self* (Amherst: University of Massachusetts Press, 1995) pp. 6–7. While I agree with the general thematic lines of Michelsen's analysis, his framing of it in the context of a discussion of realism seems to me to stretch generic boundaries to definitional breaking point. Realism becomes the *same* as fantasy or tall tale here. Michael Davitt Bell, in *The Problem of American Realism: Studies*

in the Cultural History of a Literary Idea (Chicago: University of Chicago Press, 1993), argues that 'the case for connecting *Huckleberry Finn* to the supposed tradition of American realism seems, at every point, an exceptionally weak one' (p. 57). Somewhat unexpectedly, as far as accepted critical opinion goes, he then discusses *A Connecticut Yankee* in terms both of Twain's 'conversion to realist values' (p. 69), and dramatisation of the instability of those values. I would resist the narrow limits of Bell's definitions and conclusions, and would continue to argue for the usefulness and relevance of 'realism' as a discrete generic term despite the problems that surround it. One of the best introductions to the techniques and concept of realism in the context of late nineteenth-century American literature is in June Howard's opening chapter to *Form and History in American Literary Naturalism* (Chapel Hill: University of North Carolina Press, 1985) pp. 3–35.

8. June Howard, *Form and History in American Literary Naturalism*, pp. 11–12.

9. Terry Eagleton, *Literary Theory: An Introduction* (Oxford: Basil Blackwell, 1983) p. 136. The claim that reality can be straightforwardly represented is, as any theory of realism now recognises, naive. As E. H. Gombrich, in *Art and Illusion*, writes, 'All thinking is sorting, classifying' (quoted in June Howard, *Form and History in American Literary Naturalism*, p. 15), and accordingly any representation of reality depends on, and is skewed in one way or another by, the angle of perception and the ideological and historical positioning of the subject involved.

10. 'The Country of the Blue', the introduction to Eric Sundquist (ed.), *American Realism: New Essays* (Baltimore, Md.: Johns Hopkins University Press, 1982) p. 8. This is a good general essay on realism in America as a response to 'the social and psychological effects of industrial capitalism' (p. 6).

11. Rosemary Jackson, *Fantasy: The Literature of Subversion* (London: Methuen, 1981) pp. 82–3. Or as Catherine Belsey puts it, 'Classic realism presents individuals whose traits of character, understood as essential and predominantly given, constrain the choices they make, and whose potential for development depends on what is given. . . . "The mind of man" . . . is shown in classic realism to be the source of understanding, of action and of history', *Critical Practice* (London: Methuen, 1980) pp. 74–5.

12. Lee Clark Mitchell, *Determined Fictions: American Literary Naturalism* (New York: Columbia University Press, 1989) p. xii.

13. *The Adventures of Huckleberry Finn* (Harmondsworth, Middx.: Penguin, 1987) p. 283.

14. The term is Lee Clark Mitchell's. See *Determined Fictions*, p. xii.

15. Rosemary Jackson, *Fantasy*, p. 35.

16. *The Adventures of Huckleberry Finn*, p. 141.

17. M. M. Bakhtin, *The Dialogic Imagination: Four Essays*, trans. Caryl Emerson and Michael Holquist (Austin: University of Texas Press, 1981) p. 404.

18. Tony Bennett, *Formalism and Marxism* (London: Methuen, 1979) p. 21.
19. John Carlos Rowe calls the novel a 'historical romance' in 'How the Boss Played the Game: Twain's Critique of Imperialism in *A Connecticut Yankee in King Arthur's Court*', in Forrest G. Robinson (ed.), *The Cambridge Companion to Mark Twain* (Cambridge: Cambridge University Press, 1995) p. 176. Richard Pressman discusses the relation between sentimentalism and realism in the novel in 'A Connecticut Yankee in Merlin's Cave: The Role of Contradiction in Mark Twain's Novel', *American Literary Realism 1870–1910*, vol. 16 (1983) pp. 58–72. Bruce Michelson discusses the book in terms of the 'battle lines on literary modes' (p. 156) – romance and realism – drawn in it, in *Mark Twain on the Loose*, pp. 150–1. Gregory M. Pfitzer treats it as displaced western in '"Iron Dudes and White Savages in Camelot": The Influence of Dime-Novel Sensationalism on Twain's *A Connecticut Yankee in King Arthur's Court*', *American Literary Realism*, vol. 27, no. 1 (Fall 1994) pp. 42–58. For readings of the novel as science fiction, see, for instance, John Clute, 'Time Travel Past', in Samuel L. Macey (ed.), *Encyclopedia of Time* (New York: Garland, 1994) pp. 646–7. Here Clute equates some forms of science fiction with fantasy. This suggests that the categorisations I mention are by no means exclusive. My thanks to Nick Mount for bringing Clute's entry to my attention. William J. Collins, too, discusses Twain's role as 'innovator of science fiction themes' (p. 111) in 'Hank Morgan in the Garden of Forking Paths: *A Connecticut Yankee in King Arthur's Court* as Alternative History'. His discussion of our readerly hesitation concerning the status of Hank's evidence for his journey through time also leads straight back to definitions of the fantastic.
20. See James M. Cox, who calls the novel 'inverted Utopian fantasy' in *Mark Twain: The Fate of Humor* (Princeton, NJ: Princeton University Press, 1966) p. 203. Winfried Fluck echoes him in saying that 'the novel which can be considered as an inverse utopian novel is clearly a fantasy', 'The Restructuring of History and the Intrusion of Fantasy in Mark Twain's "A Connecticut Yankee in King Arthur's Court"', in Winfried Fluck, Jurgen Peper and Willi Paul Adams (eds), *Forms and Functions of History in American Literature* (Berlin: Erich Schmidt Verlag, 1981) p. 136.
21. Rosemary Jackson, *Fantasy*, p. 34. See my 'Towards the Absurd: Mark Twain's *A Connecticut Yankee*, *Puddn'head Wilson* and *The Great Dark*' in Robert Giddings (ed.), *Mark Twain: A Sumptuous Variety* (London and Totowa, NJ: Vision and Barnes & Noble, 1985) pp. 176–98, for further analysis of the relationship between realism and fantasy, magic and science.
22. See Rosemary Jackson, *Fantasy*, pp. 25–6, 22, 23. She is drawing on the work of other critics (Tzvetan Todorov, Joanna Russ and Irene Bessiere).
23. Mark Twain, *A Connecticut Yankee in King Arthur's Court* (London: Penguin, 1986 [1889]) p. 36. Page references to follow quotes henceforth.

24. See, for instance, William J. Collins, 'Hank Morgan in the Garden of Forking Paths', pp. 112–14.
25. T. J. Jackson Lears's analysis of the 'antimodern impulse' rising out of the dissatisfaction with modern culture in late nineteenth-century America (and Europe), and the terms he uses, provide a particularly useful context for discussion of Twain's novel. See *No Place of Grace; Antimodernism and the Transformation of American Culture, 1880–1920* (New York: Pantheon, 1981).
26. Everett Carter, 'The Meaning of *A Connecticut Yankee*', *American Literature*, vol. 50 (1978–9) pp. 418–40.
27. Louis J. Budd, 'A (Better-Humored) Re-trial for Hank Morgan: Convicted Mass Murderer', *Over Here: Reviews in American Studies*, vol. 15, nos. 1 and 2, (Summer and Winter 1995) p. 6. Budd argues that 'our dismissive hindsight has distorted the interpretations of *A Connecticut Yankee*' (p. 9). I would defend my reading of the novel, while recognising the validity of alternative responses to it.
28. Everett Carter, 'The Meaning of *A Connecticut Yankee*', p. 440.
29. See Mark Seltzer, *Bodies and Machines* (New York: Routledge, 1992) pp. 6–9, 11, 94–5, 153; Martha Banta, 'The Boys and the Bosses: Twain's Double Take on Work, Play, and the Democratic Ideal', *American Literary History*, vol. 3, no. 3 (Fall 1991) pp. 487–520; Ronald T. Takaki, *Iron Cages: Race and Culture in Nineteenth-Century America* (London: Athlone Press, 1979), pp. 147–70; Cindy Weinstein, *The Literature of Labor and the Labors of Literature: Allegory in Nineteenth-Century American Fiction* (Cambridge: Cambridge University Press, 1995) pp. 129–72.
30. Ronald T. Takaki, *Iron Cages*, pp. 166, 169–70.
31. Walter Benn Michaels, *The Gold Standard and the Logic of Naturalism: American Literature at the Turn of the Century* (Berkeley: University of California Press, 1987).
32. Martha Banta, 'The Boys and the Bosses', p. 489.
33. Cindy Weinstein, *The Literature of Labor and the Labors of Literature*, p. 10. The first quote is taken directly from Michel Foucault. In *Bodies and Machines*, Mark Seltzer, too, uses a Foucaultian base to examine tensions concerning body/machine boundaries in 'turn-of-the-century American culture and beyond' (p. 3). As Weinstein indicates, and as any study of twentieth-century modernist literature would confirm, anxieties about agency and technology cannot in fact be confined to a specific 'critical cultural moment' but are generally evident from mid-nineteenth century onward. It can be argued, roughly following Seltzer, that it is toward the end of the century, in a period of considerable social turmoil, that such anxieties reach a climax.
34. Mark Seltzer, *Bodies and Machines*, p. 19.
35. For Twain criticises the hermit and his value system just as much as he does Hank, following his source in this: W. H. Lecky's *History of European Morals* (1872). Lecky focuses especially on the masochistic self-abuse, all performed in the name of self-discipline and God's greater glory, of such hermits. He gives further information on St Stylites and his actions: 'For a whole year, we are told, St Simeon stood

upon one leg, the other being covered with hideous ulcers, while his biographer was commissioned to stand by his side, to pick up the worms that fell from his body, and to replace them in the sores, the saint saying to the worm, "Eat what God has given you".' If Simeon Stylites was a Christian saint to his contemporaries, with biographer at hand to close the gap between the wounding of the self and the writing of the saintliness it signified, to Lecky writing in 1872, to Twain (his Victorian contemporary) and to Hank, such 'hideous maceration of the body', far from being 'the highest proof of excellence' was quite without point or value. The relevant passages from Lecky are quoted in the Norton Critical edition of *A Connecticut Yankee* (New York: W. W. Norton, 1982). Here, see pp. 266, 264.

36. Werner Sollors, 'Ethnicity', in Frank Lentricchia and Thomas McLaughlin (eds), *Critical Terms for Literary Study* (Chicago: University of Chicago Press, 1990) pp. 297, 294, 293.

37. Such methods were taken for granted by those whom T. J. Jackson Lears calls the 'ruling-class custodians of [Victorian] culture'. See *No Place of Grace*, p. 10.

38. Martha Banta, *Taylored Lives: Narrative Productions in the Age of Taylor, Veblen, and Ford* (Chicago: University of Chicago Press, 1993) pp. 43, ix, 235, 3.

39. Werner Sollors, 'Ethnicity', p. 295.

40. Martha Banta, *Taylored Lives*, p. 3.

41. Certainly, at any rate, conspicuous consumption and emulative display, as well as social hierarchy, explain the more decorative versions of the shirt which are produced.

42. See Martha Banta, *Taylored Lives*, p. 9. She is referring to Chaplin's *Modern Times* in her use of the phrase.

43. Again reminding of Foucault, with his emphasis on the forms of regularisation and control, the disciplinary procedures that come together to create 'docile bodies'; reminding too of his analysis of 'panopticism'. See *Discipline and Punish: The Birth of the Prison* (London: Penguin, 1991 [1975]), pp. 135–69 and 195–228.

44. I borrow Banta's terminology here. See *Taylored Lives*, p. 29. I also follow Banta earlier, in my punning on Taylor's name.

45. Mark Seltzer, *Bodies and Machines*, p. 155.

46. Martha Banta, *Taylored Lives*, p. 382.

47. See Mark Seltzer, *Bodies and Machines*, p. 157. Ford's calculations and his concern for exact numbers echo Hank's. See, too, Twain's own obsessive calculations over the Paige typesetter – those given in *Mark Twain's Notebooks & Journals, Volume 3*, p. 585, are typical.

48. Matha Banta, *Taylored Lives*, p. 280.

49. Martha Banta, 'The Boys and the Bosses', p. 487, and see pp. 497–511.

50. T. J. Jackson Lear, *No Place of Grace*, p. 7.

51. Ronald Takaki, *Iron Cages*, p. 167.

52. John Carlos Rowe focuses on this aspect of the novel in 'How the Boss Played the Game'.

53. Soap is undoubtedly (positively) associated with Hank's sanitation

programme. Twain's repeated use in his work of the phrase 'soap and civilization' in an imperialist context carries, though, negative connotations.

54. The following sign was displayed in the Colt Factory Armoury: 'Every man Employed in or about my Armoury Whether by Piecewirk or by Days Wirk is Expected to Wirk Ten Hours During the Running of the Engine [steam power] & No one who Does not Chearfully Concent to Do this need expect to be employed by me. Saml Colt.' See R. C. Wilson, *Colt: An American Legend* (New York: Abbeville, 1985) p. 75.

55. Jennifer L. Rafferty makes similar points in 'Mark Twain, Labor and Technology: *A Connecticut Yankee*, and *No. 44, The Mysterious Stranger*', *Over Here: Reviews in American Studies*, vol. 15, nos. 1 and 2 (Summer and Winter 1995) pp. 24–7.

56. See the notebook entry, written in the period July 1888–May 1889, which echoes this passage: Robert Pack Browning, Michael B. Frank and Lin Salamo (eds), *Mark Twain's Notebooks & Journals: Volume 3*, p. 422.

57. I alter 'a light' as it appears in the Penguin text to 'light' in accord with the authoritative University of California Press edition of the novel.

58. *Mark Twain's Notebooks & Journals, Volume 3*, p. 418.

59. The phrase comes from Tim Armstrong's article, 'The Electrification of the Body at the Turn of the Century', *Textual Practice*, vol. 5, no. 3 (Winter 1991) p. 304.

60. See Arnold Bleichman, 'The First Electrocution', pp. 410, 411, 417, 415.

61. See Arnold Bleichman, 'The First Electrocution', pp. 410–11.

62. See Horst H. Kruse, 'Mark Twain's *A Connecticut Yankee*: Reconsiderations and Revisions', *American Literature*, vol. 62, no. 3 (September 1990) p. 478.

63. T. J. Jackson Lears, *No Place of Grace*, p. 12.

64. As has been often pointed out, Twain alludes in this novel both to the regional differences that were to end in the American Civil War, and to the Indian wars to follow. Thus a common reading of the book is one which sees the conflict between the values of Arthurian England and of Hank in terms of a contrast between a pastoral, feudal and slave-holding ante-bellum South, and a progressive and abolitionist North. Twain's own ambivalent attitude to the South (nostalgia as well as contempt) can then be seen to carry over to his Arthurian materials. Gregory Pfitzer reads the Battle of the Sand-Belt scenes in the different (Indian wars) context; as 'a kind of Custer's Last Stand in which the Indian nation achieves a temporary victory but is ultimately defeated', '"Iron Dudes and White Savages in Camelot"', pp. 48–9.

65. T. J. Jackson Lears, *No Place of Grace*, pp. 12–13. See Lears's remarks concerning the centre of 'nineteenth-century bourgeois morality . . . the autonomous individual, whose only moral master was himself'.

66. See *No Place of Grace*, p. 8.

67. Rosemary Jackson, *Fantasy*, pp. 82, 86.

68. This occurs in a bridging passage Twain wrote for excerpts of the novel

printed in *Century* magazine. See the Norton Critical edition of *A Connecticut Yankee*, note, p. 227.

69. Werner Sollors, 'Ethnicity', p. 302. Sollors uses the instability of the oppositional boundaries constructed in the novel to build a larger argument about the 'invented character' (p. 305) of national and ethnic difference.

70. Michael Davitt Bell, *The Problem of American Realism*, p. 66.

71. Werner Sollors, 'Ethnicity', pp. 303–4, 302.

72. *The Lost Land* was one of Twain's working titles for the novel. See *Mark Twain's Notebooks & Journals, Volume 3*, p. 216.

73. Following Sollors, who writes: ' . . . the Arthurians make themselves felt as mirror images of the Yankee's hidden self: whatever HM denies in himself he may call "Arthurian" – and try to destroy', 'Ethnicity', p. 303.

74. Max Weber, 'Science as a Vocation', quoted in Douglas Tallack, *Twentieth-Century America: The Intellectual and Cultural Context* (London: Longman, 1991) p. 21.

75. Georg Lukacs, 'Narrate or Describe' (1936), in *Writer and Critic and Other Essays*, ed. and trans. Arthur Kahn (London: Merlin, 1978) pp. 133, 125.

76. His *Personal Recollections of Joan of Arc* (1896) might seem to contradict this. Bruce Michelson's comment, though, is relevant here: '*Joan of Arc* turns out to be . . . an escapist work . . . [Joan] lives and dies above the political and moral messes that not only vex everyone else but make them who and what they are', *Mark Twain on the Loose*, p. 206.

77. Maria Ornelli Marotti, *The Duplicating Imagination: Twain and the Twain Papers* (Pennsylvania State University Press, 1990) p. 46.

Chapter 7 Severed Connections: *Puddn'head Wilson and Those Extraordinary Twins*

1. Mark Twain, 'An Encounter with an Interviewer,' in *The Stolen White Elephant Etc.* (London: Chatto & Windus, 1897 [1882]) pp. 223–4.

2. Arnold L. Weinstein, *Nobody's Home: Speech, Self, Place in American Fiction from Hawthorne to DeLillo* (New York: Oxford University Press, 1993) p. 67.

3. See Hamlin Hill (ed.), *Mark Twain's Letters to His Publishers: 1867–1894* (Berkeley: University of California Press, 1967) p. 328. Twain later seems to leave the choice of title in his publisher's hands, when he refers to the book as '"Puddn'head Wilson – A Tale." (Or, "Those Extraordinary Twins," if preferable.)', p. 337.

4. Mark Twain, *Puddn'head Wilson and Those Extraordinary Twins* (Harmondsworth, Middx.: Penguin, 1981[1894]) pp. 230, 303. Page references to follow quotes henceforth.

5. A practice which became the rule, rather than the exception, for future editions of the text(s). The first British edition, however, consisted of *Puddn'head Wilson, A Tale* alone.

6. Evan Carter, 'Puddn'head Wilson and the Fiction of Law and Custom', in Eric J. Sundquist, American Realism: New Essays (Baltimore, Md.: The Johns Hopkins University Press, 1982) p. 88.

7. Susan Gillman, Dark Twins: Imposture and Identity in Mark Twain's America (Chicago: University of Chicago Press, 1989) p. 55. The emphasis is mine.

8. Twain follows accepted Victorian conventions here. Leslie Fiedler points out that '"monster" is the oldest word in our tongue for human anomolies', in Freaks: Myths and Images of the Secret Self (New York: Simon and Schuster, 1978) p. 16. Fiedler's title jars contemporary ears with its binary assumption of normality and complete abnormality. See Susan Gillman for brief comment on late nineteenth-century attitudes to Siamese twins in Dark Twins, pp. 55–6.

9. See Eric J. Sundquist, 'Mark Twain and Homer Plessy', in Susan Gillman and Forrest G. Robinson (eds), Mark Twain's Puddn'head Wilson: Race, Conflict, and Culture (Durham, NC: Duke University Press, 1990) pp. 66, 64. A revised version of this essay appears in Sundquist's To Wake the Nations: Race in the Making of American Literature (Cambridge, Mass.: Belknap Press, 1993) pp. 225–70.

10. Cindy Weinstein, The Literature of Labor and the Labors of Literature: Allegory in Nineteenth-Century American Fiction (Cambridge: Cambridge University Press, 1995) p. 139.

11. Puddn'head Wilson is still a comic text, but the dominant type of humour is a corrosive irony. I describe a general tendency here. The American Claimant (1892) combines farce and social satire, though unsteadily.

12. See Cindy Weinstein, The Literature of Labor and the Labors of Literature, pp. 138, 130, 131, 137, 150–2. I condense Weinstein's argument considerably.

13. Cindy Weinstein, The Literature of Labor and the Labors of Literature, pp. 159, 130, 160. I would see this process slightly differently. The comedy and expansiveness of the novel comes in Hank's descriptions of, and dialogue with, the medieval world he meets. His narrative accounting of his experience takes the form of an exploration of, and picaresque journey through, an unfamiliar world. As dialogue ends, and as Hank transforms this world into the image of that he already knows, so the comedy and the narrative possibilities close down also. His 'efficient making of persons' (Weinstein, p. 159) to operate as cogs in the system he has created marks the final stage of this process.

14. Arnold Weinstein argues differently. He sees character (and language) as mobile in Puddn'head Wilson, engaged in a 'counter-assault' (p. 68) on determinism. Consequently he argues against a one-dimensional 'allegorical' reading (p. 74). Weinstein's argument is strongly made and his account of the figurative play in the text is penetrating. I would, though, challenge his dismissal of the Siamese Twins story. Unlike him, too, I see webs of constraint fixing the terms of Roxy and Tom's actions throughout. Even when they do adopt disguise and shape-shift, it is always within the larger parameters of the racial boundaries which affect their every thought and move. Roxy's subversive act temporarily

upsets the racial order and reveals its arbitrary nature, but does not change its system. I acknowledge, though, the strength of Weinstein's (counter) reading. See *Nobody's Home: Speech, Self, Place in American Fiction from Hawthorne to DeLillo* (New York: Oxford University Press, 1993) pp. 65–88.

15. Eric Lott, 'Mr Clemens and Jim Crow: Twain, Race, and Blackface', in Forrest G. Robinson (ed.), *The Cambridge Companion to Mark Twain* (Cambridge: Cambridge University Press, 1995) p. 144.

16. Bruce Michelson uses this phrase. His description of Twain's subversion of 'basic rules for the framing of narratives' in both *Puddn'head Wilson* and 'The Man who Corrupted Hadleyburg', and his contextual remarks about the wider challenge to 'structural and thematic unities' taking place in 1890s' art, complement my present analysis. See *Mark Twain on the Loose: A Comic Writer and the American Self* (Amherst: University of Massachusetts Press, 1995) pp. 176, 177.

17. As I suggest in my later remarks on Tom and Roxana, Twain's position on the nature–nurture argument is never entirely consistent.

18. As I explore the Siamese twin motif, I recognise my critical debts here to the following: Susan Gillman, *Dark Twins*; Susan K. Gillman and Robert L. Patten, 'Dickens: Doubles:: Twain: Twins', *Nineteenth-Century Fiction*, vol. 39, no. 4 (March 1985) pp. 441–458; and Nancy Fredericks, 'Twain's Indelible Twins', *Nineteenth-Century Literature*, vol. 43, no. 4 (March 1989) pp. 484–99.

19. The Tocchis each had a head and arms but were joined from the sixth rib down. Their main difference from Twain's twins lies in the fact that, due to the different stages of development of their two legs, the Tocchis were unable to walk. See Leslie Fiedler, *Freaks*, p. 211.

20. Leslie Fiedler, *Freaks* pp. 217, 214, 213.

21. Hamlin Hill (ed.), *Mark Twain's Letters to his Publishers*, p. 319

22. Forrest G. Robinson, 'The Sense of Disorder in *Puddn'head Wilson*', in Susan Gillman and Forrest G. Robinson (eds), *Mark Twain's Puddn'head Wilson*, p. 32. The twins' status in terms of legal and political boundaries is particularly important.

23. Susan Gillman, *Dark Twins*, p. 63. She refers here just to the twins' 'problematic leg power'.

24. To cross between the two texts, this comment would have considerable resonance for a pre-Civil War slave, twinned in Siamese connection with a socially powerful master.

25. Arnold Weinstein, *Nobody's Home*, p. 68.

26. Again to cross to *Puddn'head Wilson*, Tom, as mulatto 'freak', can cause such disruption because Southern law and society, both ante- and post-bellum, only categorised racial difference in terms of 'black' and 'white'. The 'black–white binary that defines the US racial system and the master narrative of US race relations' contrasts with more complex systems of racial classification elsewhere. See Susan Gillman, 'Mark Twain's Travels in the Racial Occult', in Forrest G. Robinson (ed.), *The Cambridge Companion to Mark Twain*, pp. 201, 206.

27. Bruce Michelson, *Mark Twain on the Loose*, p. 200. His analysis is sharp

here: 'Joined at the waist . . . the Twins are indistinguishable in ways so gross that distinctions in identity, as this culture belabors them, become ludicrous. Luigi smokes, drinks coffee, reads heresy and votes Democrat, boozes heavily and brawls; Angelo stays a pious peaceful, nonsmoking, teetotalling Whig. Satiric fire rains upon such vices, virtues, and political inclinations, not in themselves but as preposterous indicators and measures of identity, as plausible definitions of human difference. Thus a deep-running theme of this sketch: that every Tweedledum or Tweedledee, with alterations in a few trivial habits, could really be anybody else, and that possibly everybody is fundamentally and inescapably just that: Tweedledum or Tweedledee.' See *Mark Twain on the Loose*, pp. 200–1. I make my own critical use of the Tweedledum/Tweedledee motif.

28. Eric J. Sundquist reads *Puddn'head Wilson* in the context of the *Plessy* v. *Ferguson* case (finally settled in 1896). Homer Plessy challenged the 1890 law establishing segregated railroad accommodation (in theory, but not in fact, 'equal but separate') in Louisiana. See *To Wake the Nations*, especially pp. 233–49.

29. Susan Gillman ponts out that Roxy's exchange is set in motion by her master's actions, thus 'in a peculiar way . . . the master is responsible for enslaving his own son', *Dark Twins*, pp. 63–4.

30. The fact that one twin is 'very masculine', the other 'much less so' (pp. 247–8), may accordingly connect with the crossings of gender boundaries in *Puddn'head Wilson*. Gillman notes that Twain, after this novel, 'explicitly pursue[s]' implications of the race/gender connection introduced here: 'if "male" and "female" are as readily interchanged as "black" and "white," then gender difference may prove to be as culturally constituted, as much "a fiction of law and custom" as racial difference.' *Dark Twins*, p. 79. See elsewhere in Gillman's book for other material on Twain and gender. This subject, increasingly the focus of critical interest, is explored by such scholars as Peter Stoneley in *Mark Twain and the Feminine Aesthetic* (Cambridge: Cambridge University Press, 1992), Laura Skandera-Trombley, *Mark Twain in the Company of Women* (Philadelphia: University of Pennsylvania Press, 1994), and Shelley Fisher Fishkin, 'Mark Twain and Women', in Forrest G. Robinson (ed.), *The Cambridge Companion to Mark Twain*, pp. 52–73. Particularly useful bibliographical information is contained in the footnotes to the latter essay.

31. Richard Chase, *The American Novel and Its Tradition* (1957). See *Critical Essays* in Sidney E. Berger (ed.), *Puddn'head Wilson and Those Extraordinary Twins* (New York: Norton Critical Edition, 1980) p. 247. And James Cox, '*Puddn'head Wilson* Revisited', in Susan Gillman and Forrest G. Robinson (eds), *Mark Twain's Puddn'head Wilson*, p. 18. These two collections of essays, taken together, provide a useful indicator of the changing nature of the critical response to Twain's book.

32. Quoted in Frederick Anderson, '[The Writing of *Puddn'head Wilson*]' (1968), reprinted in the Norton Critical Edition of the text, p. 293.

33. From James M. Cox, *Mark Twain: The Fate of Humor* (1966). See the

Norton Critical Edition, p. 267. Cox's argument is that the novel's irony overwhelms the attractive vernacular character of Roxy. His choice to twin Tom with Puddn'head rather than Valet suggests how widely critical readings of the text diverge.

34. John Carlos Rowe, *Through the Custom-House: Nineteenth-Century Fiction and Modern Theory* (Baltimore, Md.: The Johns Hopkins University Press, 1982) p. 167.

35. John C. Gerber, '*Puddn'head Wilson* as Fabulation' (1975), reprinted in the Norton Critical Edition, p. 361. Gerber's reference to 'the charm of fabulation' (p. 366) may indicate why I do not think this generic term a useful one to apply to Twain's novel.

36. See John Carlos Rowe, *Through the Custom-House*, p. 148.

37. That is, African-Americans as part-people and pieces of property. Cindy Weinstein uses the quoted terms in *The Literature of Labor and the Labors of Literature*, p. 140, in her discussion of the allegorical aspects of *Life on the Mississippi*. Eric J. Sundquist reminds his reader that 'the Constitution had originally counted the African American slave as three-fifths of a person', *To Save the Nations*, p. 239.

38. Susan Gillman points to 'the anguished tangle of contradictions surrounding the slave system' revealed by the trial and what follows it. As Roxy's son is redefined as property so he becomes, by definition (a 'will-less chattel') incapable of the murder he has committed, and 'not to be held accountable for human antisocial acts'. See *Dark Twins*, p. 92.

39. William Dean Howells, *A Hazard of New Fortunes* (Oxford: Oxford University Press, 1965 [1889]) p. 396. The statement comes from Basil March when he is at his most despairing about American society. It has come, though, to be generally applied to Naturalist writing.

40. Cindy Weinstein, *The Literature of Labor and the Labors of Literature*, p. 52.

41. George E. Marcus, '"What did he reckon would become of the other half if he killed his half?": Doubled, Divided, and Crossed Selves in *Puddn'head Wilson*; or, Mark Twain as Cultural Critic in His Own Times and Ours', in Susan Gillman and Forrest G. Robinson (eds), *Mark Twain's Puddn'head Wilson*, p. 197.

42. Though Arnold Weinstein approaches the novel from a different interpretive position, his reading of the symbolic resonances of the scene is particularly interesting. See *Nobody's Home*, pp. 79–80.

43. John Carlos Rowe, *Through the Custom-House*, p. 163. Rowe exempts 'that one uncanny moment in which he experiences his own divided identity as imitation black/imitation white'. Lee Clark Mitchell, too, follows Rowe in calling 'Tom' a 'deterministic machine'. He sees Roxy, too, as 'similarly a product of cultural forces'. See '"De Nigger in You": Race or Training in *Puddn'head Wilson*', *Nineteenth-Century Literature*, vol. 42, no. 3 (December 1987) pp. 304–5.

44. Susan Gillman points out that, in his working notes, 'Twain made Judge Driscoll himself the father of Tom'. See 'Mark Twain's Travels in the Racial Occult', p. 197. See too Arlin Turner, 'Mark Twain and the South: *Puddn'head Wilson*' (1968), reprinted in the Norton Critical

Edition. Turner quotes from Twain's notes and manuscript scraps to show that Twain planned at one stage to have 'Tom' confront and kill his own father: 'when his father pleads, "spare me! – I am your father!" Tom cries, "Now for *that*, you shall die," and kills him' (p. 276).

45. Though John Carlos Rowe's approach differs from mine, his comments on the 'illusion of . . . family instincts' is relevant here. See *Through the Custom-House*, p. 161.

46. Carolyn Porter, 'Roxana's Plot', in Susan Gillman and Forrest G. Robinson (eds), *Mark Twain's Puddn'head Wilson*, pp. 133, 134.

47. And contained, anyway, in its very secretness. If no one had found out that Tom was 'black', then the social system would have continued unaltered.

48. Shelley Fisher Fishkin, 'Race and Culture at the Century's End: A Social Context for Puddn'head Wilson', *Essays in Arts and Sciences*, vol. 19 (May 1990) pp. 2, 5, 6. Fishkin quotes George M. Frederickson in the definition given of the 'one-drop rule'.

49. Susan Gillman, *Dark Twins*, p. 85.

50. Standing in for his class here, 'too concerned with their speculations to notice any substitutions in the specific bodies that are the vehicles of their capital', Carolyn Porter, 'Roxana's Plot', p. 135. See John Carlos Rowe, 'Fatal Speculations: Murder, Money, and Manners in *Puddn'head Wilson*', in Susan Gillman and Forrest G. Robinson (eds), *Mark Twain's Puddn'head Wilson*, for discussion of the novel as 'a commentary on the shared economics of slavery and the new speculative economy that would carry us through the Civil War into the Gilded Age', p. 141. See too George M. Spangler, '*Puddn'head Wilson*: A Parable of Property' (1970), reprinted in the Norton Critical edition, pp. 295–303.

51. It is Roxy who uses this phrase. It can accordingly be read entirely ironically as part of Roxy's acceptance of hegemonic values.

52. See Eric Lott, 'Mr. Clemens and Jim Crow', pp. 148–9. While I agree with the general lines of Lott's argument, I differ in my conclusions.

53. In *The American Claimant* (New York: Charles L. Webster, 1892) young Lord Berkeley sees the forms and customs of European society as having become 'second nature'. They need casting off in favour of what can thus be called first or original nature – making one's own judgements and reverencing one's own ideals (pp. 99–100). In the incident which shortly follows this, when Berkeley is introduced to Puss, the daughter of the boarding-house keeper, Twain comments that 'his natural, lifelong self' which 'sprang to the front' did not know how to respond to this introduction to a chambermaid, but that his 'other self – the self which recognized the equality of all men – would have managed the thing better, if it hadn't been caught off guard' (pp. 108–9). The distinction between first and second nature, the natural self and that conditioned by environment and training, is here absolutely blurred. Cindy Weinstein similarly analyses Hank's opposition of nature and training ('that one microscopic atom that is truly *me*' versus 'training is everything', *A Connecticut Yankee*, p. 161)

to illustrate its collapse. See *The Literature of Labor and the Labors of Literature*, p. 154.

54. John Carlos Rowe, *Through the Custom-House*, p. 156. See, too, the passage in Twain's working notes for the novel where he writes, in regard to Tom's refusal of the duel, 'what was high came from either blood, & was the monopoly of neither color; but that which was base was the white blood in him debased by the brutalizing effects of a long-drawn heredity of slave-owning . . . '. Quoted in Shelley Fisher Fishkin, 'Race and Culture at the Century's End', p. 16.

55. Eric J. Sundquist, 'Mark Twain and Homer Plessy', in Susan Gillman and Forrest G. Robinson (eds), *Mark Twain's Puddn'head Wilson*, p. 71. The wording here differs from the version of the essay in *To Wake the Nations*, and is contradictory. Sundquist first claims that Tom's criminality may be *either* such aristocratic degeneration or a sign of his 'blackness', but goes on to argue that 'Tom's worst traits, like his "color" . . . can be traced neither to birth nor to training alone, neither to black nor to white'.

56. Arnold Weinstein, *Nobody's Home*, pp. 68–9.

57. Susan Gillman, *Dark Twins*, p. 78.

58. John Carlos Rowe, *Through the Custom-House*, p. 144.

59. Arnold Weinstein, *Nobody's Home*, pp. 86–7.

60. Eric Sundquist, *To Wake the Nations*, p. 228. See Sundquist's book for a reading of *Puddn'head Wilson and Those Extraordinary Twins* as 'an allegory of the 1880s and 1890s' (p. 232).

61. Arnold Weinstein, *Nobody's Home*, p. 87.

62. Sundquist describes how 'lynching in the 1890s was not reserved for African-Americans alone but had spread like an epidemic across . . . racial lines'. Focusing on the lynching of eleven Italians In New Orleans in 1891, he reads the twinned texts in terms of anti-immigrationist as well as anti-racist responses, and in terms of national as well as Southern prejudices. *To Wake the Nations*, pp. 261–3.

63. Twain adds one more element to this sense of necessary incompletion in the thematic development of the provisionality of knowledge itself. This theme appears in both *Those Extraordinary Twins* and *Puddn'head Wilson*. Unfortunately, my imposed textual limits prevent me from dealing fully with this important subject, though it returns as an issue as I discuss Twain's late writings in my final chapter. I merely indicate here, then, the grounds of an argument.

Fingerprinting in *Puddn'head Wilson* is not a neutral science ('pure' knowledge) but an ideological tool, used to confirm the racial prejudices of a particular community. The 'truth' of Tom's final identity as 'nigger' which the fingerprinting reveals, is only a fiction of law, based in turn on a fiction of race classification. 'Scientific' knowledge, in other words, is relative, dependent on the political framework that contains and produces it.

Equally Wilson's position as both a lawyer and a scientist in the trial scene raises theoretical (though only theoretical) questions about how anyone can *know* he tells the truth. In the trial scene, Wilson steps down from one role to give evidence in another. The only person with the 'scientific' knowledge to explain the case is also the one in whose professional interest (as lawyer) it is to win his case as convincingly as possible. It is clear Wilson does not falsify his evidence, but as a legal and scientific expert he does have his audience in the palm of his knowledgeable hand, should he wish to 'swindle' them (the word comes from Luigi's hoax in *Those Extraordinary Twins*, p. 261). At every turn in the text we are confronted with the potential unreliability of knowledge; the reminder that expertise and authority carry no guarantee of disinterested truth.

A final acknowledgement of the former fact lies in the play between fingerprinting and palmistry in *Puddn'head Wilson*. It is only palmistry that is seriously called a 'science' in the novel (p. 126). If we now dismiss palmistry as a science, and if fingerprinting has been validated by long practice, this was not the case as Twain wrote. In the comparative use made of the two 'sciences', the text provides a hint that knowledge is not always stable, and that our definitions of science always have something provisional about them.

For critical texts that address such issues, see especially Susan Gillman, *Dark Twins*; Evan Carter, '*Puddn'head Wilson* and the Fiction of Law and Custom'; John Carlos Rowe, *Through the Custom House*; and Brook Thomas, 'Tragedies of Race, Training, Birth and Communities of Competent Puddn'heads', *American Literary History*, vol. 1, no. 4 (Winter 1989) pp. 754–85.

Chapter 8   The Late Works: Incompletion, Instability, Contradiction

1. Mark Twain, *The Great Dark*, in John S. Tuckey (ed.), *Mark Twain's Which was the Dream? and Other Symbolic Writings of the Later Years* (Berkeley: University of California Press, 1967) p. 130. All page references from this, and *Three Thousand Years Among the Microbes* (also published in this edition), to follow quotes henceforth.
2. William R. Macnaughton, in *Mark Twain's Last Years as a Writer* (Columbia: University of Missouri Press, 1979), suggests that, from the end of 1906 till his death in 1910, 'Mark Twain seldom wrote well or finished what he began . . . ' (p. 241).
3. The best-known editorial manipulation of Twain's later work was the version of *The Mysterious Stranger* (1916) 'laundered and pasted together by Albert Bigelow Paine and Frederick A. Duneka'. See William R. Macnaughton, *Mark Twain's Last Years as a Writer*, p. 2. Maria Ornella Marotti alludes to other 'violation[s]' (p. 8) of Twain's work, discusses his self-censorings (pp. 3–6, 9–10), and gives a history of the publication of the Mark Twain Papers, in her important book, *The Duplicating Imagination: Twain and the Twain Papers* (Pennsylvania State University Press, 1990).
4. William M. Gibson (ed.), *Mark Twain's Mysterious Stranger Manuscripts* (Berkeley; University of California Press, 1969). The edition I use in this

chapter is the paperback version of this: Mark Twain, *The Mysterious Stranger*.

5. So Bruce Michelson categorises this critical tendency in *Mark Twain on the Loose: A Comic Writer and the American Self* (Amherst: University of Massachusetts Press, 1995) p. 175. See, too, his footnote, p. 253.

6. Bruce Michelson, *Mark Twain on the Loose*, pp. 173, 174, 212. Michelson's final chapter, 'The Wilderness of Ideas', discusses Twain's work after 1890. See pp. 173–229.

7. See Susan Gillman, *Dark Twins: Imposture and Identity in Mark Twain's America* (Chicago: University of Chicago Press, 1989) pp. 136–80; Susan Gillman, 'Mark Twain's Travels in the Racial Occult', in Forrest G. Robinson (ed.), *The Cambridge Companion to Mark Twain* (Cambridge: Cambridge University Press, 1995) pp. 193–219; Maria Ornella Marotti, *The Duplicating Imagination*; David R. Sewell, *Mark Twain's Languages: Discourse, Dialogue, and Linguistic Variety* (Berkeley: University of California Press, 1987) pp. 126–54. See, too, Susan K. Harris, *Mark Twain's Escape from Time: A Study of Patterns and Images* (Columbia: University of Missouri Press, 1982); Bruce Michelson, 'Deus Ludens: The Shaping of Mark Twain's Mysterious Stranger', *Novel*, vol. 14, no. 1 (Fall 1980) pp. 44–56; Cindy Weinstein, *The Literature of Labor and the Labors of Literature* (Cambridge: Cambridge University Press, 1995) pp. 160–72. I note here only those critics who have influenced my thinking. An increasing stress on the value of the late work (in all its variety) is now becoming standard.

8. Maria Ornella Marotti, *The Duplicating Imagination*, p. 62.

9. See Bruce Michelsen, *Mark Twain on the Loose*, pp. 223–5, and Maria Ornella Marotti, *The Duplicating Imagination*, pp. 31, 64, 152. Michelson uses Conrad as a 'handsome opposite' to Twain. To do so is also, though, to reveal, in terms of literary context, the nature of the difference between the two writers. If Conrad shows how Marlow's 'self press[es] on in full awareness of its own contingency' and finds a kind of healing and authority over experience in the telling of his well-shaped story (*Mark Twain on the Loose*, pp. 224–5), Twain's narratives cannot be brought to completion, and his fictional characters are often subjects who lack Marlow's self-awareness. Marotti's study focuses on fictions from all the posthumously published Twain Papers. My range is narrower. By the dream tales, I refer primarily to those fictions published in *Mark Twain's Which Was the Dream?* (though I do not discuss all the texts published there). Susan Gillman puts *The Mysterious Stranger Manuscripts* in the same category (see *Dark Twins*, p. 139). I prefer, here, to refer to *No. 44, The Mysterious Stranger* separately.

10. I would query Bruce Michelson's suggestion in *Mark Twain on the Loose* that Twain is consciously rebelling 'against cultural and rationalist expectations governing narrative and the written word' (p. 222). The large number of incomplete, fragmented and (at that time) unpublished texts suggest to me no such deliberate *intent*.

11. Dennis Welland points out that the two versions of the text were far

from identical, but that there is no evidence that Twain was aware of this. See *The Life and Times of Mark Twain* (London: Studio Editions, 1991) pp. 134–6. For fuller discussion of the differences between the two texts, see Welland's 'Mark Twain's Last Travel Book', *Bulletin of the New York Public Library*, vol. 69, no. 1 (January 1965) pp. 31–48.

12. I comment in chapter 2 on the importance of the associationist mode in Twain. The notion of 'occult travel' (p. 204) that Susan Gillman introduces in 'Mark Twain's Travels in the Racial Occult' is a reworking of the same principle, but one that also takes into account Twain's later interest in 'spirit communication and disembodied space-and-time travel, made newly respectable . . . by the investigations of psychical researchers' (p. 194). Gillman's analysis of Twain's writing on race, as, in *Following the Equator*, he mentally shifts from Bombay to his Missouri childhood home, and accordingly discovers a 'more forgiving cultural relativism' (p. 204), is astute.

13. Bruce Michelson, *Mark Twain on the Loose*, p. 77.

14. Susan Gillman, 'Mark Twain's Travels in the Racial Occult', pp. 204, 206, 194; and *Dark Twins*, pp. 99, 100. In my 'Racial and Colonial Discourse in Mark Twain's *Following the Equator*', I place emphasis, rather, on the divided nature of Twain's racial discourse in the text. See *Essays in Arts and Sciences*, vol. 22 (October 1993) pp. 67–83.

15. The repeated nature of these patterns signal, for me, a move from conventional non-fiction reportage to the deliberate patternings, equivalences and symmetries normally associated with the fictional and/or poetic. 'The Enchanted Sea-Wilderness' was, in fact, initially written as a story to be included in *Following the Equator*. See the introduction to John S. Tuckey (ed.), *Mark Twain's Which was the Dream?*, p. 8.

16. Other similar and related motifs appear in *Following the Equator* which relate to the late fictions. (i). Accounts of family disaster, the separation of families, and the loss of home (see pp. 63, 75, 99–100, 110–12, 121: not all these examples necessarily carry the psychologically disturbing or pessimistic implications of the late fiction). (ii) Relativistic uncertainty and the way different sets of coordinates, or frameworks of knowledge, meet to dislocatory effect; the failure of contact and communication (see p. 57, and the examples in my main text). (iii) Sudden reversal of fortune, both upward (pp. 141–50 – the story of Cecil Rhodes as a type of 'mysterious stranger' figure) and downward (p. 179 – I see an analogy between this description of the Adeleide crash and Twain's own financial disaster, especially in its forceful language, and in the metaphor with which he describes the story's final reversal: 'the corpse got up and danced'). On pp. 156–7 Twain alludes to the Tichborne trial: a story of twinned and confused identities, claimants, the conflicting status of dream and reality, and the loss of fortune and status.

17. Quoted in William R. Macnaughton, *Mark Twain's Last Years as a Writer*, p. 99. See too Bernard DeVoto (ed.), *Mark Twain: Letters from the Earth* (Greenwich, Conn.: Fawcett, 1962) pp. 226–7.

18. If fantasy as a genre gains its effects from hesitation concerning the nature of the 'real', an odd effect occurs at the start of *The Great Dark*. For rather than directly moving between one world (Jessie's birthday and the scientific experiment) to another (on shipboard), there is an intervening passage where the narrator talks to the Superintendent of Dreams about his projected voyage. We are left uncertain as to exactly where the rupture with 'reality' occurs; whether the narrator is already dreaming (if this is what happens to him) or not. This contributes to the sense of uncertainty over the status of the real in the text.

19. Bruce Michelson, *Mark Twain on the Loose*, p. 173.

20. Maria Ornella Marotti, in *The Duplicating Imagination*, calls the predominant mode of *The Mysterious Stranger Manuscripts* that of romance, but 'interspersed with fantastic, satirical, and burlesque motifs' (p. 99).

21. Rosemary Jackson, *Fantasy: The Literature of Subversion* (London: Methuen, 1981) p. 124. She discusses the intrusion of the Gothic in Victorian novels here, but it relates equally to the Fantastic.

22. Rosemary Jackson, *Fantasy*, pp. 45, 44.

23. Maria Ornella Marotti, *The Duplicating Imagination*, p. 92.

24. Bruce Michelson, *Mark Twain on the Loose*, p. 218.

25. See Susan Gillman, *Dark Twins*, pp. 149, 159–60. Gillman identifies Twain's representation of the dream and waking self with the theories of the psychic researcher, F. W. H. Myers. Gillman's valuable chapter on 'The Dream Writings' shows them to be 'thoroughly saturated in the context of late-nineteenth-century psychology' (p. 178), and links Twain's interest in this area to his own 'problems of authorial intentionality and control' (p. 138).

26. But, of course, also a duplication of the name of Twain's best known protagonist. In an unpublished article, 'Tom Sawyer's Capitalisms and the Destructuring of Huck Finn', Scott Michaelsen pursues the implications of this. His argument that Huck finally emerges as Tom Sawyer here, and that Huck's 'inability [in his microbic world] to resist capitalist occupation' (p. 33) provides a bleak rethinking of Twain's thirty years of work on aspiring capitalists (p. 22), should stimulate critical reassessment of the story. Michaelsen's description of the narrative's 'radical account of personhood', its portrayal of 'the self as entirely in flux' (p. 31), parallels and complements my own thinking on this subject. His further historicist move, in connecting this notion of the self to the allegorical representation of capitalism, is especially intriguing. My thanks to the author for allowing me to refer to his work.

27. For details of Eastern European immigration, see Roger Daniels, *Coming to America: A History of Immigration and Ethnicity* (New York: Harper Perennial, 1991 [1990]). Daniels writes that 'many Americans at the turn of the century felt that their way of life was threatened by what they called the "immigrant invasion"' (p. 275). Mary Douglas's remark that 'our ideas of dirt . . . express symbolic systems' is also to

the point here. See *Purity and Danger: An Analysis of Concepts of Pollution and Taboo* (London; Routledge & Kegan Paul, 1966) p. 35.

28. Catherine Belsey, *Critical Practice* (London: Methuen, 1980) p. 58.

29. Cindy Weinstein writes that 'His full name . . . registers his birth on the assembly line and his membership in an allegorical population [of workers]', *The Literature of Labor and the Labors of Literature*, p. 163. No. 44's role and identity cannot, however, be so narrowly contained.

30. Mark Twain, *The Mysterious Stranger*, edited by William M. Gibson (Berkeley: University of California Press, 1969) pp. 305, 315, 282. Page references follow quotations henceforth.

31. See my 'Afterword' to *The American Claimant* in the forthcoming edition of *The Oxford Mark Twain*. In my present interpretation of the duplicates, I take my initial cue from Cindy Weinstein in *The Literature of Labor and the Labors of Literature*. Weinstein's analysis takes a different direction, though, as she describes the confusions resulting from the failure to distinguish original from duplicate in terms of the disintegration of 'the efficiency of [Frederick Winslow] Taylor's utopia' (p. 165).

32. Though it must be said that neither these workers, nor their way of asserting their industrial rights, are presented sympathetically here. This serves to remind of Twain's deep ambivalence about labour–capital relationships.

33. The text closely parallels *Puddn'head Wilson and Those Extraordinary Twins* in its play with confused subjectivity. Similarly, it reverts to farce in the stage business about the twin wooing of Marget/Lisbet von Arnim by August and his double (see pp. 342–53).

34. Twain further complicates his narrative by giving August three selves. The Soul is the immortal spirit, capable of great force and passion, existing beyond the 'physical and mortal' properties of the other two selves. See pp. 342–3.

35. Maria Ornella Marotti, *The Duplicating Imagination*, p. 65.

36. Rosemary Jackson, *Fantasy*, p. 65.

37. *No. 44, The Mysterious Stranger*, pp. 318, 311; *The Great Dark*, pp. 104, 122, 130; *Three Thousand Years Among the Microbes*, p. 482.

38. *The Mad Passenger*, Appendix to John S. Tuckey (ed.), *Mark Twain's Which was the Dream?*, p. 567.

39. This bears all the marks of the confusions that inevitably attend the later editing of unfinished manuscripts. There seems every reason for seeing the second 'Preface' as a replacement for the first.

40. See especially Bruce Michelson, '*Deus Ludens*: The Shaping of Mark Twain's *Mysterious Stranger*', pp. 55–6; also, Maria Ornella Marotti, *The Duplicating Imagination*, pp. 126, 128.

41. See Maria Ornella Marotti, *The Duplicating Imagination*, p. 113.

42. I follow Bruce Michelson here. See '*Deus Ludens*: The Shaping of Mark Twain's *Mysterious Stranger*', p. 53. Michelson argues that, in such sequences, 'through play, a vital, enduring hopeful festivity and life have been restored to Mark Twain's fiction' (p. 56).

43. Bruce Michelson, '*Deus Ludens*: The Shaping of Mark Twain's *Mysterious Stranger*', p. 56.

44. I paraphrase Rosemary Jackson, *Fantasy*, p. 22.

45. Mark Twain, *The Mysterious Stranger*, p. 404.

46. See Eric Mottram, 'The Location of Dangerous Shoals: American Fictions on the Science of Power', *Over Here: An American Studies Journal*, vol. 3, no. 2 (Autumn 1983) p. 23. Mottram's brief but provocative reading of the text focuses on Twain's 'sense of catastrophe in the modern age': 'Henry Edwards' despair', he writes, 'increases as exploration of the unknown looks like going on for ever. . . . Adaptation to conditions causes amnesia. . . . [Henry] has become a flying Dutchman of American technological fears, dreaming of family, home, and land'.

47. Susan Gillman, *Dark Twins*, p. 167.

48. Susan Gillman, in 'Mark Twain's Travels in the Racial Occult', focuses on the historical resonances of the various versions of *The Mysterious Stranger*. She concentrates on Twain's representation of race and ethnicity, and shows how 'the black-Jewish parallel' (p. 213) made in the narratives extends into a 'final vision of universal human enslavement, containing and collapsing within it all of the historically specific nationalist, religious, and ethnic persecutions encompassed by *The Mysterious Stranger*, from the medieval witch-hunt, to the French revolution, to European missionary and colonial violence in China and India' (p. 216).

49. See Susan Gillman, *Dark Twins*, pp. 170–1.

50. Forrest G. Robinson, *In Bad Faith: The Dynamics of Deception in Mark Twain's America* (Cambridge, Mass.: Harvard University Press, 1986) p. 222. Robinson discusses the incompatibility of the free choice and determinist poles of Twain's thought, with specific reference to the late works, in the final chapter of his book.

51. Richard Boyd Hauck's discussion of Twain in *A Cheerful Nihilism: Confidence and the 'Absurd' in American Humorous Fiction* (Bloomington: Indiana University Press, 1971), pp. 133–66, is of relevance here, though I do not always agree with his conclusions.

52. Gregg Camfield, *Sentimental Twain: Samuel Clemens in the Maze of Moral Philosophy* (Philadelphia: University of Pennsylvania Press, 1994) p. 215.

53. Twain's concern with this area of American foreign policy can be traced in Jim Zwick (ed.), *Mark Twain's Weapons of Satire: Anti-Imperialist Writings on the Philippine–American War* (New York: Syracuse University Press, 1992).

54. Susan Gillman, *Dark Twins*, p. 170.

55. See David Sewell, *Mark Twain's Languages*, Chapter 7, 'Toward a Chaos of Incomprehensibilities', pp. 126–54.

56. Bruce Michelson refers, for instance, to the breezy resilience of children in Twain's late narratives (*Mark Twain on the Loose*, p. 212).

57. Indeed in his *Autobiography*, Twain did find a method that could, in its meandering variety, its free associations, repetitions and intersections, shape his materials. His formal approach there was based on the principle that 'in following no plan but the plan to follow no plan, he

allowed his memories to speak out in spite of himself' (Camfield, p. 229). The problem, though, is that if this appears to become a paradigmatic postmodernist text (the recounting of a life that formally defies closure; a 'measur[ing]' of the truth by a self who fully acknowledges the variability and inconsistency of his 'tapeline', and builds this changeable subjectivity into his text), its extreme length and necessary formal and thematic indiscipline has made it, to the present, unpublishable in any final version – though the Mark Twain Papers project is evidently preparing 'something approximating a definitive edition': see R. Kent Rasmussen, *Mark Twain A to Z: The Essential Reference to His Life and Writings* (New York: Facts on File, 1995) p. 23. Critical interest in the *Autobiography* is growing, and Gregg Camfield has a particularly interesting section on it in his *Sentimental Twain*, pp. 220–36. The quote I use to describe Twain's method has its source in (one version of) the *Autobiography* itself, where Twain writes of Susy 'measur[ing] her disasters . . . with her own tape-line': see Michael Kiskis (ed.), *Mark Twain's Own Autobiography* (Madison: University of Wisconsin Press, 1990) pp. 29–30. This reminds me, in its application to Twain's own textual methodology, of Henry Adams' historian, seeking 'no absolute truth . . . only a spool on which to wind the thread of history without breaking it', *The Education of Henry Adams* (New York: The Modern Library, 1931[1918]) p. 472.

In *Mark Twain on the Loose*, Bruce Michelson concentrates too on the 'anti-story configurations' (p. 222) of the late texts, and gives a particularly interesting reading of the neglected *Extract from Captain Stormfield's Visit to Heaven* (1909) pp. 219–23.

58. Perhaps Henry Adams, in his *The Education of Henry Adams*, provides a notable exception to this rule.
59. Alex Ayres (ed.), *The Wit and Wisdom of Mark Twain* (Harmondsworth, Middx.: Penguin [Meridian], 1987) p. 58.

Select Bibliography

This bibliography is necessarily highly selective. Twain wrote a vast amount and, since his death, much more of his work has been published, and republished, most especially in the authoritative University of California Press Editions. At least four versions of his *Autobiography* (as this suggests, a highly problematic text) have appeared, as well as various editions of his letters. The fourth volume of *Mark Twain's Letters* (1995), published in chronological sequence by the University of California Press, still only takes Twain's life up to 1871. There are also three volumes of *Mark Twain's Notebooks & Journals* (running to 1891) published by the same press. The amount of critical work, too, that has appeared on Twain is mountainous. I keep to narrow limits here, listing a selection of books that Twain produced during his lifetime, but then naming those texts that have been most useful for my own critical purposes. For a longer, up-to-date, but not overwhelming, bibliography, I would direct my reader to the 'Books by Mark Twain' and 'Suggested Reading' sections of one of the most useful reference works on Twain, R. Kent Rasmussen's *Mark Twain A to Z* (details below). I only refer to full studies of Twain's work. For information on critical articles and chapters in books, see my notes.

In my book, I use the Penguin edition of the text (when there is one) for ease of readerly access.

TWAIN'S MAJOR WORKS

The Celebrated Jumping Frog of Calaveras County and Other Sketches (1867).
The Innocents Abroad, or The New Pilgrim's Progress (1869).
Roughing It (1872).
The Gilded Age (1873).
Sketches New and Old (1875).
The Adventures of Tom Sawyer (1876).
The Prince and the Pauper (1881).
The Stolen White Elephant, Etc. (1882).
Life on the Mississippi (1883).

Adventures of Huckleberry Finn (1885).
A Connecticut Yankee in King Arthur's Court (1889).
The American Claimant (1892).
The £1,000,000 Bank-Note and Other New Stories (1893).
Puddn'head Wilson and Those Extraordinary Twins (1894).
Personal Recollections of Joan of Arc (1896).
Following the Equator (1897).
The Man that Corrupted Hadleyburg and Other Stories and Essays (1900).
Letters from the Earth (1962).
Mark Twain's Which Was the Dream? and Other Symbolic Writings of the Later Years (1967).
Mark Twain's Mysterious Stranger Manuscripts (1969).

Letters, Speeches, Etc.

Mark Twain–Howells Letters: The Correspondence of Samuel L. Clemens and William D. Howells, 1872–1910, ed. Henry Nash Smith and William M. Gibson (Cambridge, Mass.: Harvard University Press, 1960).
Mark Twain's Letters to His Publishers, 1867–1894, ed. Hamlin Hill (Berkeley: University of California Press, 1967).
Mark Twain's Correspondence with Henry Huttleston Rogers, 1893–1909, ed. Lewis Leary (Berkeley: University of California Press, 1969).
Mark Twain Speaking, ed. Paul Fatout (Ames: University of Iowa Press, 1976).

See too the various editions of *Mark Twain's Letters* and *Mark Twain's Notebooks & Journals* published by the University of California Press.

SECONDARY CRITICISM

Biographical Studies

Budd, Louis J., *Our Mark Twain: The Making of His Public Personality* (Philadelphia: University of Pennsylvania Press, 1983).
Emerson, Everett, *The Authentic Mark Twain: A Literary Biography of Samuel L. Clemens* (Philadelphia: University of Pennsylvania Press, 1976).
Hill, Hamlin, *Mark Twain: God's Fool* (New York: Harper & Row, 1973).
Hoffman, Andrew, *Inventing Mark Twain* (William Morrow, forthcoming).
Kaplan, Justin, *Mr Clemens and Mark Twain* (New York: Simon & Schuster, 1966).
Skandera-Trombley, Laura, *Mark Twain in the Company of Women* (Philadelphia: University of Pennsylvania Press, 1994).
Steinbrink, Jeffrey, *Getting to be Mark Twain* (Berkeley: University of California Press, 1991).
Welland, Dennis, *The Life and Times of Mark Twain* (London: Studio Editions, 1991).

Critical Studies

My book is deeply influenced by the generation of scholars who, in the late 1950s and 1960s, did the critical groundwork on which most later responses to Twain depend. Though I have made little direct reference to these texts, they inform much of what I have written. I list a selection of these below, and then leave a space before separately listing the more recent books which I have found most useful.

Blair, Walter, *Mark Twain & Huck Finn* (Berkeley: University of California Press, 1960).

Budd, Louis J., *Mark Twain: Social Philosopher* (Bloomington: Indiana University Press, 1962).

Cox, James M., *Mark Twain: The Fate of Humor* (Princeton, NJ: Princeton University Press, 1966).

Lynn, Kenneth S., *Mark Twain and Southwestern Humor* (Boston, Mass.: Little, Brown, 1959).

Regan, Robert, *Unpromising Heroes: Mark Twain and His Characters* (Berkeley: University of California Press, 1966).

Smith, Henry Nash, *Mark Twain: The Development of a Writer* (Cambridge, Mass.: Harvard University Press, 1962).

Bridgman, Richard, *Traveling in Mark Twain* (Berkeley: University of California Press, 1987).

Louis J. Budd (ed.), *New Essays on Adventures of Huckleberry Finn* (Cambridge: Cambridge University Press, 1985).

Camfield, Gregg, *Sentimental Twain: Samuel Clemens in the Maze of Moral Philosophy* (Philadelphia: University of Pennsylvania Press, 1994).

Champion, Laurie (ed.), *The Critical Response to Mark Twain's Huckleberry Finn* (Westport, Conn.: Greenwood Press, 1991).

Doyno, Victor A., *Writing Huck Finn: Mark Twain's Creative Process* (Philadelphia: University of Pennsylvania Press, 1991).

Fishkin, Shelley Fisher, *Was Huck Black? Mark Twain and African-American Voices* (New York: Oxford University Press, 1993).

Gillman, Susan, *Dark Twins: Imposture and Identity in Mark Twain's America* (Chicago: University of Chicago Press, 1989).

Gillman, Susan and Robinson, Forrest G. (eds), *Mark Twain's Puddn'head Wilson: Race, Conflict, and Culture* (Durham, NC: Duke University Press, 1990).

Gribben, Alan, *Mark Twain's Library: A Reconstruction*, 2 vols. (Boston: G. K. Hall, 1980).

LeMaster J. R. and Wilson, James D. (eds), *The Mark Twain Encyclopedia* (New York: Garland, 1993).

Leonard, James S., Tenney, Thomas A. and Davis, Thadious M. (eds), *Satire or Evasion? Black Perspectives on Huckleberry Finn* (Durham, NC: Duke University Press, 1991).

Marotti, Maria Ornelli, *The Duplicating Imagination: Twain and the Twain Papers* (Pennsylvania State University Press, 1990).

Michelson, Bruce, *Mark Twain on the Loose: A Comic Writer and the American Self* (Amherst: University of Massachusetts Press, 1995).

Rasmussen, R. Kent, *Mark Twain A to Z: The Essential Reference to His Life and Writings* (New York: Facts on File, 1995).

Robinson, Forrest G., *In Bad Faith: The Dynamics of Deception in Mark Twain's America* (Cambridge, Mass.: Harvard University Press, 1986).

Robinson, Forrest G. (ed.), *The Cambridge Companion to Mark Twain* (Cambridge: Cambridge University Press, 1995).

Sattelmeyer, Robert and Crowley, J. Donald (eds), *One Hundred Years of Huckleberry Finn: The Boy, His Book, and American Culture* (Columbia: University of Missouri Press, 1985).

Scharnhorst, Gary (ed.), *Critical Essays on The Adventures of Tom Sawyer* (New York: G. K. Hall, 1993).

Sewell, David R., *Mark Twain's Languages: Discourse, Dialogue, and Linguistic Variety* (Berkeley: University of California Press, 1987).

Sloane, David E. E., *Mark Twain as a Literary Comedian* (Baton Rouge: Louisiana State University Press, 1979).

Stahl, J. D., *Mark Twain, Culture and Gender: Envisioning America Through Europe* (Athens: University of Georgia Press, 1994).

Stoneley, Peter, *Mark Twain and the Feminine Aesthetic* (Cambridge: Cambridge University Press, 1992).

Sundquist, Eric J. (ed.), *Mark Twain: A Collection of Critical Essays* (Englewood Cliffs, NJ: Prentice Hall, 1994).

Tenney, Thomas A., *Mark Twain: A Reference Guide* (Boston, Mass.: G. K. Hall, 1977).

Wilson, James D., *A Reader's Guide to the Short Stories of Mark Twain* (Boston, Mass.: G. K. Hall, 1987).

Wonham, Henry B., *Mark Twain and the Art of the Tall Tale* (New York: Oxford University Press, 1993).

Index

Adventures of Huckleberry Finn 18, 20, 67, **86–109, 111–15**, 132, 133, 136, 149
'evasion' sequence 88, 89–90, 96, 99, 101, 102, 104, 109
freedom 92–8, 99, 100, 101, 104, 105, 108–9
genre 111–5
Huck's voice 87, 91–9, 101–2, 103–8, 112–13, 114–15
idyll 87–8, 103–8
Jim, representation of 87, 88, 90, 91–108
'Jim and the Dead Man' 86
narrative incompletion 87–8, 103–9
race 86–109, 111–12, 114
  positive depiction 87–8, 102–9, 132
  post-Reconstruction 88–90, 99–100, 102, 104, 105, 109, 111–12, 115
  see too Jim, representation of
realism 112–15
status of subject 112–14
Adventures of Tom Sawyer, The 1, **65–85**, 111, 133, 136
anti-modernism 65–7, 73, 76, 81, 83, 85
boy book 66, 67, 71, 76, 81, 111
Huckleberry Finn 80
Indian Joe 74, 80–2, 84–5
Jacksonianism 72–3, 75, 84
race 81, 82–5

sexuality 81–2
status of subject 76–9
theatricality 76–7
Tom as proto-capitalist 67, 70–2, 73–6
Tom as confidence man 72–4
whitewashing scene 68–72
work–play relation 70–2, 75–6
Aldrich, Thomas Bailey 67
American Claimant, The 151, 166
American West
  see *Roughing It*
Andrews, William L. 99
Arac, Jonathan 104, 105, 107
Authorial intentionality 13, 18–21, 89, 105, 111, 115–16, 117, 119, 138, 175–6

Bakhtin, Mikhail 92, 106, 115
Banta, Martha 46, 60, 118, 119, 123
Barnum, P. T. 4
Bell, Michael Davitt 131
Bennett, Tony 115
Big Bonanza, The 60
Bridgman, Richard 26
Budd, Louis J. 65

Cable, George Washington 90
Carter, Everett 117, 118, 119
Carton, Evan 135
Civil War 20, 23, 28–9, 42, 66, 68, 73, 119
Confidence Men and Painted Women 72

*Connecticut Yankee in King Arthur's
    Court, A* 19, **110–11, 115–33,**
    136–7, 151, 154, 166
  Battle of the Sand-Belt 127,
    128–9, 137
  body–machine interaction
    119–24, 126
  cultural anxieties 117–33, 154
  electrocution 110, 127–9
  fantasy 110–11, 115–33
  history 131–3
  Hank–Merlin relation 125, 130–1
  St Stylite 119–24, 126–7, 128
  status of subject 119–24, 130–1,
    136–7
  Taylorisation 122–4

De Quille, Dan 60
Douglass, Frederick 95
Doyno, Victor 100
Dream Tales 157–9, 160, 161,
    162–6, 167–70, 171–6
  *see also Enchanted Sea-Wilderness,
    The; Great Dark, The; Three
    Thousand Years Among the
    Microbes*
DuBois, W. E. B. 97, 100

Edison, Thomas 130
Eliot, T. S. 86, 89
Ellis, R. J. 90
Enchanted Sea-Wilderness, The 161
'Ethnicity' 122
European–American relations
  see Innocents Abroad

Fender, Stephen 44
Fiedler, Leslie 106
Fishkin, Shelley Fisher 90, 91, 92,
    100, 149–50
Following the Equator **159–61**
  race 160
  travel writing 159–60, 161
Foner, Eric 100
Ford, Henry 123
Foucault, Michel 119, 120
'Freedman's Case in Equity, The'
    90

Gilded Age, The 35, 132
Gillman, Susan 4, 135, 140, 150,
    152, 158, 160
Grandissimes, The 90
Great Dark, The 159, **162–4,** 166,
    168–9, 172, 175
  epistemological uncertainty
    162, 163–4, 167–9, 172, 175
  fantasy 162–3, 167–8, 171–2
  farce 162
  narrative problems 158–9, 162,
    168, 169, 172, 175
  status of the subject 162–4, 167,
    172, 175
Gribben, Alan 67
Gutwirth, Marcel 4, 8, 9, 10,
    14,15, 16

Haltunnen, Karen 72
Holland, Laurence B. 95
Homestead Strike 12
Horwitz, Howard 58
Howard, June 113
Howells, William Dean 113
Humour 1–21 and *passim*
  ambivalence about 9–13

Incidents in the Life of a Slave Girl 108
Innocents Abroad, The **22–43,** 47,
    48, 160
  aesthetics 30–1, 36, 37, 38
  Civil War 23, 28–9, 42
  Columbus's discovery 29–30
  economics 22–4, 27–8, 31, 32,
    33, 43
  ethnocentrism 28–34, 38
  epistemological uncertainty 25,
    35–6
  Milan bath-house 32–4
  Orientalism 38
  'pilgrim'–'sinner' contrast 41–3
  status of subject 24–5, 32, 34, 36
  tourism 22–4, 27, 30–1, 33
  travel writing 22–4, 26, 36–40

Jackson, Rosemary 113, 116–17, 163
Jacobson, Marcia 66, 67
Jacobs, Harriet 93, 108

'Jim Smiley and His Jumping
Frog' 2, 5

Kazin, Alfred 28, 35
Kemmler, William 128
King, Martin Luther 109

Lears, T. Jackson 77, 125
Life on the Mississippi 58, 67, 90,
135, 136
Lukacs, Georg 132
Lynn, Kenneth 51

MacLeod, Christine 108
Mailloux, Steven 19, 88, 90
Marotti, Maria Ornella 158
Michaels, Walter Benn 61, 119
Michelson, Bruce 24, 143, 158,
160, 163, 171
Mitchell, Lee Clark 53, 64, 113
Molly Maguires 12
More Tramps Abroad
see *Following the Equator*
Moreland, Richard C. 104, 105
Morrison, Toni 91
Mysterious Stranger, The,
manuscripts 11, 157, 158, 159,
162
see also *No 44, The Mysterious
Stranger*

No 44, The Mysterious Stranger 136,
159, 164, **166–7, 170–1, 172–3,
174–5**
epistemological uncertainty
162, 167–8, 170–1, 175
fantasy 162–3, 167–8, 172
narrative problems 158–9, 167,
171, 172–3, 174, 175
status of the subject 162, 164,
166–7, 172, 174, 175
Taylorisation 166–7

Oriard, Michael 71

Paige typesetter 166
Pinkerton Detective Agency 12

see also Homestead Strike, Molly
Maguires
*Puddn'head Wilson and Those
Extraordinary Twins* 18, 67, 79,
83, **134–56**, 157, 158, 159
allegory 136, 137, 138, 139, 140,
144–6, 154, 155
Chang and Eng 139–40
detective genre 136, 153, 154–5
farce 134–5, 137, 138, 140–3
finger-printing 155
narrative tensions 134, 135–6,
139, 140, 153–4, 155–6
Puddn'head Wilson 134–9, 140,
142, 143, **144–56**, 158
Puddn'head Wilson 144, 145,
146, 148, 153, 154–5
race 135, 137, 140, 143–55
post-Reconstruction 135,
143–4, 146, 149–50, 154
Roxy 144–52, 154–5
Siamese Twins 134, 137, 139–43,
153, 155
status of subject 136–7, 140,
141–3, 145–6, 148, 150–3, 155
Those Extraordinary Twins 134–9,
139–44, 145, 153, 154
Tocchi brothers 139–40
Tom Driscoll 134, 144–5, 147–55
twinnings 134–43 and *passim*
Valet de Chambre 145, 150–5

Regan, Robert 28
Robinson, Forrest G. 4
Roughing It 26, 34, **44–64**, 66, 111,
133, 160
Buck Fanshawe's funeral 50–2
American Indian 49–50
emergent capitalism 46–7, 57–63
epistemological uncertainty 46,
53–7
Great Landslide Case, The 45–6
Hawaii 56–7
Lake Tahoe 59–61
Mining 54, 60–2
Mountain Meadows Massacre
54–5
Slade 53

travel narrative 47, 56, 64, 111
see also Turner, Frederick Jackson

Said, Edward 28, 38
San Francisco *Alta* 22
Secret History of Eddypus, The 133
'Seeing the Elephant' 4
Seltzer, Mark 118, 120, 123
Sewell, David 32, 51, 158
Smith, David L. 97
'Sociable Jimmy' 91
Sollors, Werner 122, 130
Southwick, Dr Alfred 110, 128
Steinbrink, Jeffrey 48
'Stolen White Elephant, The'
  1–21, 25, 136, 155
  allegory 10–13, 20
  detective genre 1–2, 4, 5–8, 10,
    12, 17–18
  epistemological uncertainty
    2–3, 14–18
  hoax 4–6, 16, 20
  narrators 3–5, 13
  'seeing the Elephant' 4
Story of a Bad Boy, The 67
Stowe, William W. 23, 25, 43
Sundquist, Eric 77

Takaki, Ronald 118
Taylor, Frederick Winslow
  see Connecticut Yankee, A:
    Taylorisation
Taylored Lives 123
*Three Thousand Years Among the
  Microbes* 159, 160, **164–6**,
  169–70, 173–4

black humour 173, 175
epistemological uncertainty
  162, 165, 167, 169–70, 172,
  173, 175
fantasy 162–3, 164–5, 167–8,
  171–2
historical context 164–5, 173–4
narrative problems 158, 170,
  172, 173–4, 174–5
status of the subject 162, 164,
  165–6, 167, 172, 173, 175
Todorov 117
Trachtenberg, Alan 57–8
Turner, Frederick Jackson 44, 45,
  46, 47, 48, 49, 50
Twain, Mark
  as fictional persona 22, 32,
    33–4, 36–7, 48–9
  Notebooks 43, 110

Virginia City *Enterprise* 4, 60

Wallace, John H. 97
Was Huck Black? 91
Weber, Max 125, 131–2
Webster & Company 110
Weinstein, Cindy 118, 119, 136–7,
  146
*Which Was the Dream? and Other
  Symbolic Writings* 157
  *see also The Great Dark, Three
    Thousand Years Among the
    Microbes*
Whittier birthday dinner 19
Wolff, Cynthia Griffin 66